Introduction to
Human Communication

Introduction to

Allyn and Bacon, Inc.
Boston · London · Sydney

Human Communication

James C. McCroskey
Lawrence R. Wheeless
West Virginia University

Photo Credits

Page 4, Jean-Claude Lejeune, Stock, Boston; page 9, Margo Foote, M.I.T. Historical Collections; page 22, M.I.T. Historical Collections; page 27, *Boston Globe* photo; page 37, Craig W. Reynolds, Boston University Photo Service; page 39, Wide World Photos; page 46, Courtesy of the N.Y. Stock Exchange; page 52, Barth J. Falkenberg, *The Christian Science Monitor;* page 65, Christopher S. Johnson, Stock, Boston; page 66, United Nations/T. Chen; page 75, Joseph Schuyler, Stock, Boston; page 79, Gabor Demjen, Stock, Boston; page 102, Joseph Kovacs, Stock, Boston; page 111, *The New York Times*/John Soto; page 115, Culver Pictures Inc.; page 131, Wide World Photos; page 142, Dietz, Stock, Boston; page 147, Norman Hurst, Stock, Boston; page 150, George W. Reynolds, M.I.T. Historical Collections; page 157, Boston University Photo Service; page 173, Robert M. Campbell, Perkins School for the Blind; page 180, Cary Wolinsky, Stock, Boston; page 186, Nicholas Sapieha, Stock, Boston; page 190, Peter Vandermark, Stock, Boston; page 196, Calvin Campbell, M.I.T. Historical Collections; page 218, Anna Kaufman Moon, Stock, Boston; page 238, Ruth Silverman, Stock, Boston; page 248, Jean-Claude Lejeune, Stock, Boston; page 257, Ellis Herwig, Stock, Boston; page 272, Anna Kaufman Moon, Stock, Boston; page 279, *Boston Globe* Photo; page 293, Mike Mazzaschi, Stock, Boston; page 305, left, Patricia Hollander Gross, Stock, Boston, and right, Jeff Albertson; page 310, courtesy of the Massachusetts Audubon Society/Leslie A. Campbell; page 311, courtesy of the Philadelphia Museum of Art/A. J. Wyatt, Constantin Brancusi's "Bird in Space"; page 314, Owen Franken, Stock, Boston; page 332, courtesy of the Bureau de Recherches de Petrole, France; page 339, Elizabeth Hamlin, Stock, Boston; page 351, Daniel S. Brody, Stock, Boston; page 356, *Boston Globe* Photo; page 369, Boston University Photo Service; page 372, U.S. Department of Agriculture, SCS Photo/N. P. McKinstry; page 379, Wide World Photos; page 398, Daniel S. Brody, Stock, Boston; page 407, Cary Wolinsky, Stock, Boston.

Library of Congress Cataloging in Publication Data

McCroskey, James C.
   Introduction to human communication.

   Includes bibliographies and index.
   1. Communication.   I.   Wheeless, Lawrence R., joint author.   II.   Title.
P90.M2   301.14   75-31931
ISBN 0-205-05001-8

To the founders of
the International Communication Association

C. Merton Babcock
Paul Bagwell
W. Norwood Brigance
H. P. Constans
Clyde W. Dow
Franklin Knower
Edward C. Mabie
Paul McKelvey
Elwood Murray
Ralph Nichols
W. Charles Redding
Wesley Wiksell
Harold P. Zelko

You have provided us with a vehicle
for bringing together
people who study human communication
from many disciplines and countries.
We are all better because of your efforts.

Contents

Preface

Over the past three decades the amount of research concerning human communication has been increasing at a geometric rate, particularly empirical research. This knowledge explosion has paralleled similar phenomena in other hard and soft sciences. But unlike many other areas of scholarly effort, research in human communication has been a concern of many academic disciplines. So many, in fact, that many scholars are not even familiar with the work done by people in some other disciplines.

The products of over three decades of intensive empirical investigations and over two thousand years of non-empirical scholarship include a plethora of isolated facts about how human communication occurs, and a few relatively primitive theories of human communication, theories that for the most part integrate few of the available facts known and are seldom integrated with each other. There have been numerous attempts made to draw these disparate facts and theories together, most of which have helped to advance scholars' understanding of human communication. But such efforts have been directed primarily at the scholar who already knows a great deal about human communication. The person approaching the study of human communication for the first time finds such treatises very tough going.

Most books that are directed to the beginning student in human communication lack the integrative thrust of more scholarly efforts. As a result, the beginning must approach the study of human communication, usually for both the first and *last* time, through books that have a heavy disciplinary bias. Some will study human communication as interpersonal communication, some as mass communication, some as public speaking, some as news or essay writing. Each of these orientations, as well as many others, may have merit. But each tends to focus on some important element of human communication to the unfortunate exclusion of other important elements.

For many years we have felt that there is a common core of information about human communication to which all beginning students should be exposed, whether their initial exposure be in anthropology, business, communication, education, English, journalism, mass communication, psychology, social psychology, sociology, speech, or any of a number of other disciplines. Our purpose in writing this book has been to bring this core of information together in a manner that is understandable and usable for the student who wants to improve her or his own communication, but may have no previous formal background or training in the field.

The content of this book has been drawn from many sources with diverse orientations. The orientations that have influenced us the most are *systems orientation, transactional orientation,* and *functional orientation.* We have adopted none of these as an overriding view, rather, we have attempted to employ each viewpoint when it is most useful and we try to avoid slavish devotion to any one.

Similarly, three main approaches to human communication have had the most impact on us: the interpersonal communication approach, the mass communication approach, and the diffusion of innovations approach. Strong adherents of any one of these approaches, however, may feel that we do not go far enough with their favorite. We have not attempted to satisfy such desires, since this is not a book on *interpersonal* communication, on *mass* communication, or on *diffusion*; rather it is an introduction to *human* communication. Consequently, we have drawn heavily from all three of these approaches, but adopted none of the three as our own.

A word about style in which this book is written is needed. The reader will notice that we use no footnotes or APA-type internal references. In an earlier draft of the manuscript, such references were included. We took them out. We have broken from this tradition for books in the communication field for two reasons. First, many of the ideas included in the book are not the product of single scholars or research teams, but are the results of the efforts of many people. In such cases, citing one source, or even several, ignores the contributions of many others. Further, many of the ideas are our own, or the product of our integration of the ideas of others. In these instances, we really don't know whom to cite! The second reason, however, was more compelling. This is a book designed for the beginning student. We don't believe he or she cares (or should be made to care) about the names of scholars who have contributed to our knowledge about human communication. For the student who does wish to pursue further reading, however, we have suggested some major sources that should be considered for each chapter, and have also noted the major references upon which we drew to form the content of each chapter. To our colleagues whose work is not cited in the usual way, we apologize. We trust you will understand our reasons.

This book is divided into twenty chapters. The first two are designed to provide an overview of human communication and set the stage for the remainder of the book. Chapters 3 and 4 explore the various social systems of communication and the unique characteristics of each type of system. Chapters 5 through 7 focus on the individual as a communicator and the many elements that make each person's communication behavior unique to that individual. Chapters 8 through 11 examine the relational nature of communication between unique individuals. These first eleven chapters provide a basic introduction to the variables that affect human communication. The last nine chapters take a functional view of human communication and examine behaviors likely to lead to desired outcomes from communication.

You will notice that separate chapters have not been devoted to dyadic, small group, organizational, public, mediated, or cultural communication. Neither have chapters been devoted to specific skills such as message preparation, audience analysis, camera use, or layout techniques. The authors see these contexts for communication and these skills as highly interrelated. They are best presented as such for the beginning student who may have little further contact with communication studies. However, even a casual skimming of the content of the chapters will reveal information that is directly related to student applications in a variety of social contexts and to the development of a variety of specific skills. Any of the chapters beyond the first two lend themselves to be used for these purposes.

Scattered throughout the book are a series of "black boxes." In these boxes we pose questions designed to focus the reader's attention on what we consider to be more important ideas in the book and the more important applications the reader needs to make. Smaller boxes in the margin of the text key the content to the questions and applications posed by the "black boxes." For the student or teacher who likes to use cognitive or behavioral objectives as an aid to learning, most of these questions can be modified easily for this purpose.

Acknowledging all of those who have had an influence on the ideas one includes in a book is an impossibility. We won't attempt it. However, we do wish to acknowledge two very special groups of people. We are deeply indebted to our colleagues and graduate students at Illinois State University and, more recently, West Virginia University. You have provided us with an environment in which productivity is a norm and scholarship is a prerequisite to friendship, and an atmosphere where no idea is safe from challenge. We have grown because of you. We hope it shows in our book.

J.C.M.
L.R.W.

1

Human Communication and Change

The Caterpillar and Alice looked at each other for some time in silence; at last the Caterpillar took the hookah out of its mouth, and addressed her in a languid, sleepy voice.

"Who are you?" said the Caterpillar.

This was not an encouraging opening for a conversation. Alice relied, rather shyly, "I—hardly know, sir, just at present—at least I know who I was when I got up this morning, but I must have been changed several times since then."

"What do you mean by that?" said the Caterpillar sternly. "Explain yourself!"

"I can't explain myself, I'm afraid sir," said Alice, "because I'm not myself, you see."

"I don't see," said the Caterpillar.

"I'm afraid I can't put it more clearly," Alice replied very politely, "for I can't understand it myself to begin with; and being so many different sizes in a day is very confusing."

"It isn't," said the Caterpillar.

Lewis Carroll

In this brief encounter between Alice and the Caterpillar, Lewis Carroll has provided a penetrating commentary on change in society. As individuals, we are

1

always changing.   Beliefs and values that we held this morning may be in doubt this evening.   What we were yesterday, we are not today.   And often the whole process is quite confusing.   Some of us find adapting to change a difficult task.   Others are more like the Caterpillar.   We recognize change in ourselves and adapt to it readily.   Some of us are instigators of changes which affect us as individuals and stir the social systems surrounding us. The social systems of which we are a part and which are a part of us are also like Alice and the Caterpillar.   They are struggling with the dynamics of change.   They are simultaneously attempting to adapt to change and working to produce it.

So why talk of caterpillars and wonderlands and change in a book about communication?   Communication is the basic process through which change and, more importantly, adaptation to change occur.   Communication determines whether or not there are changes in our concepts of ourselves, the way we see the world around us, and the way the world around us sees us.

Significant changes are constantly occurring at all levels of society. These changes tend to be more rapid in so-called advanced societies (like ours) than in more "primitive," less developed, societies.   But change in all societies in the world is increasing at an ever-accelerating pace.   Futurists, people who attempt to predict changes so that we may be better able to adapt to them, estimate that there will be more change in all societies in the world in the next decade than has occurred in all recorded human history. Whether the futurists are right or not only time will tell for sure.   But the fact that over 90 percent of all scientists in history are still alive today certainly suggests that futurists' predictions are not simply idle speculation.

The field of human communication is an excellent example of what futurists are talking about.   Over 99 percent of all communication scientists who ever lived are working today, and most of them are still producing more research.   Over half of our total knowledge about human communication is the product of research that has been conducted in the last decade.   By the time this chapter passes from our typewriter through the publication process and reaches you, the amount of scientific knowledge about human communication will have increased by between 10 and 20 percent.

While knowledge in almost every field is exploding and change is being thrust upon us from nearly every quarter, our human capacity for assimilating knowledge and adapting to change is remaining relatively constant.   As Alvin Toffler put it, we are going into *Future Shock*.   We are becoming more like Alice.   As little children many of us learned to recite the optimistic lines: "Every day and in every way, I am becoming better and better."   Many people today would probably change the line to: "Every day and in almost every way, I am becoming worse and worse; but fortunately the people around me are worse yet!" We would prefer to put words into the mouth of the Caterpillar: "Every day and in every way, I am becoming different."

Change is inevitable. We are all changing every day. Our environment is changing every day. How are we to adapt to those changes? The primary tool for adapting to change is communication with other people. Yet, this tool, like an overage shotgun, may blow up in our faces unless it is well oiled. Unfortunately, most people attack problems of changes in themselves and their environment with rusty-barreled tools. Misconceptions about the process of human communication abound, and they are the rust in our barrels. Let us engage in some rust removal.

BLACK BOX

The "black box" is sealed and hidden. We cannot pry it open to get inside. Even if we could, what is going on in there would be obscured because it is dark. It is a puzzle.

The black box is inside your head. Communication scholars have tried for a long time to discover what happens inside, but most often we can only guess. In teaching, learning, and research, the black box remains a perturbing mystery.

Throughout this book, you will discover other black boxes. Sometimes they too will be puzzling. But we hope that these questions will help you to discover important ideas that you should store in your own "black box."

Misconceptions About Communication

Communication Will Solve All Our Problems.

For many people in today's society, communication appears to be the magic wand for solving all problems. People in business take Dale Carnegie courses, attend sensitivity training sessions, hire communication consultants, and participate in endless rounds of meetings. Politicians (or statesmen, if you prefer) seek to increase communication between countries. "If we could only get the Arabs and Israelies to sit down and discuss their prob-

3

*Human
communication is
simply the process of
one person
stimulating an idea in
another person's
mind.*

lems. . . ." Parents are advised to "talk to your teenager." The connoisseur of communication calls it the remedy for whatever ails us. In a very real sense, communication is a modern snake oil. If your marriage is in trouble, take a shot of communication. If your business is not making enough money, take a shot of communication. If you want to avoid a war, take a shot of communication.

Human communication is simply the process of one person stimulating an idea in another person's mind. Whether that process helps overcome a problem, or is the *cause* of a problem, depends on the idea that is stimulated. One of the authors once told his spouse that he thought she was a terrible housekeeper. They *really* communicated. Did that help to overcome a problem? Hardly. It caused one. On another occasion, one of the authors told his boss that he was a racial bigot. Did that help to overcome a problem? Possibly. The man who held the author's job the next year could have been unemployed otherwise.

Communication is not a panacea. It can either create or help to eliminate problems. The question is not *whether* people communicate; it is *what* they communicate that makes the difference.

The More Communication, the Better

The more a person talks (within limits) the more positively that person will be viewed by others. People who talk a lot are perceived to be more competent, more friendly, more attractive, more powerful, and better leaders than people who talk less. Even though most of us, including the authors, would like to deny this observation, it has been confirmed over and over again in both laboratory and on-the-spot studies of communication behavior. Why? People seem to equate quantity of communication with quality of communication. While more may be better when we are concerned with money or sex (depending on how hedonistic we are!), more is not necessarily better when we are concerned with communication. More and more negative communication merely leads to more and more negative results. Quantity and quality of communication have no necessary relationship. To communicate more and more with someone whom we dislike and who dislikes us probably will only intensify the dislike for both of us. Again, the question is not *how much* people communicate. It is *what* they communicate that makes the difference.

Communication Can Break Down

One of the most common devils that people try to exorcise is that little demon called "the communication breakdown." "Joe, why are you getting a divorce?" "Well, Martha and I had a communication breakdown; we just can't talk anymore." "Bill, why didn't you get that order mailed out on time?" "Sorry, Mr. Wilks, I thought it wasn't to go out until Thursday. We just had a communication breakdown." "Why are the Irish Catholics and Protestants fighting each other?" "Well, they have just had a complete communication breakdown."

All of these examples are cop-outs. Communication *can not* break down. Communication may fail to be successful in getting other people to do what you want them to, or vice versa. In fact, it can even lead to results opposite to what you desired. But that is not a breakdown—that is a failure on the part of one or both parties in the interaction. In Mr. Wilks' case, he had communicated "Thursday" to Bill. Communication was complete, but the wrong idea was communicated.

When we use the term "communication breakdown" we are often describing a situation in which communication has been very effective. In the case of Joe and Martha, what Joe may really mean is that he and Martha have found out through their communication that they really can't stand one another! Is that a breakdown? In the marriage, maybe; in the communication, no. Our Catholics and Protestants have also communicated. They understand that they may both want the same power, and that only one can have it. Communication has not broken down, there is simply no perceived need for further communication. They all know what they think they need to know.

The communication breakdown is a convenient excuse used to cover two cases where communication is not the problem: where one person fails to influence another person (for whatever reason), and where real differences exist that are communicated between people. Join with us in exorcising this *little* devil from our vocabulary so that we can turn our attention to the *big* devil that is behind the three misconceptions we have examined so far: Communication is a Good Thing.

Communication Is a Good Thing

Ask a hundred people. At least ninety-nine will praise the worth of communication. The idea that communication is a good thing is pervasive in our society. This misconception leads us to believe that communication will solve all our problems; that the more we have of it the better off we will be; and that communication can break down. Communication is *not* inherently a good thing. What? The authors of a book on communication think that communication is a bad thing? No. Communication is not a bad thing either. Communication is neither good nor bad; it is simply a tool which is available to help us cope with change in our environment. Tools are neither good nor bad universally. If I want to rake my yard, a rake would be a useful tool. I might even think of it as "good." But if I lean too heavily on the rake and dig part of my grass out by the roots, does that make the tool bad? Hardly, it is still the same rake. Or consider a pistol. A pistol is a tool. When it is used to stick up a bank, we may think of it as a bad tool. When a policeman uses it to keep an unruly crowd from burning down our house, we may think of it as a good tool. The pistol is still the same tool. Tools, then—and remember communication is a tool—are neither good nor bad. The way we use tools is what provides us with an evaluation. People who worship at the shrine of communication are misdirecting their effort. Communication is a tool to be understood and used, not to be idolized.

BLACK BOX
1

Can you explain why each of the following statements is false?
    Communication will solve all our problems.
    The more communication, the better.
    Communication can break down.
    Communication is a good thing.
    Meanings are in words.
    Communication is a natural ability.

Can you explain what communication has to do with change?

Meanings Are in Words

The biggest misconception about communication that gets in the way of understanding and using it to maximum advantage is the notion that meanings are only in words. When we operate on this misconception we greatly reduce the probability that we will be able to communicate effectively. We start operating as if *saying* something is the same thing as *communicating* it. We tell someone that we would like the report "next week" and then get incensed because it comes in Friday afternoon, instead of Monday. We blame other people when we fail to communicate accurately. Communication is the process of adapting ideas to people in order to adapt people to ideas. Ideas, thoughts, and meanings are in people's minds, and *nowhere else*. Words are simply vehicles that we have to verbalize our meanings. Our ability to use words, as well as nonverbal symbols, is in large part what distinguishes humans from lower forms of animal life. Unfortunately, because of our misconceptions about the relationships among things, words, and meanings, we are often not very distinguished.

   Meanings are in people. Words don't mean, people mean. The word is not the object. These are three of the many ways that communication scholars have attempted to state a basic concept about human communication. No word has meaning apart from the person using it. To the extent that two people have different meanings for the same word, communication between those people which uses that word will be less effective than might be possible. In large part, the success of any communication

7

effort between two people depends on the degree of shared meaning the two people have for the words (as well as the nonverbal symbols) that they use. We will return to this concept several times in later chapters, for it is central to understanding human communication. But at this point, let us use a true example which we hope will not disturb you. If it doesn't bother you, then you probably grasp the concept. If it does, our apologies; please bear with us through the book and come back and reread this material later.

In the early 1970s there was considerable interest in research concerning language development and learning among various minority groups. One researcher was doing a study that involved administering a word association test to young black children in an urban ghetto. She would read a word and then the child was to say the first word he or she thought of. A session with a six-year-old boy went like this:

Researcher:	summer
Boy:	hot
Researcher:	television
Boy:	watch
Reseacher:	sister
Boy:	brother
Researcher:	black
Boy:	beautiful
Researcher:	mother
Boy:	(long, long pause)
Researcher:	mother
Boy:	(pause) That's only half a word.

The researcher was a little surprised. Since she was from a suburban white community, she had a clear meaning for "mother" that she expected everyone to share. The little boy, however, had a different meaning for "mother" that is common in many ghettos, and is not offensive there, but which raises the hair on the back of some suburbanites' necks (and sometimes lets the red show through).

This simple example illustrates the main idea. We learn to associate meanings with words as a result of our interaction with other people in our environment. Our meanings are a product of our culture, our social class, and our experience. No two people share the same meanings for all words, because no two people completely share the same background and experiences. When we attempt to communicate with other people, therefore, our concern in the selection of words (as well as nonverbal symbols) that we will use should be on what the word actually means to the *other person,* not on what we *think* it means. This decision is best made on the basis of our knowledge of the individual person. Of course, common meanings are shared for a lot of words by large groups of people. That is what Webster and Funk & Wagnells have depended upon. But meanings, as ideas to be conveyed to another, are *not* in dictionaries; meanings are in people. And words are in dictionaries, accompanied by other words that a substantial group of people associate with those words. If you want to know what our little boy means by "mother," you have to know him. Webster will be of little help.

Communication Is a Natural Ability

One of the most pervasive misconceptions about communication is that it is an ability that comes to us naturally; "you are born with it." The result of this misconception is obvious in most of our public schools, and our private

No two people share the same meanings for all words.

9

ones as well. Communication is the most ignored area of knowledge in our schools. Some specific skills related to communication are included in the curriculum: composition, reading, typing, and occasionally speaking. But for some reason a basic understanding of the human communication process is left out of most curricula.

To communicate well is not an inborn, natural ability. It is a process to be learned. Almost everyone is born with the necessary natural abilities that provide the basis for learning to be an effective communicator. Unfortunately, few people have the opportunity to learn to use those abilities systematically.

Learning to communicate effectively requires two things: an understanding of how human communication works and an opportunity to utilize that knowledge. This book is designed to help you meet the first requirement. You will have plenty of opportunity to meet the second, because you are called upon to communicate with others in your environment every day. Both understanding and practice are essential to becoming an effective communicator. One without the other is like a chocolate sundae without ice cream—a bit sticky and not very satisfying.

Dealing with Change through Communication

Change results in communication. Communication results in change. When change occurs in our environment, we must deal with it either alone or in concert with other people. If we are to deal with it alone, we must obtain the necessary information to respond intelligently. We obtain that information through communication. If we are to deal with change in concert with other people, they must be persuaded to cooperate with us (or us with them). That persuasion must occur through communication. Whenever we communicate with another person both we and the other person are changed in some way or ways. We and/or they may know more. Our attitudes, beliefs, and/or values may be altered. Our behavior may be changed. To the extent that we understand how human communication operates, we will be able to handle these changes with little difficulty. To the extent that we operate on our misconceptions about communication, change will be threatening to us, and we will be more likely to engage in maladaptive responses like the examples in the previous section.

This is a book about communication; thus, it is a book about change. We are writing it in an attempt to produce change in *you*—the way you view communication, your understanding of the many variables involved in communication, and, most importantly, your communication behavior. We think you will like the "different" you. Are you ready to cope with such change?

2

An Overview of Human Communication

The Dean receives a letter from two irate students suggesting that a professor in the Communication Department has allowed an obscene presentation in his class. The Dean quickly grabs the phone and calls the professor to ask what is going on in his class. The professor panics.

The Dean and the professor have a hastily arranged meeting. The Dean is stiff and formal. The professor is nervous and barely articulate. The professor explains that the students in his class in nonverbal communication presented a report on how male chauvinism is evidenced by nonverbal behavior. He describes a skit in which pieces of a female mannequin were disassembled and stacked in a shopping cart. Male players in the skit then shuffled through the cart to select their "favorite parts." This was followed by a series of slides of advertisements that used pictures of females to promote products. The complaining students left class after the first slide—a picture of a prominent derriere being used to sell lawnmowers.

13

The Dean smiles and tells the professor not to worry, there is no problem. The professor relaxes, stamps out his fourth cigarette, and returns to his office. The Dean calls in the students and suggests that they should consider transferring to another school. The Dean and the professor have engaged in "communication." The Dean and the students have engaged in "communication." The students and the professor have engaged in "communication."

We have used this term "communication" for more than a chapter already, but we really have not explained what we mean by it. "Communication" is like a lot of words; it means very different things to different people. Our purpose in this chapter will be to attempt to get us on the same wavelength for this term. First we will examine a series of postulates about the nature of communication. Then we will explain the essential components in communication. Finally, we will examine each other as individual communicators and see how we function in the process.

Central Postulates about Human Communication

Communication Is a Process

The idea of process itself implies dynamics and change. In our example in chapter 1 of Alice and the Caterpillar, Alice was coming to grips with the process of life in which she was involved. She realized that she was not the same as when she got up in the morning. Lewis Carroll was expressing the thought of the philosopher Heraclitus who remarked that you can't step in the same river twice. Perhaps even more thought-provoking is the idea that you can't step in the same river *once*. In the process of stepping, both the stepper and the river change.

Analyzing a process requires that it be stopped and taken apart; however, in doing that, the process is actually changed. That is the problem involved in analyzing and giving names to things in a process. After the process is altered, other words must be used to discuss the relationships among those things. Often our assumption is that the world is made up of static objects or ideas which become activated only when something stimulates them. As a result, movement and process are not generally incorporated into our basic conception of the world. Therefore, when we talk of process, we must often utilize static concepts and terminology. The obvious conclusion to this line of reasoning is the idea that through observing a process, the process itself becomes changed. Also, we might conclude that events do not repeat themselves; only classes of events, which may be very similar, have the same pattern.

Likewise, this idea of process suggests that communication cannot be reversed or repeated exactly. Communication often evolves from previous encounters which affect the next ones to occur. In this frame of reference, some theorists argue that communication is an evolutionary process affecting the individual and social systems of which we are members. Through this process, individuals and social systems evolve, change, adapt, are replaced, or become obsolete or extinct.

The Communication Process Is Systemic

Although its structure is possibly not apparent upon first consideration, the communication process is systemic. We can define any system as an interrelated group of elements which work together as a whole to achieve certain outcomes.

The idea of *systemic process* implies some interrelationship or interdependence among elements in communication. The process itself is determined by the elements within it and how those elements interact and affect one another. The processes of combining chemicals and nuclear fission are examples of this idea. The way that elements interact determines the nature of that process. The synthesizing of water is dependent upon the relationships among components in the formula, H_2O. The solar system continues to function because of the interrelationship and interdependence of planets, moons, forces, and the sun. The Dewey Decimal System and electronic circuits in your television are also examples of this sort of arrangement and operation. In addition, all of these organized, interdependent elements are performing certain functions. Electronic circuits function to transform signals into picture and sound. The Dewey Decimal System functions to help store and retrieve information. Our circulatory system functions to circulate and revitalize our blood; our central nervous system to control and operate other bodily functions.

In the same sense, the communication process involves an organized, methodically operating group of elements. At a superficial level, those elements include: (1) a source of communication which sends (2) a message (3) through some channels or media (4) to a receiver of the communication. This system, of course, involves more elements and becomes more complex as the messages, individuals, channels, etc., increase in number.

The systems with which we are most concerned in communication are the *social systems* in which communication exchanges occur. Social systems often exist within other systems. For example, the social system of marriage, involving two people (dyad), often exists within a family system. Interpersonal dyads, such as secretary and executive, exist within organizational systems. Organizational systems exist within societal systems. The functioning of communication itself varies drastically depending upon whether the exchanges occur in highly structured business organizations, in the classroom, via mass media, or between two lovers. Also, one of the main functions of these social systems is communication and its facilitation. Therefore, in this book on communication, we view social systems as significant determinants of the nature of communciation. As such, social systems are more than merely contexts in which communication occurs; they can be viewed as *communication* systems. We will examine some of these systems in chapters 3 and 4.

The *intrapersonal system,* which we will describe a bit later, is the individual person composed of all of her or his complex, interrelated, and interdependent components. These physical and psychological elements are organized and operated methodically as a whole to perform functions for the perpetuation of that human system. These functions include eating and digesting, sensing, breathing, thinking, and *communicating.*

The Communication Process Is Interactional

Closely related to the idea of a system is the concept of interaction. When we say that the communication process is interactional, we are noting that there are dynamic exchanges among people involved in the process. We normally think of interaction as the reciprocal exchange of related messages between two people which results in change in one or both. When I buy a new car, I interact with the salesperson and both of us are changed. I have less money and a car; he has more money and a story to tell other salesmen about how he found another "sucker." Interactions during a date likewise may change both persons in more subtle ways. Later, one of the two may refuse a request for a subsequent date and the other must adapt to this change in expected (or hoped for) behavior.

Interaction has occurred when any person involved in the process is changed or adapts to the change of another as a result of communication. Obviously, when we talk with each other, both of us often are changed in terms of our ideas or behavior. However, sometimes only one of us may change apparently; the other may appear to be unaffected. Closer analysis reveals, however, that people who engage in sending and receiving messages are in the process of changing, attempting to change others, adapting to changes, or adapting to others' attempts to change them. These changes and adaptations may occur in terms of feelings, beliefs, information, decisions, actions, or other variables. Interaction has occurred if there has been an exchange of related messages which has resulted in change or adaptation to change.

In communication, the things that are exchanged are *messages*. These messages include what we write and say. But they also include the things we do, the way we dress, the length of our hair, and the kind of car that we drive. In fact, a message may be anything that stimulates or excites meaning in another person. If what we do or wear means something to another person, then we have sent a message, either intentionally or unintentionally, to that person.

Communication Can Be Intentional or Unintentional

(1) A person can intentionally send a message to another person who is intentionally receiving the message. Under this condition, communication is more likely to be effective, when compared to other possibilities. (2) A person may unintentionally send a message to another person who is intentionally receiving. Deliberately listening in to another conversation, or "eavesdropping," is an example of this type of exchange. So is a psychiatrist's observation of a client's behavior. (3) On the other hand, a person may intentionally send a message to which the other person only unconsciously or unintentionally reacts. Unfortunately, many university classrooms operate in this manner. (4) Finally, both persons may be unaware of messages being exchanged. Often our nonverbal behaviors, such as dress, constitute messages sent and received in this unintentional manner. Figure 2–1, which is coded according to the four possibilities noted above, illustrates these options.

One of the goals of this book and many basic courses in communication is to increase your understanding and awareness of communication. By doing this, more of your communication activity can be changed to occur in block 1, where both people are conscious and intent upon the exchange. Unfortunately, most people communicate most of the time in block 4, unintentional giving and receiving.

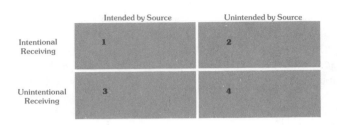

FIGURE 2–1. *Nature of intentional and unintentional communication.*

From this perspective, it is apparent that it is difficult, if not impossible, *not* to communicate. Intentionally or unintentionally, we are often sending and receiving messages. We are frequently engaging in communication which we are unaware of. *The only possibility of not communicating is when no message is consciously or unconsciously sent or received.*

The Communication Process Can Be Transactional

If you look in any number of communication books you will find as many concepts of transaction or transactional communication as there are books. Communication scholars do not agree on exactly what this concept means. One reason for this discrepancy is the fact that it is a difficult concept to define. In order to deal with the notion of transaction you must have a bit of background knowledge and a slight change in orientation, because it is not a *thing* we can point to; it is a characteristic of certain types of communication. We ask your indulgence to bear with us while we give you that background and try to shift your orientation toward communication.

Communication occurs within environments that influence not only the kind of communication occurring but also our perceptions, what we share with each other, and the level at which we communicate. We do not interact within a vacuum. We act upon one another within social systems and physical contexts which significantly alter our exchanges. What you talk about at home with your parents is different from what you talk about with your friends at the university, or what you talk about with your teachers in the classroom. More than this, however, the way that you perceive the world changes as a result of your communication within differing social systems or environments. Think of the ways in which your perceptions and beliefs have changed since you "came to college." Also, think of the different ways you see the world from your seat in a science class, through the microscope, from the bar stool at the local pub, or in church on Sunday morning. The social systems and environments in which we place ourselves change our outlook and perspective. We communicate differently as a result. We are different as a result.

In this sense, we interact not only within our environment but also *with* our environment. Moreover, we have become what we are as a result of the culture, social systems, individual exchanges, and physical environments in which we place ourselves or which have been forced upon us. As these situations change, so do we in adapting to them. As a result, our communication changes and we communicate about "reality" in different ways. In this sense, we share reality with each other through our communication. Even more important, we share something of ourselves with each other through communication. This is possible because our perceptions of the world—our reality—change, depending upon where we are in the physical environment, individual exchanges, and the social or cultural system. A number of us have had the common experience of visiting a close high school friend or having that friend visit us after we have gone to college. If this occurs after some extended separation from each other, we find that "suddenly" we have little in common. We have difficulty sharing with each other as we did before. Communication becomes strained and difficult. We are no longer in the same environment, so we have difficulty sharing through our communication. The visitor feels out of place. The intimacy of our relationship is gone. This experience illustrates that communication occurs within environments that influence the kind of communication taking place, our perceptions and adaptations to reality, what we share with each other, and the level at which we communicate.

It is important that we understand the levels at which we can communicate with others. We can communicate with others at cultural, social, and individual levels. At the cultural level we make predictions about all of the people who fall within that culture and attempt to adapt our sending and receiving of communication to those predictions. We try to perceive and predict what common beliefs, attitudes, and characteristics people within a particular culture share with each other. We can know with some certainty that Russians as a whole may share some common political beliefs, behavior characteristics, and attitudes toward religion. We can also know with some certainty that these are not shared with most Americans or Chinese. Americans, however, share other common values, beliefs, and behaviors that are unique to our culture. In highly complex ways we communicate within our culture as a whole, and as a result share common perceptions and identities. This process also occurs within subcultures arising from the ghetto, the Indian reservation, and Appalachia. Effective communication involves accurate prediction of commonalities within that culture and adaptation to those common perceptions and attitudes in the encoding and decoding of messages.

At the social level of communication we become concerned with the subgroups within a culture. Here we focus upon the ways people are divided into institutions, professions, fraternal associations, occupations, and other functional roles such as students, teachers, parents, and children. At this level we communicate with others in relation to the social roles they have selected and perform within society. We make predictions about people on the basis of commonalities they share with others performing the same function or role for society. We expect teachers to share some common orientations, mothers to hold some common values, and doctors to behave in certain ways. Neither do we say the same things to each of these types of people nor do we interpret their messages in the same way. However, based upon limited information about any one of them, we can make predictions about the commonalities shared by any group and adapt our communication. At this level, effective communication involves prediction of commonalities in the shared role of the group and adaptation of our subsequent encoding and decoding. Much of our communication with people with whom we come in contact at irregular intervals operates at this level.

At the individual level of communication we become concerned with the unique characteristics of each person. We make individualized predictions about the unique characteristics, psychological states, and specific personality of another. Then, if we are effective, we adapt our messages to the individual and interpret that individual's messages according to their uniqueness. At this level, and only at this level, does intimate communication occur in which we share private and personal information about ourselves with another. However, it is often impossible to reach this level until we have discovered and shared our cultural and social commonalities with each other.

So what do we mean when we say that the communication process can be transactional? We mean that communication does not occur in a vacuum; rather, communication can be transactional because it occurs as a part of the total environment which we share with each other. Communication can be transactional because it largely determines our perceptions of reality and is the process by which we share those perceptions and ourselves with others. It is the means by which we go beyond ourselves to share and

participate in the world of which others are a part. To the extent that our
communication is effective not only on cultural and social levels but also at the individual level, our transaction with others is more effective. In short, *communication can be transactional because it is the process by which we share our reality and ourselves with each other.* Our reality, in turn, is not only what exists "out there" but also is our perception of it.

**BLACK BOX
2**

Can you explain why communication is all of these things?
  a process   transactional
  systemic   functional
  interactional

The Communication Process Is Functional

An obvious conclusion from our discussion is that the human communication process must perform some function. We have said that the basic function of communication is change and adaptation to change. But more specifically, what kinds of changes are we concerned about in the communication process? What *specific* functions does it perform?

1. Affinity Function.   One function of communication is the establishment, maintenance, and/or change of social relationships. We communicate in order to relate to other people and to adapt to changes in those relationships. This function often involves messages which indicate the existence or absence of attraction, similarity, and commonality among people. Tom and Mary meet. Mary likes the looks of Tom. Tom likes the looks of Mary. What is the first goal of their interaction? Each tries to create messages to send that will make the other person like them better. In our example of the Dean and the professor, there was little affinity between the two at the outset of their communication. The Dean could probably handle that, but the professor, being in a subordinate role, needed to make the Dean like him better. Thus, he was not only trying to explain what had gone on in his class, but he was trying to do it in a way that would result in the Dean having affinity for him. In short, communication can function to create (increase) or destroy (decrease) affinity among persons and/or to adapt to changes in affinity.

2. Information and Understanding Function.   We commonly think of communicating in order to increase understanding or information.   One function of communication is sending and receiving information which can, in turn, affect understanding, depending upon whether or not it is accurately decoded.   We communicate in order to change the information that another has and to adapt to changes in information and understanding that we have.   The primary function that we hope this book has is to increase your information about and understanding of communication.   In the case of the Dean and the professor, the Dean initiated the communication in order to obtain information.   The professor was more than happy to help.   Communication affects information and understanding.

3. Influence Function.   Another important function of communication is influence.   We communicate in order to change people's attitudes, beliefs, values, or behavior.   Similarly, communication initiated by others can influence us.   Communication also allows us to adapt to attempts at influencing

*We often
communicate with
people who will help
us with problems we
are thinking about.*

us and to the effect of influence on others. When the students wrote to the Dean, they were attempting to influence him to do something, possibly reprimand the professor and get the professor to change what was going on in the class. When the professor met with the Dean, he was trying to get the Dean to indicate approval of what was going on in the class. Through communication, then, we influence others, are influenced, and adapt to the influence of others.

4. Decision Function. Communication also serves a decision-making function. One outcome or effect of communication is reaching a decision. We often communicate with others to help us to decide on issues or behavior we are thinking about adopting. At other times, communication functions in aiding us to adapt to decisions that affect us. In the case of our Dean, he initiated communication with the professor in order to obtain information he felt he needed in order to make a decision about what course of action he should take, if any. He decided there was nothing wrong in the class, but that there was something wrong with the students. Now the students have a decision to make.

5. Confirmation Function. The final function of communication involves continuance or discontinuance of a newly adopted idea, belief, behavior, practice, product, decision, etc. Through communication we attempt to rationalize continuing or justify discontinuing some change that we have adopted previously. Therefore, one outcome of communication is often the confirming or disconfirming of previous change. This function is probably the most closely related to the ways that we adapt to change. In the case of the Dean and the professor, the Dean later talked to the Department Chairman to see if he agreed with the decision that had been reached. He also talked to some other students in the class. Everyone told the Dean that they thought he had made the right decision (people normally do that with Deans, you know); thus, the correctness of the decision was confirmed in the Dean's mind.

All of these functions involve changes that result from communication. As such, they may be viewed as the outcomes or effects of communication. We may also consider them as the reasons that we communicate with each other. The standard by which we can determine whether communication is effective or not is whether the process performed the desired function. *If communication produces the desired change or adaptation to change, then it is functional or effective. If not, then it is ineffective or disfunctional.*

> **BLACK BOX**
> **3**
>
> Can you identify the functions that communication can perform?
>
> Can you provide an example of each function from your own everyday experiences?

Components of Communication

In our previous discussion of communication as a system, we noted that all systems are made up of components. At this point we will specify the essential components that compose any communication system: source, message, channel, and receiver. Let us consider each in turn.

Source

The source in communication is the component that originates a message. The source is usually an individual person, but a source can be two people (a dyad), a group, or even a complex organization. Our Dean and professor both served as individual-person sources; the two students who wrote to the dean were a source composed of a dyad. The role of the source in communication is threefold: determining the meaning that is (hopefully) to be communicated, encoding that meaning into messages, and transmitting those messages. Usually a single person serves in all three roles, but the roles could be served by different people, e.g., the President may determine what is to be communicated, the speech writer prepare the message, and the press secretary present it to the public.

One term that we used above may need further clarification: *encoding*. As we noted in chapter 1, meanings are in people, not in messages. We cannot transmit meanings to other people, we can transmit only messages. Encoding, then, is the process of creating messages that we believe represent the meaning to be communicated and are likely to stimulate similar meaning in the mind of a receiver. Careful encoding is vital to effective communication, because if the messages that are created do not represent the meaning we have or stimulate different meanings in other people, the exchange will not result in the desired outcome.

Message

A message is any verbal or nonverbal stimulus which can serve to evoke meaning in a receiver. What the Dean and the professor said to each other in their meeting represented their messages. The letter sent by the students was composed of a series of messages. The Dean's smile at the end of the discussion was a message. The professor's excessive smoking during the meeting was a message, probably indicating his nervousness. The smoking message illustrates an important point: not all messages are consciously encoded. Some are transmitted without the source even being aware of them. This is particularly true with many nonverbal messages.

Channel

A channel is a means by which a message is conveyed from a source to a receiver. There are many kinds of channels. In face-to-face communication, light waves and sound waves are the primary channels, as the case in the communication between our Dean and professor. Sometimes there are physical means of conveyence, such as the message of the students being carried to the Dean by the mail system. The mass media—radio, television, film, records, billboards—also serve as channels for conveying messages from sources to receivers. In some cases people serve as channels, a common occurrence in organizations: the manager tells the foreman who carries the message to the people on the assembly line. In our Dean-professor case, the Dean served as a channel between the students and the professor.

Receiver

The receiver in communication is the component that ultimately acquires the source's message. As was the case with the source, the receiver is usually an individual person, but the receiver can also be a dyad, a group, or even a complex organization. Our Dean and professor both served as individual-person receivers. The students who received the Dean's recommendation to transfer were a dyad serving as a receiver, but probably were individual receivers as well. The role of the receiver in communication is threefold: reception of messages, decoding those messages to secure meaning, and responding to that meaning. Usually a single person serves in all three

25

roles, but the roles can be served by different people, e.g., the CIA could receive the messages, the State Department could decode the messages, and the President could respond.

> **BLACK BOX**
> **4**
>
> **Can you define each of these important communication terms?**
>
> source   encoding
> message   decoding
> channel   feedback
> receiver

The term *decoding* deserves further clarification. Since messages don't have inherent meaning, it is necessary for us to process them in our minds and compare them with previous messages and our previous experience to discover what they might mean. Decoding, like encoding, is vital to effective communication. If the receiver's previous background and experience are very different from that of the source, or if the receiver allows bias to enter the decoding process, communication will very likely not lead to the desired outcome.

One final component of communication systems that we need to consider is *feedback*. We have not included feedback among the essential components of communication systems because this component may or may not be present, depending on the particular system. Feedback is composed of messages that receivers generate that can be observed by sources which may provide the source with information about how the receiver is processing the messages the source is sending. In the case of the Dean and the professor, the Dean's smile provided the professor with feedback, probably indicating that the professor was having the desired effect from his messages. Similarly, the Dean's recommendation for a transfer was feedback to the students, probably indicating they were not doing too well. In live, face-to-face communication, feedback usually is readily available. Feedback in communication systems that involve the mass media, on the other hand, is usually very limited, delayed, or absent. We will consider the problems that limited feedback produces later, and examine the various effects of feedback in some detail in chapter 8.

Finally, a word about change. In the context of the discussion above, change in the receiver determines whether or not communication has oc-

*Feedback tells the
source how the
receivers are
processing the
message.*

curred. Each outcome of communication, the function that the communication performs, is some type of change in thoughts and/or behaviors. The product of all communication systems, then, is change. To communicate is to change.

Figure 2–2 attempts to show how various components are related to each other within communication systems.

The Intrapersonal Communication System

Individual people—you and I, the Dean and the professor—serve as both sources and receivers of communication, sometimes simultaneously. We believe, therefore, that it is useful to look at the individual as a unique communication system by her or himself. Such a system can be referred to as an "intrapersonal" communication system, since the essential components of all communication systems are in operation within the single individual.

The diagram in Figure 2–2 is a representation of the individual as a communication system. The experiential and physical boundaries in the

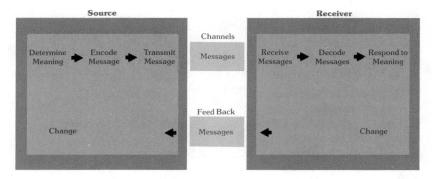

FIGURE 2–2. Basic components of communication.

diagram are intended to suggest that we are all restricted in our communication behaviors by our past experiences and physical makeup. What a person has learned or gained in all of her or his past experience determines to a large extent how that person will respond to and process messages from others, as well as how she or he will encode meaning and send messages to others. We all respond differently. Our language, culture, social status, educational and economic levels, and personal psychological orientation all have an impact on our communication behavior. A black child born and reared in an urban ghetto will not respond like a white child born and reared on a farm in South Dakota. In a similar way, our physical capabilities and limitations affect the way we communicate. Although we might wish it were otherwise, our intelligence, sex, race, stature, abilities, disabilities, personality, and other variables affect how we respond to messages of other people and how we create messages for other people.

These experiential and physical boundaries, then, serve to make each person an individual who has, to a greater or lesser degree, something in common with other individuals. However, these boundaries which define and shape each person are *open* to allow additional inputs of experience and information. These boundaries are open also to allow additional outputs of messages and behaviors directed toward others. All living systems are open, allowing for the transfer of matter and energy between the system and its environment. The kinds of inputs and outputs with which we are primarily concerned in human communication are messages, both verbal and nonverbal.

Within our experiential and physical boundaries, we function as unique information processors. We take incoming messages, decode them and process them through our psychological makeup. This often results in our generating new messages to send to others. In the process we may be changed, so that the next time a message is received, we may handle it somewhat differently. Let us consider some of the elements in the intrapersonal communication system that have a major impact on all other communication systems.

Important Elements in the Intrapersonal Communication System

Several important elements in the intrapersonal communication system are noted in Figure 2–3. These include beliefs, attitudes, motivations, values, behavior habits, and personality.

Information and *beliefs* are closely related concepts. Information refers to our learned and stored experiences or reality. Beliefs refer to our perceptions about the validity—the truth or falsity—of elements in reality. On the other hand, an *attitude* is a predisposition to respond or behave in a favorable or unfavorable way toward something in reality. In communication we are particularly concerned about our attitudes toward other individuals (sources and receivers) and our attitudes toward concepts inherent in messages. *Motivations* refer to both physiological drives (for food, shelter, sex, etc.) and social drives (for love, affection, self-esteem, etc.) of the individual. Based upon our information, beliefs, attitudes, and motivations, we consciously or unconsciously formulate *values*. *Values* are relatively long-enduring judgments about the desirability of things and behaviors.

All of these elements are also related to our *behavior habits*. For example, while we might have beliefs, attitudes, and motivations that would point to a certain behavior, our values might preclude us from engaging in

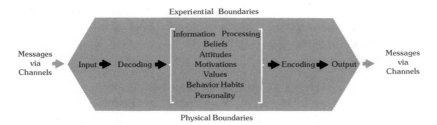

FIGURE 2–3. *The intrapersonal communication system.*

that behavior. While we may be hungry, inclined to take food from a shelf, and believe that we could do so without getting caught, our value system might prevent us from stealing. In short, *past behavior* as well as *ability to behave* in certain ways (skills) are related to these other elements within the individual. An important consideration in communication is that our past behavior affects how we decode and encode messages. Also, the encoding and decoding of messages affects how we behave. Since we consider communication to involve behavior, our learned abilities in communication (communication skills) also affect how we will encode and decode messages.

Personality refers to the total psychological makeup of the individual that is a result of the mixture of all of these elements. An individual's personality reflects her or his information, beliefs, attitudes, motivations, values, and behavior. The personality of an individual, involving all of that person's unique traits, is derived from the interplay of these elements with the environment external to the individual.

In addition, we should note the basic principle that interrelates these elements within the person. The individual attempts to maintain balanced and consistent relationships among these components. If a person's values are changed, this will result in adjustments in the other elements to achieve consistency. If a person's attitudes and beliefs are changed, for example, there may be some corresponding change in behavior to restore consistency, and visa versa. However, individuals have differing tolerance levels for inconsistency. Almost all of us are capable of maintaining some level of inconsistency; for example, between our beliefs and our behavior. By applying this principle, we can better understand how these elements affect and are affected by the encoding and decoding processes. We will address ourselves to this principle in more detail in later chapters.

The individual person is a very complex communication system. When we bring two or more of these complex systems together to form a new communication system, it is no wonder that the outcomes are often far less promising than desired. No communication that involves human beings is ever perfect, nor is it ever likely to be. While the outcome of the communication between our Dean and professor was probably very much to the liking of the professor, we might wonder what the Dean thinks of a professor who smokes four cigarettes in fifteen minutes. We might also wonder about what the professor thinks of a Dean who calls him in on such a matter without checking with the Department Chairperson first. Or we might wonder what the two students think of a Dean who recommends that they change schools.

While your communication probably can never reach a stage of perfection, our hope is that by developing an understanding of all the elements that impinge upon communication and how communication systems function, you will be able to move in that direction. Our concern in the next two chapters is directed toward the kinds of communication systems that are formed when two or more individual systems are brought together.

SUGGESTED FURTHER READINGS

1. Miller, Gerald R. and Steinberg, Mark. *Between People.* (Chicago: Science Research Associates, 1975).

   Chapter 1 discusses an interesting and novel approach to the study of interpersonal communication. Three levels of analysis (psychological, social, cultural) used in making predictions in communication are defined and discussed in some detail.

2. Rogers, Everett M. and Shoemaker, Floyd F. *Communication of Innovations: A Cross-Cultural Approach* (New York: The Free Press, 1971).

   Several chapters in this text are worth reading. The nature of communication in social change is discussed in some depth in several chapters. The process of communicating innovations to society appears to be closely allied to the functions of communication as conceptualized in this chapter and the remainder of the text.

3. Schramm, Wilbur. *The Process and Effects of Mass Communication* (Urbana: University of Illinois Press, 1954).

   The introductory chapters of this volume should be of interest at this point in your study of communication. Again, the perspective is limited to mass communication involving primarily mediated messages. While this scope is more limited than our purpose in this text, it does provide another orientation or point of view that is helpful in clarifying concepts of communication.

4. Sereno, Kenneth K. and Mortensen, C. David, eds. *Foundations of Communication Theory* (New York: Harper & Row, 1970).

   This book of readings has several articles that are relevant at this point. Parts I and II and the first reading in Part III contain basic definitions, information, concepts, and models, along with discussions of notions of process, systems, transaction, and so forth. Selection of several of these readings would constitute a valuable supplement presenting some divergent views.

5. Stewart, John, ed. *Bridges Not Walls* (Reading, Mass.: Addison-Wesley, 1973).

This book of readings contains some views and perspectives that are divergent from those presented in this chapter. Since the readings are designed to apply primarily to interpersonal communication, the orientation is necessarily more limited to scope. However, chapter one, containing three readings, might help to clarify and expand our notion of transaction.

SELECTED REFERENCES

BERLO, DAVID K. *The Process of Communication* (New York: Holt, Rinehart and Winston, 1960).

FABUN, DON. *The Dynamics of Change* (Englewood Cliffs, N.J.: Prentice-Hall, 1967).

FOTHERINGHAM, WALLACE C. *Perspectives on Persuasion* (Boston: Allyn and Bacon, 1966).

LANDIS, J. R. *Current Perspectives on Social Problems,* 3rd ed. (Belmont, Cal.: Wadsworth, 1973).

LASSWELL, HAROLD D. "The Structure and Function of Communications in Society," in *The Communication of Ideas.* Edited by L. Bryson (New York: Harper & Row, 1948).

LIN, NAN. *The Study of Human Communication* (Indianapolis: Bobbs-Merrill, 1973).

MCCROSKEY, JAMES C., LARSON, CARL E., and KNAPP, MARK L. *An Introduction to Interpersonal Communication* (Englewood Cliffs, N.J.: Prentice-Hall, 1971).

MILLER, GERALD R. and STEINBERG, MARK. *Between People* (Chicago: Science Research Associates, 1975).

MONROE, ALAN H. *Principles and Types of Speech,* 4th ed. (Chicago: Scott, Foresman, and Company, 1955).

OSGOOD, CHARLES E., ed. "Psycholinguistics: A Survey of Theory and Research Problems," *Journal of Abnormal and Social Psychology* 49 (1954), Morton Prince Memorial Supplement.

PACE, WAYNE R., BOREN, ROBERT R., and PETERSON, BRENT D. *Communication Behavior and Experiments: A Scientific Approach* (Belmont, Cal.: Wadsworth, 1975).

ROGERS, EVERETT M. and SHOEMAKER, FLOYD F. *Communication of Innovations: A Cross-Cultural Approach* (New York: The Free Press, 1971).

ROSS, RAYMOND S. *Persuasion: Communication and Interpersonal Relations* (Englewood Cliffs, N.J.: Prentice-Hall, 1974).

SCHRAMM, WILBUR. *The Process and Effects of Mass Communication* (Urbana: University of Illinois Press, 1954).

Sereno, Kenneth K. and Mortensen, C. David, eds. *Foundations of Communication Theory* (New York: Harper & Row Publishers, 1970).

Shannon, C. E. and Weaver, W. *The Mathematical Theory of Communication* (Urbana: University of Illinois Press, 1949).

Stewart, John, ed. *Bridges Not Walls* (Reading, Mass.: Addison-Wesley, 1973).

3

Interpersonal Communication Systems

When various systems of human communication are stripped of their complexity and reduced to the lowest common denominator, the nature of the human communication process can be observed as essentially the same in all systems. Human communication exists when any source, whether a single person or a group, encodes and transmits a message that is decoded by a receiver, either a single person or a group. From the simplest of all human communication systems to the most complex, this process remains basically the same. Almost four decades ago, while writing about public speaking, James Winans made the point quite clearly:

> Let us imagine all speeches and all memory of speech-making to be blotted out, so that there is no person in the world who remembers that he has ever made a speech, or heard one, or read one; and there is left no clue to this art. "Is this the end of speech-making?" Here comes a man who has

seen a great race, or has been in a battle, or perhaps is excited about his new invention, or on fire with enthusiasm for a cause. He begins to talk with a friend on the street. Others join them, five, ten, twenty, a hundred. Interest grows. He lifts his voice that all may hear; but the crowd wishes to hear and see the speaker better. "Get up on this truck," they cry; and he mounts the truck and goes on with his story or plea.

A private conversation has become a public speech; but under the circumstances imagined it is only thought of as a conversation, enlarged conversation. It does not seem abnormal, but quite the natural thing.

When does the converser become a speech-maker? When ten persons gather? Fifty? Or is it when he gets up on the truck? There is, of course, no point at which we can say the change has taken place. There is no change in the nature or the spirit of the act; it is essentially the same throughout, a conversation adapted as the speaker proceeds, to the growing number of his hearers. There may be a change, to be sure, if he becomes self-conscious; but assuming that interest in story or argument remains the dominant emotion, there is no essential change in his speaking. It is probable that with the increasing importance of his position and the increasing tension, the feeling that comes with numbers, he gradually modifies his tone and diction and permits himself to launch into a bolder strain and a wider range of ideas and feelings than in an ordinary conversation; but the change is in degree and not in kind. He is conversing with an audience.[*]

As Winans indicates, the essential nature of the communication process, from the simpler form in conversation to the complex form of public speaking, does not change. However, even if we had never given a public speech, we would be able to recognize that there is *something* different about talking to a friend and giving a talk before a large group. We would also recognize that there is something different about writing a memo to a colleague and broadcasting the evening news over CBS television. Indeed, there are major differences. But these differences are the result of the differences in social systems of communication, not differences in the human communication process itself. In this chapter we will examine some of the common interpersonal systems of human communication. In chapter 4 we will look specifically at mass communication systems.

Dyadic Communication Systems

A dyadic communication system is formed when any two people attempt to communicate with each other. The man on the street and his friend formed

[*] J. A. Winans, *Speech-Making* (New York: Appleton-Century-Crofts, 1938), pp. 11f. Reprinted by permission of Prentice-Hall, Inc.

We can recognize that there is a major difference between talking to a friend and giving a public speech.

such a system. So did our friends, the Dean and the professor, in the previous chapter. The authors of this book formed such a system in order to write the book. We all join with others to form dyadic systems in our everyday lives.

Some of these systems continue in operation for long periods of time. A marriage forms a dyadic system that continues over an extended period, although at some point it may be interrupted or terminated by divorce, separation, or death. Other dyadic systems which may extend for any period of time include a dating relationship, a teacher-student relationship, a salesman-client relationship, a doctor-patient relationship, a secretary-executive relationship, or the simplest dyad of all, two friends. In short, whenever any two people join to communicate, either temporarily or over a long period of time, a dyadic communication system is formed.

Dyads don't exist only in their own right. They also exist as parts of all other systems. Within a family there is a small-group communication system. But within that small-group system, there are several dyadic systems. Let us presume that there is a mother, a father, a son, and a daughter in the family. The following dyadic systems exist within that family: mother-

37

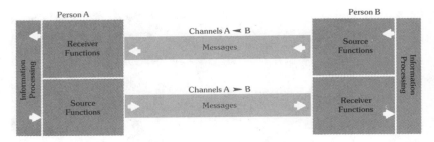

FIGURE 3–1. Basic dyadic communication system model.

father, mother-son, mother-daughter, father-daughter, father-son, and daughter-son. The communication that exists within each of these dyads will differ from all the others both in terms of content and context. However, the dyadic system of communication in each case will remain the same. Figure 3–1 presents a model of the dyadic communication system. With this model in mind, let us consider some of the essential characteristics of dyadic communication systems.

Dyadic communication systems are "coactive." By "coactive" we mean that the two people within the dyad are simultaneously functioning as sources and receivers. Each is changing the other. Each is being changed by the other. Presume Tom and Cathy have formed a dyad and are out on a date. Tom suggests stopping for a pizza after a movie. Cathy tells him she doesn't like pizza. Tom begins to wonder about their relationship. Pizza is one of his favorite foods. Cathy also begins to wonder. Tom is a bit on the plump side. "Will he keep eating pizza and get fatter? Ugh."

Each person in the dyad can also be changed by external forces. When Cathy gets back to her room, her roommate asks her why she is still dating "that slob." Such external elements inherently exist because dyadic systems always exist within larger communication systems. For example, a secretary-executive dyad exists normally as a part of a larger organizational structure which serves as a communication system as well. While the secretary and the executive communicate and produce change in one another, there are also changes produced in both of them and in their dyadic relationship by the external elements within the organization.

It should be stressed that a dyadic communication system is more than just the sum of the two people of whom it is composed. A dyad exists with a life of its own. Mary and Bill each exist independently. When they join together to form a dyad, however, they may relate to one another in ways that differ from how they relate to any other people. Essentially then,

A secretary-executive dyad is often part of a larger organizational structure that is also a communication system.

the Mary and Bill we know as individuals are different from the Mary and Bill we know as a part of their dyad.

Similarly, a dyad is a constantly changing system. As we have noted previously, change is the inherent result of communication. Consequently, when two individuals form a dyad, they are changed by that formation. When they communicate within that dyad they are also changed, and as a result the dyad itself changes. The way Mary and Bill relate to one another today may be very different from the way they will relate to one another tomorrow or a week from tomorrow or next year.

Although a dyad is a complete system within itself, it may serve as a unit in a larger system. The dyad may become a source in a larger system. For example, Tom and Cathy may decide to have a party and invite some friends in (if he gives up the pizza). They function together as a source when they send the invitation. Similarly, a dyad may serve as a receiver. Tom and Cathy send an invitation to a married couple they know, Mary and Bill. Mary and Bill as a dyad serve as a receiver, and will probably communicate about the message they received from the other dyad. "Do you want to go over to the party?" "I don't know, Tom certainly can be obnoxious. But

39

Cathy always has interesting people at her parties. Let's go." "Yeah, I'd like to go, too. Cathy sure has a nice way about her."

In some cases dyads can also serve as channels. Tom and Cathy may have put a note at the bottom of the invitation to Mary and Bill: "Bring Frank and Ellen if you can." Later Mary and Bill run into their friends Frank and Ellen and ask them if they would like to go to the party. They have served as a channel between the Tom-Cathy and Frank-Ellen dyads. Also, let us take the case where Mary and Bill run into Barb, who is a good friend of Cathy's. They ask her if she is going to the party. She says, "What party?" A message has been communicated between the Tom-Cathy dyad and Barb via the Mary-Bill channel. This type of human channel, whether it is a dyad as it was in this case, or if it is a single individual, is what we normally refer to as a "rumor" channel.

In sum, dyads are the smallest interpersonal communication systems. These systems exist in their own right and also as parts of larger systems.

Small-Group Communication Systems

Small-group communication systems exist when more than two individuals are joined, or when there is simultaneous coaction of two or more dyads within the same context. We can set no arbitrary limit on the number of individuals or dyads which may exist within a small group; however, there are boundaries. For a small group to exist it must be possible for simultaneous communication to occur among any or all of the individuals in the group. Consequently, a public speaking setting should not be viewed as a small-group communication system. In such a system it may be possible for each of the receivers to interact simultaneously with the public speaker, but it is probably impossible for all of the receivers to interact with one another at the same time. Similarly, a group composed of 100 people, such as the United States Senate, should not be considered a small group. It would be difficult, if not impossible, for all 100 senators to communicate simultaneously with one another.

Although all human communication systems exist because of some purpose or function that is necessary to the members of the system, this is particularly evident in small-group communication systems. Small groups exist for a variety of functions. Some of them may exist on a pure friendship basis, with affinity being the only function served. An example might be a group of men who live in the same dorm and often go out for a beer together in the evening. Other groups exist for the purpose of information seeking, such as study groups that may be formed to complete a class project or prepare for a test. Still others exist because there are problems that need to be solved or decisions made by the group. Examples would include committees that are appointed by student clubs or organizations, and task groups in a business. As is the case with dyads, small groups may be either transitory or long lasting. Three people waiting for a bus may form a very transitory small group, designed exclusively to serve the function of affinity. A family is a small group that exists for many, many years in most cases. Committees of an organization may also exist for extended periods of time. Such committees illustrate another important point concerning small-group communication systems: they may be a part of a larger communication system.

Characteristics of Small-Group Systems

Figure 3–2 presents a model of a small-group communication system. For the purpose of simplicity and clarity, the small group included in this model involves only three individuals. With this model in mind let us consider some of the common characteristics of small groups.

First, a small group is an *interactive* system. By this we mean that each of the individuals who make up the small group is constantly changing the other individuals and being changed by them. Similarly, the dyads which exist within the small group are constantly being changed by the communication that occurs in the small group. Tom, Cathy, Bill, and Mary interact as a small group. What goes on in the group will affect the later communication in the Tom-Cathy and Bill-Mary dyads.

Although we did not stress the point when considering dyads because the point may be obvious, whenever an individual is removed from a larger communication system, the larger communication system is changed. For example, a father-mother dyad could be radically changed by substituting the son for the mother. This principle also applies to small-group communication systems, although it may not be as immediately apparent. If one person leaves a group, or one person is replaced in a group, or a new person joins a group, the group is changed. It is not the same group that existed previously. Thus, the parts of a small group are not interchangeable or replaceable. Whenever any of the people are changed or replaced, a new group communication system is created.

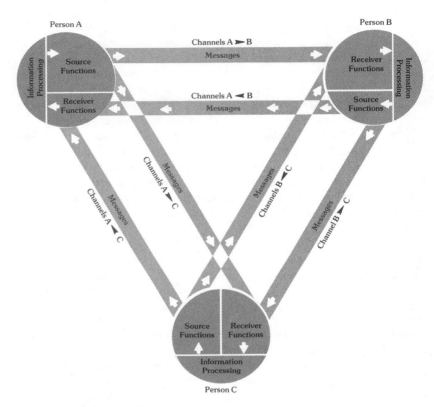

FIGURE 3–2. Basic small-group communication system model.

A small group has an existence of its own in the same sense that a dyad does. A group is not just the sum of its parts. The output of a group is not the sum of Mary's and Bill's and Tom's contributions. Nor is it simply the sum of the contribution of the dyads in the group (Mary-Bill, Mary-Tom, Bill-Tom). Since a small group is interactive, all of the individuals and dyads within the small group are changed as a result of being part of the system. The output of the group, then, may be very unlike what the output would be from any of the individuals or dyads within the group. This is sometimes referred to as the "assembly affect."

Since a group takes on a life of its own, the individual members of the group often develop an identification with the group, sometimes called *groupness*. This is particularly evident in groups that serve as units in larger communication systems. A group may serve as a receiver in larger communication systems whenever it feels that it needs to seek information. Similarly, the group may serve as a source in a larger system if it feels that units in the larger system need information that the group possesses or if units in the larger system need to be influenced in some way or another. A committee, for example, may seek to influence the larger organization to adopt recommendations of the committee. A group may also serve as a channel within a larger communication system where inputs are provided to the group by other units of the system and these are transmitted on to still other units in the larger system. An example is the committee system of Congress which collects inputs from other parts of the Congressional communication system and transmits them to still another part of that system.

Small groups and dyads have many things in common. In both systems, individuals serve as sources and receivers, often simultaneously. Both systems are formed for some purpose or function and may cease to exist once that function is performed, or no longer needed, or no longer wanted. Both systems often exist as parts of larger communication systems. Finally, both systems regularly produce change in the larger systems of which they are a part, are changed by the larger systems, and are changed by external forces.

Large-Group Communication Systems

A large-group communication system is normally referred to as an *organization*. Such a system may be of any size. Some common examples are General Motors Corporation, the Roman Catholic Church, a University Student Government, the administration and faculty members of a college, the management and employees of a restaurant. Like dyads and small groups, organizations exist for some function. The people who compose the system normally form the organization to accomplish some purpose, such as to influence other people, or to market some product.

Organizations are made up of many dyads and small groups. Many larger organizations actually have other large group communication systems as a part of the parent organization. General Motors Corporation is one of the largest group communication systems in existence. This system also has very large group communication systems that are subsystems of the parent: Chevrolet, Buick, and so forth. We can see that the reciprocal would also be true; that is, that a large-group communication system may be part of an even larger system, as Chevrolet and Buick are parts of General Motors. Similarly, we know that although the Department of Health, Education and Welfare is an enormous group communication system, it is also a part of the larger group communication system known as the Executive Branch of the United States Government.

Figure 3–3 is a relatively simple model of a large-group communication system. It is impossible within the space available in this chapter to provide a fully descriptive model of a very large organization; however, the model in Figure 3–3 illustrates the essential nature of such systems.

The Roles of Large-Group Systems

We have stressed that dyads and small groups are interactive systems. Large-group systems are generally not fully interactive; rather, they are

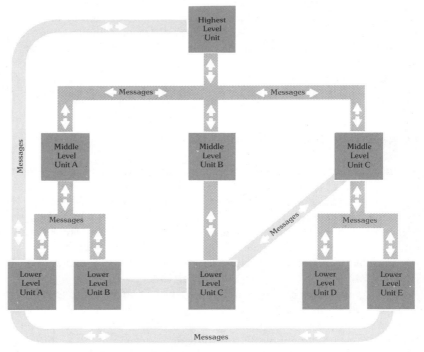

FIGURE 3–3. Simplified model of large-group communication system (solid lines indicate formal channels; broken lines indicate some of the possible grapevine or rumor channels).

"hierarchical" systems. An hierarchical system is one in which communication tends to flow primarily in one direction, rather than being reciprocal. In a business organization, for example, many messages are transmitted from the upper levels of the system to the lower levels. In many cases no response is requested or obtained from below. Similarly, messages can flow from lower levels of an organization to the upper levels without any response or interaction. Nevertheless, hierarchical communication systems such as this have one essential characteristic that is necessary for classification as a *system;* that is, each part of the structure can produce change in each of the other parts and can be changed by each of the other parts as well as by external forces. Whereas this kind of change is inherent in dyads and small groups, it is not inherent in hierarchical systems. While a measure of change is common in all parts of hierarchical systems, it is possible for some parts to remain relatively unchanged as a result of communication from other parts. An example is a large organization where the leadership (e.g., Board of Directors) is far removed from the lower levels of the organization (e.g., assembly-line worker). There may be no communication between these elements of the system and, consequently, no change.

Large-group communication systems, unlike dyads and to a degree unlike small groups, are usually very long lasting. The exceptions are organizations intended to exist for only a temporary period. For example, an organization formed to develop a protest rally in Washington, D.C., against the Vietnam War existed to accomplish that purpose. Once that rally was over, the organization ceased to function. This, however, is the exception rather than the rule.

Although large-group systems may be hard to visualize in this role because of their size, organizations may serve as sources, receivers, or channels in even larger systems. The Department of Health, Education and Welfare, for example, may serve as a source of communication to local school districts concerning innovations in educational methods. The same department may serve as a receiver of communication from the United States Congress. Similarly, HEW may serve as a channel of communication from the upper executive levels of government to the local school districts.

There is one very important characteristic of large-group communication systems that is shared by dyads and small groups. This characteristic is generally recognized by people concerned with dyads and small groups, but it is often not recognized in organizations. Individuals within organizations are not interchangeable. Whenever one person leaves a group, one person is added to the system, or one person is replaced by another person, that organization is changed. The larger the system, the less impact this

*Large-group systems
are hierarchical:
messages are
transmitted from
upper to lower levels
of the system.*

alteration will have on the total organization. Nevertheless, such change does occur. Managers in a large company often operate on the assumption that people are interchangeable parts. Thus, if one person is not working out well, that person is replaced by another person. Such a change of personnel will affect many dyadic relationships and many small groups of which the first person was a part and of which the new person becomes a part. These changes can have a major impact on communication within the organization itself.

Large-group communication systems differ from dyads and small groups primarily in the extent to which direct links among many of the people within the system do not exist. Although the chairperson of the board of General Motors and the auto worker on the assembly line are all part of the same organization, there is seldom any direct link between the two, hence seldom *any* communication between the two. Rather, there are formal channels of communication between the Board and the assembly-line worker, usually fairly extended channels that must pass through several small group and dyadic systems. Such extended systematic patterns do not normally result in effective communication, because too much information is lost along the line. This type of communication system is clearly not in-

---

**BLACK BOX
5**

**Can you identify the elements that all interpersonal communication
systems have in common?**

**Can you distinguish between each of the following pairs of communica-
tion systems:
dyadic and small group;
dyadic and large group;
small group and large group.**

**Provide an example of each type of interpersonal communication sys-
tem from your everyday experiences.**

---

teractive. A message may be sent from the upper levels to the lower levels, but little feedback is likely to occur. Since communication within the formal channels of the hierarchical system in organizations is very difficult, and even sometimes impossible, it is normal for informal communication channels to be created outside of the formal system. These informal patterns must be considered as part of the large-group communication system if we are to understand how communication occurs within an organization. Most of us are familiar with terms such as "rumor" and "grapevine." Both terms refer to the informal communication systems that exist within the large-group communication system as a whole. In many cases the communication that occurs via the grapevine or rumor is very effective and very accurate. In other cases, it is neither effective nor accurate.

Interpersonal and Mass Communication

In this chapter we have focused on three communication systems that we have labeled interpersonal: dyadic, small-group, and large-group communication systems. We have stressed the ways that the three differ from each other, and indeed, they do differ substantially. But they are still more similar to one another than they are to other systems; hence, our decision to place them within the same category—interpersonal.

The essence of interpersonal communication is *potential for interaction, two-way communication, and mutual influence.* Dyads, small groups, and organizations all share this potential, although it is less often fully realized in large organizations than in the other two systems.

Mass communication systems lack the full potential for interaction, two-way communication, and mutual influence. So mass communication systems are not interpersonal. Rather, mass communication systems involve primarily linear, one-way communication, with little or no opportunity for receivers to have an impact on mass communication sources. We will examine such systems in more detail in the next chapter.

SUGGESTED FURTHER READINGS

1. Harms, L. S. *Human Communication: The New Fundamentals* (New York: Harper & Row, 1974).
   Chapters 4 and 5 of this book expand some of the concepts we set forth in this chapter.

2. Laszlo, E. *The Systems View of the World* (New York: George Braziller, Inc., 1972).
   This book gives a general introduction to the systems orientation which influenced our approach in this and the following chapter. If you have not been exposed to this orientation previously, this is a good book to get you started.

SELECTED REFERENCES

BARNLUND, D. C. *Interpersonal Communication* (Boston: Houghton-Mifflin, 1968).

BERTALANFFY, L. VON. *General Systems Theory, Foundations, Development, Applications* (New York: George Braziller, 1968).

BROCK, B. L., CHESEBRO, J. W., CRAGAN, J. F., and KLUMPP, J. F. *Public Policy Decision-Making* (New York: Harper & Row, 1973).

BURGOON, M., HESTON, J. K., and McCROSKEY, J. C. *Small Group Communication* (New York: Holt, Rinehart and Winston, 1974).

GOLDHABER, G. M. *Organizational Communication* (Dubuque: W. C. Brown, 1974).

HARMS, L. S. *Human Communication: The New Fundamentals* (New York: Harper & Row, 1974).

KATZ, D. and KAHN, R. L. *The Social Psychology of Organizations* (New York: John Wiley, 1966).

LASZLO, E. *The Systems View of the World* (New York: George Braziller, 1972).

McCROSKEY, J. C., LARSON, C. E., and KNAPP, M. L. *An Introduction to Interpersonal Communication* (Englewood Cliffs, N.J.: Prentice-Hall, 1971).

SEILER, J. A. *Systems Analysis in Organizational Behavior* (Homewood, Ill.: Irwin, 1967).

YOUNG, O. R. "A Survey of General Systems Theory." *General Systems Handbook* 9 (1964): 61–80.

4

Mass Communication Systems

Walt and Donna get up at 7:30 in the morning. While Walt is shaving he listens to the local radio station to see what the weather will be like today. While Donna is waiting for the coffee to perk, she turns on the *Today Show* and catches the news. On the way to work, Walt and Donna listen to music and several advertisements on the car radio.

Walt drops Donna at her office and goes on toward his. He notices a billboard advertising a national motel chain. In the middle of the morning Walt has to give a speech to forty new employees concerning the company's employee benefits program. He picks up the company newsletter and thumbs through it while waiting for them to arrive.

Donna has to meet with a representative of her company's ad agency to go over a new sales campaign. She looks up the number of the agency in the phone book and calls for an appointment. Finding that she can see someone soon, she catches a cab to the agency's offices. She notes the sign on

*In a one-to-many
system, there is one
source but many
receivers.*

top of the cab advertising a local restaurant. While she is waiting for her appointment, she picks up a copy of *Time* and flips through it.

After a hard day's work, Walt and Donna sit down to relax. Donna goes through the day's mail, tossing an ad for mail-order jewelry in the waste basket, and decides to read the evening newspaper. Walt picks up a book and reads for a while. Later both watch television, catching a movie they had missed when it appeared in the local theater.

All day and evening, Walt and Donna, just like you and I, have been involved constantly in mass communication. Mass communication permeates our environment. We can't avoid it even if we want to, and usually we don't want to. It is our primary source of information and entertainment.

"Mass communication" is a generic term for several different types of communication systems which differ from one another in a number of important ways. We will look at three major types of mass communication systems.

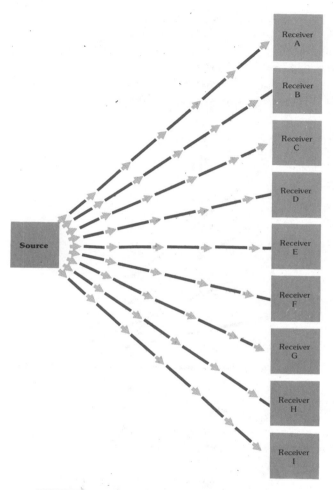

FIGURE 4–1. One-to-many communication model.

One-to-Many Systems

One-to-many communication is probably the most common form of mass communication. In such a system there is one source but many receivers. Figure 4–1 presents a simplified model of a one-to-many communication system. The source in this type of communication system may be an individual, a dyad, a small group, or a large group. The receivers may be individuals, dyads, small groups, or large groups. Public speaking is probably the most obvious example of this type of mass communication; however, television, radio, books, magazines, records, and films also provide examples. Another very common example of this type of mass communication is

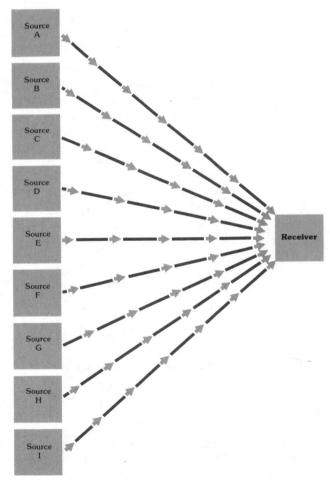

FIGURE 4–2. Many-to-one communication model.

the house organ that is published by many business concerns. In each of these examples there is one source, which may be either an individual or a group of one type or another, that is providing a message or a group of messages simultaneously to a large number of receivers.

Many-to-One Systems

Many-to-one systems are almost the exact reverse of one-to-many systems. Figure 4–2 provides a simplified model of such a system. In many-to-one communication there is only one receiver but many sources. Again, the receiver or any of the sources may be composed of individuals, dyads, small groups, or large groups. The social protest movements during the 1960s were many-to-one systems, particularly the protest movement against the Vietnam War. There were large numbers of sources trying to influence the President (receiver) to change his policy concerning the war in Vietnam. Similarly, the question of birth control has produced a many-to-one communication system that focuses on the Pope of the Roman Catholic Church, where many people and groups, both Catholic and non-Catholic, are exerting a concerted effort to influence the Pope to change his mind on the question of artificial birth control.

Many-to-Many Systems

Many-to-many communication systems are probably the most complex systems to understand. Figure 4–3 provides a model of this type of communication system. As we note in that model, there can be any number of sources and any number of receivers within such a system. The best example of this type of communication system in operation is the process of

> **BLACK BOX**
> **6**
>
> Can you describe the distinguishing characteristics of these communication systems and provide an example of each from your own experience to illustrate your definition: one-to-many systems; many-to-one systems; and many-to-many systems?

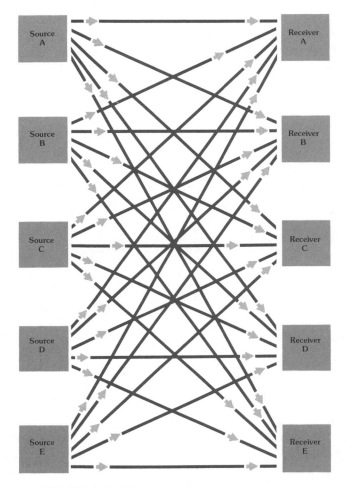

FIGURE 4–3. Many-to-many communication model.

news diffusion in the United States. All of the people, dyads, and groups within the society serve as receivers, and all the various mass media (television, radio, newspaper, magazines, and so forth) serve as sources. Each of the sources and receivers operates as an individual unit within the system. There is seldom a significant collaboration among these units. Rather, this is a highly diffused communication system with most of the parts being relatively unfamiliar with what the other parts of the system are doing.

The Nature of Mass Communication Systems

Although the differences among the three mass communication systems described above are rather obvious, there are a number of similarities among these systems that we need to stress. The most important similarity, and a characteristic which distinguishes mass communication systems from other systems, is the almost complete lack of interaction between source and receiver in mass communication systems. Very little mass communication occurs in face-to-face transactions. The exception is public speaking. But even in this instance, there is generally little interaction between source and receiver.

A second important characteristic of mass communication systems is that they often involve media, the print and electronic methods we use to transmit a message from its source to a receiver, such as television, radio, books, magazines, billboards, etc. The presence of the media in any communication system eliminates, for all intents and purposes, the possibility of direct interaction within that system. Thus, if we examine mass communication systems for interactions without looking very carefully to the total system, we may see no connection present at all. Closer examination of these systems will indicate that there is a great deal of interaction normally present, but that interaction is not normally present between the ultimate source and the ultimate receiver.

Models of Mass Communication Process

Frequently, mass communication systems are "multi-transactional" in nature. People become links in a chain within the overall system. To understand this phenomena we need to examine some of the models of mass communication systems which have been considered in the past.

The original model which was used to attempt to explain the mass communication system has been referred to as the *hypodermic needle model*. This model is represented in Figure 4–4. It is a very simplistic model of mass communication. Essentially it suggests that messages flow from a communication source, generally through the media, to the receiver. Thus if we wish to find out the effect of any particular attempt at mass communication, we could observe what the source did and measure the impact on the receiver. Unfortunately, mass communication systems do not always operate in this simple manner. Only part of the effect of the

FIGURE 4-4. Hypodermic needle model of mass communication.

source on the ultimate receiver can be explained through this type of a model.

A second approach to explaining how mass communication operates is exemplified in the model in Figure 4–5. This model introduces the concept of the *opinion leader.* An opinion leader is someone within our peer group, with whom we have formed a dyad, from whom we receive information and advice about a particular topic. An opinion leader would be the person we turn to for an opinion about a new movie before we go to see it, or a person whom we ask about a new cologne before we buy it.

The model in Figure 4–5 suggests that messages flow from the original source, usually via media, to opinion leaders, who in turn pass these messages on to the rest of the population. This model has been referred to as the *two-step flow model* of mass communication. This model better explains how communication occurs within a mass communication system than the hypodermic needle model. It notes that although there is the presence of the media in most cases, there is also face-to-face communication that occurs as part of the process. Unfortunately, the model indicates only part of this face-to-face communication.

Figure 4–6 presents a more contemporary model which can be used to explain how communication occurs within a mass communication system. We may refer to this model as a *two-cycle, two-step flow model.* In this model the original source will transmit messages, normally via the media, to both opinion leaders and other receivers simultaneously. Then communication may be initiated either by the opinion leader or the other receiver concerning the source's message. Thus, it is not uncommon to find a situation where a receiver has heard or read the message from the source and then goes to that person's opinion leader to ask for more information or

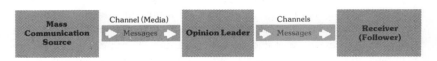

FIGURE 4-5. Two-step flow model of mass communication.

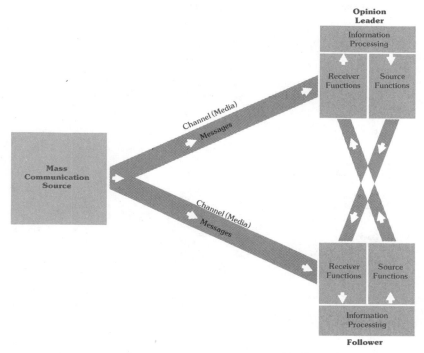

FIGURE 4–6. Two-cycle, two-step flow model of mass communication.

advice. Similarly, the opinion leader may see or hear the message and seek out the other receiver to provide her or his opinion or advice. To exemplify this process, let's imagine that a toothpaste manufacturer comes out with a new product, "Cream Toothpaste," and advertises it on television. Both my dentist and I see the advertisement. She will probably receive other information, and maybe a sample, in the mail. I visit my dentist, who is my opinion leader on toothpaste, for my regular checkup and while there ask her what she thinks of "Cream Toothpaste." She will tell me what she knows about "Cream" and give me her advice without my asking for it, particularly if she thinks that "Cream" is unusually good or bad and that I need to know about it.

While the two-cycle, two-step flow model accurately explains how much of the impact of mass communication functions, it still overlooks one important element, the possibility of more than two steps being present.

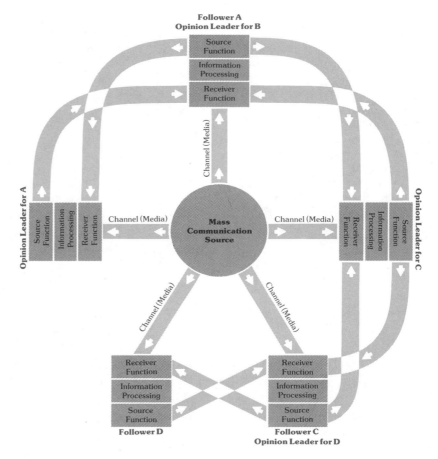

FIGURE 4–7. *Multi-cycle, multi-step flow model of mass communication.*

Figure 4–7 is the most adequate model that we have developed to explain how mass communication systems function. This may be referred to as a *multi-cycle, multi-step flow model.* While very similar to the model in Figure 4–6, this model notes that mass communication may involve several series of opinion leader-follower interactions. Thus, ultimate receivers may obtain information and influence through interaction with their opinion leaders, who have in turn been informed and influenced by interaction with *their* opinion leaders, and on and on through any number of opinion leader-follower steps. The key point is that impact in a mass communication system is often principally produced by the dyadic interpersonal communication that occurs, rather than as a process of a message coming directly from an original source to the ultimate receiver.

To understand why and how messages from mass communication sources, particularly those involving the media, have so little impact on ultimate receivers, but interpersonal communication, which may be produced as a result of a message from a mass source, does have a major impact, we need to examine carefully the concepts of interpersonal similarity and opinion leadership.

Similarity of Source and Receiver

The degree of similarity between sources and receivers—technically referred to as *homophily*—has a substantial impact on communication. If a source and receiver are similar, communication is likely to be more effective. If Tom and John are from the same area, use the same language, were educated in the same way, share a lot of common beliefs, attitudes, and values, then they are much more likely to be able to communicate with each other effectively than either would be able to communicate with Walter Cronkite or any other mass communication source whom they have likely never met and who may have a drastically different background from theirs. This strong tendency for communication between people who are highly similar and noncommunication between people who are greatly different has been referred to as the *principle of homophily*. Most of our communication patterns reflect this principle. We communicate most often with others who are similar to us.

Another way of visualizing this principle is to talk about *overlap*. To the extent that the attitudes, beliefs, experiences, education, background, culture, and so forth, of the source and the receiver overlap, they are more likely to attempt communication with each other, and equally as important, they are more likely to be effective in their communication attempts. The diagrams in Figure 4–8 illustrate this principle.

One problem enters here, one that may not be readily apparent at first glance. When we are highly similar to another person, we have less *need* to communicate with each other. Jack and Charlie grew up together, went to the same schools, attend the same church, married sisters, and work in the same office. They should be able to communicate very effectively with one another—but about what? Jack needs to communicate with his

61

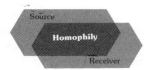

FIGURE 4–8. *Source-receiver similarity.*

(a) Similar source and receiver with overlapping boundaries of experience, etc. Prediction: effective communication.

(b) Dissimilar source and receiver with little overlap of boundaries of experience, etc. Prediction: ineffective, or no, communication.

boss—a person who grew up in another part of the country, attends a different church, is not married, and makes twice as much money as Jack. The dissimilarity between Jack and his boss is technically referred to as *heterophily.* Jack's boss is not unlike the typical source Jack encounters in the mass media: very dissimilar to himself. The likelihood of successful communication between such dissimilar people is very limited. What is needed is someone in between who can communicate with both of them. Such a person is sometimes called an *opinion leader.*

Opinion Leadership

Opinion leaders are the heart and soul of mass communication. Our opinion leaders are similar to us on many dimensions (we will consider those dimensions in chapter 6), but they tend to have more competence or information on a given topic than we do. These people have a major influence on us, particularly on the decisions that we make.

Dorcas and Marion live in the same neighborhood and their husbands make similar salaries. Neither has a job at present, nor is seeking one. Dorcas has traveled widely and is thought of in the neighborhood as someone who is "with it." Marion is watching the Tonight Show one evening and hears that a new resort has opened in the Caribbean. Does she run to the phone and call her travel agent for reservations? Not likely. But the next day when she is having coffee with Dorcas she inquires what Dorcas thinks about that resort.

What is happening in the Dorcas-Marion example is typical of the relationships among mass media sources, opinion leaders, and ultimate

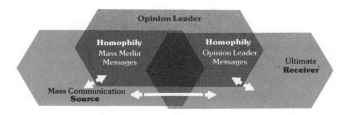

FIGURE 4–9. Opinion leadership in mass communication.

receivers. Dorcas is Marion's opinion leader on travel. Since Dorcas is "known" in her neighborhood as being "with it," Marion credits her with being informed about fashionable resorts. The message from the mass media caused Marion to seek information and advice. But the advice of the opinion leader, Dorcas, not the guests on the Tonight Show, will determine whether Marion decides to investigate the resort further.

Figure 4–9 illustrates the relationships in our opinion leader example. Included are the mass communication source (guests on the Tonight Show), the opinion leader (Dorcas), and the ultimate receiver (Marion). A mass communication source initiates the process of communication by sending a message(s). The message(s) could well fall outside the realm of common experience for the ultimate receiver, but fall into the realm of common experience for the opinion leader. Take, for example, a political speech delivered by the President on television concerning the problems of inflation. As an individual voter, I am one of the targeted receivers. But I don't really understand economics very well. Thus, before I decide to agree or disagree with the President, I may turn to my opinion leader on such matters. He or she can understand the President's views, can tell me what they mean to me since my opinion leader and I have a common base of experience, and advise me on what attitude I should have.

As is the case in both our travel and inflation examples, most of the impact of the mass communication process is felt not as a result of the message presented by the mass communication source, but as an effect of the interpersonal communication between opinion leaders and their followers. This is the most central point you should grasp to understand how mass communication works. While messages from mass communication sources can be very effective in diffusing information, particularly when presented via one of the media, decisions and behavioral choices are almost always a result of interpersonal communication between opinion leaders and their followers.

The Gatekeeper

There is one very important element in mass communication systems that we have not yet considered and that is not represented in any of our models. This element always exists in mass communication that involves the media, and is often present even when the media are not involved. This element is known as the *gatekeeper*. A gatekeeper can be an individual, a dyad, a small group, or a large group through which messages must pass from a source to a receiver. The gatekeeper is analogous to the fare collector on a toll bridge. All of us must pass through the tollgate in order to get on the bridge. If we don't have money, we don't get on the bridge. When television and radio are involved, and to a lesser extent all of the printed media, the gatekeeper must perform an extremely important function within the mass communication system. This is the function of screening, rejecting, and selecting messages that will be permitted to pass through the media. Thus, when a mass communication system is concerned with the diffusion of news, the gatekeeper must decide what news will and will not be diffused.

If we take the example of a network television news program, we can recognize the necessity for the gatekeeper and possibly develop some feeling for her or his overall impact. Far more news events take place in the world during any twenty-four-hour period than can be broadcast in one thirty-minute television newscast. Someone must decide what will be

---

**BLACK BOX
7**

Can you explain the importance of each of the following elements of
mass communication systems?
source-receiver homophily
opinion leadership
gatekeepers

---

broadcast and what will not. The gatekeeper, in this instance, is not a single individual but a whole news bureau. The first gatekeeper is the reporter on the spot who must decide whether or not to report the information through her or his news bureau. Once a report comes in, the news bureau staff must screen all of the reports that they receive to determine which ones are

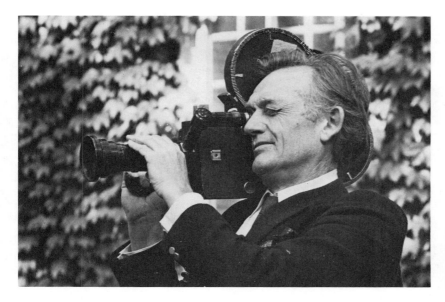

The gatekeeper screens, rejects, and selects messages that will pass through the media.

important enough to be included in the news broadcast. This process of filtering occurs until shortly before the newscast goes on the air. What we see in our living room, then, is a very heavily screened version of the news that has occurred during a given day.

In our discussion of the gatekeeper, we have been concerned primarily with the gatekeeper's function to screen messages from a source to ultimate receivers. In this instance we have thought of the source as unitary while there are many receivers. This system operates similarly in reverse when there are many potential sources and only a single receiver. In a large organization, for example, the executive at the top generally cannot possibly receive and process all of the information that people below that level might wish to transmit to the executive. Thus this material must be screened by people at lower levels. In some instances this process involves screening *people* out. For example, the secretary of an executive will frequently serve as a gatekeeper to keep some people away from the executive while permitting others through. Thus, the gatekeeper is an extremely important element in any communication system that involves large numbers of people.

To this point, we have been stressing the important differences between mass communication systems and other communication systems. We should not lose sight, however, of elements that all of these systems have in common. First, the structure of the process of communication has not changed from the simplest dyadic system to the most complex mass communication system. In each, there is a source, a receiver, and channels between the source and receiver. Messages are created and transmitted by sources and received and responded to by receivers. In addition, mass communication systems, like other communication systems, exist to perform some function. In general, mass communication systems exist for the purpose of either influence or information dissemination.

Intersocietal Communication Systems

The largest communication systems are intersocietal systems and are usually classified as mass communication systems. An intersocietal communication system exists whenever two or more societies attempt to communicate. Even though this represents enormous size with accompanying complexity, this type of system is not unlike other communication systems. Individual units within the system will serve as source, receiver, and often, as channel.

Although intersocietal communication systems are always in operation on the contemporary scene, there have been several examples in recent

*The U.N. is a
large-group
communication
system that is also an
intersocietal
communication
system.*

years that may serve to illustrate well what we mean when we refer to this type of system. During the late 1960s and early 1970s an extended intersocietal communication system operated in an attempt to resolve the problems of war in Southeast Asia. The United States, North Vietnam, the government of the Republic of South Vietnam, and the government representing the PRG of South Vietnam were all parties to this intersocietal communication system. The representatives of several million people were in constant communication in an attempt to resolve the disputes that forced the war to continue. Eventually, however, the communication system focused on an apparently dyadic relationship between Henry Kissinger, representing the United States, and Le Duc Tho, representing North Vietnam.

**BLACK BOX
8**

Can you explain the major differences between interpersonal and mass communication systems?

The communication between these two individuals could be looked at as a strictly dyadic communication system, but this would ignore many pertinent distinctions between this particular dyadic interchange and other more common ones. Neither Dr. Kissinger nor Le Duc Tho was speaking for himself; rather, they were representatives of extremely large organizations representing the governments of millions of people. Thus, these two individuals were merely two units of a much larger communication system.

Another somewhat similar exchange occurred during the Middle East Peace Negotiations in 1973 and 1974. Israel and Egypt found it necessary to communicate with one another in order to reach some kind of an agreement to withdraw their troops from front-line combat positions and establish some kind of cease-fire. Dr. Henry Kissinger was again involved in these negotiations. In this instance, however, Dr. Kissinger was not a true participant in the negotiations in the sense that he was in the Southeast Asian War negotiations. Although he was representing the United States once again, the United States was not a direct party to the negotiations. As a result, Dr. Kissinger served primarily as a channel of communication between the Israeli society and the Egyptian society.

A final example of intersocietal communication is the most enduring one in modern times: the United Nations. The United Nations serves as a large-group communication system that is also an intersocietal structure of communication. The representatives of the numerous societies of the world all come together at the United Nations to communicate about their various concerns. The United Nations may serve as the best example of how intersocietal communication systems differ from other communication systems. That difference is primarily one of degree and complexity. When communication must cross cultural barriers, as it almost always does when intersocietal communication is involved, there are additional problems introduced into the communication system. Neither words nor actions will necessarily stimulate the same meaning from one culture to another. We will note a variety of examples of this phenomena in later chapters.

Summary

With the exception of the intrapersonal communication system (the individual person), all communication systems are made up of smaller communication systems. The more complex the system, the more probable it is that some element within the system will function improperly. This is likely to lead to ineffective or disfunctional communication. Nevertheless, the primary elements in any communication system have important similarities. There are always sources, receivers, and channels between these sources and receivers. In addition, there are always messages that pass from sources through channels to receivers. The purpose of the next seven chapters is to examine the common elements in communication systems— people and messages—and their interrelationships, so that we may better understand how these elements can function together to produce effective communication.

SUGGESTED FURTHER READINGS

1. KATZ, E. and LAZARSFELD, P. F. *Personal Influence* (New York: The Free Press, 1955).

   A classic book on the effects of the mass media and the process of mass communication through interpersonal communication systems.

2. ROGERS, E. M. and SHOEMAKER, F. F. *Communication of Innovations* (New York: The Free Press, 1971).

An excellent summary of theory and research concerning the diffusion of new ideas and techniques through societies. The focus is on the interaction of mass and interpersonal communication systems in the diffusion process.

3. SCRAMM, W. and ROBERTS, D. F., eds. *The Process and Effects of Mass Communication,* rev. ed. (Urbana: University of Illinois Press, 1971).

A valuable anthology of readings on mass communication by several of the leading scholars in the field.

SELECTED REFERENCES

BERTALANFFY, L. VON. *General Systems Theory, Foundations, Development, Applications* (New York: George Braziller, 1968).

BROCK, B. L., CHESEBRO, J. W., CRAGAN, J. F., and KLUMPP, J. F. *Public Policy Decision-Making* (New York: Harper & Row, 1973).

KATZ, D. and KAHN, R. L. *The Social Psychology of Organization* (New York: John Wiley, 1966).

KATZ, E. and LAZARSFELD, P. F. *Personal Influence* (New York: The Free Press, 1955).

McCROSKEY, J. C. *An Introduction to Rhetorical Communication,* 2nd ed. (Englewood Cliffs, N.J.: Prentice-Hall, 1972).

ROGERS, E. M. and SHOEMAKER, F. F. *Communication of Innovations* (New York: The Free Press, 1971).

SCHRAMM, W. and ROBERTS, D. F., eds. *The Process and Effects of Mass Communication,* rev. ed. (Urbana: University of Illinois Press, 1971).

SEILER, J. A. *Systems Analysis in Organizational Behavior* (Homewood, Ill.: Irwin, 1967).

TROLDAHL, V. C. "A Field Test of a Modified Two-Step Flow of Communication Model." *Public Opinion Quarterly* 30 (1967); 609–623.

YOUNG, O. R. "A Survey of General Systems Theory." *General Systems Yearbook* 9 (1964); 61–80.

5

Communication Motivations

Dave, Kellie, Mark, and Ruth are the planning committee for the dance that their coed dorm intends to sponsor during registration week for the second semester. Their meeting has already begun. Let's listen in for a bit.

Kellie: *Since we have so little money, we have to decide whether to spend most of it on the band or get a cheaper band and more refreshments.*

Mark: *I'm for a better band; we can bring our own "refreshments."*

Kellie: *What do you think, Ruth?*

Ruth: *I'm not sure.*

Kellie: *Maybe we should determine first how much bands cost. Dave, you were going to look into that. What did you find out?*

Dave: *I didn't get around to it.*

Mark: *How the hell are we going to make a decision when we don't know what everything costs? Man, we only asked you to do one thing, and you didn't even do that!*

Dave (to Mark): *Why don't you bug off . . .*

Kellie: *Please, Dave. That won't help us make a decision. Mark, we know we can get some kind of band for about $150. Why don't we figure on using $150 to $200 on the band?*

Dave (aside to Ruth): *We ought to tell them to stick that dance in their ear. Who wants to spend a whole evening with a bunch of dorm freaks anyhow?*

Ruth: *What time is it?*

Mark: *I guess that would be okay, Kellie. But you had better check soon to see if we can get a good band for that money.*

Kellie: *Is that our decision then?*

Dave: *Okay by me. Who cares anyway?*

Mark: *Yeah, that's okay.*

Ruth: *(silence).*

Kellie: *What do you think Ruth?*

Ruth: *I don't know. Does anybody know what time I am supposed to register?*

Our dance committee has just engaged in "communication." The outcome may or may not be satisfactory to the other inhabitants of the dorm; that remains to be seen. The outcome, however, was probably not equally satisfactory to all of the members of the committee, because each was motivated in disparate ways and each communicated differently within the group. These problems can be attributed in large part to differences in motivations of the individuals.

To communicate or not to communicate is *not* the question. To be human is almost synonomous with "to communicate." But all human beings do not communicate to the same degree, as we saw in our committee meeting above. Some people are involved in communicating from the moment they get up in the morning until the moment they go to bed at night. Other people are involved in very few communication experiences in a given day. Communication is a constant for all human beings, but the *amount* of communicating that a person does is highly variable from one human being to another. In this chapter we will examine some of the variables that account for the amount of communication in which various people engage.

The Motivation to Communicate

A sizable portion of our total communication experience in a given day is initiated by people other than ourselves. Frequently we have little choice about whether or not we communicate. Someone walks into our room or our office and asks us a question. We must communicate in return, even if all we do is ignore the other person. That behavior in itself will certainly communicate. Nevertheless, we do exert considerable control over the extent to which we communicate. In some instances we may choose to communicate and other instances we may choose not to. The question posed here is why we act in some cases while in others we do not.

Our choice of whether or not to communicate is normally based upon our projection of the outcome of communicating in the given instance. Generally, if we predict that the outcome will be to our advantage, we will choose to communicate. If our projection is negative, however, we will be more likely to avoid communication. The outcomes with which we are concerned are affinity, information or understanding, influence, decision, and confirmation. Chapters 12 through 20 are devoted to in-depth consideration of these outcomes, so we will not discuss them in detail here. Rather, we will simply introduce these outcomes briefly so that we may be able to see the relationship between them and the motivations to communicate.

Affinity

Affinity between two people is often a desired outcome of communication. If person A likes and respects person B, then person A has affinity for person B. Most of us have an inner need for warm relationships with other people. We do not want to be isolated from our fellow human beings. Consequently, we often seek to communicate with other people in order to establish such affinity relationships with them. Some people have less need for affinity than others, and they will probably seek less communication on a social level than will people with higher affinity needs. In our committee meeting Mark exhibited a fairly low affinity need when he snapped at Dave. Dave snapped back, but evidenced some need for affinity by turning to Ruth for support. Of course, he didn't get it. Some people have extremely high affinity needs, and they may try excessively hard to communicate with other people. Such excessive needs can result in overexuberance, the "trying too hard" syndrome, or the "yes man," communication pattern. It has been estimated that between 50 and 90 percent of all interpersonal communication exists primarily because of the participants' motivation to seek affinity with one another. Even when other outcomes may be the principle ones desired in a communication relationship, seldom is affinity completely irrelevant to the relationship. Even Walter Cronkite wants to be loved.

Information or Understanding

It has been said that "knowledge is power." In many cases this may be true. To know that the stock market will go up gives us the power to make money quickly. In other cases, whether knowledge is power or not, knowledge is necessary. Consequently, when we need information to understand something or to make a decision, this need is very likely to motivate us to communicate to obtain that information. Our committee chairwoman evidenced this need when she turned to Dave to ask about the cost of bands. Mark also indicated that he felt this need when he snapped at Dave because he couldn't provide the information requested. The need for information is a common motivator behind communication. Students come to class and/or read textbooks (at least in some instances), because they feel a need for information or understanding. We read the newspaper and watch television in order to find out about what is going on in the world. In short, we often talk to other people or read their works in order to obtain information, and other people may seek to talk with us or read our work in order to obtain information they feel they need.

Influence

As we have emphasized throughout this book, change is an important outcome of communication. We often wish to change the attitudes or behaviors of other people, or to *influence* them. Human beings can control their own environment to some extent, but they must depend upon other human beings for cooperation to exercise efficient control over the environment to maintain the society in which we live. Primitive human beings often found the need to work together for a common purpose, necessitating one individual's influencing another individual's behavior.

*People read because
they feel a need for
information or
understanding.*

The outcome of influence should not be confused with the motivation to manipulate. Although we may manipulate people when we are influencing them, manipulation is not a necessary condition of influence. The outcome of influence merely means to change the attitude or behavior of another individual. That change may be in the interests of the other person, in the interest of ourselves, or in the mutual interests of both parties. It is an outcome that is essential in contemporary society.

In our committee meeting, Kellie appeared to have a strong need to influence. She took over the meeting right away and attempted to direct the group to a decision by making statements and asking for agreement. In the end, her decision was the one the group accepted. Earlier, however, Mark attempted to influence the group in a different way—toward an expensive band—but that influence attempt seemed to have little or no impact. Both Dave and Ruth gave little evidence of a need to influence in the meeting. Dave seemed not to care, and Ruth hardly participated at all.

Decision

Whenever we are confronted with a choice, we must make a decision. In some cases we simply wish to have information that other people can provide us and other opinions prior to making our own decision. In other cases, we engage in communication with people so that we may reach a decision jointly. This outcome is a very common goal of small-group communication. Such was the case in our committee meeting. The group existed to decide how to handle the proposed dance.

Confirmation

After we make a decision it is common for us to seek communication with other people to be certain that our decision was the correct one. We seek confirmation from the opinions of other people and the information they can provide. You will recall that our committee decided to spend $150 to $200 on the band, but left Kellie with the responsibility of confirming that decision as a wise one later. Since Mark wanted a more expensive band, it is likely that he will try to confirm that the decision reached will result in having a good band without spending the extra money. To do this he will probably try to talk to people who have heard the band that is selected before to see if they like it.

When we choose from a variety of alternatives (better band or more refreshments), particularly when more than one of those alternatives is attractive, we are often disturbed by having had to reject one desirable alternative to accept another. (I can't afford both to travel to Europe this summer and return to school in the fall.) To reduce this psychological stress, we often communicate with other people to confirm that they would have made a similar choice had they been in our position.

In summary, the normal motivations to communicate focus on five major outcomes of human communication. The normal person needs affinity and information, wants to influence, needs to make decisions, and desires confirmation for past decisions. We communicate to fulfill these needs.

The Motivation *NOT* to Communicate

As we have indicated, there are many reasons for a person to seek communication with other human beings. Nevertheless, some people engage in much less communication than others. In some instances, this reduced level of communication is normal and in other instances it is abnormal. Let us consider both.

Normal Withdrawal from Communication

The normal person will avoid communication under some circumstances. There are two conditions that are particularly likely to result in a reduced level of communication. The first is a desire to be left alone. Almost all of us have experienced the feeling that we simply wish to withdraw from communication at times. This may be expressed by taking a vacation away from our job or community and going somewhere where we don't know many people and few people are likely to initiate communication with us. This feeling is also evidenced by people who simply take their telephone off the hook for an hour or so. These behaviors are not unusual, and most of us engage in them at one time or another. We may even build our homes in such a way as to make this withdrawal behavior more plausible. We may build a study in our home where we can go and be away from everyone else for a period of time and avoid communication. Or we may simply go to our bedroom and lock the door.

Another normal reason for not initiating communication is to avoid disclosing something about ourselves. We will consider self-disclosure in some depth in chapter 11. At this point we will note only two important points. First, people have a need to disclose their feelings, worries, concerns, and aspirations to someone else. Such disclosure is highly related to the development of affinity between people. However, second, people normally engage in this kind of behavior with only a relatively small number of other people. While self-disclosure can help to develop warm, friendly relationships, opposite effects are also possible.

As we have noted before, information often is power. In some instances we may not wish to let another individual know too much about ourselves. In order to avoid disclosing information about ourselves to the other individual, we may withdraw from communication contact. In both this instance and the one noted above, the avoiding behavior should be considered normal. It is a kind of behavior we would expect most human beings to engage in at one time or another. It is the many people who seek to avoid communication for other reasons whose behavior is abnormal.

Before going further, we wish to clarify our use of the term *normal.* Normal is a very relative concept. If we meet someone on the street who is walking along with a finger placed firmly in his or her left ear, and we see the person engaging in the same behavior day after day, we would conclude that the person is not behaving "normally." However, if in our culture almost everyone were to walk around with their finger in their ear, then the person who did not do that would be abnormal. In reference to communication behavior, then, *normal* is related to what most people in our culture do. *Abnormal* is the term we use to describe behavior that deviates from what most people do. Abnormal does not necessarily mean there is something wrong, but as we use it here it does have that connotation.

Abnormal Withdrawal from Communication

There are two personality characteristics that have been found to result in abnormal withdrawal from communication. The first is called "anomie" or "alienation." Anomie is a state marked by a failure to understand or accept society's norms and values. A person with this type of personality is likely to be inordinately insecure, and in extreme cases may even be suicidal. The person frequently has feelings of meaningless, powerlessness, aloneness, and hopelessness. In general, he or she tends to reject accepted norms and retreats from society. Many young people in the 1960s were alienated from the social and political systems. Some dropped out of school and society and sought fulfillment in rural, remote areas.

The norms of society with reference to communication are reflected in specific motivations, and the alienated individual tends to reject those motivations and withdraw from communication. Since the goals to be achieved by communication are not desirable to such an individual, things that would motivate the normal person to communicate have little or no effect on the alienated person. Although some research has suggested that this syndrome is more characteristic of people in low socioeconomic status groups in our society, it is important to note that the syndrome is present in the spectrum of socioeconomic classes. The anomic tendency is a personality characteristic that is not directly related to communication, but one that has a major impact of the communication behavior of the affected person. Communication is only one of many normal behaviors within a society that are rejected by this individual. When such a person does communicate it can be expected that the type of communication in which he or she engages would be sharply different from the communication behavior of others. But the most important characteristic of this individual with relation to commun-

Almost all of us have experienced the need to withdraw from communication at times.

ication is simple withdrawal. The alienated person is not motivated to communicate by the same things that impel others. Consequently, there is little reason to seek interaction with other people.

BLACK BOX
9

Can you explain why:
  most people seek communication;
  most people avoid communication sometimes;
  some people avoid communication most of the time?

Alienation may be either a general personality characteristic, as we have considered it above, or it may apply to only a given group in which the individual finds her or himself, or even only to a given task. In our committee meeting, Dave showed strong signs of alienation. He had little interest in the decision to be made and expressed strongly negative feelings about the other people who live with him in the dorm. We can not tell whether Dave has an alienated personality or is just alienated from his dorm mates without observing his communication in many other settings. Ruth also gave some indication of alienation; she withdrew almost completely from the discussion. However, the hostility that accompanies alienation was not present, so it is more likely that the second personality characteristic that leads to withdrawal would apply in her case.

The second characteristic that leads individuals to avoid and withdraw from communication is *communication apprehension*. This characteristic has also been referred to by a number of other labels such as "speech fright," "stage fright," "speech anxiety," and "reticence." All of these labels apply to at least part of the characteristic that we refer to here as communication apprehension. The individual suffering from communication apprehension is a person for whom apprehension about participating in communication outweighs any projection of gain from communicating in a given situation. Such people are motivated to communicate by the same elements that motivate any other human being, which we have discussed previously, but they are blocked from acting upon that motivation by an apprehension about the communication act itself. The communication apprehensive individual anticipates negative feelings and outcomes from communication, and thus either avoids communication, if possible, or suffers from a variety of anxiety related feelings while communicating. Because of the extent of this characteristic within our society and its major impact on human communication behavior, we will consider this characteristic in more detail below.

The Nature and Effects of Communication Apprehension

At the outset, let us make it clear that communication apprehension has only to do with apprehension about communicating, either orally or in writing. It should not be confused with a generally anxious personality. Generally, anxiety and communication apprehension are not highly related (the correlation is about .30 between them). Thus, a person can be very normal in all other respects, but be highly apprehensive about communication. On the other hand, a person could be highly neurotic, afraid of her or his own shadow, and still not be a communication apprehensive.

You may be asking yourself at this point, "Why should I know about communication apprehension? I'm not a communication apprehensive." To begin with, the chances are about one in five that you *are*. Extensive research has indicated that between 10 and 20 percent of all college students suffer from extreme communication apprehension, and that the percentages are about the same in groups all the way from junior high school students to senior citizens. But let us assume for the moment that you are not a communication apprehensive (chances are at least four out of five that our assumption is correct!). Why, then, should you be concerned?

Communication apprehension severely disrupts the communication of the person with the problem. It affects both source functions and receiver functions. Since the individual is disrupted, any communication system (dyad, small group, organization) of which the person is a part is also disrupted. Recall our committee meeting. Ruth gave every indication of being a communication apprehensive. What did she contribute to the group? Whatever good ideas she may have had were not shared with the group. The decision was not better as a result of her being in the group. She might as well have stayed in her room. Have you ever been in a group with a Ruth? Odds are that you have been in many. Ruth and other communication apprehensives may have as much to offer as anyone else in the group (there is no correlation between communication apprehension and intelligence), but they don't offer it. Thus, the product of our group with Ruth's input is not as good as it could be.

Communication apprehension leads to ineffective encoding by the individual when she or he is functioning as a source. Since the person is more concerned with the anxiety associated with communication than with the outcome of the communication, encoding choices may be made on the basis of avoiding anxiety rather than enhancing the probability of the desired outcome. The most common manifestation of this feeling is withdrawal, or noncommunication. Simply put, the person doesn't talk. Communication apprehension can also have a negative impact on the communicator as a receiver. If the individual is concerned about having to perform as a source, this may dominate the individual's thinking so that she or he cannot properly function as a receiver either.

Communication apprehension is a pervasive characteristic that has implications for all types of communication systems. It appears that it may be more severe in some settings than in others, but severely apprehensive individuals are affected by communication apprehension whenever they are involved in any kind of communication, particularly where they may have to serve as a source of communication. It should be stressed here that communication apprehension is characteristic of all human beings, but to varying degrees for individual human beings. Almost everyone feels some apprehension when confronted by a very formal communication demand, such as formal public speaking. The type of person that we label here a communication apprehensive will, however, feel much more apprehension in such settings than will the normal person, and even more importantly, will feel considerable apprehension even in very informal communication, such as an interview for a job, an interaction among a small group, or even talking with one or two friends.

We have already noted that the main behavioral outcome of communication apprehension is a withdrawal from communication. But we need to explain what is meant by "withdrawal." In some cases withdrawal is very obvious, such as the person who refuses to give a public speech, or, someone like Ruth, who won't talk in a small group. Other withdrawal symptoms are less obvious, and in some cases are almost unnoticed by the average person. For example, communication apprehensive individuals tend to select a different type of housing than will less apprehensive individuals. When given a free choice, the high apprehensive will choose housing that provides the least opportunity for people to impose communication demands on her or him. For example, in a dormatory setting the high apprehensive will usually choose to live at the end of a hallway, out of the mainstream of social interaction on the dorm floor, and away from stairwells that would cause people to have to pass by his or her room. Less apprehensive people, on the other hand, are prone to seek rooms where interaction is more likely—near an entrance, near a communal rest room, or near the stairwell. Similarly, in a housing or apartment complex the highly apprehensive individual will prefer houses that are removed from social interaction points in the development, such as playgrounds or washing facilities, while less apprehensive individuals will seek such busy interaction areas as well as preferring backyards that connect with those of other people so that "talking over the fence" is easy.

As indicated in Figure 5–1, in a small group setting there are often seating positions where the apprehensive person will not have to engage in as much communication as he or she would in other seats. Notice where Ruth chose to sit. Her behavior was typical of the high apprehensive. Kellie's choice was typical of the low apprehensive, as was Mark's. The high apprehensive will also normally avoid seating positions where leadership would be expected, such as at the head or foot of the table, whereas less apprehensive people tend to gravitate to those seats.

The kind of behavior we have been describing in the last two paragraphs is probably unconsciously motivated for the most part. Neither the high nor the low apprehensive is likely to make low conflict choices with full awareness of the implications. Nevertheless, these choices are made and an environment is created that reduces the amount of communication the high apprehensive will be forced into.

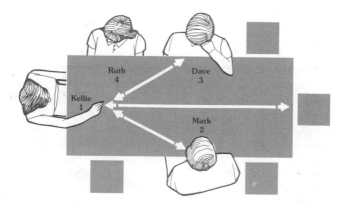

FIGURE 5–1. Interaction patterns in small groups. Arrows indicate most frequent interaction patterns for all seats. Numbers indicate the amount of leadership expected for the occupied seats.

No matter how hard the communication apprehensive individual tries, of course, she or he will have to engage in some communication in our modern society. Observation of such people in interaction settings, however, indicates that these individuals will still talk far less than will less apprehensive individuals. This pattern holds true whether we are talking about a dyadic relationship, a small-group communication relationship, or any other communication system. Further, when highly apprehensive individuals do communicate they evidence much more tension in their interaction than do less apprehensive individuals. In addition, the contributions made by highly apprehensive individuals tend to display less interest in the topic under discussion and to be less relevant to the subject being discussed than do the contributions of less apprehensive individuals. Recall Ruth's behavior in the meeting. When Dave tried to get her involved in a side interaction, she simply asked what time it was. When she was asked to concur with the group's decision, she expressed her concern for her registration schedule. Such reactions tend to discourage others from seeking further communication with the apprehensive, whereas directly relevant comments can result in responses of disagreement or questions that pressure the apprehensive to talk even more.

It has also been found that in dyads and small groups highly apprehensive individuals tend to take less risk in their communication with other people and to avoid disclosing information about themselves more than do less apprehensive individuals. Such people are harder to get to know, and thus, are harder to communicate with than less apprehensive individuals. Consequently, the probability of ineffective communication is much higher with communication apprehensive individuals than with more normal people.

BLACK BOX
10

After having read the descriptions of how high apprehensives behave in communication, if you suspect that you may be a high apprehensive, or are simply curious about your own level of apprehension, we suggest that you fill out the following two questionnaires. The first is the "Personal Report of Communication Apprehension." The PRCA is designed to measure your level of apprehension about oral communication. The "Writing Apprehension Test" is designed to measure your level of apprehension about writing. Both the PRCA and the WAT have been extensively tested and used in numerous research studies. If you score (instructions for scoring are below) above 75 on the PRCA or above 60 on the WAT, this is an indication of some communication apprehension. But unless your score is above 88 on the PRCA or above 72 on the WAT, you are probably not a high communication apprehensive.

Should your score on either questionnaire suggest that you may be a high communication apprehensive, we suggest that you seek help to overcome this problem. If your English, Speech, or Communication department has a program for helping people with communication apprehension, you should seek help there first. If no such program is available, you should check with your school's counseling service. Most colleges and universities have people in their counseling service who are trained professionals who can provide systematic desensitization or whatever other treatment might be most appropriate. The decision to seek help, if you have this problem, may be the most important decision you ever make. Quite literally, it may change your whole life.

Scoring the PRCA and WAT

To compute your PRCA score, follow these 3 steps.

1. Add up your scores for items 1, 3, 5, 8, 9, 10, 12, 13, 15, 16, 19, 20, 22, and 24.
2. Add up your scores for items 2, 4, 6, 7, 11, 14, 17, 18, 21, 23, and 25.
3. Complete the following formula:
   PRCA Score = 84 — (total from step 1) + (total from step 2)

To compute your WAT score, follow these 3 steps.

1. Add up your scores for items 1, 4, 5, 10, 13, 18, 19, and 20.
2. Add up your scores for items 2, 3, 6, 7, 8, 9, 11, 12, 14, 15, 16, and 17.
3. Complete the following formula:
   WAT Score = 48 — (total from step 1) + (total from step 2)

BLACK BOX
11

PRCA

DIRECTIONS: This instrument is composed of twenty-five statements concerning feelings about communicating with other people. Please indicate the degree to which each statement applies to you by marking whether you (1) Strongly Agree, (2) Agree, (3) Are Undecided, (4) Disagree, or (5) Strongly Disagree with each statement. There are no right or wrong answers. Work quickly, just record your first impression.

		SA	A	UN	D	SD
1.	While participating in a conversation with a new acquaintance I feel very nervous.	1	2	3	4	5
2.	I have no fear of facing an audience.	1	2	3	4	5
3.	I talk less because I'm shy.	1	2	3	4	5
4.	I look forward to expressing my opinions at meetings.	1	2	3	4	5
5.	I am afraid to express myself in a group.	1	2	3	4	5
6.	I look forward to an opportunity to speak in public.	1	2	3	4	5
7.	I find the prospect of speaking mildly pleasant.	1	2	3	4	5
8.	When communicating, my posture feels strained and unnatural.	1	2	3	4	5
9.	I am tense and nervous while participating in group discussion.	1	2	3	4	5
10.	Although I talk fluently with friends I am at a loss for words on the platform.	1	2	3	4	5
11.	I have no fear about expressing myself in a group.	1	2	3	4	5
12.	My hands tremble when I try to handle objects on the platform.	1	2	3	4	5
13.	I always avoid speaking in public if possible.	1	2	3	4	5
14.	I feel that I am more fluent when talking to people than most other people are.	1	2	3	4	5
15.	I am fearful and tense all the while I am speaking before a group of people.	1	2	3	4	5
16.	My thoughts become confused and jumbled when I speak before an audience.	1	2	3	4	5
17.	I like to get involved in group discussions.	1	2	3	4	5
18.	Although I am nervous just before getting up, I soon forget my fears and enjoy the experience.	1	2	3	4	5
19.	Conversing with people who hold positions of authority causes me to be fearful and tense.	1	2	3	4	5
20.	I dislike to use my body and voice expressively.	1	2	3	4	5
21.	I feel relaxed and comfortable while speaking.	1	2	3	4	5
22.	I feel self-conscious when I am called upon to answer a question or give an opinion in class.	1	2	3	4	5
23.	I face the prospect of making a speech with complete confidence.	1	2	3	4	5
24.	I'm afraid to speak up in conversations.	1	2	3	4	5
25.	I would enjoy presenting a speech on a local television show.	1	2	3	4	5

BLACK BOX
12

WAT

Directions: Below are a series of statements about writing. There are no right or wrong answers to these statements. Please indicate the degree to which each statement applies to you by marking whether you (1) Strongly Agree, (2) Agree, (3) Are Uncertain, (4) Disagree, or (5) Strongly Disagree with the statement. While some of these statements may seem repetitious, take your time and try to be as honest as possible.

	SA	A	UN	D	SD
1. I avoid writing.	1	2	3	4	5
2. I have no fear of my writing being evaluated.	1	2	3	4	5
3. I look forward to writing down my ideas.	1	2	3	4	5
4. My mind seems to go blank when I start to work on a composition.	1	2	3	4	5
5. Expressing ideas through writing seems to be a waste of time.	1	2	3	4	5
6. I would enjoy submitting my writing to magazines for evaluation and publication.	1	2	3	4	5
7. I like to write my ideas down.	1	2	3	4	5
8. I feel confident in my ability to clearly express my ideas in writing.	1	2	3	4	5
9. I like to have my friends read what I have written.	1	2	3	4	5
10. I'm nervous about writing.	1	2	3	4	5
11. People seem to enjoy what I write.	1	2	3	4	5
12. I enjoy writing.	1	2	3	4	5
13. I never seem to be able to clearly write down my ideas.	1	2	3	4	5
14. Writing is a lot of fun.	1	2	3	4	5
15. I like seeing my thoughts on paper.	1	2	3	4	5
16. Discussing my writing with others is an enjoyable experience.	1	2	3	4	5
17. It's easy for me to write good compositions.	1	2	3	4	5
18. I don't think I write as well as most other people.	1	2	3	4	5
19. I don't like my compositions to be evaluated.	1	2	3	4	5
20. I'm no good at writing.	1	2	3	4	5

The WAT was developed and validated by our former colleagues, John A. Daly and Michael D. Miller. We are grateful to them for allowing us to include this instrument in our book.

Since the communication apprehension phenomenon has a major impact on the communication behavior of individuals, it might be expected that this would have an impact on the way people are perceived as a result of their communication. Research has confirmed this expectation. Communication apprehensive people are much less likely to be perceived as leaders by their peers. They are viewed as less competent, less sociable, and less extroverted by their peers. They also are seen as less composed, less task-attractive, less socially attractive, and in some cases even less physically attractive. They are perceived as less desirable dates and potential marriage partners. In short, the highly communication apprehensive individual engages in less communication and as a result is perceived in a generally negative way by other individuals, whether these other people are communication apprehensives themselves or whether they are more normal.

**BLACK BOX
13**

Can you distinguish between high and low communication apprehensives in terms of:
the amount of communication attempted
choice of housing
choice of seat in a small group setting
their interaction behaviors
the ways they are perceived by others?

The causes of communication apprehension are not yet fully known; however, the characteristic has not been related to heredity. Rather, it is produced in the individual by the environment in which he or she grows and matures. The best explanation for the existence of the communication apprehension syndrome that has been advanced to date is one of "patterned conditioning." It is thought that communication apprehension is developed from early childhood by the process of reinforcement. If a child is not reinforced for communicating with his or her parents, peers, or teachers, it is likely that the child will develop communication apprehension. This development may in itself be reinforced by rewarding the child for not communicating. The home in which a child is told to be quiet and not talk at the dinner table is a good example. The talkative child may be likely to be punished rather than rewarded for attempting to initiate communication whereas the quiet child may be reinforced for that behavior. The quiet child in our culture is much more likely to be described as "well behaved." This is true both in the home and in the school.

Considerable research has been done in the area of communication apprehension to determine how extensive the problem is. The results of these investigations indicate that probably between 10 and 20 percent of the American population suffers from severe, debilitating communication apprehension; that is, the normal functioning and communicating of these individuals is severely restricted by their high apprehension about communication. Further, it is estimated that an additional 20 percent of the population suffers from communication apprehension to a degree substantial enough to interfere to some extent with their normal functioning. In short, communication apprehension is probably the most common handicap that is suffered by people in contemporary American society. Unfortunately, this handicap is generally ignored in schools, both at lower levels and all the way through college. Relatively few attempts have been made to develop methods for overcoming the problem and freeing individuals from communication apprehension. The most commonly employed methods are used in speech and English classes. Unfortunately, the approach operates from the faulty assumption that people are anxious about speaking or writing situations because they do not have the knowledge or experience about communication that will permit them to relax and communicate normally. Thus the "treatment" commonly involves requiring the student to give a number of public speeches after instruction in speech making, or writing a number of compositions after instruction in composition. While this approach is very helpful to people who are not severely handicapped by communication apprehension, it is much more likely to make the problem more severe for the highly apprehensive individual. Since the apprehensive is most likely to communicate ineffectively in this demanding setting, it will simply be another unrewarding, failure experience which will further condition the individual to be apprehensive about communicating rather than easing the stress connected with communicating. An awareness of this flaw in speech and composition training has been increasing in higher education over the past decade, but is as yet generally unrecognized at secondary and elementary levels.

Alternative methods for helping people who suffer from severe communication apprehension have been explored more vigorously in recent years. Several methods have been found to be helpful, most notably a behavior therapy known as *systematic desensitization*. Research has indicated that between 80 and 90 percent of the people severely handicapped by communication apprehension can be helped to a major extent, or even cured, by this particular treatment. Of course, neither this nor any other single treatment method is a magical "sure-cure." Different people need to be helped in different ways. Unfortunately, few English, Speech, or Communication departments in higher education are equipped to provide the help with communication apprehension that their students need. Until such help is made readily available to all those who need and want it, a very large proportion of our population will continue to suffer from communication apprehension, and, as a result, they and we will suffer from the loss of effective communication with them.

When involved in almost any communication system, we must keep in mind that there are a large number of communication apprehensives around us, even if we are not highly apprehensive ourselves. While most people are motivated to seek communication with others to achieve certain desired outcomes (affinity, information or understanding, influence, decision making, confirmation), communication apprehensives are primarily motivated by their desire to avoid communication. In short, many of the people with whom we are motivated to communicate do not share our motivations. When we are trying to communicate with a person who is a high apprehensive, we must take care to avoid projecting our motivations on the other person. If we are to communicate successfully we must try to make our communication with the other person as nonthreatening as possible. To the extent that we can succeed in that attempt, we can create an atmosphere where a person can communicate without apprehension blocking those essential efforts.

SUGGESTED FURTHER READINGS

1. Clevenger, T., Jr. "An Analysis of Variance of the Relationship of Experienced Stage Fright to Selected Psychometric Inventions."

   Unpublished Doctoral Dissertation, Florida State University, 1958. An extensive summary of the early research related to oral communication apprehension.

2. Daly, J. A. and Miller, M. D. "The Development of a Measure of Writing Apprehension." *Research in the Teaching of English* 1975 (in press).

   The original report of the Writing Apprehension Test with a rationale for the importance of studying this form of communication apprehension.

3. Griffin, K. and Gilham, S. M. "Relationships Between Speech Anxiety and Motivation." *Speech Monographs* 38 (1971): 70–73.

   This paper sets forth a theoretical explanation for oral communication apprehension.

4. McCroskey, J. C. "Measures of Communication Bound Anxiety." *Speech Monographs* 37 (1970): 269–277.

   The original report on the development of the Personal Report of Communication Apprehension.

5. McCroskey, J. C. "The Implementation of a Large Scale Program of Systematic Desensitization for Communication Apprehension." *The Speech Teacher* 21 (1972): 255–264.

   A report of an extensive treatment program for communication apprehension and discussion of how a similar program can be implemented in other places.

6. Phillips, G. M. "Reticence: Pathology of the Normal Speaker." *Speech Monographs* 35 (1968): 39–49.

   A theoretical discussion of the causes and effects of oral communication apprehension.

SELECTED REFERENCES

BARRICK, J. E., McCROSKEY, J. C., and RALPH, D. "The Effects of Systematic Desensitization on Speech and Test Anxiety." Paper presented at the Annual Convention of the Speech Communication Association, Chicago, 1968.

BASHORE, D. N. "Relationships Among Speech Anxiety, Trait Anxiety, IQ, and High School Achievement." Unpublished Masters Thesis, Illinois State University, 1971.

BEHNKE, R. R. and CARLILE, L. W. "Heart Rate as an Index of Speech Anxiety." *Speech Monographs* 39 (1971): 62–67.

BURGOON, J. K. and BURGOON, M. "Unwillingness to Communicate, Anomia-Alienation, and Communication Apprehension as Predictors of Small Group Communication." *Journal of Psychology* 88 (1974): 31–38.

CHENOWETH, E. C. "The Adjustment of College Freshmen to the Speaking Situation." *Quarterly Journal of Speech* 26 (1940): 585–588.

CLEVENGER, T., JR. "A Definition of Stage Fright." *Central States Speech Journal* 7 (1955): 26–30.

————. "A Synthesis of Experimental Research in Stage Fright." *Quarterly Journal of Speech* 55 (1959): 124–145.

CLEVENGER, T., JR. and PHIFER, G. "What Do Beginning College Speech Texts Say About Stage Fright." *Speech Teacher* 8 (1959): 1–7.

DALY, J. A. and McCROSKEY, J. C. "Occupational Desirability and Choice as a Function of Communication Apprehension." *Journal of Counseling Psychology* 22 (1975): 309–313.

DALY, J. A. and MILLER, M. D. "Apprehension of Writing as a Predictor of Message Intensity." *Journal of Psychology* 89 (1975): 175–177

————. "The Development of a Measure of Writing Apprehension." *Research in the Teaching of English* 1975 (in press).

DYMACEK, D. A. "Effects of Number of Classroom Speeches on Anxiety Reduction and Performance Improvement." Paper presented at the Annual Convention of the Speech Communication Association, San Francisco, 1971.

FISHER, J. Y. and INFANTE, D. A. "The Relation Between Communication Anxiety and Human Motivation Variables." *Central States Speech Journal* 24 (1973): 246–252.

FRIEDRICH, G. W. "An Empirical Explication of a Concept of Self-Reported Speech Anxiety." *Speech Monographs* 37 (1970): 67–72.

GIFFIN, K. and BRADLEY, K. "An Exploratory Study of Group Counseling for Speech Anxiety." *Journal of Clinical Psychology* 25 (1969): 98–101.

GIFFIN, K. and GILHAM, S. M. "Relationships Between Speech Anxiety and Motivation." *Speech Monographs* 38 (1971): 70–73.

GIFFIN, K. and MASTERSON, S. "A Theoretical Model of the Relationships Between Motivation and Self-Confidence in Communication." *Communication Spectrum* 7 (1968): 311–316.

GILKINSON, H. "Social Fears as Reported by Students in College Speech Classes." *Speech Monographs* 9 (1942): 141–160.

HAMILTON, W. "A Review of Experimental Studies on Stage Fright." *Pennsylvania Speech Annual* 17 (1960): 41–48.

JOHNSON, C. *Speech Reticence* (Fort Collins, Col.: Shields Publishing, 1973).

JOHNSON, T., TYLER, V., THOMPSON, R., and JONES, E. "Systematic Desensitization and Assertive Training in the Treatment of Speech Anxiety in Middle School Students." *Psychology in the Schools* 8 (1971): 263–267.

LAMB, D. H. "Speech Anxiety: Towards a Theoretical Conceptualization and Preliminary Scale Development." *Speech Monographs* 39 (1972): 62–67.

McCROSKEY, J. C. "Measures of Communication Bound Anxiety." *Speech Monographs* 37 (1970): 269–277.

————. "The Implementation of a Large Scale Program of Systematic Desensitization for Communicaton Apprehension." *Speech Teacher* 21 (1972): 255–264.

McCROSKEY, J. C. and LEPPARD, T. "The Effects of Communication Apprehension on

Nonverbal Behavior." Paper presented at the Annual Convention of the Eastern Communication Association, New York, 1975.

McCroskey, J. C., Ralph, D. C., and Barrick, J. E. "The Effect of Systematic Desensitization on Speech Anxiety." *Speech Teacher* 19 (1970): 32–36.

Meichenbaum, D. H., Gilmore, J. B., and Fedoravicius, A. "Group Insight Versus Group Desensitization in Treating Speech Anxiety." *Journal of Consulting and Clinical Psychology* 36 (1971): 410–421.

Mulac, A. and Sherman, A. R. "Behavioral Assessment of Speech Anxiety." *Quarterly Journal of Speech* 60 (1974): 134–143.

Paul, G. L. *Insight Versus Desensitization in Psychotherapy* (Stanford, Cal.: Stanford University Press, 1966).

Pedersen, D. J. *Report to the Alameda County School District and Title III, Area J. of Pennsylvania of the Incidence of Reticence in Their Respective School District.* Alameda County, PACE Center, 1968.

Phillips, G. M. "The Problem of Reticence," *Pennsylvania Speech Annual* 22 (1965): 22–38.

———. "Reticence: Pathology of the Normal Speaker." *Speech Monographs* 35 (1968): 39–49.

——— and Butt, D. "Reticence Revisited." *Pennsylvania Speech Annual* 23 (1966): 40–57.

Phillips, G. M. and Metzger, N. J. "The Reticent Syndrome: Some Theoretical Considerations About Etiology and Treatment." *Speech Monographs* 40 (1973): 220–230.

Porter, D. T. "Self Report Scales of Communication Apprehension and Autonomic Arousal (Heart Rate): A Test of Construct Validity." *Speech Monographs* 41 (1974): 267–276.

Porter, D. T. and Burns, G. P. "A Criticism of 'Heart Rate as an Index of Speech Anxiety'." *Speech Monographs* 40 (1973).

Quiggins, J. G. "Effects of High and Low Communication Apprehension on Small Group Member Source Credibility and Interpersonal Attraction." Unpublished Masters Thesis, Illinois State University, 1972.

Shaw, I. R. "Speech Fright in the Elementary School, Its Relationship to Speech Ability and Its Possible Implications for Speech Readiness." *Speech Monographs* 34 (1967): 319.

Sikkink, D. E. "An Experimental Study Comparing Improvers and Non-Improvers in the Beginning Speech Course." *Western Speech* 19 (1955): 201–205.

Sorensen, G. A. "The Use of Personality Traits and Communication Apprehension in Predicting Interaction Behavior in Small Groups." Unpublished Masters Thesis, Illinois State University, 1972.

Thoreson, C. E. "Oral Non-Participation in College Students: A Survey of Characteristics." *American Educational Research Journal* 8 (1966): 199.

COMMUNICATION
MOTIVATIONS

WELLS, J. and LASHBROOK, W. B. "A Study of the Effects of Systematic Desensitization of the Communicative Anxiety of Individuals in Small Groups." Paper presented at the Annual Convention of the SCA, New Orleans, 1970.

WHEELESS, L. R. "Communication Apprehension in the Elementary School." *Speech Teacher* 10 (1971): 297–299.

WOLPE, J. and LAZARUS, A. A. *Behavior Therapy Techniques* (New York: Pergamon Press, 1966).

6

Perceptions of One Another

Let's follow Ted around his world for part of a day. Ted wakes up about 7:30, shaves, showers, and comes downstairs to get some coffee. Joyce is sitting in the kitchen having a cup of coffee and getting ready to go to work. Joyce smiles, says, "Good Morning" and gives Ted a kiss as he bends over to her. Ted makes a mental note of the good mood that Joyce seems to be in. Joyce notices how handsome Ted looks in his new suit. She thinks, "Too bad we both have to go to work. Sure would like to stay home for an hour or so!" Ted pours himself a cup of coffee and sits down with Joyce.

Ted mentions to Joyce that one of the executives in his company is leaving at the end of the week. Joyce comments that she would like to apply for the job, it pays more than she is making now. Ted suggests that she probably wouldn't care for the work and probably would be happier where she is.

Both Ted and Joyce leave for work. When Ted enters his office building he meets Dave, the head of the company. Dave ignores Ted. Ted thinks, "That creep. Just because his father left him this company, he thinks he can treat people any way he wants to." Ted goes into his office and sits down at his desk. At the next desk is Harold. Ted and Harold exchange greetings. Ted thinks, "Too bad Harold isn't head of this company. He knows twice as much as Dave, and you can trust him."

Ted looks over the papers on his desk. He is not sure how one of the forms should be completed. He takes the form into his supervisor, Bill, to find out. Bill explains the form to him. Ted recalls when he was going to high school and that Bill lived two doors down and was a year older. They had a lot of fun together. He is pleased that they still do. He notes that one of the best times he has had in a long while was last month when he and Bill went to that political convention together. He thinks, "I'm glad to see Bill is letting his hair grow longer. Now people may stop kidding me about my long hair." He asks Bill if he is going to the meeting at the church this evening, and offers to stop by and give him a ride. Bill accepts. As Ted is leaving Bill's office, Bill reminds Ted that the contracts for the Bixler account have to be sent out today. Ted makes a mental note to work on them first thing after lunch.

Ted completes the form and takes it to one of the accountants. He accepts it nervously; he is new on the job. Ted thinks, "What a mouse. He'll never last here."

On his way to lunch, Ted runs into Jim. Jim slaps him on the back and says, "How's it going, fella?" Ted thinks, "That loud-mouth. I'd like to punch him out. But, I guess I had better be pleasant; he's Joyce's cousin." After he gets away from Jim, Ted decides to stop for a cocktail before lunch. He goes into the bar and asks Freddie for a dry martini on the rocks. Freddie brings the drink and takes Ted's money. Ted takes a sip and thinks, "Good, as usual. Freddie sure is a good bartender." Freddie brings back Ted's change. Ted counts it carefully. "Freddie would cheat his own grandmother if he had the chance."

Ted has been doing what we all do every day. He has been perceiving other people in his environment. And those perceptions have influenced the way he has behaved toward those people, the way that he communicates with the other people, and probably the way they communicate with him in return. Whenever we communicate with another person, the way we view that person will have a major impact on our communication. As sources, the way we perceive our receivers will have an impact on the way that we attempt to communicate with them. Similarly, as receivers the way we perceive sources will have a major impact on the way we respond to those sources. Our attitudes toward other communicators have a major impact on our communication in four areas: exposure, perception, learning, and influence. We will consider each of these in turn.

Effects of Perception on Communication

Exposure

One of the most important effects of our attitudes toward other communicators is our choice of whether to open ourselves to communication with the other person. If we have a positive attitude toward an individual, we are more likely to expose ourselves to communication with that individual, both as a source and as a receiver. This effect works both at a dyadic level and at all other levels of communication, even mass communication. We tend to listen to the news commentator we have the most positive attitude toward, for example. We talk more with our friends than we do with people with whom we have not established a friendly relationship. Ted had positive attitudes toward Joyce, Harold, and Bill, and would be likely to seek communication with all of them. His attitude toward Dave, Jim, and the new accountant, however, was negative, so he would be unlikely to seek or desire communication with any one of them. Since exposure is necessary for any communication outcome to be possible, these attitudes toward others can obviously affect all outcomes.

Perception

Our attitude toward another communicator will have an impact both on the way we perceive messages from that other person and on the way in which we expect our messages to be perceived by that other person. For example, if we believe a person is dishonest, we may discredit what he or she says and simply not perceive whatever is said to be true. For example, Ted would probably be reluctant to believe what Freddie, the bartender, would tell him. Similarly, if we perceive another person to have a strong attitude on a question, we may interpret what the person says in light of that attitude rather than specifically on the basis of the message itself. For example, if we believe a person is highly prejudiced against a particular race or ethnic group, we will interpret whatever that persons says about that race or ethnic group in light of the way we perceive that person's attitude. Messages in communication, therefore, are always mediated by our attitude toward the person or persons who have provided us with those messages. Such an influence on our perceptions, of course, can have an impact on what kind of information we acquire from the other person, and an even greater impact on the degree of influence another person can have on us.

Learning

Our attitudes toward other communicators have a major impact on how much we learn from them, and, in turn, how much they learn from us. This effect appears to be related to attention. We pay more attention to people toward whom we have a positive attitude and process more of the messages that such people provide us. Consequently, we learn more from those messages. Obviously, the process works in reverse as well. Other people who have positive attitudes toward us pay more attention to our messages and thus will learn more from us. This is particularly important in the educational environment. If a student has a positive attitude toward the teacher, the student is much more likely to learn material from the teacher than she or he would otherwise. But this effect is also important in other communication environments. In almost any organization it is necessary for the individuals within the organization to learn from one another. To the extent that the individuals have positive attitudes toward one another, this learning outcome is enhanced.

In the case of Ted, it would be very likely that he would learn from

---

**BLACK BOX
14**

Can you explain the impact of the ways people perceive other people on these elements?
exposure to communication   learning
perception of messages   influence

Can you draw an example of each of these effects from your own experiences?

from Bill and Harold. In fact, he did learn how to complete the form from Bill. But he would be very unlikely to learn from Dave, "the creep." We will examine the relationship between our attitude toward other people and information acquisition in more detail in chapter 14.

Influence

Given our discussion of learning, it is probably obvious to you that the way we perceive other people has a major impact on how likely they are to be able to influence us, to cause us to modify our beliefs, our attitudes, and/or our behavior. Joyce, Harold, and Bill would have a high probability of influencing Ted. Dave, Jim, Freddie, and the new accountant would not. We will go into more depth concerning the relationship between influence and the attitudes communicators have toward each other in chapters 16 and 17.

Up to this point, we have referred to the perception of one communicator on the part of another communicator as our "attitude." This is a general term that we need to break down into more specific concepts to better understand how this process operates. There are four major categories of perceptions that communicators have of other communicators. These categories have been referred to as credibility, attraction, homophily, and power. We shall consider each of these in turn.

Dimensions of Communicator Perception

Credibility

There has probably been more research on the effects of credibility on communication than on any other single variable in the communication process. Although most of this research has been focused on the effects of the source's credibility on the receiver's response, we will look at this subject more broadly, because in most communication systems the individual people involved shift in their roles from source to receiver rather than maintain a specific role. Of course, in mass communication that is mediated, and in public speaking, the source and receiver distinctions are more clear.

The term *credibility* represents a construct that is multidimensional. Both the nature and the number of these dimensions have been the subject

*During the Vietnam
War the credibility
gap between the
government and the
public was a
character gap.*

of numerous research studies. The results of this research suggest that there are at least five dimensions of credibility; by that we mean five ways that communicators perceive other communicators' credibility. These have been labeled competence, character, sociability, composure, and extroversion.

Competence refers to the degree to which a person is perceived to be knowledgeable or expert on the subject matter under discussion. If one person perceives another person to have little knowledge about the subject, that second person will probably have little impact on the first person's thinking as a result of their communicating. For example, in Ted's case, messages coming from Dave would probably have little impact on Ted's thinking; but messages from Bill or Harold would be expected to have considerable impact. Perceptions of competence can range across a continuum from completely incompetent to extremely competent. But these perceptions are mediated by the receiver's perception of his or her own competence. If we visualize competence to be on a scale of zero to ten, and I consider myself to be a seven, if I perceive you to be an eight, you are probably quite competent in my mind. However, if I perceive myself to be a nine, and I perceive you to be an eight, you are probably not judged as very competent in my mind. To illustrate, let's take Freddie the bartender. Ted perceived Freddie to be competent as a bartender. A young man or woman ordering a first drink in a bar would probably perceive Freddie to be *extremely* competent. But would another bartender feel the same way if he or she came into Freddie's place for a drink? Quite possibly not.

Competence is a very important element in most communication attempts. We tend to accept opinions of people whom we judge to be more competent than we are and to follow their advice. On the other hand, if we judge ourselves to be less competent than another person on a given topic, it is not as likely that we will attempt to influence that person on that particular topic.

Although the first judgment we may make about another communicator's credibility is competence, the second dimension of credibility, *character,* is frequently as important or more important. We judge a communicator's character in terms of the essential goodness, trustworthiness, and decency of the individual. Even though we may recognize that a person is highly competent on a topic, if we do not believe that we can trust the person to tell us the truth about what she or he knows, we will tend to perceive the individual as low in credibility. To use our example of Ted and Freddie again, even though Ted judged Freddie high on competence as a bartender, he did not trust him and judged Freddie low on character. Another example is the often discussed "credibility gap" between government and the public. During the Vietnam conflict few people questioned whether the President and his advisors knew what was going on, but many people did not trust the President and his spokesmen to tell the truth about the war. The credibility gap was a character gap. While competence is judged on a scale of incompetence to highly competent, and mediated by a communicator's perception of him or herself, character is perceived on a similar continuum, but is probably not mediated by self-perceived character. By that we mean that we tend to evaluate the character of another communicator on an absolute scale. How trustworthy we are is not necessarily taken into account when we are judging the trustworthiness of another person. The old saying about there being honor among thieves has some apparent validity. Even a totally dishonest person will tend to discount communication from another person whom she or he perceives is dishonest. In sum, we tend to discount messages from communicators whom we believe to have low character. On the other side of the coin, most people tend to engage in much less communication with such people. We find little motivation to initiate communication with people whom we distrust because we cannot predict that they will cooperate with us to achieve mutual ends, and often we anticipate that our communication will be distorted by them and may even be used against us.

103

A very important dimension of credibility in interpersonal—particularly dyadic—communication is *sociability*. Sociability refers to the degree that we perceive another person to be friendly, likeable, and pleasant. In general, we will seek dyadic contact with people whom we perceive to be highly sociable, but will normally avoid dyadic contact with others whom we perceive to be less sociable. This is particularly important when the desired primary outcome of a communication is affinity. We tend to avoid making friends with unfriendly people. Sociability is also important for communication that is concerned with outcomes other than affinity. If we judge a person to be competent and of high character, but perceive the person to be unpleasant, we may not turn to him or her for advice because of the negative aspects of the communication that we might anticipate. Similarly, we may choose not to turn to a person whom we judge to be of high character but less competent than we for the purpose of influencing that person, because we don't like the unsociable individual and tend not to be concerned with informing or persuading the individual on a given topic.

The element of sociability in credibility is recognized by advertisers, particularly those on television. When you examine television advertisements you will notice that in most cases the advertiser seeks to have a very pleasant, warm person present its message rather than someone who might be perceived as unsociable. The sociability of the actor may capture our attention and get us to listen to the advertisement, whereas the less sociable person may be immediately rejected by us and thus have no impact. We recall seeing an ad for panty hose on television a few years ago. Now, neither of us is accustomed to wearing, or buying, panty hose. But the ad caught our attention because Joe Namath was in it and he was at his friendly, outgoing, sociable best. If someone were to ask us to pick up a pair of panty hose for her, the impact of this ad could well be for us to select the brand advertised.

The first three dimensions of credibility that we have discussed are clearly evaluative in nature; there is a "good" perception and a "bad" perception. The fourth dimension involves a different kind of appraisal. *Composure* refers to the degree of emotional control that we perceive another person to have, whether the person is poised, relaxed, and confident as opposed to nervous, tense, or uptight. When Ted gave the form to the new accountant, he perceived him to have a lack of composure and concluded that he probably wouldn't be successful in that office.

Generally, we perceive the person who is more composed to be more credible, but there is such a thing as *too* much composure. A person who is so completely in control of his or her emotions as to be at the extreme end of the composure scale is likely to be perceived as cold and unfriendly. We have all met people who could be described as "cold fish." While few people would perceive a President who lacked composure in a situation threatening war as credible, the same people might perceive a sportscaster who got carried away and used four-letter words to describe an important and exciting play to be more credible as a result of her or his lack of composure.

One of the reasons that high communication apprehensives may be perceived as less credible than other people is because of their usual weakness on the composure dimension. When they are forced to communicate, they are very likely to exhibit tension and lack of confidence. This can easily be spotted by others, interpreted as a lack of composure, and negatively influence the person's credibility.

The final dimension of credibility, *extroversion,* is even less evaluative in nature than composure. Extroversion refers to the degree that we perceive another communicator to be talkative, bold, and outgoing. The very introverted or shy person is generally perceived to be less credible, as we indicated in chapter 5 when discussing the communication apprehensive individual. On the other end of the scale, the person who is extremely extroverted may be perceived as less credible. We may perceive this kind of a person in the same way as the stereotyped used-car salesman. The individual may be just too outgoing to the point of being overbearing. You will recall Ted's reaction to Joyce's cousin, Jim, "the loud mouth." The most credible communicator is probably the one who is somewhere near the middle of the extroversion continuum; probably a little more extroverted than introverted, but not too much so.

Credibility is a perception of one communicator on the part of another communicator. It is important that we clearly understand that this is a perception, rather than a reality. A person can be extremely competent, but if that person is not perceived to be competent by the other communicator, the person is not credible. Since credibility is a multidimensional set of perceptions, a person can be perceived positively on some of the dimensions and not on others, and thus not be perceived as credible. For example, we may perceive a person to be very friendly, composed, and moderately extroverted, but to be a compulsive liar. We will not tend to accept the opinions or information provided by that other person. Or we may view someone as highly competent and trustworthy, as well as composed and moderately extroverted, but also unfriendly. Thus, we are not as likely to seek communication with that person and establish any kind of communication system with that individual. To be completely credible, therefore, a communicator must be perceived as competent, of high character, sociable, composed, and at least moderately extroverted. If any of these circumstances are not present, the communicator is perceived as lower in credibility.

Let us take the now-classic case of Richard Nixon. During the 1972 election Nixon was perceived as very credible by most people. Even though his opponent referred to the Nixon-Agnew Administration as "the most corrupt in American history," the majority of the voters didn't buy McGovern's accusations. With the exception of Massachusetts (and the District of Columbia), every state in the union voted for Nixon. What happened in the following months dramatized one of the most significant changes in credibility that has ever occurred in public life. As a result of the Congressional hearings on the "Watergate" burglary and the release of tapes of the President talking to his advisors, people changed their perception of Nixon's character. This resulted in his almost total rejection by the American people. Little that he could say or do had any effect whatsoever.

As we have noted, if a person is perceived low in credibility, we are likely to misperceive the messages that the communicator gives us; we are less likely to expose ourselves to that person; we are less likely to learn something from that person; and we are less likely to be influenced by that person. Similarly, we are less likely to attempt to provide information or influence to that person, and we will probably expect that our messages will be misperceived. Credibility, therefore, is a very important variable in human communication. We will discuss the implications of this variable in much more depth in later chapters, particularly those concerned with information acquisition and influence.

Attraction

Attraction, like credibility, is a multidimensional perception of one communicator on the part of another communicator. There are at least three dimensions of attraction: physical, task, and social.

Physical attraction is the first dimension of appeal that has an impact on human communication. Physical attraction relates specifically to our perception of someone in terms of that person's physical appearance. During initial communication encounters we tend to look at the other person more as an object than as a human being, and the implications of this habit for the outcome of affinity are very important. Research has clearly indicated that physical attraction is the single most important perception in initial communication encounters. Thus, if there is negative physical attraction there is also little likelihood that affinity will be developed. In fact, in many instances there will be no communication at all unless there is at least some initial physical attraction between people, particularly when they are of the opposite sex. This dimension of attraction becomes less important as communicators become more familiar with one another. Over time, the other dimensions of attraction increase in importance; however, initially the physical dimension is vital. It is a popular axiom within American culture to discount the importance of physical appearance; we say things like "beauty is only skin deep." But our behavior belies this cultural truism. As one friend of ours put it, "beauty is only skin deep, but most people are only interested in skin!"

Physical attraction is affected not only by the actual physical makeup of a person's body, but also by clothing and accessories. You will recall Joyce's physical attraction for Ted when she noted the new suit he was wearing. You will also recall Ted's positive reaction to Bill's appearance when he noted that Bill was letting his hair grow longer. In each case the physical attraction felt probably contributed to increased affinity between the two persons.

Remember, when we initially encounter another human being the only information we have concerning that other human being is what we can see. Thus, we make decisions about communication with that other individual on the basis of that physical apprarance. If we are physically attracted to that individual, we are highly likely to attempt to initiate communication. If we find the other person not physically attractive, we are not only unlikely to attempt to initiate communication ourselves, but we are also likely to be highly resistant to communication attempts by that person.

Task attraction refers to the degree to which we perceive it to be desirable to establish a work relationship with another communicator. If we view another as one with whom it would be easy to work, who would probably be productive in that work, and who is motivated to achieve communication outcomes similar to those we are motivated to achieve, then we are likely to perceive that person to be task attractive. When there is task attraction between two communicators it is very likely that their communication will be goal-directed and quite effective. If we perceive someone to be task attractive we will perceive that working with that individual will result in a desirable outcome. If this perception is shared by the communicators in a communication system, it is likely to be a self-fulfilling prophecy. Since we expect to communicate effectively, we are much more likely to actually do so.

The third dimension of attraction is *social attraction.* Social attraction refers to the degree to which one communicator perceives another communicator to be someone with whom she or he would like to spend time at a social level. This dimension of attraction is particularly important when the outcome of the potential communication transaction is affinity. Again, if there is social attraction between communicators in the transaction, the communicators expect to have a socially satisfying relationship and this tends to be a self-fulfilling prophecy.

While it is possible for one communicator to perceive another as highly attractive on all three dimensions, it is not necessary for a person to be attractive on one dimension in order to be attractive on another. For example, in a classroom it is not uncommon to assign group projects. We may find a classmate physically unattractive and not someone we would like to date, but we may also see that person as bright and capable on the topic of the group assignment and be very attracted to working with that individual to achieve a common goal. Similarly, we may find it extremely desirable to establish a social relationship with a certain man, but would never want to work with him. A glaring example of this situation is the stereotyped chauvinistic male attitude toward females. The male may find the female very physically and socially attractive, but view the idea of working in the same office with her as totally repulsive. How about our old chauvinistic friend, Ted? He certainly finds Joyce both physically and socially attractive. But when she tried to suggest that she would like to apply for a job in his office, what did Ted do? He tried to give her excuses for not trying for the job.

As this example indicates (hopefully), we are dealing here with perceptions rather than with reality. Although society has defined some standards of attraction, there is no reality in attraction beyond the perception of communicators. A person is attractive if that person is perceived as attrac-

---

BLACK BOX
15

Can you identify the dimensions of these perceptions in human communication?

attraction   credibility
homophily

From your own experience, name some people whom you perceive to be particularly high and particularly low on each of these dimensions.

tive, otherwise that person simply is not attractive. The person we perceive as attractive is much more likely to find us sharing ourselves with that individual for communication. If we have a shared attraction we are much more apt to learn from one another and be influenced by one another, and to the extent that we find one another attractive we are more likely to perceive one another's messages in a desirable, if not more accurate, manner.

Homophily

Homophily, as we noted in chapter 4, refers to the degree of similarity between communicators on any given attribute or group of attributes. The term *homophily* may be roughly translated as "similarity." You will probably recall the "principle of homophily" which we discussed in relation to mass communication and opinion leaders. Because of the importance of this principle we will restate it here: the more similar two communicators are, the more likely they are to interact with one another, and the more likely it is that their communication will be successful. Homophily has a major impact in communication, particularly on affinity, information acquisition, and influence outcomes. Simply put, we tend to be more attracted to people similar to us than to others; we tend to learn more from such people, and they are a great influence on us.

Homophily may be considered from two vantage points: (1) on the basis of what an external observer can perceive, what we might call "real" homophily; or (2) on the basis of what communicators perceive about one another, or "perceived" homophily. Let us examine both approaches.

Many of the similarities between communicators can be observed by people outside the communication system. The degree to which people share the same sex, age, culture, religion, race, and other variables is an indication of the degree to which they are homophilous. We can make many predictions about the probable success of a communication system on the basis of such observable characteristics of homophily present in the system. And many of these predictions will be found to be accurate. For example, we can predict that a black who has grown up in a black ghetto could return to that ghetto as a change agent and produce more change, more rapidly, than could a white who was born and raised in suburbia. Although such a prediction may be obvious given our knowledge of the principle of homophily in human communication, this prediction apparently was not made several years ago when Federal programs were being developed to try to help people in urban ghettos. The initial change agents who were sent into this atmosphere shared few characteristics with the people whom they had hoped to help. For the most part, these programs were miserable failures. Only later were attempts made to employ change agents who were highly similar to the people whom they were supposed to help. These programs have been much more successful in improving at least some conditions in ghetto neighborhoods.

Most of the early research on the effects of homophily on human communication examined the concept in the manner discussed above; that is, the degree of homophily was determined by observers outside the communication system. More recently, attention has been focused more on *perceived* homophily within the communication system. Like credibility and attraction, perceived homophily has been found to be multidimensional. There are at least four dimensions of perceived homophily: appearance, background, attitude, and value.

One of the first homophily perceptions that communicators make is based on the *appearance* of another communicator. We perceive ourselves to be more similar to another person if we look somewhat alike. Obviously, sex is involved in this dimension since it is more difficult to discern a person of the opposite sex looking like us. But given this reservation, research suggests that people who are small tend to perceive other small people as more similar than they do tall people, and the reverse is also true. Long-haired people tend to perceive other long-haired people as more similar than short-haired people; short-haired people consider themselves to be more similar to other short-haired people than they do to long-haired people. People who dress in conservative styles see others who dress in conservative styles as more similar to them. This perception of homophily, therefore, leads to more communication between people who have similar appearance than between people who differ substantially in appearance.

Another early perception that has a major impact on perceived homophily is perceived similarity in *background.* We perceive those people who have backgrounds similar to our own as more homophilous to us than people with different backgrounds. College graduates find other college graduates more similar than noncollege graduates. People from New York City perceive other New Yorkers as more similar than people from the Middle West. People born and raised in a ghetto see other ghetto-dwellers as more similar than suburbanites. Americans perceive other Americans to be more similar than they perceive Russians to be. A person with a southern accent identifies another person with a southern accent as more similar than a person with a midwestern accent. All of these perceptions lead

We perceive ourselves to be more similar to another person if we look alike.

communicators to an increase in perceived homophily, more communication with one another, and subsequently they are more likely to be effective in that communication.

While perceptions of appearance and background homophily may actually be generated prior to any real communication between two individuals, and these perceptions may be maintained over long periods of time, attitude and value homophily are generally not perceived until some communication has occurred between the individuals involved. *Attitude* homophily refers to the degree to which two communicators perceive their feelings, beliefs about reality, and general information level to be similar. *Value* homophily refers to the degree to which two communicators perceive their basic orientations on such things as moral questions to be similar. (We will explore the meanings of "attitude" and "value" further in chapter 7.) Since it is generally impossible to know another person completely, no matter how much communication occurs between two people, attitude and value homophily perceptions tend to fluctuate over the life of a communication system. During an initial interaction, for example, I may discover that another communicator is a member of the same political party that I am, adheres to the same religion, and has some of the same opinions about life. I may, therefore, perceive a considerable degree of attitude and value homophily with that person. In our case of Ted and his supervisor, Bill, it is

111

highly likely that they have a great deal of attitude and value homophily since both are active in the same political party and attend the same church. It is possible, however, even in the case of Ted and Bill, who also share strong background homophily, that communication between people who initially perceive themselves to be highly similar may result in the discovery of areas in which their attitudes and/or values may differ. When this occurs, their perceived homophily may decline rather sharply. This leads to an important reservation concerning the principle of homophily that we need to explain carefully.

The principle of homophily suggests that the more two people perceive themselves to be similar, the more likely they are to communicate, the more likely they are to communicate effectively, and the more similar they will become. Thus, if a male and a female are attracted to one another and discover that they have a lot of things in common, they will probably perceive a considerable degree of homophily. This may result in extended communication between the individuals, and possibly even the formation of a formalized dyadic communication system known as marriage. Based upon the principle of homophily, we would predict that when this occurs, communication would continue to be highly effective between these people and they would become more and more similar as time passed. Are there exceptions? We are all familiar with divorce. On the surface at least, divorce indicates a fatal flaw in the principle of homophily. But it may be merely suggestive of a limitation on the principle. Even if perceptions of homophily are not correct, that is, they do not square with reality, they still may lead to increased communication and apparently more effective communication. But if this continues over a period of time, it is most likely that the individuals involved will begin to discover that their attitudes and values are not as similar as they believed initially. This kind of impact from communication should not be taken as unusual if the two people have established a close affinity relationship. Such a relationship, as we will discuss further in chapter 11, tends to lead to increased self-disclosure. In early stages of a relationship, people tend to self-disclose comparatively little, and then primarily only positive things. Over an extended period of time, however, increased self-disclosure can likely lead to an increase in the disclosure of negative things. Thus, over time, the perception of homophily may be changed to the point where people may no longer perceive themselves to be similar. At that point we would predict that the communication system would begin to deteriorate or possibly collapse completely, as in the case of divorce. Consequently, it is important that we realize that the principle of homophily only applies if *real* homophily exists, or only as long as perceived homophily is not confronted and altered by reality.

Many writers concerned with interpersonal communication argue strongly for high disclosure among people about their inner feelings, desires, and motivations. Other people argue that such disclosures may cause an interpersonal relationship to be destroyed. In a sense, both positions are correct. It is a matter of timing. It has been said, probably with some substance in fact, that there would be very few marriages in the world if the two people involved really knew one another. High disclosure will normally indicate a lack of homophily between people, simply because people are not alike in many respects. Most of us have recognized in courting relationships that there are some things about us that we prefer that the other person not know. We fear that if our true self were known, nobody would really want us. This, of course, supports those people who argue against high disclosure in interpersonal communication. On the other hand, over an extended life of a communication system, it is almost impossible not to reveal a great deal more about one's self. Such disclosures may result in weakening the bonds among the people in the communication system. It can be argued, therefore, that high disclosure in the initial stage of the life of the communication system could have prevented that system existing beyond its point of usefulness. There is clearly some truth on both sides of this question. We will consider the impact of self-disclosure on communication in more depth in chapter 11.

Before we turn our attention to the next area, we need to restress the importance of homophily in human communication. To the extent that we perceive another communicator to be similar to us, we are increasingly likely to attempt to communicate with that person. To the extent that our perception of homophily is accurate we will have a much greater likelihood of having effective communication, primarily because the more similar we are the more likely we are to perceive both verbal and nonverbal messages in a similar manner. The relationships established by perceptions of homophily usually enhance communication so that the outcomes of affinity, information acquisition, and influence are more likely. In many communication systems, homophily tends to dominate the system. We simply prefer to talk with people whom we perceive to be similar to us, and our normal tendency is to avoid communication with people whom we perceive to be dissimilar.

Power

Power refers to the degree to which one person has the ability to influence another person's existence beyond that person's control. While many people would prefer that power would have no impact on communication systems, we all know that it does. Power is particularly important in hierarchical systems such as large-group communication systems or organizations. We do not communicate with people whom we perceive to have power over our lives in the same way that we communicate with people whom we think have no power over us. Similarly, we do not communicate in the same way with people over whom we have power as we do with people over whom we have no power. Like homophily, power can be examined either on a basis of "reality" or on the basis of perception. We will consider both approaches.

Real power in a communication system has an impact on that system whenever the power is used in a coercive manner or whenever the threat of coercion is present. The presence of power tends to inhibit communication. Often if we have power over another individual we will perceive less need to communicate with them, particularly as a receiver. We will simply indicate our wishes to them and presume that our power over them will result in conformity to our request. On the other side of the coin, if a person has power over us, we will often avoid communication with them in order to circumvent their power over us. We may perceive that if we communicate with them, it will be an unpleasant experience since we will be inhibited in our communication behavior for fear of receiving punishments which that individual is in a position to exercise upon us.

Power probably has its biggest impact on the influence outcome of communication; however, it can also have a substantial impact on the outcome of affinity. Perceived power is likely to have an even greater impact upon a communication system than real power. Perceived power refers to the degree to which one communicator perceives another communicator as having the ability to influence his or her existence beyond his or her control.

The crucial context of this perception is whether or not the individual understands the other person's power to be *legitimate* or *illegitimate*. In a democratic society we make a major delineation between a person who is granted legitimate power and one who assumes power that is not granted to

**BLACK BOX
16**

Can you explain the difference in people's attitudes toward President Nixon before and after the Watergate disclosures in terms of legitimate and illegitimate power?

Real power affects a communication system whenever it is used in a coercive manner or when the threat of coercion is present.

that individual by the persons over whom she or he is to exert the power. We believe in democratic elections, for example. Even though our candidate does not win, we usually still perceive the elected person to have assumed power legitimately and tend to follow the requests or demands of the individual. In the work environment, we often perceive our superior to have legitimate power because we have accepted the job. We have the choice, if we don't like the way that power is exerted, to resign and take a position elsewhere. Small children generally perceive their parents to have legitimate power over them and follow their requests because the parent has made them. As the child moves into the teenage years, this perception of legitimacy tends to diminish to the point in some cases where the teenager does not perceive the parent as having *any* legitimate power whatsoever.

The distinction between legitimate and illegitimate power perceptions can be made clearer by returning to our old friend, Ted. During our visit with him, Ted came upon two people who had some power over him: Dave, the head of the company ("the creep") and Bill, Ted's supervisor and childhood friend. While we may be putting thoughts in old Ted's head, we would guess that he perceives Dave's power as illegitimate, particularly since he attributes Dave's success to his father's money.   On the other hand, Ted probably thinks Bill has legitimate power, since they seem to be such good friends in spite of their supervisor-subordinate roles.

The impacts of legitimate and illegitimate perceived power are quite different.   To the extent that we perceive that a person has legitimate power over us, we will follow the instructions and requests of that individual without giving them too much consideration.   In fact, we will often turn to that individual and ask for directives, particularly in the work environment.   Perceived legitimate power, therefore, can be very helpful to a communication system in terms of its efficiency.   That appears to be the kind of relationship that exists between Ted and Bill.   Perceived illegitimate power, however, produces a very different result.   To the extent that we perceive a person to be exercising illegitimate power over us, we attempt to avoid influence from that individual and to circumvent the regulations and instructions that communicator gives us.   This is highly disruptive within communication systems, since true communication between those individuals is very unlikely.   The projection for the life of a communication system in which illegitimate power is perceived to be present is not good.   People seek to leave communication systems if they believe that illegitimate power is being placed upon them.

Summary

Throughout this book we have stressed the complexity of the human communication process.   In this chapter we have considered one of the most important, if not *the* most important element in that process: the ways people perceive each other.   In all, we have considered thirteen dimensions of the perceptions that we can have of one another, and there are probably others that we have overlooked.   The sheer number of possible perceptions may make you feel like throwing up your hands and exclaiming, "How on earth can anyone ever control all of those perceptions?"   Good question.   You probably can't, at least most of the time.   We know we can't.   Fortunately, not all of these perceptions are equally important for all communication exchanges.   Some are more important for affinity (physical attraction, sociability, homophily), while others are more important for information acquisition (competence, character, task attraction), and still others are more important for other outcomes.   We have attempted to suggest the outcomes for which perceptions are most important in this chapter, but we will deal with this subject in much more detail in chapters 12 through 20 when we focus our attention on the outcomes themselves.

At this point you should be aware that to the extent that we are sensitive to the way we are perceived by other communicators, we can adapt and attempt to change their perceptions of us, and enhance our communication with other people. To the extent that we ignore the impact of the way people perceive other people in communication, the probability that we will have successful communication is reduced.

SUGGESTED FURTHER READINGS

1. ANDERSEN, K. and CLEVENGER, T., JR. "A Summary of Experimental Research in Ethos." *Speech Monographs* 30 (1963): 59–78.

   An excellent synthesis of the early research on source credibility.

2. BERSCHEID, E. and WALSTER, E. *Interpersonal Attraction* (Reading, Mass.: Addison-Wesley, 1969).

   A brief but thorough summary of the early research and theory concerning interpersonal attraction.

3. ROGERS, E. M. and BHOWMIK, D. K. "Homophily-Heterophily: Relational Concepts for Communication Research," in *Speech Communication Behavior,* L. L. Barker and R. J. Kibler, eds. (Englewood Cliffs, N.J.: Prentice-Hall, 1971), 206–225.

   A brief but thorough explanation of the principle of homophily and the research supporting the principle.

SELECTED REFERENCES

ABRAHAMSON, M. *Interpersonal Accommodation* (Princeton, N.J.: D. Van Nostrand Co., 1966).

ALPERT, M. I. and ANDERSEN, W. T., JR. "Optimal Heterophily and Communication Effectiveness: Some Empirical Findings." *Journal of Communication* 23 (1973): 328–343.

ANDERSEN, K. and CLEVENGER, T., JR. "A Summary of Experimental Research in Ethos." *Speech Monographs* 30 (1963): 59–78.

ARONSON, E. and COPE, V. "My Enemy's Enemy Is My Friend." *Journal of Personality and Social Psychology* 8 (1968): 8–12.

ARONSON, E. and GOLDEN, B. W. "The Effect of Relevant and Irrelevant Aspects of Communicator Credibility on Opinion Change." *Journal of Personality* 30 (1962): 135–146.

BERGER, C. R. and CALABRESE, R. J. "Some Explorations in Initial Interaction and Beyond: Toward a Developmental Theory of Interpersonal Communication." *Human Communication Research* 1 (1975): 99–112.

BERGER, E. M. "The Relation Between Expressed Acceptance of Self and Expressed Acceptance of Others." *Journal of Abnormal and Social Psychology* 47 (1952): 778–782.

BERLO, D. K., LEMERT, J. B., and MERTZ, R. "Dimensions for Evaluating the Acceptability of Message Sources." *Public Opinion Quarterly* 33 (1969): 563–576.

BERSCHEID, E., BOYE, D., and DARLEY, J. "Effect of Forced Association Upon Voluntary Choice to Associate." *Journal of Personality and Social Psychology* 8 (1968): 13–19.

BERSCHEID, E. and WALSTER, E. *Interpersonal Attraction* (Reading, Mass.: Addison-Wesley, 1969).

BREWER, R. E. "Attitude Change, Interpersonal Attraction, and Communication in a Dyadic Situation." *Journal of Social Psychology* 75 (1968): 127–134.

BREWER, R. E. and BREWER, M. B. "Attraction and Accuracy of Perception in Dyads," *Journal of Personality and Social Psychology* 8 (1968): 188–193.

BRISLIN, R. W. and LEWIS, S. A. "Dating and Physical Attractiveness." *Psychological Reports* 22 (1968): 976, et passim.

BYRNE, D. and GRIFFITT, W. "A Developmental Investigation of the Law of Attraction." *Journal of Personality and Social Psychology* 4 (1966): 699–703.

————. "Similarity Versus Liking: A Clarification." *Psychonomic Science* 6 (1966): 295–296.

BYRNE, D., LONDON, O., and REEVES, K. "The Effects of Physical Attractiveness, Sex, and Attitude Similarity on Interpersonal Attraction." *Journal of Personality* 36 (1968): 259–271.

CLORE, G. L. and BALDRIDGE, B. "Interpersonal Attraction: The Role of Agreement and Topic Interest." *Journal of Personality and Social Psychology* 9 (1968): 340–346.

DALY, J. A., McCROSKEY, J. C., and RICHMOND, V. P. "The Relationship Between Vocal Activity and Perception of Communicators in Small Group Interaction." Paper presented to the convention of the Speech Communication Association, Chicago, 1974.

FESTINGER, L., SCHACHTER, S., and BACK, K. *Social Pressures in Informal Groups* (New York: Harper and Brothers, 1950).

HAIMAN, F. "An Experimental Study of the Effects of Ethos in Public Speaking." *Speech Monographs* 16 (1949): 190–202.

HEIDER, F. *The Psychology of Interpersonal Relations* (New York: John Wiley, 1958).

HOROWITZ, H. "Interpersonal Choice in American Adolescents." *Psychological Reports* 19 (1966): 371–374.

HOVLAND, C. I., JANIS, I. L., and KELLEY, H. H. *Communication and Persuasion* (New Haven, Conn.: Yale University Press, 1953).

HOVLAND, C. I. and WEISS, W. "The Influence of Source Credibility on Communication Effectiveness." *Public Opinion Quarterly* 15 (1951): 635–650.

ILIFFE, A. H. "A Study of Preferences in Feminine Beauty." *British Journal of Psychology* 51 (1960): 267–273.

INGLIS, R. "The Effects of Personality Similarity on Empathy and Interpersonal Attraction." Ph.D. Dissertation, Duke University, 1965.

IVERSON, M. A. "Attraction Toward Flatterers of Different Statuses." *Journal of Social Psychology* 74 (1968): 181–187.

KATZ, A. M. and HILL, R. "Residential Propinquity and Marital Selection: A Review of Theory, Method, and Fact." *Marriage and Family Living* 20 (1958): 27–35.

KATZ, E. and LAZARSFELD, P. F. *Personal Influence* (New York: The Free Press, 1955).

LANDY, D. and ARONSON, E. "Liking for an Evaluator as a Function of His Discernment." *Journal of Personality and Social Psychology* 9 (1968): 133–141.

McCROSKEY, J. C. "Scales for the Measurement of Ethos." *Speech Monographs* 33 (1966): 65–72.

McCROSKEY, J. C., HAMILTON, P. R., and WEINER, A. N. "The Effect of Interaction Behavior on Source Credibility, Homophily, and Interpersonal Attraction." *Human Communication Research* 1 (1974): 42–52.

McCROSKEY, J. C., HOLDRIDGE, W. E., and TOOMB, J. K. "An Instrument for Measuring the Source Credibility of Basic Speech Communication Instructors." *Speech Teacher* 23 (1974): 26–33.

McCROSKEY, J. C., JENSEN, T., and TODD, C. "The Generalizability of Source Credibility Scales for Public Figures." Paper presented at the Speech Communication Association Convention, Chicago, December, 1972.

McCROSKEY, J. C., JENSEN, T., TODD, C., and TOOMB, J. K. "Measurement of the Credibility of Organization Sources." Paper presented at the Western Speech Communication Association Convention, Honolulu, November, 1972.

McCROSKEY, J. C. and JENSEN, T. "Measurement of the Credibility of Mass Media Sources." *Journal of Broadcasting* 19 (1975): 169–180.

————. "Measurement of the Credibility of Peers and Spouses." Paper presented at the International Communication Association, Montreal, April 1973(b).

McCroskey, J. C. and McCain, T. A. "The Measurement of Interpersonal Attraction." *Speech Monographs* 41 (1974): 261–266.

McCroskey, J. C., Richmond, V. P., and Daly, J. A. "The Measurement of Perceived Homophily in Interpersonal Communication." *Human Communication Research* 1 (1975).

McCroskey, J. C., Scott, M. D., and Young, T. J. "The Dimensions of Source Credibility for Spouses and Peers." Paper presented at the Western Speech Communication Association convention, Fresno, California, November, 1971.

Meyer, W. J. and Barbour, M. A. "Generality of Individual and Group Social Attractiveness Over Several Rating Situations." *Journal of Genetic Psychology* 113 (1968): 101–108.

Mills, J. and Aronson, E. "Opinion Change as a Function of the Communicator's Attractiveness and Desire to Influence." *Journal of Personality and Social Psychology* 1 (1965): 173–177.

Newcomb, T. M. *The Acquaintance Process* (New York: Holt, Rinehart and Winston, 1961).

Priest, R. F. and Sawyer, J. "Proxemity and Peership: Bases of Balance in Interpersonal Attraction." *The American Journal of Sociology* 72 (1967): 633–649.

Rogers, E. M. and Shoemaker, F. F. *Communication of Innovations* (New York: The Free Press, 1971).

Shrauger, J. S. and Jones, S. C. "Social Validation and Interpersonal Evaluations." *Journal of Experimental Social Psychology* 4 (1968): 315–323.

Walster, E., Aronson, V., Abrahams, D., and Rottmann, L. "Importance of Physical Attractiveness in Dating Behavior." *Journal of Personality and Social Psychology* 4 (1966): 508–516.

Warr, P. B. and Knapper, C. *The Perception of People and Events* (New York: John Wiley, 1968).

Widgery, R. N. and Webster, B. "The Effects of Physical Attractiveness Upon Perceived Initial Credibility." *Michigan Speech Association Journal* 4 (1969).

7

Personal Orientations and Personality

There are several men engaged in an animated discussion in the lounge. Let's listen in.

Pat: *I think the main cause of our oil shortage is the Arabs. They have enough oil to supply the world for several hundred years, but they just want to rob everybody.*

Juan: *I don't agree. We have a lot of oil in my country. But it is all owned by American oil companies, and they just leave most of it in the ground. I think it is the big oil companies that are causing the problem.*

Barry: *We can't blame either the Arabs or the oil companies. They are supplying more oil than ever before. It is the ecology freaks that are causing the problem. Without those ridiculous gadgets on our cars we could get almost double the mileage from a gallon of gas. Then there wouldn't be a shortage at all.*

George: *Well, I don't think there is any shortage. Did you know that the oil companies have enough oil stored around the country right now to supply us with all the oil we need for the next six months?*

Pat: *I didn't know that.*

Juan: *I didn't either.*

Barry: *I don't think you are right about that, George. I think that the supply would be enough for our cars for six months, but that would be ignoring all trucks, busses, industrial and heating oil users. We have to have a storage supply for winter, because we can't refine oil as fast as we use it then.*

Pat: *Well, I don't care what anybody says; I think we should blast hell out of those Arabs and take over their oil fields. If we don't, sooner or later the Russians will.*

Juan: *You want to do that to the Latin Americans too?*

Pat: *Naw. You guys will give us your oil if we need it.*

Tom: *Well, I sure wish I knew what was going to happen. I haven't bought a new car for four years. Until we know whether we are going to have more oil or the cars are going to get better mileage, I just can't decide what to do. That really worries me.*

George: *I can understand how you feel, Tom. It is about time the government made some decisions. We sure can't solve this problem by ourselves.*

Pat: *Right on, George.*

Barry: *That's for sure.*

Juan: *Yes, a government policy decision is necessary.*

Tom: *Well, I sure hope they hurry up about it. I can't go on like this much longer.*

George: *By the way, where is Kevin? I thought he was going to join us.*

Pat: *He isn't coming. He has a mid-term in the morning.*

Like our friends in the lounge, people do not all think the same. If they did, communication would certainly be easy and effective, but there might be little or no reason to communicate at all! The real reason why communication plays such a large part in human behavior is because people do not think alike. People hold different attitudes, beliefs, and values, and, as a result, choose to expose themselves to different communication experiences, learn different things, perceive the world in different ways, and engage in different behaviors. We will consider how these personal orientations affect the way people engage in communication interactions and transactions in the next chapter and how they are related to communication outcomes in chapters 12 through 20. At this point we need to explain what these orientations are and how they differ from one another so that our later discussion will be meaningful to you.

Personal Orientations

Attitudes

Our attitudes are predispositions to respond or behave in specific ways toward people, ideas, and objects. Essentially, our attitudes represent our evaluations of things in our external world. By "evaluation" we mean a continuum ranging from good to bad, or desirable to undesirable. In our lounge discussion, Pat expressed a negative attitude toward Arabs, Juan expressed a negative attitude toward oil companies, and Barry expressed a negative attitude toward pollution control devices. Everyone expressed a positive attitude toward government decisions, with Pat indicating favor for military action. Kevin apparently had a more positive attitude toward studying for his mid-term than discussing oil; he didn't show up.

Attitudes, as well as beliefs and values, vary on three psychological dimensions: direction, intensity, and salience. Throughout our explanation of personal orientations, we will maintain a running example of the controversy concerning ecology and air pollution. We hope that this will help you sort out these different orientations and fix the concepts more firmly in your mind.

The *direction* of an attitude may be favorable, unfavorable, or neutral. For example, people may vary in the direction of their attitude concerning certain programs designed to protect our environment. We may be for a new pollution control device on an automobile, we may be against it, or we may be neutral or undecided. Our friend, Barry, was clearly against such devices. In general, we expect people to behave in a manner consistent with the direction of their attitude. People who feel positively toward something generally will do things in support of it, while people who are opposed to something will do things in opposition to it, and people who are undecided will generally engage in little or no related behavior. We would expect, for example, that Barry would try to get government regulations on pollution devices removed. We would not expect to see him in a pro-ecology demonstration!

The *intensity* of an attitude is the degree of strength with which an individual holds the attitude. The more intense an attitude, the more extreme that attitude is. If we presume that two people are both favorable toward a certain ecological program, but one holds that attitude very intensely while the other one is more moderate, we would expect more behavior—and more extreme behavior—from the person who holds the intense attitude than from the one who holds a more moderate attitude. The "ecology freaks" to whom Barry referred are probably people who feel very intensely about the ecology, and thus, engage in behaviors designed to protect the ecology.

The *salience* of an attitude refers to the importance of the attitude to the person holding it. We are much more likely to behave in accordance with our attitudes if they are important to us than if they are not. Consider two people who are both favorable toward control of air pollution in the environment. One person lives in Los Angeles and the other lives in a remote mountain area of Montana. While both people may share the same attitude in terms of direction and intensity, we would expect the person in Los Angeles to engage in more behavior related to that attitude, since air pollution is a far greater problem in Los Angeles than it is in Montana.

Belief

Beliefs are perceptions about reality in the external environment. Although such beliefs may lead to evaluations, beliefs are not as inherently evaluative as attitudes. While attitude varies on a good-bad continuum, belief varies on a true-false continuum. In our lounge discussion George expressed the belief that there was enough oil stored to last six months. Barry expressed the contrary belief that the oil stored would not be sufficient for that period.

The *direction* of a belief refers to whether the individual thinks that something is true, false, or unclear. George believed there was six-months' worth of oil stored; Barry did not. Consider another example. There are some people who believe that cigarette smoke in a room is harmful to both smokers and nonsmokers alike. Other people believe that second-hand smoke is harmless. Still other people are undecided.

Intensity refers to the strength with which an individual holds a belief. Intensity of belief and attitude are essentially the same. Intensity of belief can run from a very moderate level to a very extreme level. In essence, intensity of belief refers to the certainty with which we believe something. When we hear words like "probably," "possibly," and "certainly" we are given cues about the intensity of a person's belief. If someone says it "possibly" will rain, we can recognize that as a less intense belief than if the person had said that it will "certainly" rain. In general, the more intensely a person holds a belief, the more likely that belief is to influence that person's behavior.

Salience of belief, like salience of attitude, has to do with the importance of the belief to the individual holding it. For example, if two people believe that second-hand cigarette smoke is dangerous to nonsmokers, but one of the people is in excellent health and the other one has emphysema, we would expect the person suffering from emphysema to engage in behaviors consistent with the belief to a greater degree than the person in good health. The person with emphysema might seek to leave the room or to encourage other people to stop smoking in his or her presence. The person in good health would be less likely to engage in either of these behaviors.

Value

Our values are relatively long-enduring judgments about the desirability of ideas and behaviors. Values form the basis for most of our behavioral habits. They establish our criteria for forming attitudes and beliefs about people and things in our external environment. Although attitudes and beliefs are regularly subject to change, particularly if someone exerts influence on them to change, values are highly resistant to alteration and tend to endure over very long periods of time, even over a complete life span.

The *direction* of a value is very similar in nature to the direction of an attitude; that is, the values range on a good-bad continuum. We can value something positively, we can value it negatively, or we can have a neutral value or missing value related to something. For example, we can hold human life in high esteem, thus having a positive value for it, or we can consider human life relatively meaningless, and thus hold a negative value for it. Similarly, we can feel that money is a very desirable thing to have, and thus have positive value for money, or we can consider money to be a negative element in our existence.

Intensity of value is essentially the same as intensity of attitude or belief: it refers to the strength with which a person holds a judgment. Intensity of value differs somewhat from other degrees of feelings, however, since most values are held quite strongly. Nevertheless, we do vary to some extent in the intensity with which we hold our values.

Salience of value is determined by the importance of a value to us in a given circumstance. Since most of our behavioral actions involve choices between conflicting values, the salience of a value is especially important. For example, most people hold positive values both for human life and for acquiring wealth. The salience of these two values becomes very important when we are confronted with a behavioral choice that involves sacrifice of wealth in order to protect life or risk to life in order to obtain or maintain wealth. An example of this type of behavior choice may be taken from the appeal of ecology. Most of us believe that air pollution produced by automobiles is dangerous to our health. Thus we wish to reduce that pollution in order to protect our lives. But air pollution control devices sharply increase the cost of an automobile, and we wish to keep the price we must pay for an automobile as low as possible. We can't fully support either value without sacrificing one thing in terms of another. In a highly polluted city environment, therefore, a person may find human life value to be more salient than financial value. In a more remote rural area, the same person may find financial value to be more salient than life value. In either case, we would expect people to behave in accordance with the value most salient to the given behavioral choice.

**BLACK BOX
17**

Can you distinguish between attitudes, beliefs, and values? Give examples of each based on your own orientation.

In sum, attitudes are our evaluations of things; beliefs are our conceptions of reality; and values are our enduring conceptions of what is good and what is bad. Each of these orientations can vary in direction, intensity, and salience. These orientations are highly related to human behavior. They are also interrelated with each other. We will explore these interrelationships in detail in chapter 16 when we consider the outcome of influence. However, at this point we need to stress that these personal orientations are integrally associated with one another. Thus, as individuals, we develop certain habitual patterns of approaching life. These ways of behaving and looking at our environment have been referred to as *personality variables*. Contrasts in personality result in major differences in communication behavior and have a strong impact on all of the communication outcomes we will consider in later chapters.

Personality Variables in Human Communication

People differ substantially in the way they operate within communication systems. Communication between Person A and Person B may be very different from communication between Person C and Person D. Attitudes, beliefs, and values aren't always complementary, and this results in differences in people's communication behavior. In addition, some of these differences can be accounted for by such rather obvious variables as sex, age, and race. In later chapters we will discuss some of the impacts that can be attributed to such general characteristics. Far more important, however, are the characteristics of the individual which make that human being unique. We have described these characteristics as personality variables. Literally dozens of personality variables have been isolated by personality psychologists, although their impact on communication is yet to be studied. Our attention will be directed here to a relatively small group of personality variables about whose impact we have some information: Machiavellianism, dogmatism, self-esteem, tolerance for ambiguity, emotional maturity, adventurousness, sensitivity, eccentricity, radicalism, and general anxiety.

Machiavellianism

The highly Machiavellian personality views other people as objects to be manipulated for her or his own purposes. Not only are high-Machs willing to manipulate other people, but they also tend to be very successful at such manipulation, and, further, they seem to enjoy such attempts. The impact of this personality type on communication is probably obvious. The high-Mach communicates with willful intent to influence other people and does so with glee. An important corollary of the Machiavellian orientation toward communication is that the Machiavellian tends to show little concern for conventional morality and has little emotional involvement in the communication encounters in which she or he is engaged. Machiavellians tend to distrust other people. In fact, research has indicated that highly Machiavellian individuals do not even form perceptions of other people on the character dimension of credibility; rather, they tend simply to distrust everyone. High Machiavellians tend to be very pragmatic in their orientation, focusing on immediate outcomes rather than long-range ones. They are often hostile and in some cases alienated. While the highly Machiavellian individual is quite successful in influencing other people, he or she is less likely to be influenced by anyone else. In general, in communication relationships the Machiavellian displays a low regard for others, treats them as objects, and is generally unconcerned with the humanness of the other person. When a highly Machiavellian individual is placed in a communication system that is primarily populated by people with less Machiavellian personalities, the high-Mach normally controls the product of the system. High-Machs tend to rise to the top of the communication system while low-Machs tend to settle to the bottom if the system is hierarchical.

Dogmatism

Dogmatism is a personality characteristic that is best described as "closed-mindedness." In our lounge discussion, Pat and Barry appear to be dogmatics. The dogmatic individual is ideologically rigid, and as a result tends to be highly inflexible in his or her communication behavior and quite intolerant of those who hold contrary views. Dogmatics are also referred to as "authoritarian" because they hold an unusually high respect for persons in authority, and tend to be dominated by the views of those whom they perceive to be authorities. Dogmatic individuals are also characterized by feelings of anxiety and insecurity. They are more likely to respond to communication that is irrelevant to the question under consideration, based on emotions, than they are to respond to rational discourse. If a dogmatic person believes that blacks are inferior to whites, no degree of evidence to the contrary is likely to change the dogmatic's mind. However, that position might well be changed if a person in an authority position were to tell the dogmatic that her or his view is incorrect and should be changed. The dogmatic also tends to view everything in extremes. If someone disagrees with the dogmatic even slightly, the dogmatic individual will tend to perceive the disagreement to be major. Finally, the dogmatic will tend to conform to group influence attempts more than he or she will to an individual attempt, unless that attempt comes from an authoritarian source. In short, communicating with highly dogmatic individuals is not much fun, and usually is not very productive either. To see dogmatism dramatized, watch "All in the Family." Archie Bunker and his son-in-law characterize dogmatism of the political right and left.

Self-Esteem

Self-esteem refers to the view a person has of him or herself in terms of overall worth. People with low self-esteem tend to lack confidence in their own ability and to evaluate their own competence negatively on almost any question. They expect failure in their lives, including their communication

*The dogmatic person
is ideologically rigid.*

attempts. Communication apprehensives frequently have low self-esteem.
The person with high self-esteem, in contrast, is confident, expects to succeed, and expects to communicate well. People with low self-esteem tend
to be followers in any communication system. They tend to accept other
people's views readily because they consider their own views to be of less
value than those to which they are exposed from others. People with high
self-esteem, on the other hand, are generally leaders in a communication
system. If people differing on the self-esteem personality variable are
placed in a dyad, it is highly probable that the person with higher self-esteem
will completely dominate the dyad.

Tolerance for Ambiguity

Some people have a personality that permits them to operate in a communication system in which there is a great deal of uncertainty. Others have almost no tolerance for the ambiguous or uncertain situation. In our lounge discussion, Tom indicated a very low tolerance for ambiguity. People with low tolerance for ambiguity have a need to identify all questions as either good or bad, right or wrong. They are in constant search for correctness and closure. Thus, in an ongoing communication system, the person with low tolerance for ambiguity would rather make a decision today than seek information for a better decision tomorrow. The person with high tolerance for ambiguity has less need for having things resolved and thus can continue communication over an extended period of time without ever reaching resolution. Differences on this personality variable can cause considerable conflict among communicators. If one seeks resolution when another sees no need for it, the interaction that occurs between the two persons can only euphemistically be called communication.

The preceding four personality variables have been most clearly indicated through research as having a major impact on communication. Although less research has been conducted on the following personality variables, these also seem to have some impact. Our generalizations about these variables must, therefore, be more tentative than those above.

Emotional Maturity

Emotional maturity refers to a range of personalities from those who are changeable, dissatisfied, and easily annoyed to those who are stable, calm, and well-balanced. More emotionally mature individuals show much greater flexibility in their communication with other people. Such people are willing to admit when they are wrong and change when necessary. They also seem to be much more task-oriented in their communication behavior and do not have as much need for less relevant social stimulation.

Adventurousness

The person who is high on the personality variable of adventurousness is one who is very ready to try new things, is sociable, and tends to show an abundance of emotional responses. Pat seemed to be adventurous in the lounge discussion. The person low on adventurousness tends to be cautious, withdrawn, and have feelings of inferiority. More adventurous people tend to show more interest in their communication with other individuals, to discuss things with more relevant contributions to the topic, and to have a fairly high task orientation. They also tend to be somewhat more talkative than people who are less adventurous in many circumstances.

Sensitivity

The personality variable of sensitivity distinguishes between persons who tend to be practical, realistic, and cynical and those who appear to be imaginative, artistic, and fastidious. As might be expected, people high in sensitivity tend to evidence considerable interest in other communicators during interactions. They are also somewhat more likely to make relevant contributions to a discussion. There is some indication that highly sensitive people also tend to be more tense in communication with other people than people with less sensitivity.

Eccentricity

Eccentricity is a personality variable which distinguishes those people who are conformists from those who are generally unconventional. To a great extent, people high in eccentricity are similar to people who are low dogmatics. Eccentrics tend to enjoy communication and be quite willing to change their mind on an issue, in some cases with little apparent reason visible to other people.

Radicalism

Radicalism distinguishes the personalities of the people who tend to resist change and be traditional in their orientation from those who are willing to experiment, tolerant of new ideas, and anxious to try something different. People who are highly radical, like Pat in the oil discussion, tend to be much more talkative than people who are less radical. There is also some indication that radicals are more tense in their interaction with other people and less likely to stick to the topic of discussion than people with less radical orientations.

General Anxiety

It is important that this personality characteristic not be confused with communication apprehension. General anxiety differentiates between persons who tend to be tense, restless, and impatient in their general lives and those who generally tend to be calm, relaxed, and composed. Although the person with high general anxiety is more likely to be communication apprehensive than the person who is low in general anxiety, there is not a high correlation between these two characteristics. The individual with high general anxiety is likely to show more tension in communication, is less likely to talk than a person with lower general anxiety, tends to be more socially oriented than task-oriented, and evidences less interest in most topics of communication than do people with less general anxiety.

BLACK BOX
18

Can you explain the impact of the following personality variables on communication behavior?

Machiavellianism	adventurousness
dogmatism	sensitivity
self-esteem	eccentricity
tolerance for ambiguity	radicalism
emotional maturity	general anxiety

Estimate how high or low you are on each of these personality characteristics.

Can you identify people in your environment who appear to be particularly high and particularly low on each of these characteristics?

Summary

In this and two previous chapters we have focused our attention on the individual communicator. We have examined the motivations that lead the individual to communicate or not to communicate; we have looked at the ways individual communicators perceive one another; and we have considered some of the internal variables that make the communication behavior of each individual unique. In the next four chapters our attention shifts to the relationships between communicators and the messages people employ when they communicate. The remainder of this book attempts to integrate the individual orientation developed to this point with the collective orientation to be explained in chapters 8 through 11. By doing this we hope to explain how human communication functions within various communication systems in order to achieve outcomes people desire.

SUGGESTED FURTHER READINGS

1. Rokeach, M. *The Open and Closed Mind* (New York: Basic Books, 1960).
   A thorough explanation of the concept of dogmatism.

2. Cristie, R. and Geis, F. L. *Studies in Machiavellianism* (New York: Academic Press, 1970).
   A summary of research and theory relating to Machiavellianism.

3. McCroskey, J. C., Larson, C. E., and Knapp, M. L. *An Introduction to Interpersonal Communication* (Englewood Cliffs, N.J.: Prentice-Hall, 1971), chapter four, 54–76
   A summary and synthesis of a variety of attitude theories.

SELECTED REFERENCES

ABELSON, R. P. and LESSER, G. S. "The Developmental Theory of Persuasibility," and JANIS, I. L. and RIFE, D. "Persuasibility and Emotional Disorder," in *Personality and Persuasibility,* C. I. Hovland and I. L. Janis, eds. (New Haven: Yale University Press, 1959), 121–166.

BARKER, E. N. "Authoritarianism of the Political Right, Center, and Left." *Journal of Social Issues* 19 (1963): 63–74.

CHRISTIE, R. and GEIS, F. L. *Studies in Machiavellianism* (New York: Academic Press, 1970).

COOPER, E. and JOHODA, M. "The Evasion of Propaganda; How Prejudiced People Respond to Anti-Prejudice Propaganda." *Journal of Psychology* 23 (1947): 15–25.

EHRLICH, H. J. and LEE, D. "Dogmatism, Learning, and Resistance to Change: A Review and a New Paradigm." *Psychological Bulletin* 71 (1969): 249–260.

135

FESTINGER, L. *A Theory of Cognitive Dissonance* (New York: Row, Peterson, 1957).

FISHBEIN, M. "A Consideration of Beliefs, Attitudes, and Their Relationship," in *Current Studies in Social Psychology,* I. D. Steiner and M. Fishbein, eds. (New York: Holt, Rinehart and Winston, 1965), 107–120.

HAIMAN, F. S. "Effects of Training in Group Processes on Open-Mindedness." *Journal of Communication* 13 (1963): 236–245.

HANSON, D. J. "Dogmatism and Authoritarianism." *Journal of Social Psychology* 76 (1968): 89–95.

HEIDER, F. "Attitudes and Cognitive Organization." *Journal of Psychology* 21 (1946): 107–112.

HOVLAND, C. L. and JANIS, I. L. *Personality and Persuasibility* (New Haven, Conn.: Yale University Press, 1959).

HOVLAND, C. I. and SHERIF, M. *Social Judgment* (New Haven, Conn.: Yale University Press, 1961).

HUNT, M. and MILLER, G. "Open- and Closed-Mindedness, Belief-Discrepant Communication Behavior, and Tolerance for Dissonance." Paper presented at the Speech Association of America Convention, New York, December, 1965.

JANIS, I. L. "Personality as a Factor in Susceptibility to Persuasion," in *The Science of Human Communication.* Wilbur Schramm, ed. (New York: Basic Books, 1963).

KERLINGER, F. and ROKEACH, M. "The Factorial Nature of the F and D Scales." *Journal of Personality and Social Psychology* 4 (1966): 391–399.

KORN, H. A. and GIDDAN, N. S. "Scoring Methods and Construct Validity of the Dogmatism Scale." *Educational and Psychological Measurement* 24 (1964): 867–874.

LEVENTHAL, H. and PERLOE, S. I. "A Relationship Between Self-Esteem and Persuasibility." *Journal of Abnormal and Social Psychology* 64, 5 (1962): 385–388.

MILLER, G. R. and BURGOON, M. *The Techniques of Persuasion* (New York: Harper & Row, 1973): 21–23.

MILLS, J., ARONSON, , E., and ROBINSON, H. "Selectivity in Exposure to Information." *Journal of Abnormal and Social Psychology* 59 (1959): 250–253.

NEWCOMB, T. M. "Attitude Development as a Function of Reference Groups; The Bennington Study," in *Readings in Social Psychology,* E. E. Maccoby, T. M. Newcomb, and E. L. Hartley, eds., (New York: Holt, Rinehart and Winston, 1958), 265–275.

OSGOOD, C. E. and TANNENBAUM, P. H. "The Principle of Congruity in the Prediction of Attitude Change." *Psychological Review* 62 (1955): 42–55.

PLANT, W. T. "Rokeach's Dogmatism Scale as a Measure of General Authoritarianism." *Psychological Reports* 6 (1960): 164.

PLANT, W. T., TELFORD, C. W., and THOMAS, J. A. "Some Personality Differences

Between Dogmatic and Non-Dogmatic Groups." *Journal of Social Psychology* 67 (1965): 67–75.

POWELL, F. Q. "Open- and Closed-Mindedness and the Ability to Differentiate Source and Message." *Journal of Abnormal and Social Psychology* 65 (1962): 61–64.

REBHUN, M. T. "Parental Attitudes and the Closed Belief-Disbelief System." *Psychological Reports* 20 (1967): 260–262.

ROKEACH, M. *The Open and Closed Mind* (New York: Basic Books, 1960).

―――. "The Nature and Meaning of Dogmatism." *Psychological Review* 61 (1954): 194–204.

SHERIF, M., SHERIF, C., and NEBERGALL, R. *Attitude and Attitude Change* (Philadelphia: W. B. Saunders Co., 1965).

SIMONS, H. W. and BERKOWITZ, N. N. "Rokeach's Dogmatism Scale and Leftist Bias." *Speech Monographs* 36 (1969): 459–463.

VACCHIANO, R. B., STRAUSS, P. S., and HOCHMAN, L. "The Open and Closed Mind: A Review of Dogmatism." *Psychological Bulletin* 71 (1969): 261–273.

VACCHIANO, R. B., STRAUSS, P. S., and SCHIFFMAN, D. C. "Personality Correlates of Dogmatism." *Journal of Consulting and Clinical Psychology* 32 (1968): 83–85.

WHITTAKER, J. O. "Resolution of the Communication Discrepancy Issue in Attitude Change," in *Attitude, Ego-Involvement and Change,* C. W. Sherif and M. Sherif, eds. (New York: John Wiley, 1967), 159–177.

WRIGHT, J. M. and HARVEY, O. J. "Attitude Change as a Function of Authoritarianism and Positiveness." *Journal of Personality and Social Psychology* 1 (1965): 177–181.

8

Interaction and Transaction

Our examination of the individual as a communication system has enabled us to see the complex forces that affect each person's unique communication behaviors. But people do not communicate in a vacuum. When Pete is talking to himself in his room, that is not communication, at least not as we have defined communication in this book. But if Pete is talking in his room, and Jan walks in—change! Communication is occurring. What kind of communication depends on the uniqueness of Pete, the uniqueness of Jan, and, most importantly, how Pete and Jan relate to each other. The relational nature of human communication is our concern in this chapter.

Interaction Versus Transaction

Interactional exchanges are characterized as having reciprocal messages exchanged between sources and receivers; that is, each participant functions both as a receiver and a source of communication and alternately exchanges related messages. Someone may function primarily as source or primarily as receiver, but some type of related, reciprocal exchange must occur for there to be interaction. In interpersonal-dyadic communication, source and receiver functions are often fairly well-balanced in the individual. The time a person spends as a source is almost equal to the time spent as a receiver. In small groups and increasingly more so in organizations, an individual may assume a more unbalanced role, becoming predominantly either a source or a receiver, generally the latter. In mediated mass communication, of course, the distinction between media-source and media-receiver is quite clear, and there is seldom any true interaction as we have defined it above.

To understand the nature of interaction better, it may be useful to look at a category system for analyzing interaction developed several years ago by R. F. Bales. This system was developed in order to code communication behaviors for research. Bales called the system "Interaction Process Analysis." For our purposes, the system illustrates the kinds of behavior that occur in what we call "interaction," and may give us a more concrete meaning for that term.

Bales believed that the messages that people produce in interaction—the things they say or do—can be classified into twelve categories. Let us consider each one briefly.

1. *Shows solidarity,* raises the other person's status, gives help, rewards. "That is a good point, Mary." "You really understand this don't you, Bill?" "That approach is very helpful, Carol."

2. *Shows tension release,* jokes, laughs, shows satisfaction. "That reminds me of the story about Pat and Mike..." "Whew, that is a load off my mind."

3. *Agrees,* shows passive acceptance, understand, concurs, complies. "I agree with you, Pete." "Now I understand that point." "O.K., I'll do that right away."

4. *Gives suggestion,* direction, implies autonomy for the other person. "I think we might want to consider the problem first." "You may want to go to that movie; I think you will like it."

5. *Gives opinion,* evaluation, analysis, expresses feeling, wish. "I think the oil companies are at fault." "That technique is a good one." "Somehow that approach makes me uncomfortable." "I wish we didn't have to do that."

6. *Gives orientation,* information, repeats, clarifies, confirms. "That figure is 42 percent." "By that I mean less than half of the people." "Yes, that is what I meant."

7. *Asks for orientation,* requests information, repetition, confirma-

tion. "How much money is available for this?" "Do you mean almost everyone would be involved?" "Should we expect it on Saturday, then?"

8. *Asks for opinion,* requests evaluation, expression of feeling. "What do you think, Karen?" "How does that idea appeal to you, Lisa?"

9. *Asks for suggestion,* direction, possible ways of acting. "Tom, what do you think we ought to do?" "Well, what options do we have open to us?"

10. *Disagrees,* shows passive rejection, withholds help. "I just can't buy that idea, Barry." "That is just not acceptable to me." "No, I don't want to work on that committee."

11. *Shows tension,* asks for help, withdraws. "I'm sorry, I just can't cope with this." "Can someone help me figure this out?"

12. *Shows antagonism,* deflates other person's status, defends or asserts self. "Terry, that is a stupid idea." "I know more about this than you do!"

These categories probably do not exhaust all the possible messages that could be generated in interaction, but they are at least highly illustrative of many. When we have statements like these, we can tell that they are either responsive to what someone else said or call for another to respond. This kind of interchange is what we describe as an *interaction.*

The kinds of messages exemplified above are also likely to occur in communication *transactions.* All human communication is to a lesser or greater degree "transactional." Most transactional exchanges are characterized as having the same properties as interactions, but an additional element is introduced. In transactional communication, the related messages that are exchanged include information about the people engaging in the transaction. They are sharing themselves and their perceptions of reality, as well as some other topic. For example, when wife and husband express their real feelings to each other and share their perceptions of how their children are developing, they demonstrate that communication can be transactional. Their views will likely differ; however, they are sharing themselves and their perceptions of reality in a marriage context or environment that has helped shape them and their perceptions. These types of exchanges are most likely to occur in dyads and sometimes in small, intimate groups. The larger or more formal the social system in which communication occurs, the less likely transactional communication is to occur. Transactional communication always includes a degree of self-disclosure (a topic we will address in depth in chapter 11). Thus, when we are engaged in communication that is transactional we "give something of ourselves" to the other person in exchange for that person "giving something of her or him-

*In transactional
communication we
adapt and target our
message at the
individual
psychological level.*

self" to us. To the extent that this kind of honest, intimate exchange occurs, communication moves from being simply interactional toward being more fully transactional.

Social and Psychological Dimensions of Interaction and Transaction

In communication exchanges we make predictions about others and adapt our communication in accordance with those predictions. For example, we may predict that another will have difficulty understanding some idea, so we adapt our communication by explaining and providing examples. Often these predictions are on a more impersonal, social, or cultural level. We frequently predict needs and reactions of others according to social roles that they and we are playing. We often interact with doctors, teachers, mothers, and service station attendants quite effectively by having knowledge of the expectations related to those roles. We may interact with classmates in the role of student, with friends of the opposite sex in dating or friendship roles, and with storekeepers or waiters in the role of customer or consumer. Knowledge of these sociocultural roles allows us to judge what the expectancies are in the specific situation involved, make fairly accurate predictions of responses, and effectively adapt our messages to achieve our goals in that situation. We think of communication exchanges which are characterized by predictions and adaptation according to social or cultural roles, as being primarily *interactional* in nature.

In other environments for communication, we make predictions and adaptations on an individualized, psychological level. We predict psychological (as opposed to social) needs and responses of others. We attempt to adapt to the other individual on the basis of our knowledge of her or him as a unique human being. We talk with this person as one whom we know outside of, and in addition to, the many roles assumed in her or his life. We adapt and target our messages at the individual, psychological level, rather than at the social or cultural role level. For example, we may know that a particular individual becomes upset easily when a particular topic is discussed. Therefore, we approach that topic with great care or even avoid it when communicating with this specific person. We establish a personal relationship which defines the nature of the communication involved. Communication which is characterized by prediction and adaptation at a personal, psychological level, is often likely to be more *transactional* in nature. For obvious reasons (the difficulty of predicting and adapting to more than one person at a time), this type of communication occurs most frequently in dyads.

The concept of transaction also assumes that people are not the same in different social relationships and situations. We change and adapt to our social, cultural, and physical environments. Because of this, an individual's communicative behavior, including her or his responses to other people's communication, is not nearly so predictable as the general behavior of a group or social class of individuals. The unique behavior of individuals in groups is often lost in the gross, statistical estimates of group behaviors. Consequently, predictions about a specific individual necessitate knowledge not only about that person's cultural and social group affiliations, but also about that person as a unique human being. Our expectancies often must be individualized and tested through communication with that individual.

In a sense we can never know another person unless we engage in communication with that person at a transactional level. Some argue that this is the only way we can get to know ourselves as well. We are constantly changing, growing, and becoming. In the transactional view, "we *are* who we are *becoming*." We are becoming someone only in relation to others with whom we are communicating. For example, when two friends share a great deal of themselves with each other over a period of time, they both change through that communication. We are not merely static persons who interact. The way in which we know who we are becoming, and who another is becoming, is through our communication with others at a *transactional* level. We communicate with each other, stripped of protective social roles, and share our experiences of reality with another.

A problem arises in exchanges when one individual is communicating at a personal, psychological level and another participant is communicating at a cultural or social role level. These mixed interactions often produce misunderstanding and even antipathy or conflict. Our ability to recognize and shift from one level to another is critical to effective communication. While highly transactional communication probably is the most personally rewarding, it is not always appropriate. Although executive-secretary, professor-student, boss-employee, and wife-husband may engage in transactional communication at times, role-based interaction is demanded at other times. Consider the relationship between the executive and the secretary. This relationship involves a superior-subordinate role distinction. To get the work done in the office the distinction between superior and subordinate roles probably must be maintained. However, if they become close friends or begin dating, problems in the office may result. Once a transactional relationship is established between the two people, it may be extremely difficult to switch back to the appropriate work roles. Maybe one will be able to switch back, but the other won't. Maybe neither will be able to. This is probably why there is an unwritten rule in many offices that supervisor and supervisee never date or engage in extensive social activity together.

A Way of Knowing

As we indicated above, some scholars view transaction as a way of knowing about ourselves and others. They claim that we exist in the relationships that we experience and share with others. In addition, reality for the individual, to a large extent, is what that person experiences and perceives to be real. Carl Rogers expressed this view when he noted that we exist in a dynamic and constantly changing world. To a large extent, we perceive ourselves as the center of that world. We experience reality as we act and react within our world. What we perceive *is* our world. The way that we know something about ourselves or others is through the experience of ourselves in relation to others. Within this context, the best frame for understanding another person is to attempt to understand that person's world as she or he experiences it. Part of that world is the way that a person experiences her or himself, experiences others, and experiences her or himself in relation to others. To some extent, then, we must understand the subjective reality of individuals—self and others—for communication transaction. Certainly, objective reality impinges upon our communicative behavior. However, subjective reality *also* governs our communication.

Both subjective and objective reality constitute the environments in which we find ourselves. Take a mother and daughter who are attending the same social gathering. They are likely to perceive many different things occurring. The mother may see the group as rowdy and unruly, while the daughter may perceive the group as happy and fun-loving. Both mother and daughter are objectively at the same party at the same time and at the same place. Both subjective and objective environments serve to define whom we are and whom we become. As they change, our perceptions of reality and our sharing of that reality through communication change.

Even though communication with another person may advance to the transactional level, it always begins with interaction. Thus, to understand both levels of communication we need to consider communication behaviors they have in common. During this discussion we will be talking specifically about *interaction,* but you should keep in mind that if the communicative relationship advances to the transactional level, what we are saying applies there as well.

**BLACK BOX
19**

Can you describe interaction in terms of Bales' categories?

Can you make a distinction between interaction and transaction and identify the relationships and differences between these two types of communications systems?

Can you discuss how sharing, perceptions, and the social environment are related to your communication?

Can you supply examples of both interactional and transactional communication from your own experience?

The Decision to Interact: Initial Encounters

A number of factors affect our decision whether or not to interact with others. We examined these in detail in chapters 5 through 7. As we noted there, we often weigh the cost of interaction in relation to the expected value of the outcome. Our choice to seek out a professor for advice and help on a course, to call someone special for a date, or to contest a parking ticket in court may appear to cost more than the expected value of the outcome. When the value of the expected outcome exceeds the anticipated personal costs, we are likely to initiate interaction with others. However, we enter each interaction with some uncertainty about the outcome. Often we interact to reduce that uncertainty. We want to know where we stand. Therefore, we discuss our grades with our professors, clear up our checking account with the bank teller, and seek out the friend we argued with last night. To the extent that we are highly involved with another, we are more likely to seek that person out for interaction. To the extent that we are highly involved on issues, we are likely to seek out forums for exchange of ideas, whether the exchanges relate to hobbies, politics, finances, or personal problems.

In most conscious or unconscious decisions to interact, there are some key variables involved. These are considered in detail under the topic of selective exposure in chapter 14. One of these is attraction. Simply stated, we choose to interact with those to whom we are attracted. Although we may be attracted to others in terms of physical, task, or social desires, the perceived physical attractiveness of another is probably the most influential element facilitating the initial decision to interact. This is particularly true in male-female interactions. Although this fact may be undesirable and socially discredited, it remains as an accurate predictor of initiation of communication exchanges.

As mentioned previously, the anxiety and communication apprehension that we have may determine whether or not we seek our interaction with some persons in some situations. This element may also determine whether or not we interact in situations in which we find ourselves. Some individuals, for example, may have difficulty seeking interaction with persons in authority or with persons who have power to reward or punish.

As we have repeatedly noted in previous chapters, homophily serves as a strong determiner of our interaction patterns. Most interaction is between people who are, or at least perceive themselves to be, highly similar. Individuals of similar education, social status, economic level, general appearance, morals, values, and general attitudes interact with each other

*Group memberships
we create with our
established exchange
patterns determine
future decisions to
interact.*

most often. Less often do we go beyond these boundaries in seeking social or task-oriented interactions. To some extent, then, our interaction choices are "locked into" certain patterns that may or may not be desirable for us as individuals. When was the last time you contacted the president of your university to interact about your perceptions of the university? Or when was the last time you discussed your preference in beverages with the "wino" who hangs out down the street?

The social structures and group memberships we create with our established exchange patterns further determine our future decisions to interact. We are not likely to extend our interactions very far beyond familiar social structures and groups with which we are affiliated. As a result, many of our existing notions, values, and beliefs will receive continued reinforcement and support. The production of change in individuals and social systems often necessitates making changes in interaction patterns. Would you have changed as much if you had not decided to attend college? New information, attitudes, and behaviors may not occur until interaction patterns are changed. In organizations, for example, this sometimes requires changing the formal structure of the organization or shifting personnel to new positions in order to correct some problem. Stable interaction

147

patterns often maintain things as they are—the *status quo*. Breaking these patterns is sometimes necessary for change and innovation in ideas, practices, and products.

Initial interactions with new individuals involve a "feeling-out" period in which we test reactions and establish a relationship through which we can predict future reactions. Early interactions are likely to be related to impersonal topics of casual conversation. During this phase, we often exchange impersonal, biographical kinds of demographic information with each other. "Hi, my name is Frank ... Where are you from?" On this basis, then, we begin to predict beliefs, attitudes and values of another. Then we test those predictions by interacting on rather impersonal areas where we have beliefs and attitudes. "What do you think of the parking problem ... the president ... the school?" We may discuss government, politics, education, business, and other areas where we have opinions. A frequent phase following exchange of opinions is discussion of other people. "Do you know Howard and Mary?" Following this phase, and depending upon its outcome, we may progress into more personal attitudes and opinions, tastes or interest, work or studies, or perhaps even money and finances. "I've really been having trouble in courses this semester. Of course, I'm working part-time." As these interactions become more intimate, they become more transactional in nature. We may eventually choose to interact (transact) about our personality likes and dislikes, our bodies, or sexual attitudes and desires. "There are somethings about myself I don't like ..." It should be reemphasized that we can interact on any of these more intimate topics without moving into a highly transactional exchange. However, when we begin exchanging *self-disclosive* messages (see chapter 11), we definitely have begun more transactional communication.

In human communication exchanges, then, a sequential pattern usually develops. First, we decide to interact or to expose ourselves to some communication sources. This may occur consciously or unconsciously. The next stage usually involves actual interaction and adjustment of roles and expectancies. Much communication never progresses beyond this point. We have neither the time nor the inclination to go beyond this level in our exchanges with most people. The third stage involves transaction through the exchange of intentionally self-disclosing messages of a personal nature. Seldom do we engage in this stage of communication with a large number of people. As noted above, our social systems also demand other types of role-defined communicative behavior.

Understanding and utilization of these types of patterns allows us to examine our interactions and interactions of others. To that extent, consideration of these patterns is useful, not only in research, but also in under-standing interactions in which we are involved. In this sense, we can gain control of our own interactions when we are consciously aware of them and understand what is going on.

**BLACK BOX
20**

Can you name five things that prompt interaction between people?

What are the usual stages in the acquaintance process?

From your own experience, can you recall any unsuccessful interactions that did not follow the usual stages in acquaintance?

Feedback

At the heart of the interaction process is *feedback*. In chapter 2 we defined feedback and provided a model to indicate how it operates within a com-munication system. Feedback is often conceived as the reciprocal, related message that a receiver sends back to the source. This message may be verbal agreement or disagreement, opinions, suggestions, or other indica-tions or reactions. This message may also be a nonverbal nod, laugh, or sympathetic pat on the shoulder. This related, reciprocal message is the heart of interaction. Often feedback functions to tell the source how well he or she is communicating. The receptive lecturer will recognize the students' puzzled looks as feedback telling her or him how well the message is being communicated. The young lady who indicates that she has a "splitting headache" may be providing similar feedback to her date.

Feedback as a Regulator

Feedback may be viewed as a regulator. The thermostat on the wall pro-vides feedback to the furnace or air conditioner in order to regulate a constant temperature state in the room. In a similar way, we provide feed-back into communication systems to regulate, achieve, and maintain certain

*"Hand jive" is part
of the feedback this
receiver sends back
to a source.*

constant states that we desire. The teacher provides feedback to class members on how well they did on the exam in order to regulate behavior and to achieve or maintain some desired level of achievement. Similarly, the class gives feedback to the instructor about how difficult the exam was in order to achieve some desired state of test difficulty. The wise husband or wife may not express real, disagreeable opinions about some new article of clothing the other has purchased. The feedback given may have as its goal the maintenance of the balanced state of desirable personal relationships between the two. In a similar fashion, an employee may not actually tell the boss that he thinks the boss's idea is bad. Rather he might choose to maintain some desirable constant relationship with an easily offended employer: "It looks like a good idea to me, but maybe we ought to test it out on others before it's implemented." In this manner, we often use the feedback we supply others to regulate desired states relevant to our relationships with them. Communicative interactions within social systems often perform this function.

Feedback as a Stimulator

Feedback can also be viewed from the opposite perspective: it may be used to stimulate change in social systems. In this sense, feedback may be labeled "feedforward." Social protest movements often perform this kind of feedback into our social and governmental systems. Their goal is not to maintain some preexisting or presently existing condition; rather, their interactions are an attempt to abolish some existing conditions or ideas. In the same manner stimulative feedback may produce new ideas and concepts, new directions or courses of action. Likewise, this "feedforward" tends to break up relationships rather than preserve existing ones. Sometimes this process leads to new relationships and conditions. For example, a couple may interact so as to "break up" their relationship with each other leading to the establishment of new relationships with others. In a similar manner, a professor may provide stimulative feedback to you which breaks down existing ideas and comfortable notions in the hopes of stimulating new ways of thinking.

Feedback as a Reinforcer

Another way of conceptualizing feedback is as a means of rewarding or punishing. Rewarding another usually leads to stabilizing the behavior that is being rewarded while punishing usually leads to extinction or reduction of the behavior being punished. If the feedback we provide is rewarding, reinforcing, and supportive, then we tend to stabilize that communication behavior. For example, a person is likely to continue talking when we verbalize agreements and nod affirmatively. From this point of view, then, feedback may be *positive* or *negative;* that is, feedback may vary between being rewarding and punishing. The feedback may indicate, "Yes, that's a great idea," or "That's the 'dumbest' thing I ever heard." Also, we may conceptualize *zero* feedback as no response. However, zero feedback is almost always interpreted as some type of feedback, usually negative.

Conditions Affecting the Success of Feedback

As humans, we have varying psychological needs for feedback. Most of us need others to tell us how well we are doing. If we do not receive sufficient feedback over a period of time, we will often seek it out through interaction with others. The lack of feedback appears to produce some anxiety or imbalanced state within us which we try to resolve by seeking reactions from others. This need for feedback is also true of social systems such as small groups and organizations. Most often we desire reinforcing, positive feedback to reduce this imbalance. However if we have already received sufficient feedback or have little need for it upon occasion, then the effect of subsequent feedback provided by others will be reduced. It will not have as forceful an impact upon us. Therefore, the *need* for feedback is itself a condition which affects the success of the feedback supplied. When feedback is conceptualized as a reinforcer, other conditions also affect the success of that feedback. These conditions are noted below:

1. Frequency of the feedback-reinforcement. Intermittent reinforcement through feedback produces stronger and more stable responses than constant reward through feedback 100 percent of the time. We are less frustrated by instances when we do not receive positive feedback if we have some experiences of nonreinforcement. Remember the effects of grades that your professors feedback to you.

2. Conflict may reduce the effectiveness of feedback in producing some desired behavior. Under situations of conflict and stress, the number of potential responses is reduced, the effectiveness of our message cues is degraded, and discrimination between different types of verbal and non-verbal cues is impaired. You have probably had the experience of having your feedback to another misinterpreted under conflict conditions. You may have said, "You don't understand; I'm agreeing with you."

3. Habits may interfere with the effectiveness of some reinforcement. We may respond to approximations of a stimulus as if it were the stimulus itself. For example, because we have habitually interpreted verbal or nonverbal cues from another as positive reinforcement, we may more easily misinterpret *similar* cues also as positive feedback, even though they may be intended to be negative. One of the authors had a student who slept intermittently in class and he interpreted that as negative feedback out of habit. However, the student worked as a night-watchman the night before the class met and was making no qualitative judgment: he was simply displaying his fatigue.

4. Knowledge of expected results and principles of reinforcing feedback increases the effectiveness of feedback in producing a desired behavior. If we know what is expected or what the other person wants, then we can more easily respond in the desired way when we receive differing feedback. For example, we can respond to a teacher's feedback better if we know what is expected.

5. The method of feedback or reinforcement also determines its effectiveness. There is some evidence that suggests that positive feedback which rewards a desired behavior will be more effective than negative feedback which punishes undesired behaviors. People are more receptive and responsive to reward than

to punishment. For example, if you receive positive feedback from a teacher for good work, you are more motivated to do what is required than if you receive negative feedback for poor work.

6. The amount of reinforcing feedback also determines its effectiveness. Generally, the greater the reward, the more the desired behavior is strengthened. If we could give you $20 every time you did the thing desired, rather than $1, we could have more impact. However, excessive feedback that is perceived as too exaggerated can produce responses opposite to those expected.

7. The effort required to make the response which the feedback is attempting to elicit often affects this type of interaction. Individuals tend to make responses that require less effort and avoid responses that require much effort. Rewarding feedback may not produce the desired response or change in another if the response requires too much effort. For example, we probably could not get you to do certain things or change your behavior (e.g., stop smoking) through mere words. Under these conditions, it may become necessary to approach the desired response through a number of steps or stages, thereby slowly working up to the new behavior that we are trying to elicit.

8. The person supplying the feedback or reinforcement has a significant effect upon whether or not the feedback will have the intended impact. If that person is highly credible and attractive to us, then the feedback will have increased impact upon us. However, if we do not like the person giving us feedback or do not think he or she is competent, for example, then we might well reject the feedback supplied. For example, think of the person you like the least and the impact that person's feedback has on you. Do you do what that person wants? In this case you might even strengthen some views or behaviors which are opposite to what the feedback attempts to elicit.

General Effects of Feedback

In a now-classic experiment, researchers had a speaker describe a geometrical pattern which the receivers were to reproduce on paper. During four trials, the amount of feedback permitted was varied from none to completely free choice on the part of the receivers. The results indicated that the no-feedback condition was by the far the most efficient, in the sense that it consumed the least amount of time. Also, the communication in the no-feedback condition appeared to represent the most "orderly" process; that is, the no-feedback trial looked like a "nice, orderly, well-disciplined class" (the type most elementary school principals allegedly like to see in their schools). However, across the four trials, as feedback and interaction increased, so did the accuracy of the drawings, the confidence level of the speaker, and the confidence level of the receivers that they were drawing the designs accurately.

From this and similar studies, we can draw the general conclusions that feedback (1) increases accuracy of understanding and confidence in the communicators that understanding is being achieved, but (2) requires increased expenditure of time and sacrifices apparent orderliness. Feedback also has an impact on verbal and nonverbal behavior, attitudes, and group behavior. Let's look at these effects in turn.

Verbal and Nonverbal Effects. Negative feedback usually increases a speaker's nonfluencies—uhs, ahs, unnecessary pauses—while positive feedback generally decreases them. Negative feedback will frequently reduce our rate of speaking and reduce the length of time that we talk. On the other hand, positive feedback appears to make us talk louder, faster, and longer. Obviously, if feedback became negative enough, we might lose our tempers and speak louder and faster. Within ranges, however, these general effects seem to hold true.

The verbal content is also affected by the positive or negative feedback that we receive. In the process of adapting to feedback to facilitate understanding, we often change the content of the message. This frequently occurs, for example, in political campaigns when response to a candidate becomes negative. If feedback is positive, we tend to exert more of our own opinions in a message; when negative, we have less of a tendency to express our opinions but rather we tend to rely upon "facts" and to use opinions of others. Also, when we receive positive feedback we make more plural or multiple responses to the feedback. Rather than one answer, for example, we may give several.

Attitude Effects. In addition to overt, verbal, and nonverbal changes, feedback may produce internal attitudinal changes within interacting participants. The source of communication in a one-to-many setting generally has a more positive attitude toward receivers who are supplying positive feedback and a more negative attitude toward receivers supplying negative feedback. The lecturer or public speaker will often direct her or his message toward those who are responding favorably and will develop a more negative attitude to the apathetics and "complainers" in the audience. Likewise, this feedback from receivers can affect a person's attitudes toward her or himself, especially when the feedback is almost exclusively positive or exclusively negative. Sustained negative feedback to an individual over a period of time can reduce the person's self-esteem and self-concept. When this becomes severe enough, an individual may develop anxiety and communication apprehension. (This idea is developed in some detail in chapter 5.)

On the other hand, sustained positive feedback appears to facilitate an opposite effect.

Sometimes the distinctions between source and receiver are not as clear as they would appear in the preceeding paragraph. In an interesting study, the researcher placed confederates in an audience. He instructed these secretly planted audience members to supply positive feedback on one occasion and negative feedback at another point. The feedback was found to affect other receiver's attitudes toward the source and the source's message and also to affect the source's attitude toward the audience. When the secretly placed audience members provided positive feedback, other audience members had a more favorable attitude toward the source and the ideas. Likewise, the source had a more favorable attitude toward the receivers. However, when the secretly instructed audience members responded negatively, this response reduced attitude change, the source's credibility with the audience, and the source's attitude toward the audience. Therefore, the selected audience members served as additional sources of communication for the unsuspecting audience members by supplying feedback to the "original source." Another study found similar effects on viewers when they used television to display source and audience response.

In a one-to-many setting, sources' attitudes toward their own content may be affected by the type of feedback received. In brief, sources strengthen their attitudes and beliefs in what they are arguing when they are rewarded through positive feedback. This tendency appears to be true also in situations where the source is playing "devil's advocate" by arguing an opposite view from the one he or she really believes. Under these conditions, if a source receives negative feedback, then there is typically no change in attitudes or else the person's original attitudes are strengthened.

Effects on Task Behavior. In less formal settings such as small-group discussion, feedback appears to have similar effects. For example, one of the authors served on a curriculum committee charged with revising the department's course offerings. Most of the feedback from the rest of the faculty teaching the existing courses was, understandably, negative. As a result, the committee perceived its task as more difficult and the revision took much longer than it might have. In addition, committee members became defensive and more hostile, not only to those outside the committee, but among themselves. The type of feedback received effects task behaviors and perceptions of task difficulty. Positive feedback, often in the form of personalized approval of a group, appears to decrease feelings of rejection, hostility, and defensiveness and therefore increases group task efficiency.

Efficiency of task performance and aspirations toward completion of the task are lowered when coupled with negative feedback. Generally, nonsupportive feedback to a group will increase perceptions of task difficulty and reduce task efficiency by inhibiting the quantity and quality of interaction within that group.

BLACK BOX
21

Can you identify the functions of feedback and the conditions affecting the success of feedback?

Can you try to predict the effects of feedback on:
time-required for total communication
apparent orderliness
accuracy
confidence of sources and receivers?

What are the effects of positive and negative feedback on:
verbal and nonverbal behaviors of others and yourself;
attitudes of others and yourself;
task behaviors?

Can you recall examples of these effects from your own experience?

Nonverbal Regulators of Interaction

In chapter 10 we will consider in some depth the nonverbal messages that impinge upon interaction. At this point we wish to examine some nonverbal behaviors that serve to control interaction at a broader level than individual messages. Nonverbal behaviors which maintain or regulate interaction among people are typically called *regulators*. Some of the more important nonverbal regulators are the use of space, eye behavior, and bodily movement.

Use of Space

A major regulator of our initial and even our continued interaction with others is our proximity to them. We generally interact more with persons with whom we share rooms, who attend the same classes, and who generally hang out in the same places that we do. If someone is separated from us by great distances, we tend not to interact as frequently by phone or other means as we do with those not physically separated from us. Some research has shown that marriages generally occur among those who are more closely associated in terms of distance. Studies of housing projects (apartments, etc.) have found that persons located near each other generally interact more than those who are separated. However, the main persons with whom we interact are those who occupy strategic positions near stairways, mail boxes, and the center of some line of dwellings. As we noted in chapter 5, people who are high communication apprehensives select housing with lower interaction possibilities than do other people.

Violations of the life space or personal life-bubbles that we carry around with us may affect our interaction. The setting in which interaction occurs, of course, affects the amount of space that we would like to maintain. Whether we are at a party, at a drive-in movie, or in the library studying may determine how much space we wish to maintain. When this space is violated, however, the resulting interaction is often negative in nature.

Seating arrangements also affect space relationships and thus interactions. People seated in rows in a large auditorium may not interact

The seats chosen around this conference table affect the interaction patterns of the participants.

significantly; people seated in a circle, however, may interact much more because of their face-to-face relationship with a larger number of participants. In typical seating arrangements around conference tables, the seats chosen often affect interaction patterns of the participants. End positions of the rectangular table frequently are perceived as "leadership" positions and draw a significant amount of interaction. The person who chooses this position can see most of the participants easily and is capable of easily supplying nonverbal feedback to them. Side corner positions at the rectangular table are normally selected by individuals with less willingness to communicate, sometimes because of communication apprehension (as noted in chapter 5). When a number of participants are seated at the conference table, interaction most frequently occurs between those directly opposite, those seated at diagonals, and those at the end position. Much less often do we interact with those seated beside us. In most situations involving interactions around a table, people seem to prefer to interact with those who are immediately opposite or at a diagonal across the corner of the table. Given a free choice, two interacting individuals will frequently take these positions at a table. The notable exception appears to be in bars and social encounters. In these instances, people appear to prefer side by side seating for interaction. These types of patterns can vary slightly depending upon the sex of the interactants.

Eye and Body Movement

We generally regulate interaction and feedback through eye and body behavior, particularly movements involving the head and face. People seeking positive feedback or approval will often engage in nodding, smiling, and increased gesturing. We also use various parts of our body and postural shifts to indicate the end of some statement or to provide a transition to another statement. Leaning forward or backward and accompanying such movement with head-nodding or head-shaking serve to provide positive or negative feedback to others and tends as a result to regulate their interaction. Gross shifts in posture often indicate a change in our own thoughts or reinforcement of messages from others.

Eye and head behavior, alone, appear to be the most important regulators of interpersonal interaction. We normally attempt to *prevent interruption* by not looking at the other interactant while we are talking. On the other hand, we may indicate that it is the other person's turn to talk by returning our eye contact to her or him. Often we seek feedback by making eye contact with another. This kind of behavior can signal that a channel of communication is now open. Head-nodding generally encourages the other to continue speaking. Head-nodding to excess, however, may be an attempt to cut off the person through agreement in order to gain a turn. As feedback, such behavior may facilitate or inhibit interaction by other participants. For example, reestablishing eye contact and pausing will very often produce reciprocal exchange from the other participant.

**BLACK BOX
22**

Can you explain how the use of space, eye movement, and body movement regulate interaction?

Can you regulate interaction with these nonverbal cues?

Can you name other factors affecting interaction? If not, read the next section.

Other Factors Affecting Interaction

Small-group communication scholars have examined interaction in groups for some time. They have found that the type of leadership, the social climate, attraction among participants, and the goals of the group all effect the type and frequency of interaction among participants. The effects of these factors are fairly easy to predict and probably need no explanation. However, some related ideas are worth brief consideration.

All group members do not participate equally. What are some of the reasons for this? First, high communication apprehension is directly related to low participation in groups. Also, the person who interacts most elicits the most interactions from other participants. The persons who will likely initiate most interactions will initially have higher status and power than the other group members. When this power and status are established (e.g., she or he is the boss), participants will direct more interactions to that person. She or he will, in turn, exert more influence and control over group participation and goals-outcomes of the interaction. When the power and status relationships are not established, those seeking power and group

159

status will initiate more interactions; however, participants in this situation will more likely interact with others on the basis of their homophily, competence, and proxemic relationships.

Throughout this chapter we have focused on the relationships between communicators in interactions and transactions. We found these related processes to be significantly affected by the feedback occurring. The outcomes of interaction or transaction were found to depend heavily upon the nature of the verbal and nonverbal feedback received. However, we have paid comparatively little attention to an important component of communicative exchanges—messages the communicators use. That will be the focus of the next three chapters.

SUGGESTED FURTHER READINGS

1. Altman, I. and Taylor, D. A. *Social Penetration: The Development of Interpersonal Relationships* (New York: Holt, Rinehart and Winston, 1973).

   This book describes and explains the acquaintance and social penetration process in detail. This interesting approach develops a number of stages, levels, or layers through which people progress in getting to know each other well. Other articles and papers, such as those by Berger and the one by Taylor et al., present briefer summaries of this process and further research. They are listed in the chapter references that follow.

2. Bales, R. F. *Interaction Process Analysis: A Method for the Study of Small Groups* (Cambridge, Mass.: Addison-Wesley, 1950).

   The book presents a complete discussion and analysis of Interaction Process Analysis (IPA) in Small Group Communication. Both the research and the resulting rating instrument are provided. This reading has materials that are very useful in analysis of small group discussions.

3. Gardiner, J.C. "A Synthesis of Experimental Studies of Speech Communication Feedback." *Journal of Communication* 21 (1971): 17–35.

   Gardiner's article presents a fairly complete summary of research on feedback. The discussion focuses on the effects of differing types of feedback in a variety of social settings. Although research on reinforcement and learning is excluded, this reading provides more depth and additional sources of information in the area of feedback. Other studies are listed in the chapter references.

4. Haney, W. V. "A Comparative Study of Unilateral and Bilateral Communication." *Academy of Management Journal* 7 (1964): 128–136; and Leavitt, H. J. and Mueller, R. A. H. "Some Effects of Feedback on Communication." *Human Relations* 4 (1951): 237–249.

These articles present now-classic studies of feedback. The research discussed focuses upon the presence and absence of feedback. Subsequent effects on accuracy, time consumed, and satisfaction are discussed. Other studies are listed in the chapter references.

5. Hill, W. F. *Learning* (Scranton: Chandler Publishing Company, 1971).

   In several chapters, the text develops the reinforcement approach to learning and conditions that affect reinforcement. Those interested in this approach to human communication will find Hill's discussion valuable.

6. Pemberton, W. "Semantics and Communication." *ETC,* 23:3 (Sept., 1966): 350–353.

   Sections of this article discuss the concept of transaction as it relates to our language and meaning used in human communication. The notion that transaction involves the relationship of the perceptions of individuals along with the characteristics of the "thing-person-environment" perceived is developed in some depth. The relationship of the nervous system to this transactional process is also discussed.

7. Toch, H. and MacLean, M. S., Jr. "Perception and Communication: A Transactional View." *Audio Visual Communication Review* 10 (1967): 55–77.

   The first part of this article provides an excellent discussion of the nature and derivation of the concept of transaction. Its relevance to the process of communication, the notion of interaction, and the ways we know or perceive reality are discussed.

SELECTED REFERENCES

ALTMAN, I. and TAYLOR, D. A. *Social Penetration: The Development of Interpersonal Relationships* (New York: Holt, Rinehart and Winston, 1973).

BALES, R. F. *Interaction Process Analysis: A Method for the Study of Small Groups* (Cambridge, Mass.: Addison-Wesley, 1950).

BARNLUND, D. C. "A Transactional Model of Communication," in *Foundations of Communication Theory,* K. Sereno and C. D. Mortensen (New York: Harper & Row, 1970), 83–102.

BERGER, C. R. "Proactive and Retroactive Attribution Processes in Interpersonal Communication." Paper presented at the International Communication Association Convention, Chicago, April, 1975.

BERGER, C.R. "The Acquaintance Process Revisited: Explorations in Initial Interaction." Paper presented at the speech Communication Association Convention, New York, November, 1973.

CANTRIL, H. "Perception and Interpersonal Relations." *American Journal of Psychiatry* 114 (1957): 119–126.

CANTRIL, H., AMES, A., HASTORF, A. H., and ITTELSON, W. H. "Psychology and Scientific Research," in *Explorations in Transactional Psychology*, F. P. Kilpatrick (New York: New York University, 1961), 6–35.

COLLINS, B. E. and GUETZKOW, H. *A Psychology of Group Processes for Decision Making* (New York: John Wiley, 1964).

COZBY, P. C. "Self-Disclosure: A Literature Review," *Psychological Bulletin,* 79 (1973), 73–91.

CULBERT, S. A. *The Interpersonal Process of Self-Disclosure: It Takes Two to See One* (New York: Renaissance Editions, Inc., 1968). Also short version in *Explorations in Applied Behavioral Science,* NTL Institute for Applied Behavioral Science, Washington, D.C. (1967).

DEWEY, J. and BENTLEY, A. F. *Knowing and the Known* (Boston: Beacon Press, 1949).

EISENBERG, A. M. and SMITH, R. R., JR. *Nonverbal Communication* (Indianapolis: Bobbs-Merrill, 1972).

GARDINER, J. C. "A Synthesis of Experimental Studies of Speech Communication Feedback." *Journal of Communication* 21 (1971): 17–35.

GANGE, R. M. *The Conditions of Learning* (New York: Holt, Rinehart, and Winston, 1965).

GERGEN, K. "Social Reinforcement of Self-Presentation Behavior," unpublished Ph.D. Dissertation, Duke University, 1962.

GILBERT, S. J. "The Communication of Intimacy: A Negative Finding." Paper presented at the International Communication Association Convention, New Orleans, Louisiana, April, 1974.

GOFFMAN, E. *The Presentation of Self in Everyday Life* (Garden City: Doubleday, Anchor Books, 1959).

HANEY, W. V. "A Comparative Study of Unilateral and Bilateral Communication." *Academy of Management Journal* 7 (1964): 128–136.

HILL, W. F. *Learning* (Scranton: Chandler Publishing Company, 1971).

HYLTON, C. "The Effects of Observable Audience Response on Attitude Change and Source Credibility." Paper presented at the Speech Association of America Convention, New York, December, 1969.

JOURARD, S. M. *Self-Disclosure: An Experimental Analysis of the Transparent Self* (New York: John Wiley, 1971).

KNAPP, M. L. *Nonverbal Communication in Human Interaction* (New York: Holt Rinehart and Winston, 1972).

LARSON, D. E. "Speech Communication Research on Small Groups." *Speech Teacher* 20 (1971): 335–340.

LEATHERS, D. G. "Process Disruption and Measurement in Small Group Communication." *Quarterly Journal of Speech* 55 (1969): 287–300.

LEAVITT, H. J. and MUELLER, R. A. H. "Some Effects of Feedback on Communication." *Human Relations* 4 (1951): 401–410.

McCROSKEY, J. C., LARSON, C. E., and KNAPP, M. L. *An Introduction to Interpersonal Communication* (Englewood Cliffs, N.J.: Prentice-Hall, 1971), chapter nine.

McCROSKEY, J. C., RICHMOND, V. P., and DALY, JOHN A. "Toward the Measurement of Perceived Homophily in Interpersonal Communication." Paper presented at the International Communication Association Convention, New Orleans, Louisiana, April, 1974.

McCROSKEY, J. C. and WRIGHT, D. W. "The Development of an Instrument for Measuring Interaction, Behavior in Small Groups." *Speech Monographs* 38 (1971): 335–340.

McGRATH, J. E. and ALTMAN, I. *Small Group Research: A Synthesis and Critique of the Field* (New York: Holt, Rinehart and Winston, 1966).

MEHRLEY, R. S. and ANDERSON, L. "An Experimental Study of Feedback." Paper presented at the Speech Association of American Convention, Chicago, December, 1968.

NEWCOMB, T. M. "An approach to the Study of Communicative Acts." *Psychological Review* 60 (1953): 393–404.

———. *The Acquaintance Process* (New York: Holt, Rinehart and Winston, 1961).

PEARCE, W. B. and SHARP, S. M. "Self-Disclosing Communication." *Journal of Communication* 23 (1973): 409–425.

PEMBERTON, W. "Semantics and Communication." *ETC,* 23:3 (September, 1966): 350–353.

RICHMOND, V. P., McCROSKEY, J. C., and DALY, J. A. "The Generalizability of a Measure of Perceived Homophily in Interpersonal Communication." Paper presented at the International Communication Association Convention, Chicago, April, 1975.

ROGERS, C. R. "The Characteristics of a Helping Relationship," in *On Becoming a Person* (Boston: Houghton Mifflin, 1961).

———. "The Necessary and Sufficient Conditions of Psychotherapeutic Personality Change." *Journal of Consulting Psychology* 21 (1957): 95–103.

ROGERS, E. M. and SHOEMAKER, F. F. *Communication of Innovations: A Cross-Cultural Approach* (New York: The Free Press, 1971).

RUESCH, J. *Therapeutic Communication* (New York: W. W. Norton, 1961).

SCHULMAN, J., KASPAR, J., and BARGER, P. *The Therapeutic Dialogue: A Method for the Analysis of Verbal Interaction* (Springfield: Charles C Thomas, 1964).

SHANNON, C. E. and WEAVER, WARREN. *The Mathematical Theory of Communication*

(Urbana: University of Illinois Press, 1948), p. 9.

TAYLOR, D. A., ALTMAN, I., and SORRENTINO, R. "Interpersonal Exchange as a Function of Rewards and Costs and Situational Factors: Expectancy Confirmation-Disconfirmation." *Journal of Experimental Social Psychology* 5 (1969): 324–339.

TOCH, H. and MACLEAN, M. S., JR. "Perception and Communication: A Transactional View." *Audio Visual Communication Review* 10 (1967): 55–77.

WENBURG, J. R. and WILMOT, W. W. *The Personal Communication Process* (New York: John Wiley, 1973), chapter fourteen.

WORTHY, M., GARY, A. L., and KAHN, G. M. "Self-Disclosure as an Exchange Process." *Journal of Personality and Social Psychology* 13 (1969): 59–63.

ZAGONA, S. V. and ZURCHER, L. A. "Participation, Interaction, and Role Behavior in Groups Selected from the Extremes of Open-Closed Cognitive Continuum." *Journal of Psychology* 58 (1964): 255–264.

9

Messages and Meaning

In large measure, there are only two major ingredients in most human communication systems: people and messages. Although people on the whole differ greatly from one another, the individual person remains relatively constant over a substantial period of time; thus, it is difficult to control the people variables within any communication system. Messages are not constant; they are highly variable and flexible. Consequently, messages are much easier to control within any communication system. They are the most important single ingredient in any human communication system.

Although there are many different types of messages in human communication, we may roughly classify all messages into two categories, verbal and nonverbal. Simply defined, verbal messages are concerned with words and groups of words; nonverbal messages involve everything else. One of the major distinctions between human beings and lower forms of animal life is our ability to communicate

167

with one another through the use of words. For the most part, we cannot communicate with animals verbally, except on very basic command levels. But we are able to communicate with many animals on a nonverbal level. While our words have little or no meaning for animals, our tone of voice and our touch, for example, can convey messages.

In human communication systems there is also a major limitation on our ability to communicate with another person verbally. A necessary condition for the existence of verbal communication is the sharing of a common language. If Person A speaks only English and Person B speaks only Arabic, there is no chance for verbal communication between the two people. This limitation is not as severe for communication employing nonverbal message codes. Although the ways people employ nonverbal messages vary greatly from one culture to another, and even among subgroups within the same culture, some nonverbal messages produce similar meanings across wide cultural groupings. For example, a smile and a warm touch is generally recognized as an indication of friendship in almost every culture.

The limitation on our ability to communicate through words is more severe than many people recognize immediately. Even though we may share a common language with another person, this does not necessarily mean that we have shared meanings for all or even many words within that language. Take a simple word like "cat" as an example. This is a very common English word. But would it have the same meaning for each of the following people? An elderly spinster, a heavy equipment operator, a zoo keeper, and a jazz trombonist? Each of these people may use "cat" and have a very different meaning for the word. A common language, therefore, does not insure that people have common meanings for all of the words in that language. Although there are also differences among people on the meanings of nonverbal messages, within a given cultural grouping there appears to be substantially less variation at the nonverbal level than there is at the verbal level. It is not too surprising, therefore, that research in the area of nonverbal communication has indicated that nonverbal messages tend to account for much more of the meaning that is stimulated in human communication than is accounted for by verbal messages. In fact, some of the estimates run to well over 90 percent of the social meaning being stimulated by nonverbal messages and less than 10 percent being stimulated by verbal messages. To illustrate this point we may turn to the field of drama. What is it that makes a person like George C. Scott an outstanding actor, while some other person fades into theatrical obscurity? In most instances, Scott does not write the script for the movies in which he appears. The words are given to him, and he adds all the necessary nonverbal messages in order to make his acting a success. Many of us have seen presentations of Shakespeare's plays. Why is it that an amateur production done by a high school is not perceived as well as a production presented by a Broadway group? The words in both presentations are the same. The difference involves the nonverbal skills and messages employed by the actors and actresses. As in the case of the theater, nonverbal messages tend to predominate over verbal messages in most human communication exchanges.

There is, however, a major difference between the ways that children and adults respond to verbal and nonverbal messages. Up to about the age of twelve, children normally will respond primarily to the words that are said and be relatively uninfluenced by the nonverbal message which accompanies the verbal message if the two are in conflict. Much satire, for example, will pass over the child's head, since satire is based upon a conflict between nonverbal and verbal messages and the real meaning intended is carried by the nonverbal message. On the other hand, adults tend to respond primarily to the nonverbal message when the verbal and nonverbal message are in conflict. A sign of maturity in an individual, then, is the ability to perceive nonverbal messages and recognize when they are in conflict with verbal messages and respond appropriately. Most adults seem to recognize intuitively that it is much harder to lie nonverbally than it is to lie verbally. Evidence of untruthfulness, as well as evidence of satire, is primarily communicated nonverbally. To the extent that we can perceive these message cues we can improve the quality of our communication with other people.

Communication education in the United States has long been misdirected because educators have not recognized the essential nature of messages in human communication systems. We say that "a picture is worth a thousand words," but we teach almost no one in our schools how to communicate with pictoral messages. We say "every movement has a meaning all its own," but we teach almost no one the findings of kinesics— the science of body movement. Rather, we teach verbal skills from kindergarten through graduate school. We require verbal English of everyone, but we offer training in the use of nonverbal messages within our culture to almost no one. In many foreign language courses we teach verbal Italian, but ignore the gestural messages that enrich the Italian culture. We teach German, but our students of German learn to speak it with an American accent that a German could hardly recognize. We do not wish to belabor this point here, but we stress it because in this and the following chapter we hope to avoid this common error in the study of communication. Words are only one type of message in human communication, and probably not even the most important type. Thus, in the next chapter we will examine the various types of messages, and place primary emphasis on those types which seem to account for the most impact in human communication: namely, nonverbal messages.

The Nature of Message Codes

To understand the nature of message codes, we must first understand "meaning." Beginning early in elementary school we are taught to seek the meaning of words in the dictionary. With all due respects to Mr. Webster, meanings are not in dictionaries or in words or in any other form of message. Meanings are in people. Meaning is what we think, not what we say, not what we do. When we send someone a message in human communication, we have some meaning in our mind for that message and we hope to stimulate some meaning in the other person's mind as a result of receiving that message. But we cannot transfer meaning from one person to another. All we can do is send and receive messages. In this sense, then, messages are coded meanings. To the extent, therefore, that two people employ the same code for a given meaning, there will be accurate communication between those two people. However, people may use the same code to represent different meanings, and thus fail to communicate. Remember our "cat" example? Return to that example and see if you can determine which of our four people might use the following sentences: "I have to feed my cats before six o'clock." "That cat is a real cool dude, man." "Pull that cat back here out of the way." Here we have an instance of the same code being used in several different ways, and very probably stimulating very different meanings in the minds of receivers of the various messages.

Nonverbal message codes provide us with many of the same problems that are apparent with verbal message codes, like cat. During the Vietnam War, the evening news reports often showed American servicemen riding on trucks and waving a particular gesture at the news cameras. This gesture involved two fingers extending from a closed fist, in the shape of a V. Most people who watched these news reports had no trouble recognizing that code; however, people interpreted it differently. Some recognized this message code as a symbolic gesture indicating victory, primarily those people who were old enough to remember the second World War where this was a common victory gesture. Younger people recognized this gesture as a symbol for peace. What did this gesture mean? To know for sure, we would have to ask the people who were doing the meaning!

A classic example of messages having different meanings for different people is the case involving the crew members of the U.S. alleged spy-ship, Pueblo. The Pueblo was captured off the shore of North Korea in the late 1960s. The crew members were held as prisoners of war by the North Koreans. There was great concern on the part of many Americans for the safety and return of these servicemen. The North Koreans forced the prisoners to pose for pictures for propaganda purposes. The prisoners did so but each person in the group posed with his middle finger protruding upward. In our culture this gesture would be immediately recognized as an obscene gesture and an act of defiance, but the gesture had no similar meaning for the North Koreans. Consequently, they released this famous photograph to the world. The gesture communicated nothing to the North Koreans, but it was a very powerful message that relayed the prisoner's feelings about their captors to Americans.

The point of the examples is very simple. Both verbal and nonverbal messages are simply codes that we use to represent meaning that we have in mind. To the extent the people who observe our codes have a meaning for them similar to our own, we can communicate with them. Similarly, to the extent that we have meanings for the codes employed by other people, they communicate with us.

We have stressed that messages are an essential element in human communication systems, and the next chapter is devoted to an examination of the various types of message codes that are available to us. But we should recognize that human communication science is still in its infancy. There is more about human communication that we do not know than there is that we know. It is very probable that there are forms of human communication that do not involve messages as we will be considering them in this book. It is an established fact that there is communication between human beings that we now call "extrasensory perception." There has even been a case where ESP was documented as occurring between an astronaut on the way to the moon and a person here on Earth. ESP is an all-encompassing term which refers to a potentially vast amount of communication which we simply do not understand.

Communication of this type is often referred to as "psi" (short for psychic) communication. One subset of the psi phenomena, psi gamma, clearly meets our definition of human communication, but we don't know how it occurs. Telepathy is communication in which meaning is stimulated

171

in a receiver through the conscious efforts of a source by some, as yet unknown, means. In telepathy the receiver gets the message, but may not even be consciously aware that she or he is engaging in the process. On the other side of the coin is clairvoyance, another form of psi gamma. Clairvoyance is communication in which a receiver consciously obtains a message from a source by some, as yet unknown, means. Such messages are not consciously sent by the source. In telepathy we know that meaning can be stimulated in the mind of Person B by intentional attempts on the part of Person A. In clairvoyance we know that Person B can pick up meaning from Person A even without Person A consciously doing anything. The only reason that we have to coin a new term like *extrasensory perception* for these processes is that none of the message codes which we will be discussing in the next chapter are present in this type of communication. As human communication science matures over the next several decades, it is quite likely that a new message code, a new channel, or possibly even many new message codes and channels will be discovered and the term symbolizing our ignorance, extrasensory perception, will no longer be necessary.

Isomorphism of Message Codes

"Isomorphism" is the degree to which two things are similar. In this case, isomorphism refers to the degree to which a message code is similar to the thing which the code represents. In general, the more isomorphic a message code is with the thing that it represents the more effective the communication employing that message code will be. Although in most cases nonverbal message codes are more isomorphic than verbal message codes, there is substantial variation in isomorphism within both. Consequently, we need to categorize message codes in a different way in order to clarify this important concept. For this purpose, we will divide message codes into the categories of "analogic" and "digital."

Analogic Message Codes

Analogic codes are essentially representations of the things to which they refer. This can probably best be explained by several examples. A map is a representation of an area, such as a state. If we want to find out how to drive from a metropolitan city to a distant city, we are very likely to secure a

*Sign language used
by the blind is an
analogic message
code that represents
the object or concept
to which it refers.*

map of the highway system between the two places. The map is an analogic code. Although we can not actually see the highways on which we will drive, we can see representations of those highways on the map and get some idea in our mind what the nature of our trip can be. A picture is also an analogic message code. A picture is a two-dimensional representation of a person or thing. Gesture can also be used as an analogic code. In a game of charades, we may gesturally dramatize a thing that we want to communicate. We may wave our arms, for example, to symbolize flying. Most words are not analogic message codes, but a few are. For example, to say "arf" or "woof" as a message code for the sound of a dog barking is to use an analogic message code.

Analogic message codes have a high degree of isomorphism with the object they represent. It is usually more difficult for a source of a message to find or create an analogic code than it is to find or create a digital code. However, it is much easier for a receiver to decode a message that is analogic than one that is digital. In general, therefore, analogic message codes tend to produce more accurate communication between source and receiver than digital codes.

> **BLACK BOX
> 23**
>
> **Why might nonverbal messages stimulate more meaning than verbal
> messages in some communication exchanges?**
>
> **Can you distinguish between analogic and digital message codes?
> Provide examples of each code from your own experience.**

Digital Message Codes

Whereas analogic message codes are representations of things and are
strongly tied to physical reality, digital message codes are arbitrary. Digital
codes involve some form of language. Thus words are digital codes. Other
digital codes include semaphore, the gestural language of the deaf, Morse
Code, and the electronic binary code for communicating with computers.
All digital codes are arbitrary. In English we may use the code word "cat,"
while in French we would use a different code word, and still another one in
Russian. Because of its arbitrary nature, a digital message code has extremely low isomorphism with the thing that it represents. It is much easier
for a source of communication to find or choose a digital code than an
analogic code in most cases. However, it is generally harder for a receiver
to decode a digital message than an analogic message. Consequently,
whenever digital codes are employed, the probability of inaccurate communication is greatly increased. An example, for anyone who has ever
worked with a computer, is the extreme difficulty of communicating with the
computer in its binary receiving system. A computer can respond only to
digital codes, and it is the most demanding receiver that any source can
come in contact with. It has zero tolerance for error. Thus, if the digital
code that we use to communicate with the computer is not perfect, we may
have a total failure to communicate. It is most important, whenever a code
is employed, for both source and receiver to know the same code and to use
the code in the same way. Unfortunately, no two people use language in
exactly the same way, so a certain degree of inaccuracy in communication is
inherent when a digital code is employed.

It is probably clear from this discussion that the use of analogic codes
leads to more effective communication than the use of digital codes. However, we must stress that no matter what code is employed, some meaning is

lost in the communication process. A statement often used by general semanticists to emphasize this point is that "the map is not the territory." Their point is well taken. No matter how elaborate an analogic code is, something is still lost. Even this country's premier creator of analogic codes, Walt Disney, could not overcome this inherent problem. Although Disney was able to create a physical representation of Abraham Lincoln that looked like Lincoln, moved somewhat like Lincoln, and talked somewhat like Lincoln, it still was not Abraham Lincoln. Thus, the visitor to the Hall of Presidents at Disney World may come away with some feeling of what Abraham Lincoln was like, but the visitor also comes away with a great deal of inaccurate meaning for Abraham Lincoln. An important point to remember here is that because of the inherent limitations of all message codes, perfect communication between human beings is impossible (with the possible exception of ESP). No matter how carefully we choose our words in this book, and no matter how many illustrations and pictures that we include to try to make our message and meaning more isomorphic, it is not possible for you to have exactly the same meaning that we do. Fortunately, human beings have more tolerance for error than do computers. Consequently, if our message codes result in approximately the same meaning for one another, our communication may be accurate enough for your and our purposes.

SUGGESTED FURTHER READINGS

1. Harrison, R. P. *Beyond Words* (Englewood Cliffs, N.J.: Prentice-Hall, 1974).

   Chapter four expands our concept of the nature of message codes and their relationship to verbal and nonverbal communication.

2. Hayakawa, S. I. *Language in Thought and Action,* 2nd ed. (New York: Harcourt, Brace and World, 1964).

   Our orientation toward messages and meanings is rooted in the work of general semanticists. This book expands on our concept and introduces other important notions concerning messages in communication.

(Selected references for chapters 9 and 10 appear on pages 200–202.)

10

Types of Messages

Mike walked into the bar on the way home from the office. As he sat down on the bar stool he yawned. The bartender said, "Have a hard day?"   "Yeah. The boss spent half the day in my office.   Give me a double martini, forget the vermouth."   "Coming up."

Mike picked up his drink, took a sip, and winced. Then he leaned back and looked around the room. He spotted an attractive brunette sitting alone at a nearby table. Mike caught her eye and smiled. She smiled back briefly, and then looked away. Mike asked the bartender to give her another drink. When the bartender brought it to her he said something and pointed to Mike. The brunette smiled at Mike; he waved at her, picked up his drink, walked to her table and said, "Mind if I join you?" "Please do."

Mike was late for dinner that night.

In this little story there are a lot of messages, but not very many words. It is an example of effective use

177

of messages in communication, though Mike's wife might not agree. The example also illustrates another important point: Different types of messages can be used to communicate different things.

There are at least ten types of message codes which humans use consistently in communication. Our purpose in this chapter is to identify these codes and to provide some basic information concerning each one. We wish to stress that the material included is only an overview of these message codes and their effects on human communication. A thorough treatment of each of these codes is not possible within the confines of this book; rather, the reader who is interested in learning more about these primary message codes should turn to volumes specifically directed toward nonverbal communication or language behavior. The codes which we consider in this section are illustrated in Figure 10–1

BLACK BOX
24

Can you find examples of at least five of the primary message codes in the communication between Mike, the bartender, and the brunette?

Personal Space

Research in the area of *proxemics,* the study of people's needs and interaction with space, indicates that the way people use space when they are communicating conveys a very potent message. To understand the role of space in human communication we need to distinguish between *territoriality* and *personal space.*

Territory refers to space that has a specific geographical location. By that we mean that territory is stable. Where it is today is where it will be tomorrow. *Territoriality* refers to the instinct in both human and lower forms of animal life to secure and defend territory. While animals generally carve out their territory on an individual basis, human beings tend to carve out their territory both as groups and as individuals. The terrritory of a given nation is considered by that nation to be almost sacred. When that territory is threatened or invaded the probability of violent response is extremely high. Individual human beings respond similarly. We may have

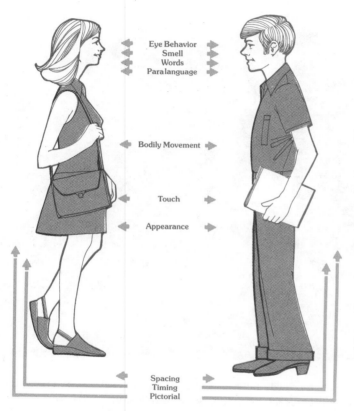

Eye Behavior
Smell
Words
Paralanguage

Bodily Movement

Touch

Appearance

Spacing
Timing
Pictorial

FIGURE 10–1. *Primary message codes.*

our own apartment, or room, or house with a lot. This we define as ours, and we will defend it against the encroachment of other people except by our specific invitation. Within our home we are also likely to carve out a territory that is distinctly ours as opposed to that of the other people who live in the home. A teenage daughter or son needs to have her or his own room. Commonly there is one chair that is "father's chair," similar to Archie's chair in "All in the Family." In the traditional home the kitchen may be the domain of the mother, and is invaded by others at their peril.

Personal space, unlike territory, has no fixed geographical boundary. Rather, it is an invisible bubble that travels with the individual person and may expand in size or contract depending upon the given situation. For

179

People's use of space communicates a great deal about them to others.

example, in a crowded elevator or classroom the size of the personal space bubble will contract to a very small dimension. However, the personal space bubble may increase in size by many times if we are walking down the street alone or sitting in the library trying to study. Whatever the given situation, the area inside the personal space bubble is considered to be the property, although only temporarily, of the individual person. It will be protected and defended to the same extent that a person's immobile territory will be defended.

People's use of space communicates a great deal about them to other people. The executive with a large office is immediately perceived to be more important than the executive with a small office. The family with the largest house and lot in the neighborhood is thought to be more wealthy than neighbors with smaller accommodations. The most important message that is conveyed in interpersonal encounters is conveyed by spatial invasion. When one person invades another person's territory, or more frequently their personal space bubble, this invasion can have a major impact on the communication between the two people. When a person's territory or personal space is violated, that person's tension level generally is sharply increased. Should the invasion continue, the person is very likely either to take flight or to respond aggressively to reclaim her or his territory or personal space. Such invasions are usually unintentional, but they greatly disrupt the communication between the people involved. Both the invader and the invadee are likely to develop highly negative conceptions of the other person. The cause of these perceptions may not be understood consciously by either person involved, and usually are not consistent with the real nature of the other person.

There are major differences from culture to culture in the way people use personal space. What is a spatial invasion in one culture may be inoffensive in another culture. For example, in general North American culture, normal conversation between friends usually involves a spatial separation of about 3 to 4½ feet. Closer spacing is reserved for highly intimate conversations. In Latin America, however, the appropriate distance for a normal conversation is much closer, well within the distance range reserved for intimate conversation in the North American culture. This difference between the two cultures is relatively unimportant unless people with the two different cultural backgrounds come into contact with one another. When this happens, the Latin American probably is going to try to establish the "normal" interpersonal distance which will be much too close for the North American. The North American, in turn, will also be trying to establish the "normal" distance, which will be too far away for the Latin American. The result of this interaction is very likely to be a perception of the North American as being distant and unfriendly, and a perception of the Latin American as being pushy and overly aggressive. When such perceptions are present, of course, many other messages in the communication transaction are likely to be distorted and misinterpreted. The probability of successful communication between such individuals, unless they are aware of the potent message that space utilization conveys, is essentially negative.

BLACK BOX
25

Can you distinguish between "territoriality" and "personal space?"

Can you provide an example from your own experience of how someone has used personal space to communicate something to you?

One does not have to travel to a distant country with a different cultural orientation, however, to confront problems of differences in use of space in communication. Such differences exist within most cultures on the basis of sex and race. Research has indicated that men prefer to stand almost twice as far away from other men in interaction as women stand from women or as either men or women prefer in interacting with a member of the opposite sex. Similarly, at least in the United States, research has indicated that whites prefer to stand or sit almost twice as far away from blacks as either whites prefer to stand or sit from other whites or blacks prefer to sit or stand from other blacks. With just this small amount of information we can predict certain problems that are likely to occur in everyday business settings in the United States. Presume that we have a white businessman interviewing a black man and woman for positions in the business. The white businessman will prefer a substantial distance between himself and the interviewees, particularly with the male interviewee. On the other hand, the female black interviewee, being both female and black, will prefer a very close distance for normal conversation. Whatever distance is established is highly likely to be wrong for at least one of the participants. The white businessman is very likely to be perceived as cold and distant, and to expect a perception of anti-black would not be unreasonable. On the other hand, the black job applicants are very likely to be perceived as overly aggressive and militant. Unless the participants in this encounter are aware of the potent message that space utilization can convey, and the differences in their own natural orientation within the culture, the rest of their communication transaction may suffer or may even completely fail.

Timing

The study of the use of time has been referred to as *chronemics*. Research here shows that, as one writer has expressed it, "time talks." The time at which we choose to communicate conveys a message in itself, and so does the way we use time while we are communicating.

Within a given culture people generally recognize appropriate times for certain kinds of communication. For example, in the United States one would seldom make a business call at two o'clock in the morning. Nor would we normally call a business acquaintance at 10:30 in the morning to simply chat for half an hour. Adolescents quickly learn that right after dad has punished them for misbehavior is not the best time to ask him for use of

for a raise

the family car for the evening. The young woman who receives a telephone call at four o'clock on the afternoon of the day of the biggest dance of the year from a young man requesting a date is quite likely to perceive she was not his first choice. All of these timing norms are generally learned by the individuals in a given culture through experience, generally by trial and error as a youngster. People who do not learn the norms, or those who learn them but don't follow them anyway, convey very strong and usually negative messages to other people. Obviously, the usual response from the other person is a highly negative perception of the individual who does not conform to time norms.

Within a given communication transaction time also plays an important role. For example, we use pauses in our interaction to signal the other person that it is time for her or him to talk. These pause times are highly culture specific. In the general North American culture the pause time to signal the other person to talk is relatively short, compared with a number of other cultures. Consequently, North Americans who travel to other cultures very often carry their short-pause time with them and tend to be extremely dominant in interpersonal encounters. They wait the "normal" period for the other person to begin talking, then become very uncomfortable, and begin talking again themselves. The person from the other culture can't understand why the North American never lets them get a word in edgewise.

Waiting time is a very important variable in many human communication encounters. In the United States if we are made to wait for more than five or ten minutes when we have a scheduled meeting with someone, we tend to become highly agitated. Forcing someone to wait beyond this period requires an apology and an explanation before the communication encounter can really begin, or there will be hard feelings on the part of the person who was made to wait too long. Acceptable waiting time in the United States is much less than that acceptable in many other cultures, particularly Latin America. Our five-minute waiting time is approximately equal to a forty-five-minute waiting time in Latin America. Consider the plight of the Latin American who has kept the North American waiting forty-five minutes for a scheduled appointment. The North American is likely to be highly offended, but the Latin American will be unlikely to know why this offense has been taken. If either or both of these individuals was aware of the powerful message that waiting time conveys this situation could be overcome without serious negative effects. Unfortunately, most people in both cultures are unaware of this powerful nonverbal message.

Arrival time is another important nonverbal message. When should one arrive for a business appointment? For a dinner invitation? For a cocktail party? There are no answers to these questions that will apply universally. Rather the answers to these questions will differ sharply from one culture to another, and even within a given culture. For example, within the United States arrival time for a cocktail party scheduled for 5:30 can vary as much as one full hour. In New York City a 5:30 arrival could cause severe embarrassment to everyone concerned, because the host and hostess both would be very unlikely to expect anyone before 6:00 to 6:15, with most of the people arriving around 6:30. In many parts of western United States, particularly those heavily influenced by the Mormon culture, arrival would be expected at or even slightly before 5:30, and a 6:30 arrival would be considered in very bad taste.

**BLACK BOX
26**

Specify the "right time" in your own locality for each of these activities.
  to call another person to ask for a date?
  to arrive for a dinner scheduled for 7:30 P.M.?
  to arrive for a 10:30 A.M. business appointment?

Can you identify some "sparrows" and "owls" among your friends and acquaintances? Which category do you think you fit in?

Before we move on to another area, we should consider one more important aspect of how time relates to human communication. This is the area of bodily time. Biological research has indicated that people vary sharply in terms of when they are at their peak and when they are in a valley. Although it is somewhat of an oversimplification, people can be divided into two general categories, facetiously referred to as "sparrows" and "owls." Sparrows are early risers who are at their peak early in the day and tend to tail off to severe fatigue by evening. Owls operate in an almost contrary manner. Owls drag themselves out of bed as late as possible, and get better all day until reaching their peak in the evening. These distinctly different biological patterns can have a tremendous impact on communication. Attempting to communicate with another person when he or she is in the valley of the day may be futile or ineffective. Sparrows should communicate with one another in the morning, owls should communicate with one another in the evening, and if a sparrow and an owl need to communicate with one another, the best time for both is a compromise afternoon arrangement. Although in any culture there is a large number of both owls and sparrows, some cultures take on a distinct orientation of one or the other. Most of Latin America, for example, follows the owl pattern. Most of North America follows, almost religiously in some instances, the sparrow pattern. These cultural patterns can cause real problems for "the other group." The owl child, for example, who must arise and catch a bus at 6:30 in order to get to the school that starts at 7:45, is certainly at an extreme disadvantage in her or his education. Similarly, the sparrow who is required to take or teach a three-hour evening class has a high probability of failure. Unfortunately, both owls and sparrows tend to be somewhat intolerant of the natural behavior of each other. For our part, we are both owls. We know a lot of sparrows, and have even found one or two that we like. They have told us that indeed the early bird catches the worm. But we don't much care for worms. Besides that, sparrows sure are dull in the evening.

Bodily Movement

Bodily movement provides the greatest range of potential messages of any of the primary message codes. Research concerning bodily movement in communication, referred to as *kinesics,* indicates that there are over seven hundred thousand distinct physical movements available to us that can stimulate different meanings to other people. That is clearly more signs than the total number of words that most of us have in our vocabulary. The potential combinations of all of these signs approach infinity in number. It would probably not even be possible for a single human being to engage in all the possible combinations of bodily movements within an entire lifetime. And yet, each of these possible combinations is available to all of us at any given time and we use many of them without being aware that we are doing so. An example of the potential of this message code and its complexity is the fact that there are twenty-three distinct eyebrow positions that have been isolated and found to stimulate differential meaning in other people. The person who consciously employs these twenty-three eyebrow positions probably does not exist, yet these positions are available to all of us and we are likely to use all of these positions at one time or another. When we expand beyond the eyebrow position to all of the rest of what we may refer to as facial expression, include hand and arm movements, foot and leg movements, torso movements, and bodily positioning, we can begin to develop a sense of the richness of this message code. We can also begin to

185

The clenched first symbol of black power is an easily recognized gesture.

understand why no human being will ever truly master this message code in its entirety.

Although there are very few (if any) bodily movements that have universal meaning across cultures, within a given culture certain norms develop that are reasonably consistent for the members of that culture, particularly in the area of gesture. Within the United States culture most of us would recognize counting gestures, waving, a black power sign, or an obscene gesture involving a single finger. Our tendency, however, is to believe that other people always use gestures the same way that we do. A simple example from the United States culture would indicate the falsity of that assumption. You will recall the example of the victory or peace sign that we discussed in the previous chapter. When we cross into another culture, the problem becomes much more severe in interpreting the meaning of bodily movement messages. We may illustrate this distinction with a couple of very common gestures. In the United States when we wish to indicate that we agree or understand we nod our head up and down. If we wish to indicate that we do not agree or we do not understand, we shake our head from side to side. In parts of Africa, the Middle East and Asia, these gestures are exactly reversed. In the United States to point to an adult is quite normal, but the pointing gesture that we use is reserved exclusively for children in Ethiopia. To point to an adult in our normal way is highly offensive. Reversing the process, in Ethiopia when people wish to indicate disagreement with what others are saying, they will shake their index fingers from side to side whether the others are adult or children. In the United States, this gesture is used only for children and is quite offensive if used to show disagreement with an adult.

**BLACK BOX
27**

List some of the gestures commonly used in your culture to indicate:
emphasis   counting   stopping
disagreement   approval

The potential for offense in the use of gestures when moving from one culture to another is extremely high. Very often gestures mean radically different things to people in different cultures. In our culture we commonly use a gesture with our index finger touching our thumb and our other three fingers protruding to indicate OK. In much of Latin America this gesture is highly obscene and roughly equivalent to our single uprised index finger in the United States. Thus, it is important that we constantly remember, whether we are engaged in cross-cultural communication or communication with someone from our own culture, that bodily movement is highly related to the individual culture of the person engaging in the movement, but will also vary a great deal even within the same culture. The way a person uses his or her body to communicate may be the single most distinguishing characteristic of the individuality of that person.

Eye Behavior

Not a great deal of research has focused on the way that people employ eye behavior in human communication. What research has been done in this area, technically referred to as *oculesics,* have been closely associated with kinesics research that has been concerned with facial expression. Consequently, we will not focus on the results of the research that are available—since much of it is highly technical—except to point out that that the findings do indicate that when we are looking at something in which we are interested, the pupils in our eyes tend to expand. Instead, we will look at some normative eye behavior patterns that are readily apparent within the North American culture.

One very strong norm in the North American culture is that we should look at a person if we are paying attention to them. If we look away from another person while they are talking to us, we send a strong message indicating our lack of interest or respect. We teach our children at an early age to look directly into our eyes when we are talking to them. We even go as far as to establish an alleged norm for telling the truth: a person who can't look you in the eye is lying to you. Actually, research indicates that whether or not a person looks another person in the eye is a totally unreliable predictor of whether or not he or she is telling the truth. But the absence of direct eye contact is very likely to signal a lack of interest, attention, or truthfulness because of the norms of the society. These norms are definitely the product of the North American culture, and do not necessarily extend to other cultures, particularly those in Africa and Asia. In many countries of the world direct eye contact with a superior is quite unacceptable.

BLACK BOX
28

Can you explain what looking at someone in the North American culture may suggest to that other person?

Eye behavior is also employed in personal contacts in order to control conversation. The general pattern that we follow is to begin talking to a person, look away while we continue talking, and return to establish contact when we are finished. During this period the other person is looking at us constantly so that he or she will be able to catch our signal that we are finished when we look back at her or him. Our looking behavior, then, sends a strong message about the nature of the conversation to the other person.

Eye behavior is also used in the early stages of courtship between a male and a female who are not well acquainted, and in some cases even by those who are. The norm here is for the male to attempt to establish prolonged eye contact at some distance away from the female. This is a signal that he is interested in communicating further with the female. If she is also interested she will maintain the contact, and probably smile. (Remember the initial contact between Mike and the brunette in the bar?) If she is not interested in further communication with the male, she will break the eye contact sharply. This type of eye behavior is characteristic of behaviors that are used to bridge spatial gaps. Eye contact brings people psychologically closer to one another. Herein lies a problem, however. If people are at a normal distance for interaction, prolonged direct eye contact can cause either or both parties to become very uncomfortable. In essence, eye contact can have the same impact as the physical invasion of territory or personal space. And violation of eye behavior norms will produce reactions very similar to territorial or personal space invasion. One way that you can experience the effects of spatial invasion with another person as a result of eye contact is to enter a crowded elevator and stand with your back to the door facing the other people. Without saying anything, just look directly into the eyes of the other people. You will be able to observe a great deal of discomfort on their part, so you should not continue this for any extended period or you may be the object of very aggressive responses.

Touch

The use of touch in human communication may be the single most potent message code, at least in the North American culture. Research in the area of *haptics*, touching behavior, suggests that the use of touch carries very strong overtones of emotion in most cultures. However, the types of touch which are permissible or even encouraged in one culture can be totally unacceptable in another culture.

The North American cultural norm involves very little touch between participants in human communication. Touch is generally considered a very intimate message in communication in this culture, and in the North American culture touch has taken on very strong sexual overtones. One exception is shaking hands. Consequently, males in this culture very seldom touch one another, except to shake hands, or possibly to pat one another on the back in some circumstances. Females engage in somewhat more touch than do males, but even their touching behavior is sharply restricted, except with their children.

Since touch in the North American culture has such a strong sexual overtone, it is a very potent message to indicate intimacy. It has been argued by many that people in this culture are severely deprived of an important form of communicative message because of these cultural restrictions, and the argument is continued to suggest that people need to be taught to touch each other more. We will not enter that controversy except to say that the more that touch is used the less potent it will be as a form of intimate communicative message.

Whereas the North American culture involves very little touching behavior, most other cultures are much more touch oriented. Hand holding, hugging, and kissing, even between two males, is not at all uncommon in

Touch may be the single most potent human message code.

most of the rest of the cultures in the world. Witness the hugging and kissing that occurs between male athletes in international competition, like the Olympic Games. These behaviors are not related to sexual attraction, unless they are engaged in under special circumstances; however, they would be likely to be perceived that way by a North American observer. One of the authors had the opportunity to meet and become well acquainted with a Russian poet who was visiting the United States. When he took the poet to the airport to catch a plane, he was treated to a full kiss on the lips. That behavior was quite normal for the Russian culture, but almost sent the author into cardiac arrest.

There is a fairly generally established norm in the early stages of traditional courtship communication between young males and females which involves permissible touch. In the early stages of classical courtship in our culture, such as at a first meeting, the female is generally not permitted to suggest verbally to the male that she would like to carry on their relationship. She must do so nonverbally. On the other hand, the male is expected to say directly that he would like to get together with the female again, and he is definitely not expected to engage in much touching behavior. It is important, therefore, for the female to be able to signal the male that she is interested in him. The most common way to do this is through touch. If the couple is standing and talking to one another, the female can

---

BLACK BOX
29

Identify the eye and touching behaviors that are normal in early stages of traditional courtship in your culture.

---

signal this interest by just a gentle touch on the forearm of the male. If they are seated, the similar touch on the forearm or on the outside of the thigh is generally recognized by males as a signal of interest. The female who is not aware of this norm is very likely to wonder why males in whom she is interested seldom call her after that first meeting. Similarly, males who are unaware of this norm may either be oblivious to the signs of interest that young women are giving him, or conclude that they are much more interested than they really are simply because he was touched. All of this illustrates the point that when norms are violated concerning touch, there is apt to be a real failure to communicate. Perceptions may go wild, and other messages may be completely ignored. Touch, therefore, is a very powerful message code to indicate interest and intimacy, but it is also wrought with potential for miscommunication, particularly in low-touch cultures.

Vocal Behavior

When we talk to other people we say words, but we also engage in a lot of nonverbal activity. The language we speak is accompanied by our tone of voice, our inflection, the variety with which we speak, our voice quality, etc. This accompanying vocal behavior has been referred to as "paralanguage." The study of paralanguage, known as *vocalics*, has indicated that much more is conveyed by this message code than is communicated by the words themselves.

To begin with, the mere amount of vocalization in which we engage has a tremendous impact on the way in which we are perceived. Folklore has it that some people talk too much, and so we don't care for them. Research does not support this belief. Rather, it has been observed that people who talk more are generally perceived as more credible, more attractive, having more power, and exerting more leadership than people who talk less. Obviously, there probably is a point at which a person could talk too much, but this point is at such an extreme level that it is unlikely that many people ever reach that point.

Although paralanguage has many other impacts, one of its main influences is as a substitute for punctuation and indications of emphasis that are unavailable in the written language. Imagine how many different ways you could say the following sentence: "I didn't know that about her." No matter how many different ways you could say the sentence, you would still be saying the same six words over and over. But the meaning that would be stimulated in the other person's mind could be drastically different, simply because of the paralanguage message code.

BLACK BOX
30

Can you identify some of the perceptions stimulated by paralanguage:
   that are based on stereotypes?
   that tend to be accurate?

We not only determine much of the meaning of words through paralanguage, but we also generate many of our perceptions of people based on their paralanguage. Some of these perceptions have a basis in reality, and others are stereotypes. Let us consider stereotypes first. Research has indicated that without ever seeing or knowing a person, consistent perceptions across a wide variety of people about a speaker's sexuality, sincerity, strength, and attractiveness are generated by the speaker's paralanguage. Unfortunately, these perceptions are simply stereotypes that have been built up in the culture and have no basis in reality. By that we mean that a lot of receivers would agree on their perception of the source of the paralanguage, but their agreement would not correlate with the way the source really is.

On the other hand, many perceptions of people can be made accurately from their paralanguage behavior alone. Research has indicated that paralanguage can accurately indicate a person's sex, size, age, race, as well as the person's level of education, region of origin, social status, and to some extent the person's emotional state at the time.

The major problem with the way people perceive other people on the basis of their paralanguage behavior is that both accurate and inaccurate perceptions can be generated simultaneously. Accents and regional inflections are typical of this problem. Within the United States there is a wide variety of regional dialects of English. No one of these dialects has any natural superiority over any of the others. Nor are the people of one region necessarily more competent, friendly, or of higher character than any other group. Nevertheless, a research study conducted in the Middle West indicated that people who spoke with a Southern accent were perceived to be less competent than any other group studied, but at the same time much more friendly and sociable. This same group of Middle Westerners perceived people with a New York accent to be more competent than people with any other accent, but at the same time to have lower character or trustworthiness. In these instances the Midwest research subjects were perceiving accurately the region the person came from, but drawing unwarranted conclusions about the people based upon their stereotypes of Southerners and New Yorkers.

The main point to remember from this discussion is that most of the meaning for words that we communicate to other people is stimulated by our paralanguage behavior, rather than the words themselves. And at the same time, our paralanguage behavior will generate many perceptions of us in the eyes of the people with whom we are communicating, some of which will be accurate, some of which will be based on stereotypes related to our paralanguage behavior.

Appearance

No matter how much we might wish that it were otherwise, we all innately recognize that the way we look has an impact on the way that other people communicate with us. We may mouth phrases like "beauty is only skin deep" and "beauty is in the eye of the beholder," but research has confirmed what many of us knew before. Physical attractiveness is the primary predictor of whether or not people will even initiate communication with one another. In contrast to several of the other nonverbal message codes that we have discussed, most of us are very sensitive to this messsge code. We are very concerned about our appearance, and attempt to modify it in ways that will make us more attractive to other people. In doing so we are manipulating messages that we are sending to others. It is most appropriate that we engage in this behavior, because initial interactions are always predicated upon the initial attraction of the other person as a physical object. We know the other person as an object before we know the other person as a person. Research has indicated that if we do not find the person-object to be physically attractive, we are much less likely to ever get to know the person at all.

There are a wide variety of messages that we manipulate with regard to our appearance. Our clothing is a major appearance message. We have to decide whether we should wear clothing that is modern or conservative. If we are female, should we wear a skirt or not. If we are male, should we wear a tie or not. Very often we will make different decisions with regard to our clothing, given differences in people and the projected outcome of the communication in which we plan to engage. Another message choice that we have available with regard to appearance is our hair. What style should we wear it in? If we are male, should we wear long hair or short hair? For anyone who lived through the late sixties, it would be unnecessary to explain the impact that long versus short hair can have on a person's life. Beyond these obvious factors of appearance, there are a wide range of other things that we can do to our bodies to make them more attractive, as evidenced by a multimillion dollar cosmetics industry. Similarly, if we examine the extensive research on color, we will find that there are certain colors that we can wear that will stimulate different meanings in the people with whom we come in contact. Finally, we add things to our apparel and our person to establish a certain kind of appearance. We can choose to wear a flag pin in our lapel, we can choose whether or not to carry a briefcase or a purse, to wear a slide rule in our belt, to carry IBM cards in our shirt pocket. All of these elements contribute to the appearance message that we send to other people which has an impact on how they respond to us and to our other messages.

BLACK BOX
31

Can you provide examples from your own behavior in which you have used appearance and smell to communicate with someone else?

Smell

Although the message code of smell is often overlooked in the study of human communication, and indeed probably does not have as large an impact as many of the other message codes, the existence of a multimillion dollar perfume, cologne, and after-shave lotion industry suggests that most of us are well aware of the impact that smell can have in human communication. In the United States we have "learned" that body odor is something offensive to other people, and consequently, we attempt to cover up our natural odors with artificial odors which will communicate a more positive message to people with whom we come in contact. Most other cultures do not find the natural odor of human beings to be offensive, and they find little need for the use of perfumes to mask their natural odor. However, the United States culture has "progressed" to the point where at the time of this writing it has been announced in a trade magazine that a whole new series of products shortly will be forthcoming. These products will be T-shirts and blouses that have a variety of odors built into the material that will be retained through numerous washings. Even as members of the United States culture and active participants in this normative behavior for the culture, we may smile at the extent to which our concern with personal odor has gone. Nevertheless, we do employ various odors in our communication. For example, if we are having guests for an evening we may reject certain foods for dinner because they leave an unpleasant after-odor that would interfere with our communication later. Similarly, we may burn incense or use certain types of aerosol sprays to change the odor of the environment in which we are going to communicate. All of this behavior is predicated upon the accurate assumption that the sense of smell is capable of receiving and permitting interpretation of a variety of messages.

BLACK BOX
32

Can you distinguish between the two kinds of messages presented by pictures?

Pictorial Messages

How a photographer takes a photo can drastically affect our perception of the scene.

All of the previous message codes that we have discussed have direct application to interpersonal communication as well as to several other human communication contexts. Pictorial messages are used infrequently in interpersonal communication, but are extensively used in mass communication. Pictorial messages may involve still photographics, drawings, television, or film. Pictorial messages inherently carry two simultaneous messages. The first message, and the most obvious one, is the actual thing being pictured.

The second message involves the way the thing is being pictured. To those who are not familiar with photography or art, probably the best way to explain this distinction is to look at television and film. In television or film the thing or person being photographed is capable of engaging in movement that will be recorded and presented to observers. This is the first level of the pictorial message. The second level involves how the photographer chooses to shoot the television or film picture. The choices that the photographer is confronted with include whether or not the picture should be a close-up, a medium range, or a long shot; should the object be pictured from above, on an eye-to-eye level, or from below; should the picture be in color or black and white; and should there be a variety of shots of the object.

A thorough study of pictorial messages is far beyond the scope of the present volume. To be fully capable of handling pictorial messages a person needs intensive training in photography, art, and TV and film production. Our purpose here is simply to stress that when we do look at a picture, whether it is still or in motion, we are looking both at the thing being pictured and the artist's interpretation of that thing which is reflected in the way in which the subject is reproduced. Probably the best example for clarity in this regard is the political cartoon. By examining the cartoon we discern that it is the President who is being drawn, but we also get the cartoonist's impression of the President from the drawing. The two messages are received simultaneously by us and are not completely distinguishable.

Words

The final type of message code that we will consider is words, the message code that most people probably think of as being the most important or the only message code involved in human communication. That illusion hopefully no longer exists in your mind after reading the previous material. Words are clearly not the most important message variables in human communication, but in many instances they are essential for any human communication. Linguistics, an extensively developed science, has provided a great deal of information about the ways that people use words, far more information than we could possibly include in this short volume. So we will focus on the importance of words within the totality of human communication and stress the uniqueness of this particular message.

While it is true that words cannot be expressed to another person without the source of communication engaging in paralinguistic behavior (or

BLACK BOX
33

Can you give an example of an idea that would require words for communication?

the written equivalent), it is also true that some ideas cannot be communicated to other people without the use of words. Can you imagine trying to communicate the meaning of "democracy" to a person unfamiliar with the concept without utilizing words? It may be possible to communicate emotions and very concrete ideas to other people without the use of words; however, communication of abstract or complex ideas requires the use of words in conjunction with other message codes. Cognitive or intellectual meaning is difficult if not impossible to stimulate in another person without the use of words.

In our use of words we make essentially two choices. First we choose the word or set of words that we are going to use to stimulate some meaning in another. We sometimes choose those words very carefully, knowing how the other person is likely to respond to them. When a police officer stops us for speeding we are careful to call him "officer" rather than other names we sometimes use. The act of choosing a word or words is called *lexical choice*. The second choice we make is how we arrange those words into sentences and paragraphs when necessary. Often this arranging seems to come quite easily, as in our normal conversation. At other times, when we are writing an English theme for example, we take great care in ordering and arranging words. The ordering and arranging of words into sentences is called *syntax*.

These two choices that we make in communication with words do affect how others respond to our messages. The choices we make may affect how much we are believed or understood. Sometimes, through careful choices, we are able to change people's attitudes and behaviors. The reason for this is that through lexical and syntactical choices we are able to create certain important elements in our messages. For example, we are able to create metaphors and analogies that help to clarify abstract concepts. We are able to offer evidence for our point of view or argue with more intense language. In addition, we are able to structure our message so that it gets attention and is easier to follow. These and many other important elements which may facilitate effective communication are possible through careful choice and arrangement of words. These choices are treated in more detail in later chapters dealing with information, influence, and decision making.

To understand fully the nature of message codes in human communication one must engage in intensive study of all ten of the message codes that we have discussed here. It is certainly not possible within an introductory volume such as this one to go into each of these message codes in great detail. Rather, it has been our purpose to provide a brief introduction to each of these message codes so that their importance and basic nature can be understood. The individual who is interested in developing a further understanding of these codes should turn to the specialized volumes on nonverbal behavior and linguistics which are designed for this purpose.

Message Awareness and Response

In chapter 2 we attempted to distinguish between four different levels of communication based upon the intent and awareness of the source and receiver of messages. Now that we have examined messages in more detail, let us return to those four levels of communication.

Level 1. Both the source and receiver are fully aware of the messages being exchanged.

Level 2. The source is fully aware of the messages being exchanged; the receiver is not fully aware.

Level 3. The receiver is fully aware of the messages being exchanged; the source is not fully aware.

Level 4. Neither the source nor the receiver is fully aware of the messages that are being exchanged.

We indicated previously that the ideal state for human communication is at Level 1. Unfortunately, it is very difficult for us to operate at this level except in comparatively rare circumstances. However, to the extent that we move from Level 4, the normal condition of most human communication, toward Level 1, we have improved our communication skills and abilities. An awareness of the primary message codes can enhance this movement from Level 4 upward. To the extent that we can become fully aware of all of the messages that we are sending to another person, we can increase the probability of communicating the meaning we intend to communicate to the other person. Similarly, to the extent to which we can be sensitive to all the messages that another person is sending us, we can improve the probability that we will be able to interpret the meaning that the other individual is attempting to send.

SUGGESTED FURTHER READINGS

1. Harrison, R. P. *Beyond Words* (Englewood Cliffs, N.J.: Prentice-Hall, 1974).
   An interestingly written introduction to nonverbal communication.

2. Knapp, M. L. *Nonverbal Communication in Human Interaction* (New York: Holt, Rinehart and Winston, 1972).
   An excellent summary of theory and research concerning nonverbal communication.

SELECTED REFERENCES

ADDINGTON, D. W. "The Effect of Vocal Variations on Ratings of Source Credibility." *Speech Monographs* 38 (1971): 242–247.

ALLPORT, G. and CANTRIL, H. "Judging Personality from Voice." *Journal of Social Psychology* 5 (1934): 37–54.

BALL, J. and BYRNES, F. C. *Principles and Practices in Visual Communication* (Washington, D.C.: Department of Audiovisual Instruction, National Education Association, 1964).

BIRDWHISTELL, R. L. *Kinesics and Context* (Philadelphia: University of Pennsylvania Press, 1970).

BOSMAJIAN, H. A., ed. *The Rhetoric of Nonverbal Communication* (Glenview, Ill.: Scott, Foresman, 1971).

DARWIN, C. *The Expression of Emotions in Man and Animals* (London: John Murray, 1872).

DAVITZ, J. R. *The Communication of Emotional Meaning* (New York: McGraw-Hill, 1964).

DITTMANN, A. T. and LLEWELLYN, L. G. "Body Movement and Speech Rhythm in Social Conversation." *Journal of Personality and Social Psychology* 11 (1969): 98–106.

DUNCAN, S., JR. "Nonverbal Communication." *Psychological Bulletin* 72 (1969): 118–137.

EFRON, D. *Gesture and Environment* (New York: King's Crown, 1941).

EISENBERG, A. M. and SMITH, R. R. *Nonverbal Communication* (Indianapolis: Bobbs-Merrill, 1971).

EKMAN, P. "Universals and Cultural Differences in Facial Expressions of Emotion," in *Nebraska Symposium on Motivation,* J. Cole, ed. (Lincoln: University of Nebraska Press, 1972).

EKMAN, P. and FRIESEN, W. V. "The Repertoire of Nonverbal Behavior: Categories, Origins, Usage, and Coding." *Semiotica* 1 (1969): 49–98.

EXLINE, R. "Explorations in the Process of Person Perception: Visual Interaction in Relation to Competition, Sex and Need for Affiliation." *Journal of Personality* 31 (1963): 1–20.

FRANK, L. K. "Tactile Communication." *Genetic Psychology Monographs* 56 (1957): 209–255.

GOFFMAN, E. *Behavior in Public Places* (New York: The Free Press, 1963).

HALL, E. T. *The Silent Language* (New York: Doubleday, 1959).

————. *The Hidden Dimension* (Garden City, L.I.: Doubleday, 1966).

HARMS, L. S. "Listener Judgments of Status Cues in Speech." *Quarterly Journal of Speech* 47 (1961): 164–168.

HARRISON, R. P. *Beyond Words* (Englewood Cliffs, N.J.: Prentice-Hall, 1974).

HARRISON, R. "Nonverbal Communication," in *Handbook of Communication,* I. DeSola Pool, W. Schramm, N. Maccoby, F. Fry, E. B. Parker and L. Fein, eds. (Chicago: Rand-McNally, 1973).

HINDE, R. A. *Non-Verbal Communication* (Cambridge: Cambridge University Press, 1972).

IZARD, C. E. *Face of Emotion* (New York: Appleton-Century-Crofts, 1971).

Journal of Communication, December, 1972.

KNAPP, M. L. *Nonverbal Communication in Human Interaction* (New York: Holt, Rinehart and Winston, 1972).

MEHRABIAN, A. *Silent Messages* (Belmont, Cal.: Wadsworth, 1971).

————. *Nonverbal Communication* (Aldine-Atherton, 1972).

MEYER, L. B. *Emotion and Meaning in Music* (Chicago: University of Chicago Press, 1956).

MONTAGU, A. *Touching: The Human Significance of Skin* (New York: Columbia University Press, 1971).

PEARCE, W. B. and CONKLIN, F. "Nonverbal Vocalic Communication and Perceptions of a Speaker." *Speech Monographs* 38 (1971): 235–241.

RUESCH, J. and KEES, W. *Nonverbal Communication: Notes on the Visual Perception of Human Relations* (Berkeley: University of California Press, 1956).

RYAN, M. S. *Clothing: A Study in Human Behavior* (New York: Holt, Rinehart and Winston, 1966).

SCHEFLEN, A. E. *Body Language and the Social Order* (Englewood Cliffs, N.J.: Prentice-Hall, 1972).

SCHUTZ, W. *Joy* (New York: Grove Press, 1967).

SOMMER, R. *Personal Space* (Englewood Cliffs, N.J.: Prentice-Hall, 1969).

————. *Design Awareness* (San Francisco: Holt, Rinehart and Winston, 1972).

STARKWEATHER, J. "Content-Free Speech as a Source of Information about the Speaker." *Journal of Abnormal and Social Psychology* 52 (1956): 394–402.

WATSON, O. M. *Proxemic Behavior: A Cross-Cultural Study (The Hague: Mouton, 1970).*

WEINER, M., DEVOE, S., RUBINOW, S., and GELLER, J. "Nonverbal Behavior and Nonverbal Communication." *Psychological Review* 79 (1972): 185–214.

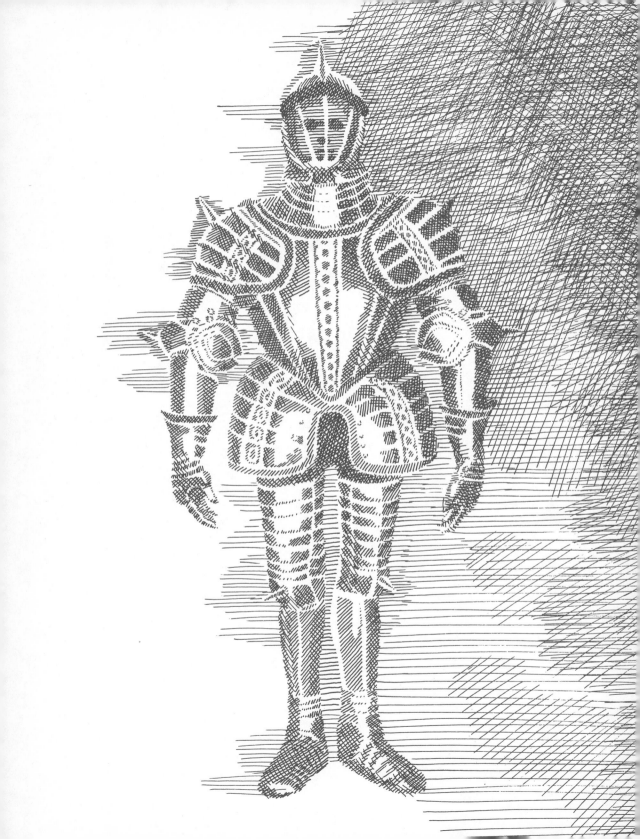

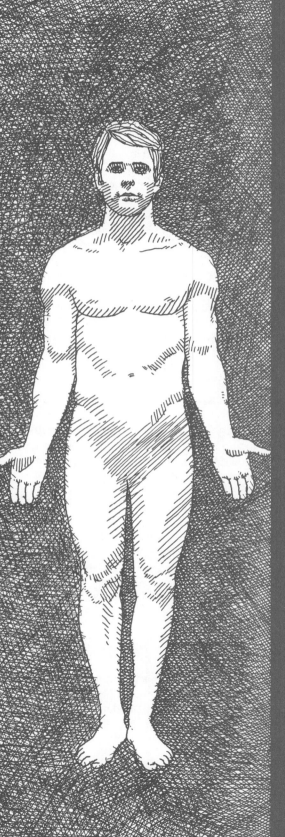

11

Self-Disclosive Messages

Through messages we are able to communicate and share our experience with others. We have seen that a great deal of these are unintended, nonverbal messages. Through these nonverbal means we reveal a great deal about ourselves to others, intentionally or unintentionally. In the same sense, we disclose who we are and what we feel to others through verbal messages. Sometimes we do this without realizing it. The next time you are engaged in conversation with a friend, consciously count the number of times you reveal your feelings about yourself, your feelings about your friend, and other information about yourself. You will be surprised at how often you engage in self-disclosure through your verbal messages. Even when we think we are not disclosing such information, others frequently "read between the lines" of what we say. In this chapter we hope to make you more aware of your own disclosure patterns and the disclosure of others around you.

The next time someone asks "How are you?", tell them in detail and observe their reaction. You will probably have engaged in self-disclosure at an inappropriate time when the other person did not really want to know about you. Although we share ourselves and our experience with others through our communication, we gauge how much it is best to reveal depending upon the situation and the person to whom we are talking.

At the heart of more intimate communication are self-disclosive messages. Because we become individuals only in relation to others, giving of self between individuals is necessary. Self-disclosure is the means by which we give ourselves to others and the means by which others share themselves with us. Self-disclosure is generally thought of as the honest revelation of information about oneself which is of a more confidential or intimate nature. This information is, of course, based to a large extent upon an individual's perceptions of reality as she or he experiences it.

Causes and Effects of Self-Disclosure

Not all people disclose equally: some people disclose a lot; some, very little. The same person may disclose a great deal in one situation, and comparatively little in another. We would like very much, at this point, to be able to enumerate all of the causes of these variations in disclosure behavior. Unfortunately, our understanding of self-disclosure in human communication does not allow us to identify causes and effects at this point. The question of whether certain characteristics cause self-disclosure or whether self-disclosure produces certain characteristics is not always answerable at this stage of our knowledge. Often self-disclosure appears to be reciprocally related to other things. Such characteristics and conditions that are closely related to self-disclosure we call *correlates* of self-disclosure behavior. Let us consider several of these.

Self-Disclosure

One of the situations that seems to correlate with self-disclosure behavior by one individual appears to be reciprocal disclosure by the other individual. Simply put, disclosure begets disclosure. Although this finding is not universal, typically this reciprocal relationship appears to exist. For example, you have probably had the experience of telling another about your feelings or some recent experience. The other person then began relating to you similar feelings and experiences that you did not know about. As a result, you may have been surprised or even shocked by those disclosures. A notable exception to this rule is disclosure among spouses. In this case, high disclosure by one partner may inhibit disclosure by the other, depending of course on the topic of disclosure. Apparently, whether the disclosure is positive or negative may also have some impact. If the self-disclosure is negative, and highly intimate, the other person may experience anxiety as a result of the expectation that she or he reveal similar information about her or himself. However, in most settings in which confederates have revealed greater amounts and more intimate items through self-disclosure, the responding persons have increased their self-disclosures correspondingly.

Obviously, the nature of the other person and the specific social situation may prohibit such reciprocal self-disclosure when the individual initiating the disclosure is perceived to lack discretion or trustworthiness. However, the reception of self-disclosure appears to be rewarding since disclosure itself implies trust and confidence in the person receiving the intimate information. Also, making self-disclosures is often rewarding in itself to the individual doing the disclosing. This may be why people will disclose despite the anxiety that might be involved in honest, intimate revelations about the self. Many of us have a need to tell others about such things.

Competence

A study of interpersonal and professional competence among nurses found a substantial relationship of competence to self-disclosure. First, nurses who were rated higher in communication competence with their patients were found to be higher self-disclosers. Also, their cumulative grade-point averages while they were sophomore nursing students were found to be substantially related to disclosure with their mothers and friends of the same sex. Grades for nursing students were derived not only from tests but also competence in actual nursing practices. You probably know some highly competent people whom you respect who freely reveal personal information, even some of their mistakes, without seeming to worry about such disclosures. You may feel that such revelations make them "human" like the rest of us.

It may very well be that people who are more competent also perceive themselves to be more competent, and thus have the self-confidence necessary to take more chances with self-disclosure. Or, even more likely, competent people may simply have more positive things about themselves to disclose than less competent people.

Trustworthiness

In the literature on self-disclosure, it is almost an axiom that self-disclosure only occurs between individuals who trust each other. Not only must we perceive another as sufficiently trustworthy and honest before we will self-disclose, but subsequent self-disclosure appears to increase perceptions of trust and honesty. Indeed, there appears to be a reciprocal relationship between trust and self-disclosive messages. However, we must note that we do not self-disclose to everyone whom we trust.

It is not difficult to understand this relationship. Much of what we can self-disclose to another we do not want everyone else to know about us. We must trust the other person to keep our information confidential. If that trust is violated, self-disclosure may cease. One of the authors recalls an instance in which he disclosed some highly personal information to a friend-colleague. Within two days, everyone in his department knew the information. That was the last time the author engaged in self-disclosure to that person!

Mental Health and Personal Growth

Some advocates of self-disclosure claim that higher self-disclosure is directly related to better mental health. Some even claim that higher self-disclosure increases mental health and personal growth. However, there is no clear indication about whether disclosure produces mental health or visa versa. In addition, there is no clear indication that high self-disclosure is even directly related to mental health. Studies of many indices of mental health in relation to self-disclosure have generally produced low correlations. Substantial relationships between mental health growth and self-disclosure have not been established. It may well be that extremes of either high or low disclosure are signs of poor mental health. We believe this to be the case. For example, you have seen others depressed and refusing to disclose. On the other hand you have known others who tell everything about their feelings for no apparent reason other than some characteristic mental or emotional problem. Therefore, we suggest that each individual should establish some optimal level of self-disclosure for her or himself which facilitates her or his own mental growth and self-actualization.

Personality

Closely related to these studies of mental health are the studies of personality as it relates to self-disclosure. The results of these studies are also similar. Although self-disclosure has been studied in conjunction with almost every personality characteristic, few meaningful relationships have been found. Usually only low-level relationships have been discovered and many contradictory findings have been reported. For example, studies of dogmatic individuals have found increased dogmatism to be directly related to increased self-disclosure, while other studies have found the opposite to be true. In one area, however, there appears to be some more consistent relationships. Think of several people in your past who have been most open and disclosive to you. Chances are these persons have sociable and extroverted personalities. Higher *sociability* and *extraversion* have been found to be directly related to higher self-disclosure. These two personality characteristics (not credibility dimensions) appear to facilitate more open communication. Some studies have failed to find this result but none has found contradictory relationships to exist.

Anxiety and Communication Apprehension

An individual's anxiety, communication apprehension, or composure appear to be related to self-disclosive communication. People apparently have varying levels of anxiety and fear related to revealing highly intimate information that they would rather keep private. At an interaction level of communication, fear of communication significantly affects willingness and frequency of communication. The motivation not to communicate which we discussed in chapter 5 substantially decreases even nondisclosive communication. How much more must it affect communication about highly revealing information through self-disclosure! We think the effect of communication apprehension on self-disclosure is even more drastic. The reward of self-disclosure must outweigh the communication apprehension involved. Certainly, the reward is not sufficient for an individual who is already highly apprehensive in typical, noninvolving interactions.

On the other hand, general anxiety may have somewhat different effects. A person who is highly anxious in general, or even highly anxious about something in particular, may have extremes in self-disclosure. This person's messages may be extremely disclosive or almost completely non-disclosive. One of the authors who has had the opportunity to advise a large number of undergraduates has observed this behavior. On some occasions students who are highly anxious about some grade, requirement, job, or graduation, pour out their lives. About as many anxious students state the problem and ask, "What can you do about this?" Many times it is difficult to even understand the anxiety producing problem because the individual doesn't want to reveal it or talk personally in such anxious situations. Certainly, such high anxiety affects us differently, but it is most likely to make us extremely disclosive or extremely nondisclosive.

Liking and Loving

Self-disclosure appears to be closely related to liking another individual. In general, the more we like another the more disclosure is present in the relationship. Which motive causes which is not clear. Apparently a reciprocal relationship exists between disclosure and liking. Research has demonstrated that liking leads to greater self-disclosure, and that self-disclosure from another will lead to greater liking of that person. However, this may not always be true for males. Research has not consistently found this disclosure-liking relationship among men. It is quite possible that the culturally defined male role of strong, silent, and somewhat distrustful is so ingrained that disclosive relationships are difficult to establish. Also, some research has demonstrated that high self-disclosure of overly intimate information may have a negative effect on liking. Moderate to high levels of disclosure that avoid the overly intimate appear to facilitate liking relationships. The effects of disclosure on liking, of course, vary with the social setting and the target person. For example, high disclosure in the work setting appears to reduce liking. Also, liking and self-disclosure seem to be most clearly related when the target person for the disclosure is a friend of the same sex or the father of the disclosee. Further, although disclosure to spouse appears to be greater than for most target-persons, the type of disclosure involved certainly affects liking or loving outcomes. For example, if I were to tell my wife I had a mistress, I might expect to be less liked! However, the fact that higher disclosure usually occurs among spouses may indicate that loving facilitates self-disclosure more than mere liking of another. If the other spouse is capable of dealing with the disclosures revealed, then increased loving may result.

As we would expect, positive reinforcement (feedback) and social support lead to increased self-disclosure. Also, when individuals are dependent upon each other to fulfill certain goals or needs, disclosure appears to be greater. Finally, the proxemic relationship with another varies with the duration-time of self-disclosure involved. Longer self-disclosure is directly related to decreased distance between participants. Although other non-verbal cues are undoubtedly related to self-disclosure, the nature of these relationships has not been explored in any detail at this point in time.

**BLACK BOX
34**

Can you define self-disclosure? Try to describe the relationships of these correlates to self-disclosure:

competence   personality
trustworthiness   anxiety and communication apprehension
personal growth   liking and loving

Can you identify any other variables that may be related to self-disclosure?

Dimensions of Self-Disclosure

Although we cautioned at the outset of the previous section that our understanding of self-disclosure at this point in time permits very little inference about causes of behavior, we should also stress that the reason the information generated to date by research on self-disclosure is often inconclusive is not because of a shortage of research or because of unusually low quality in the research. Rather, the difficulty lies in determining when self-disclosure actually occurs when we are observing an interaction. If self-disclosure involved only one aspect or one component of communicating, then it would be a simple matter to determine when self-disclosure was occurring. However, self-disclosure may involve several dimensions. As a result, it is seldom an either-or question as to whether or not a particular message is self-disclosive. At least seven of these dimensions deserve our considera-

tion. Before we examine them, we want you to become acquainted with two
friends of ours.

Pete and Jan had met each other only two weeks before graduation.
Now, less than three weeks later, they are in love. Neither knows what he or
she is going to do after college. Pete is from a working-class neighborhood
where many of the residents or their parents are recent immigrants to the
U.S. His father can't understand why he doesn't just get a job like "everybody else." Pete sometimes becomes worried and moody when he thinks
about it. Although he was in the top of his graduating class in the business
school, he had not been able to find a job he liked. Pete is quietly good
looking and introspective.

Jan, on the other hand, is from a upper-middle class neighborhood
with split-level homes and at least three cars in each garage. Her father is
an M.D. She had majored in music and although her grades were only
average, she was well liked and popular on campus. She is outgoing and
attractive.

"I was glad to meet your parents at graduation," Jan said. "I liked them
a lot."

"Yeah," responded Pete.

Conscious Intent to Disclose

"Say, I've got an idea," Jan said cautiously. "You know a lot about
business and I know something, at least, about music. I've been thinking about
this for some time. Why don't we see if we can open a little music shop across
from campus?"

"Hey, that sounds like an interesting idea. I think I really would like to
run my own business," Pete responded.

"Our business?" questioned Jan.

"Yeah, you're right. I'm sorry. But. . . ."

"But, what?"

"Oh, nothing," Pete shrugged.

"Come on, what's wrong?"

"It's the financial part. I don't want to talk about it."

Jan was not worried about the money. What she read—through
what Pete was saying—bothered her more. Did he really feel so ashamed of

his social and economic background? Why had he said, "My business?" Did he really feel that way?

Undoubtedly much if not all of our communication is self-revealing. Whenever we communicate with others we consciously or unconsciously reveal things about ourselves which others are capable of perceiving. Communication may become more self-disclosing, however, when we enter into transactions with the conscious intent of disclosing. Conscious attempts at nondisclosure or at concealment more often accompany role-based interaction. But are conscious and unconscious self-disclosures "the same kind of beast?" We suggest that they probably are not. When we recognize that another person is consciously trying to disclose to us, we may take that as a sign of true sincerity and develop greater affinity for that person. Or we may suspect the motives or the honesty of the person and reject the message as not "true" disclosure. If we receive what we perceive to be an unconsciously sent self-disclosive message, on the other hand, we are probably more likely to believe it, but it may not have as strong an impact on our affinity for the other person.

Honesty of Disclosure

"Well, I don't have a lot of money either, but I think we could scrape up enough to get us started." Jan said.

From his point of view, Pete knew her family had money, but he didn't want to use her's to start their music shop.

"Oh, I could get the money. I know enough people in town. I'm just not sure the investment would pay off."

Jan was sure that he knew he couldn't come up with the amount of money needed.

Self-disclosure may be more or less honest and open in nature. To the extent that we are direct and open about ourselves, then the transaction becomes more self-disclosive. This is not always simply a matter of conscious choice on our part. Sometimes it is difficult to be honest with ourselves and others even though we are attempting to be. At other times we may lie more deliberately. We have probably all had the experience of someone asking us, "What's the matter?" Instead of really revealing our feelings we say, "Nothing," or make up some other problem such as a headache.

Accuracy of Disclosure

"Well, I really know a lot about music and what we need to stock in the shop. Also, I'm really good at budgeting. I really had to learn that to make it through school. We could make it pay," Jan argued.

Pete was not so sure if she really did know music that well and he was positive that she had never had to worry about budgeting her money.

"Look, I'm sure you think you really know how to budget, but you had at least a couple of hundred dollars spending money every month, plus your Dad's credit cards."

"But. . . ."

"Wait! I'm the one who really knows about business. I'm really good at accounting and marketing was one of my best course areas," Pete disclosed.

"I still think I'm good at that sort of thing, but you may be better. I could certainly help out on the music side, though."

Closely related to the idea of honesty of disclosure is the idea of accuracy. In order for disclosures to be accurate, we must know ourselves to some extent. However, it is often through the process of transaction that we come to know ourselves as others act and react with us. The accuracy of our disclosures also is determined to some extent by the precision of our perceptions. However, conceptions of self and others are often subjective, and accuracy of perception assumes that our perceptions can be objectively checked against some standard. In transaction, objectivity of perceptions is often checked by comparing them to the subjective perceptions of others for consensus.

Depth of Disclosure

"I'm not trying to hurt you. I love you! I love your body. That's the problem! I'd want to be in the back of the shop making-out all the time," Pete said in a low voice as he moved toward her.

"Not now Pete! You stay away until we finish discussing this."

"I thought we had finished."

"Please, Pete! Listen to me. I really need to try this. I don't have much confidence in myself. Sometimes I think I'm weak and don't really have what it *takes. I'm afraid I might sometime just get married to find someone to take care of me. I've been taken care of most of my life."*

"Don't you love me?" Pete worried.

"Oh, Silly, you know I do. Very much! I just have to try to prove something to myself."

"You don't need to prove anything to me."

Although self-disclosure may be consciously intended, honest, and accurate, it may at the same time lack depth or intimacy. To the extent that the information is less available, more private and confidential, or more intimate, then the transaction is more self-disclosive. The depth of self-disclosure is often related to the topics we are talking about. For example, some research suggests that attitudes and opinions about such things as religious views, government, racial integration, drinking, sexual morality, and standards of beauty are not terribly intimate. Personal disclosures about tastes and interests, work or studies, money and finances, our personality, and our bodies become increasingly more self-disclosive. More in-depth self-disclosures may relate to aspects of our own personality, personal dislikes, uncontrollable feelings, means of sexual gratification, guilts, revelation of sexual partners, feelings about our own bodies, physical measurements, sexual adequacy, health concerns, and numerous other possibilities. The point is that the more depth or intimacy there is, the more self-disclosure is occurring in the transaction.

Amount of Disclosure

"I guess I could learn to control my urges," Pete confessed.

"Only at the store, okay? We both have the same urges."

In a similar sense, the frequency with which we make personal revelations directly relates to self-disclosive transactions. Although the disclosure may be highly intimate, honest, etc., we may choose to disclose only one brief item of information at infrequent intervals. The more items of disclosive information we exchange, the more self-disclosure normally occurs in the transaction. But sometimes very little discloses a great deal. Closely related to frequency of disclosure is the duration or amount of time that we spend in the process; however, it is possible to spend a longer period of time on fewer items of information. It is also possible to disclose for long durations with little intimacy, honesty, or accuracy. Given those characteristics, however, the greater the duration, the greater the self-disclosure. Note how much of this conversation has been disclosive.

Positive or Negative Nature of the Disclosure

> "I'll call Dad about the money then?"
>
> "I don't have any money to put in," he said. "I just couldn't do it this way. I would never feel right about it."
>
> "We'll get him to loan it to both of us on a legal note and we'll pay him back. Come on, let's do it!"

Self-disclosure may also be positive or negative; that is, we may reveal good things or bad things about ourselves. Obviously, it is often easier to self-disclose if we limit those disclosures to things we feel are good or desirable about ourselves. For some people, however, the opposite is true. They can only see bad things and overlook the good within them. Some have suggested that self-disclosure must have some balance among these two extremes. The effects of disclosure can be profoundly different depending upon its positive or negative nature.

> "O.K. We'll give it a try," he replied. "I know I'm good enough to make it work."
>
> "I know I can do my part."

Relevance of Disclosure

> "But I can't cook. You've grown up to like those weird foods," she said.
>
> "Don't worry, I can! Come here."
>
> "We'll do it then?"
>
> "Yes, come here."
>
> "No, you come here! Now.".
>
> (Silence)

Sometimes transactions involve exchanges about ideas or events that weren't involved in the original transaction. Any topic of conversation may be included. When our self-disclosure is about ourselves in relation to that topic, then it is relevant self-disclosure. If we are talking about each other, then all self-disclosures are relevant to some topic of conversation. However, if we are talking about *war,* then only those self-disclosures about war are relevant. Self-disclosures about sexual partners may not be relevant. In brief, we can converse about a number of things and in the process self disclose items of information that are relevant or irrelevant to those topics. When we reveal positive things about ourselves on the topic, we may be perceived as more credible. Irrelevant disclosure may serve other purposes as it did above.

Summary

To summarize, we suggest that self-disclosure is not an either–or proposition. There are varying degrees of self-disclosure. The degree of self-disclosure is often dependent upon varying degrees of conscious intent, honesty, accuracy, depth, amount, positiveness or negativeness, and relevance. Human communication transactions, in turn, are somewhat dependent upon the degree of self-disclosure involved in the exchange.

**BLACK BOX
35**

Can you list and explain each dimension of self-disclosure?

Can you recall an example of each dimension from your own personal experience?

Patterns of Self-Disclosure

Although establishing causal links between self-disclosure and anything else is difficult at best, social and cultural relationships appear to provide one significant connection. These relationships, frequently expressed as roles, seem to have a major influence on our disclosure patterns. The prominence of some role behaviors may preclude self-disclosive transaction, but other roles—mother, spouse, counselor—may initially facilitate self-disclosive exchanges. In other words, it may be easier to begin self-disclosure in some socially defined relationships than in others. Let us examine some disclosure patterns that seem to be affected by these relationships.

Family Patterns

Some research has shown that family interaction patterns, methods of child-rearing, and social relationships affect self-disclosure patterns. Apparently these factors are important in determining both the amount of disclosure and the person(s) to whom one discloses. These tendencies probably affected Pete in our illustration. For example, firstborns and only children are lower self-disclosers than later-born children. Also, disclosure to parents is usually higher when they are perceived as close, warm, friendly, and accepting. When parents are rated low on such characteristics, children are more likely to be willing to disclose to strangers, acquaintances, and good friends. Generally, the more liked parents are, the more disclosures are made to them. Young unmarried individuals self-disclose most with mother and less with father and friends of both sexes. This is probably due

Family relationships often are a major influence on adult disclosure patterns.

to early established interaction patterns with mother. Some data indicate that middle-class mothers verbalize more and respond to more of a child's vocalizations than lower-class mothers. This suggests that reinforced patterns of early behavior may carry over into adulthood. Why do you think these patterns exist?

Marriage Patterns

Closely related are disclosure patterns among married persons and persons living in "marriage-like" situations. Married persons usually disclose less to mother, father, and friends of the same sex than do their unmarried counterparts. Instead, married persons usually reveal more to their spouse than any other person. Apparently, marriage relationships *assume* and perhaps *fulfill* much of the individual's disclosure needs. This tendency may not be as desirable as it appears, especially when we examine the typical nature of disclosure between spouses.

Transactions in marriage, as in other social systems, are based to a large extent upon our perceptions. Wives generally perceive husbands as disinterested, relatively unresponsive, and unconcerned about the wife's interests. They also see their husbands as disciplinary, argumentative, controlling, competitive, cautious, worried about them, having little confidence in them, expecting a lot of them, impatient, inhibiting them, and embarrassing them. Husbands on the other hand generally perceive themselves as understanding, trusting, honest, kind, reassuring, and acting in their wives' interests. They also express having attraction, liking, and patience for their wives, while at the same time agreeing, caring, giving in to, and reassuring them. These discrepancies in perceptions probably confirm the idea that culturally defined roles tend to inhibit affection, tenderness, and intimacy in self-disclosure and other acts. Perhaps as a result of these roles, wives tend to be higher disclosers of personal feelings and husbands tend to be lower disclosers, even in relatively "healthy" marriages. Wives disclose more personal feelings, personal anxieties, and respond more openly to violations of expectancies than husbands. Jan and Pete's disclosure patterns are likely to become more discrepant from each other in the future.

On the other side of the disclosure issue, highly satisfied couples tend to disclose more, discuss more marital topics more freely, and to agree more on evaluations of *self*. A moderate level of reciprocal self-disclosure of feelings appears to be directly related to marital satisfaction. Great discrepancies in self-disclosure between husband and wife are often indica-

219

tive of dissatisfaction and unhappiness. The areas of self-disclosure that appear to be the most closely related to marital satisfaction are disclosures about "shared activity," "children," and "careers." Pete and Jan were on the right track by disclosing about shared activities and careers. This made their disclosure more effective in producing satisfaction. Disclosures related to the kind of activities that they wish to engage in together, beliefs and approaches to child rearing, and future plans related to personal goals appear to facilitate marital satisfaction and growth. Self-disclosure on all topics may not be desirable. Excessive negative disclosures, especially about past acts or things that cannot be changed, may indeed be detrimental.

Sexual Patterns of Disclosure

In our society, women are higher disclosers than men. While not all studies have found women to be significantly higher disclosers, none have found men to be higher. Women sometimes self-disclose a greater amount, of greater duration, and more intimate items of information. Furthermore, they are less guarded and more honest in their revelation of negative information and feelings. Research results are not always consistent in this area, and there is some reason to believe that these sex differences in disclosure may be related to social-economic-educational levels as well as geographic region. For example, some elite or prestige universities show no difference in amount of disclosure between sexes. Also American females generally disclose more than English females. If and when there are differences, however, research has consistently found women, not men, to be the higher disclosers. Do you have some ideas about why this is the usual pattern?

Racial and Ethnic Patterns of Disclosure

Some research has examined disclosure patterns within and between differing racial and ethnic groups. For example, some studies indicate higher disclosure among Jewish males than Baptists, Methodists, and Catholics but few differences between religious "liberals" and "conservatives." Other studies indicate that whites disclose more than blacks, and blacks disclose more than Mexican-Americans. As we might expect, however, these tendencies may be more a result of social-economic class than of racial-ethnic origin. Studies of lower economic levels generally fail to find such racial-ethnic differences in disclosure; however, disclosure does appear to increase somewhat with higher social and economic levels. Maybe these kinds of differences affected Jan and Pete's disclosure differences. Few studies have examined disclosure across cultures of differing racial and ethnic makeups. However, some differences have been observed. Americans generally appear to disclose as much or more than most of the other cultures-societies that have been used for comparison. What do you think causes these typical differences in disclosure patterns?

Age and Self-Disclosure

Age appears to be a fairly clear indicator of self-disclosure patterns. Generally, as people get older they disclose less to parents and friends of the same sex. Self-disclosure to spouse, friends of the opposite sex, and selected other target-persons increases from about age seventeen up to around fifty and then begins to drop off rather rapidly. Jourard, who has done much of the research on disclosure patterns, suggests that older persons may be attempting to disengage themselves from others as they begin to approach old age and eventual death. What reasons do you suggest?

**BLACK BOX
36**

Can you describe and discuss patterns of self-disclosure that are typical of the following relationships?
the family
marriage
sexual roles

Describe and discuss patterns of self-disclosure as they relate to:
racial background
ethnic background
age

Can you identify any other self-disclosure patterns?

Can you explain why these self-disclosure patterns exist?

Other Self-Disclosure Patterns

Although most of our interactions with others seldom involve high levels of self-disclosure, our transactions do involve at least some modest levels of this communication. During some transactions, high levels of disclosure are likely to occur. High self-disclosure is more likely to occur in dyads, such as Pete and Jan's, than in other social systems involving more individuals. When the relationship between two persons is socially as well as psychologically supportive and reinforcing, higher levels of self-disclosure are facilitated. Disclosure in this setting begets disclosure; that is, Person A facilitates disclosure from Person B by disclosing her or himself. As a consequence, the amount and intimacy of disclosure by both are usually quite similar. Most often, self-disclosure increases gradually in depth, amount, duration, honesty, and relevance over a period of time. However, we will often disclose quite completely with strangers in a bar or on a train when we expect never to see them again. In this situation, trust is unnecessary. Disclosure patterns, therefore, appear to vary substantially depending upon who the target person is. What other reasons might change disclosure patterns?

Assumptions, Benefits, and Risks
of Self-Disclosure

Probably the greatest claimed benefit of self-disclosure is increased understanding of others and self. If we do indeed self-disclose to others, they can know us in a more in-depth way. But the assumption that self-disclosure to others is necessary for self-understanding may not be true for all people. Certainly, many individuals must actually verbalize their feelings about themselves in order to come to grips with those feelings and begin to understand them. However, other individuals are capable of disclosing directly to themselves at an intrapersonal level. The understanding of self for them may be more related to comparing their intrapersonal disclosures to their knowledge of others.

Another widely claimed benefit of self-disclosure is personal growth or self-actualization. Certainly, self-disclosure may have the potential for increasing personal growth. However, research in this area has not established relationships between disclosure and growth. Simply because a person discloses does not mean that she or he will grow personally. It may be that some level of personal growth is indeed prerequisite to self-disclosure. Also, personal growth would depend heavily upon the nature of the disclosure occurring and the kind of response made by the other person involved. For example, self-disclosure of highly negative aspects about one's self which are reinforced and agreed with by the other person may have detrimental effects on an individual.

Finally, advocates of self-disclosure suggest that we have an innate need to self-disclose, even though such self-disclosure may not necessarily help individuals adapt to their society and cultural roles. However, the psychological need to self-disclose appears to vary with individuals and classes of individuals as our discussion of disclosure patterns would indicate. Disclosure needs appear to some extent to be learned in the context of the social roles which we portray.

A better way of viewing disclosure may be from the conditions that appear necessary for it to occur. Some of these are: (1) a willingness to self-disclose; (2) trust in the other person; (3) willingness to accept responsibility for what is disclosed; (4) a social relationship involving support and reinforcement; (5) sufficient self-confidence and composure among participants; (6) some confidence in the competence or intelligence of the other participant; and (7) the discovery of a person with whom these relationships can be established. To the extent that these conditions are met, then disclosure of useful and perhaps carefully selected items of information should help an individual to adapt to society and culture. If not, then the disclosure process should help to enable individuals to change or to make changes in their social relationships or in social systems that would allow them to fulfill their own needs. Adaptation involves both the changes which allow an individual to fit into existing roles and the changing of roles and social systems themselves.

**BLACK BOX
37**

There are undoubtedly risks and benefits with self-disclosure.

Can you list and explain some that you see?

Can you identify the typical conditions for self-disclosure?

SUGGESTED FURTHER READINGS

1. Cozby, P. "Self-Disclosure: A Literature Review." *Psychological Bulletin* 79 (1973): 73–91.

   This summary and critique of self-disclosure literature is very complete and up to date as of 1973. Also, the article categorizes the research into easily comprehended sections and lists related research for further study. Cozby's summary is one of the best available.

2. Cozby, P. "Self-Disclosure, Reciprocity, and Liking." *Sociometry* 35 (1972): 151–160.

   Cozby discusses the results of research related to two important issues in self-disclosure research. Again, this article provides more in-depth treatment and is a good introduction to reading research in this area.

3. Jourard, S. M. *The Transparent Self* (New York: Van Nostrand Reinhold, 1971).

   Jourard presents an interesting and popular discussion of self-disclosure in this readable book. Although some claims might be challenged, the book is generally good at providing the psychologist's perspective.

4. Pearce, W. and Sharp, S. "Self-Disclosing Communication." *The Journal of Communication* 23:4 (1973): 409–425.

   This summary is rather unique in orientation. It focuses upon self-disclosure within a transactional perspective. The relevant literature is synthesized under five statements which characterize self-disclosing communication.

5. Taylor, D. A., Altman, I., and Sorrentino, R. "Interpersonal Exchange as a Function of Reward and Costs and Situational Factors: Expectancy, Confirmation-Disconfirmation." *Journal of Experimental Social Psychology* 5 (1969): 324–339.

   This article examines social exchange and related areas of self-disclosure from the perspective of social penetration theory. As such, it provides in-depth supplementary reading for those interested in both social penetration and self-disclosure.

SELECTED REFERENCES

ALTMAN, I. and TAYLOR, D. A. *Social Penetration: The Development of Interpersonal Relationships* (New York: Holt, Rinehart and Winston, 1973).

BLOCK, E. and GOODSTEIN, L. "Comment on Influence of an Interviewer's Disclosure on the Self-Disclosing Behavior of Interviewees." *Journal of Counseling Psychology* 18 (1971): 595–597.

CERTNER, B. C. "Exchange of Self-Disclosures in Same-Sexed Groups of Strangers." *Journal of Consulting and Clinical Psychology* 40 (1973): 292–297.

————. "The Exchange of Self-Disclosures in Same-Sexed and Heterosexual Groups of Strangers." Dissertation Abstracts International 31 (9A) (1971): 4885.

CHITTICK, E. V. and HIMELSTEIN, P. "The Manipulation of Self-Disclosure." *The Journal of Psychology* 65 (1967), 117–121.

COLSON, W. N. "Self-Disclosure as Function of Social Approval." Unpublished M. A. thesis, Howard University, 1968.

COZBY, P. "Self-Disclosure: A Literature Review." *Psychological Bulletin* 79 (1973): 73–91.

————. "Self-Disclosure, Reciprocity, and Liking." *Sociometry* 35 (1972): 151–160.

CULBERT, S. A. *The Interpersonal Process of Self-Disclosure: It Takes Two to See One* (New York: Renaissance Editions, 1968).

DeLEON, P. H. "Concomitants of Self-Disclosing Behavior." *Dissertation Abstracts International* 30 (11B) (1970): 5235.

DIES, R. R. "Group Therapist Self-Disclosure: An Evaluation by Clients." *Journal of Counseling Psychology* 20 (1973) 4: 344–348.

DIMOND, R. E. and HELLKAMP, D. T. "Race, Sex, Ordinal Position of Birth and Self-Disclosure in High School Students." *Psychological Reports* 23: 1–4.

DIMOND, R. E. and MUNZ, D. C. "Ordinal Position of Birth and Self-Disclosure in High School Students." *Psychological Reports* 21 (1967): 829–883.

EGAN, G. *Encounter: Group Processes for Interpersonal Growth* (Belmont, California: Wadsworth, 1970).

————. *Face to Face: The Small Group Experience and Interpersonal Growth* (Monterey, California: Brooks/Cole Publishing, 1973).

FITZGERALD, M. P. "Self-Disclosure and Expressed Self-Esteem, Social Distance and Areas of the Self Revealed." *Journal of Psychology* 56 (1963): 405–412.

FRITCHEY, K. H. "The Effects of Anxiety and Threat on Self-Disclosure." *Dissertation Abstracts International* 31 (1971): 4336.

GOFFMAN, E. *The Presentation of Self in Everyday Life* (Garden City L.I.: Doubleday, Anchor Books, 1959).

GREEN, R. A. and MURRAY, E. J. "Investigation to Aggression as a Function of Self-Disclosure and Threat to Self-Esteem." *Journal of Consulting and Clinical Psychology* 40 (1973): 440–443.

HAASE, R. and TEPPER, D. "Non-Verbal Components of Empathic Communication." *Journal of Counseling Psychology* 19 (1972): 417–424.

HALVERSON, C. and SHORE, R. "Self-Disclosure and Interpersonal Functioning." *Journal of Counseling and Clinical Psychology* 33 (1969): 213–217.

HAMILTON, P. R. "The Effects of Risk-Proneness on Small Group Interaction, Communication Apprehension and Self-Disclosure." M. A. thesis, Illinois State University, 1972.

HIGBEE, K. L. "Group Influence on Self-Disclosure." *Psychological Reports* 32 (1973): 903–909.

HIMELSTEIN, P. and KIMBROUGH, W., JR. "A Study of Self-Disclosure in the Classroom." *Journal of Psychology* 55 (1963): 437–440.

HORROCKS, J. and JACKSON, D. *Self and Role: A Theory of Self Process and Role Behavior* (Boston: Houghton Mifflin, 1972).

HURLEY and HURLEY. "Toward Authenticity in Measuring Self-Disclosure." *Journal of Counseling Psychology* 16 (1969): 271–274.

JOHANNESEN, R. L. "The Emerging Concept of Communication as Dialogue." *The Quarterly Journal of Speech* 57 (1971): 373.

JOHNSON, D. and NOONAN, M. "Effects of Acceptance and Reciprocation of Self-Disclosures on the Development of Trust." *Journal of Counseling Psychology* 19 (5) (1972): 411–416.

JONES, L. K. "Relationship Between Self-Disclosure and Positive Mental Health Modeled Self-Disclosure and Socioeconomic Status." *Dissertation Abstracts International,* 32 (5A) (1972): 4953–4954.

JOURARD, S. M. *Disclosing Man to Himself* (New York: Van Nostrand Reinhold, 1968).

————. *Self-Disclosure: An Experimental Analysis of the Transparent Self* (New York: Wiley-Interscience, 1971).

————. *The Transparent Self* (New York: Van Nostrand Reinhold, 1971), 456.

JOURARD, S. M. and LASAKOW, P. "Some Factors in Self-Disclosure." *Journal of Abnormal and Social Psychology* 56 (1958): 91–98.

LAING, R. D. *Self and Others* (New York: Random House, 1969).

LAWLESS, W. and NOWICKI, S. "Role of Self-Disclosure on Interpersonal Attraction." *Journal of Consulting and Clinical Psychology* 38 (1972): 300.

LEVINGER, G. and SENN, D. J. "Disclosure of Feelings in Marriage." *Merrill-Palmer Quarterly* 13 (1967): 237–249.

McCROSKEY, J. C., LARSON, C. E., and KNAPP, M. L. *An Introduction to Interpersonal Communication* (Englewood Cliffs, N. J.: Prentice-Hall, 1971).

MASLOW, A. *Toward a Psychology of Being* (New York: Van Nostrand Reinhold, 1962).

MAY, O. P. and THOMPSON, C. L. "Perceived Levels of Self-Disclosure, Mental Health and Helpfulness of Group Leaders." *Journal of Counseling Psychology* 20 (1973): 349–352.

MAYER, J. E. "Disclosing Marital Problems." *Social Casework* 48 (1967): 342–351.

MURPHY, N. C. and STRONG, S. R. "Some Effects of Similarity Self-Disclosure." *Journal of Counseling Psychology* 19 (1972): 121–124.

NEWCOMB, T. M. *The Acquaintance Process* (New York: Holt, Rinehart and Winston, 1961).

NOPFSTEIN, J. H. and NOPFSTEIN, D. "Correlates of Self-Disclosure in College Students." *Journal of Consulting and Clinical Psychology* 41 (1973): 163.

OFFENSTEIN, R. E. "Self-Actualization: A Construct Validation." *Dissertation Abstract International* 33 (5B) (1972): 2379.

PALMORE, E. and LUIKART, C. "Health and Social Factors Related to Life Satisfaction." *Journal of Health and Social Behavior* 13 (1972): 68–80.

PANYARD, C. M. "Self-Disclosure Between Friends: A Validity Study." *Journal of Counseling Psychology* 20 (1973): 66–68.

PEARCE, W. and SHARP, S. "Self-Disclosing Communication." *The Journal of Communication* 23:4 (1973): 409–425.

PEARCE, W. B., WRIGHT, P. H., SHAPP, S. M., and SLAMA, K. M. "Affection and Reciprocity in Self-Disclosing Communication." *Human Communication Research* 1 (1974): 5–14.

PEARSON, P. H. "A Rational Analysis of Roger's Concept of Openness to Experience." *Journal of Personality* 40 (1972) 3: 349–365.

———. "Openness to Experience As Related to Organismic Valuing." *Journal of Personality* 37 (1969) 3: 481–496.

PEDERSEN, D. M. and HIGBEE, K. L. "Personality Correlates of Self-Disclosure." *Journal of Social Psychology* 78 (1969): 81–89.

———. "Self-Disclosure and the Relationship to the Target Person." *Merrill-Palmer Quarterly of Behavioral Development,* 15(2) (1969): 213–220.

PETERSON, D. J. "The Relationship Between Self-Disclosure and Self-Concept of Under-Achieving College Students in Group Counseling." *Dissertation Abstracts International* 33 (5B) (1972): 2354.

POLANSKY, N. A. "On Duplicity in the Interview." *American Journal of Orthopsychiatry* 37 (1967): 568–580.

———. "The Concept of Verbal Accessibility." *Smith College Studies in Social Work* 36 (1965): 1–4.

POLANSKY, N. A. and BROWN, S. "Verbal Accessibility and Fusion Fantasy in a Mountain County." *American Journal of Orthopsychiatry* 37 (1967): 651.

RICKERS-OVSIANKINA, M. A. "Social Accessibility in Three Age Groups." *Psychological Reports* 2 (1956): 283–294.

RICKERS-OVSIANKINA, M. A. and KUSMIN, A. A. "Individual Differences in Social Assessibility." *Psychological Reports* 4 (1958): 391–406.

ROTTER, J. B. "A New Scale for Measurement of Interpersonal Trust." *Journal of Personality* 35(4) (1967): 651–665.

SAVICKI, V. "Outcomes of Non-Reciprocal Self-Disclosure Strategies." *Journal of Personality and Social Psychology* 23 (1972): 271–276.

SERMAT, V. and SMYTH, M. "Content Analysis of Verbal Communication in the Development of a Relationship: Conditions Influencing Self-Disclosure." *Journal of Personality and Social Psychology* 26 (1973): 332–346.

SOUSA-POZA, J. F., ROHRBERG, R., and SHULMAN, E. "Field Dependence and Self-Disclosure." *Perceptual and Motor Skills* 36 (1973): 735–738.

STOTLAND, E., STANLEY, E., and SHAVER, K. *Empathy and Birth Order: Some Experimental Explorations* (Lincoln: University of Nebraska Press, 1971).

STRAUSS, A. *Mirrors and Masks: The Search for Identity* (Glencoe: The Free Press, 1959).

TAYLOR, D. A., ALTMAN, I., and SORRENTINO, R. "Interpersonal Exchange as a Function of Reward and Costs and Situational Factors: Expectancy, Confirmation-Disconfirmation." *Journal of Experimental Social Psychology* 5 (1969): 324–339.

TRUAX, C. B., and WITTMER, J. "Self-Disclosure and Personality Adjustment." *Journal of Clinical Psychology* 27 (1971): 535–537.

VONDRACEK, F. W. "Behavioral Measurement of Self-Disclosure." *Psychological Reports* 25 (1969): 914.

VONDRACEK, F. W. and MARSHALL, M. J. "Self-Disclosure and Interpersonal Trust: An Exploratory Study." *Psychological Reports* 28 (1971): 235–240.

VONDRACEK, S. and VONDRACEK, F. W. "The Manipulation and Measurement of Self-Disclosure in Preadolescents." *Merrill-Palmer Quarterly of Behavioral Development* 17(1) (1971): 51–58.

VOSS, F. "The Relationships of Disclosure to Marital Satisfaction: An Exploratory Study." Master's Thesis, University of Wisconsin-Milwaukee, 1969.

WEIGEL, R. G., DINGES, N., DYER, R., and STRAUMFJORD, A. "Perceived Self-Disclosure, Mental Health and Who Is Liked in Group Treatment." *Journal of Counseling Psychology* 19 (1972): 47–52.

WHEELESS, L. R. and GROTZ, J. "Self-Disclosure and Trust: Conceptualization, Measurement, and Inter-Relationships." Paper presented at the International Communication Association Convention, Chicago, April, 1975.

WHEELESS, L. R. and WILIAMS, B. "Reciprocity, Amount of Disclosure, and Person Perception: Replication and Extension." Paper presented at the Western Speech Communication Association Convention, Seattle, November, 1975.

WILLINGHAM, M. E. "The Relationship Between Self-Concept, Self-Disclosure and Peer Selection." *Dissertation Abstracts International* 32(8A) (1971): 378–387.

WORTHY, M., GARY, A. L., and KAHN, G. M. "Self-Disclosure as an Exchange Process." *Journal of Personality and Social Psychology* 13 (1969): 59–63.

WUNDERLICH, R. A. "Personality Correlates of Obese Persons." *Psychological Reports* 27 (1973).

ZIEF, R. M. "Values and Self-Disclosure." Unpublished Honors Thesis, Howard University, 1962.

12

Developing Affinity

We have spent the previous eleven chapters trying to set forth and explain the many complex elements that have an impact upon human communication. By the time you get this far you should have a good handle on the human communication process and understand, at least at the abstract level, how communication works. From this point on we want to focus more attention on communication designed for specific outcomes. We will begin that task with the outcome that is central to all the rest—affinity.

In chapter 6 we included an extended discussion of the many and varied ways—thirteen to be exact—that one person can perceive another. We will not go over these in detail again here; reread chapter 6 if you don't have all of these clearly in mind. We will begin with a definition of affinity and move right on to how it can be developed.

Affinity is a positive attitude toward another person. Another person has affinity for you if that person perceives you as credible, attractive, similar to her or himself, or perceives that you have legitimate power over her or him. At the risk of oversimplification, another person has affinity for you if she or he likes you.

The Principle of Affinity

At the heart of being able to develop affinity with another person is understanding the principle of affinity. This principle is as follows: Generally, the more people believe that we like them, the more they are inclined to like us. Of course, there are exceptions—the fact that Attila the Hun likes us may not make us like him any better—but the principle holds over the vast majority of cases.

A quick look at our own behavior will give us a hint as to why this principle is usually correct. Here is a man with whom I am communicating. He obviously likes me and respects me. (Of course, he should, I'm a nice person!) "I think I like him, he sure had good taste." And then there is a girl. I sure would like to be friendly with her, but she ignores me and spends all of her time with George. "Well, George can have her, she isn't much anyway." Does your mind ever function like that? Well, if it doesn't you are unusual (or you are fibbing to yourself). That is the way most of us work. Thus, the best way to develop affinity with another person is to extend affinity to the other person. The motto, "The best way to make a friend is to be one," hits the nail right on the head.

But to "extend affinity" or "be a friend" as we are advising requires us to communicate. What do we specifically say or do? We will address that question directly, but before we do we need to understand how perceptions of people are formed so that we will know what goes on between our communication behavior and the other person's developing affinity for us, or failing to do so.

The Person Perception Process

Affinity is the direct result of how another person perceives us. People will like us or dislike us based on the way they see us. Generally, people form perceptions of other people in three ways: (1) they observe our *object properties* (remember from chapter 6 that people communicate as objects before they communicate as people?). The properties include such things as age, weight, length of hair, color of skin, facial features, type of clothing, body odor, etc. From these perceptions people draw initial estimates of our personality, our attitudes, and our disposition. (2) People also observe our *social behaviors*. These observations include such things as smiling, frowning, verbal statements, and angry outbursts. Based upon such observation they reinforce or change their perceptions of our personality, our attitudes, and our disposition. Finally, (3) the other people make a judgment, or a series of judgments, about us based on their perceptions of the way we are as an individual. This, then, is their impression of us, for good or ill.

This resulting impression may be individualized and based exclusively upon our special, unique characteristics. This is frequently the case among our close friends, parents, brothers and sisters, and our spouse. When the impressions are formed in this way, they are likely to be accurate. However, many times people do not take so much care in forming their impressions. In fact, it would be impossible for any person to go through such a careful impression formation process with every other person with whom she or he came in contact. You don't really know Walter Cronkite, each American Indian, or the president of your university well enough to form specific, unique impressions of them. But you do have impressions of them, right?

Since people must form impressions of others, even if they can't go to the trouble of doing so on the basis of individual, specific characteristics, they usually skip the final step in impression formation and make their judgment simply on the basis of object properties and a very limited sample of social behaviors. For example, we may come in contact with a person who speaks English with a Spanish accent and jump to an impression of that person based upon the personality characteristics that we ascribe to Mexican Americans. In fact, people carry around in their heads a large number of human categories with ready-formulated characteristics that they can put on people in a moment's notice. These ready-made "boxes" are what we call *stereotypes*. And forming impressions of people with little data about them as individuals is what we call *stereotyping*. If the characteristics the

---

**BLACK BOX
38**

Can you state and defend the principle of affinity?

Can you explain how stereotyping affects affinity?

---

people are carrying around are good for the box we are stereotyped in, they will have some affinity for us. If we get placed in a bad box, we are in trouble. The problem, of course, is not in the fact that stereotyping occurs, but in the fact that people have a notorious knack for stereotyping other people inaccurately. Our task, then, is to attempt to get the other person to focus on us as a unique individual. The way we do that is through our communication behavior.

Communication Behavior and Affinity Development

When we talk about developing affinity through our communication behavior, we are talking about manipulating our verbal and nonverbal messages to produce a predetermined reaction in another person. We are, in a very real sense, in the "public relations" business. That may bother you on moral grounds, so let's address that question head on. People can perceive you as worse than you are, as you are, or better than you are—in fact they can have any of these perceptions without your conscious manipulation of *anything*. Few people would question your morality if you manipulated your verbal and nonverbal behavior to get people to see you just as you really are, or worse than you really are, but some might question your intelligence in the latter case! Where the moral question comes in is when you try to get people to see you as better than you are. We are not going to provide an answer to that question; you will have to handle it for yourself. But we don't stay up nights worrying about the problem. Since so little of your communication behavior is under your full, conscious control, messages that let out truth are so natural that we think the probability of anyone severely distorting other people's perceptions of them over a sustained period of time is most unlikely. In any case, the communication behaviors that we will recommend below are intended to be used honestly in the development of warm, human relationships. If you choose to use them for some other purpose, please don't tell anyone you got the idea here!

Control Physical Appearance

Since people react first to us as an object, we have to begin with our nonverbal, object-communication. We should be aware of ourselves as an object, realistically aware. What are our good points? Can these be emphasized? What are our bad points? Can they be altered or concealed? We have to be concerned with the type of image we wish to portray. Should a man wear shoulder-length hair when he goes for an interview for a job with IBM? Should a woman wear a severely low-cut blouse or sweater when applying for a job as a mortuary receptionist? How often do you consider whether the latest styles are *really* what makes you look best? Have you ever met anyone who looks their best in faded jeans with patches on the seat?

We will not belabor the physical appearance issue. Suffice it to say that if you use good taste and good sense, your nonverbal object-communication will usually increase the probability of the other person developing more affinity for you.

Increase Positive Self-Disclosure

As we noted in the previous chapter, increased self-disclosure generally leads to increased liking. This is particularly true when the self-disclosure is limited to positive elements. When interacting with another person, then, you should try to find things about yourself that the other person doesn't know but have a high probability of being perceived favorably by that person. You find out that Mary likes farms. Ah ha! "Did you know that I grew up on a farm, Mary?" "Really?" "Yes. I lived on the farm until I came to college. I would like to go back someday if I can." You find out that Tom is a pacifist. "Did you know that no one in my family for seven generations has ever been in the Army?" "Really?" "Yeah. In fact the reason my great grandfather came to this country was to stay out of a war."

We should stress that prior to engaging in self-disclosure you should try to determine what self-disclosures would be well received. My self-disclosure to Tom above might cause me to be perceived as a "seventh-generation chicken" if Tom and his father were both graduates of West Point! Engage in more self-disclosure to increase your affinity, but do so selectively so that you don't do yourself more harm than good.

Stress Areas of Positive Similarity

In previous chapters we have stressed the principle of homophily, that people who are highly similar are more likely to communicate and to be more successful in communication. This principle applies very strongly to the development of affinity. Find out about the background of the other person, and call her or his attention to any similarities with your background. Probe to find out the other person's attitudes, and talk about the attitudes you share. Do the same with values: stress the values you hold in common. Often this will involve self-disclosure, so remember the point we made above: know the other person before you disclose too much about yourself. Otherwise you may bring out areas of strong dissimilarity and have a negative effect on affinity instead of the positive one you desire.

Provide Positive Reinforcement

Remember the principle of affinity. If you want to be reinforced with positive affinity, provide it to the other person. Reinforce other people's expressed attitudes and behaviors. If they say something with which you agree, let them know it. If they do something that you like let them know it. Such reinforcement may take the form of either verbal or nonverbal messages. "I agree." "That is a good point." "I think you are right. I hadn't thought about it that way." "Right on." All of these are obvious positive verbal reinforcers. But more subtle nonverbal messages may be even more reinforcing. A smile. A warm but gentle touch. Looking at the other person while they are talking. Not interrupting the other person. Speaking to them in a pleasant tone of voice. Standing or sitting next to them. Leaning toward them while listening to them. Being on time to meet with them. Taking extra care to look nice when you are going somewhere together. Providing them a comfortable place to sit when they come to talk to you. All of these nonverbal messages reinforce the other person and let them know that you care for them. Each enhances the probability that they will have more affinity for you as a result.

Express Cooperation

People who work well together generally develop increased affinity for one another. If we work on something together, we develop a common goal, and to the extent that the outcome of our work affects both of us we have a common fate. When we express a willingness to cooperate with another person we are indicating our regard for the other person, because we are giving up some of our own independence to that other person. Even if the product of our cooperative effort is not positive, we will still have shared a cooperative relationship, and this generally increases affinity. In fact, in many instances failure of a cooperative effort draws people even closer (to ward off the common enemy) than success.

Comply with the Other Person's Wishes

In many cases other people may want us to do something that we don't really care to do. They may want to stop for a pizza, and we don't like pizza. They may want to watch the program on Channel 9, but we would prefer the one on Channel 4. They may want us to dress in "good" clothes, but we would prefer to wear jeans. They may want to have dinner at 5:30, but we would rather have it at 8:00. Within limits, complying with other's wishes when they know we would prefer not to will show our concern and affection for them, and they are very likely to reciprocate with increased affinity for us. We stress the "within limits" qualification. If we overdo this, we are likely to be perceived as a door mat and affinity may decrease rather than increase. How can you love a door mat?

Fulfill the Other Person's Needs

Everyone has many needs that have to be fulfilled. Some of them are basic physical needs. Others are more psychologically based. To the extent that the other person sees you as one who helps meet his or her needs, that person will have increased affinity for you.

Except in very close, intimate relationships, we are usually not in a position to provide a major input to the satisfaction of other people's physical needs. We may provide food or shelter to a spouse or children, but this is not common behavior in which we can engage with other people. Of course, we can buy them a hamburger or a drink, but this will probably not have a major impact on our level of affinity.

There are three psychologically based needs, however, that provide an excellent opportunity for us to enhance our affinity with another person: the need for companionship, the need for affection, and the need for self-esteem. Let us consider each.

People need other people. They need to be around other people. While almost everyone wants to be left alone at times, few people would choose the hermit's life if they had the chance. People need the companionship of and communication with other people to be comfortable and know that their world is still all right. Consequently, just being available for

Accessibility to communication fulfills people's need for companionship and affection.

communication and companionship *when other people need it* tends to make them increase their affinity for us.   It is easy when we are busy or out of sorts to try to cut off communication with other people.   But if we are concerned about their affinity for us, we will take the time and effort to be around when we are needed.   They will like us more as a result.

People also need something more than mere companionship.   They need affection.   They need to know that someone else cares about them and is concerned about their welfare.   Again, remember the principle of affinity.   The more other people think we`like them, the more they are likely to like us.   This principle is tied very closely to need for affection.   If you want a man to have more affinity for you, express your affection for him (if you really have affection for him, of course).   Express it often and in as many ways, both verbally and nonverbally, as you know how.   Don't just tell the person you like or love him. Show him by considerate nonverbal behavior. In less intimate relationships, the nonverbal approach is often the only acceptable one. If Tom tells Buddy he loves him, Buddy may take off for the hills! But Tom can express his affection for Buddy with a pleasant smile, by defending Buddy in front of other people, by picking up the lunch check when he knows Buddy is a little short, and so forth. Expressions of affection beget affinity.

One of the strongest necessities people have is the need for self-esteem, the need to be able to think of one's self as worthwhile and important. Our self-esteem is almost completely a product of our interaction with other people. Unless we are psychologically out of kilter, we don't usually seek to communicate with people who make us feel inferior. We reject such people and try our best to keep away from their messages. Thus, if you want someone to develop affinity for you, let them know that you think she or he is worthwhile. Note her competence in doing a good job whenever you can. Compliment him on his appearance. Take notice of any worthy deed he or she performs, for you or anyone else. Remember, as you build the other person up in their own eyes, you are also building an affinity for yourself. If you tear the other person down, you are being torn down at the same time.

**BLACK BOX
39**

Can you identify the seven communication behaviors that are likely to lead to increased affinity?

Provide a positive example of each of these behaviors from your own communication with other people.

Can you provide an example from your own communication with other people where each of these behaviors was inappropriately employed?

The Problem of Ingratiation

We dare not close this chapter without confronting the problem of ingratiation. Ingratiation is simply engaging in any of the behaviors recommended in the previous section in such a way that the other person thinks we are doing so with some ulterior motive in mind. The classic example is the "yes-man" (or woman) in the business organization. This person acts like the boss can do no wrong. Generally, such a person is rejected by the other people in the organization, including the boss. Self-serving "yessing" does not increase affinity. Any of the behaviors we recommended above can be carried to an extreme and be perceived as ingratiation. To try too hard may be as bad as to not try at all. One way you can be reasonably sure you don't fall into the ingratiation trap is to never engage in any of the recommended behaviors unless you are sincere about it. In short, don't ever overlook an opportunity to be nice to a person when you want to increase their affinity for you, but don't ever force the opportunity either.

SUGGESTED FURTHER READINGS

1. Byrne, D. *The Attraction Paradigm* (New York: Academic Press, 1971).

   This book summarizes and critiques attraction research in several chapters. Byrne also discusses a number of issues related to attraction within a reasonable, conceptual framework.

2. Hastorf, A. H., Schneider, D. J., and Prolefka, J. *Person Perception* (Reading, Mass.: Addison-Wesley 1970).

   This short volume summarizes a great deal of the literature relevant to the process of person perception. The two chapters devoted to attribution and impression formation provide further depth in these two approaches.

3. Kiesler, C. A. and Kiesler, S. B. *Conformity* (Reading, Mass.: Addison-Wesley, 1969).

   An interesting corollary to person perception and attraction is explored in this brief book. The relationship of group pressure, cooperation, compliance, and other factors to affinity or liking are discussed in brief sections in the book.

4. McCroskey, J. C. and McCain, T. A. "The Measurement of Interpersonal Attraction." *Speech Monographs* 41 (1974): 261–266.

   In this article, the authors briefly survey some of the attraction research and report the development of a method of measuring interpersonal attraction. Components of physical attraction, social attraction, and task attraction are discussed.

SELECTED REFERENCES

ABRAHAMSON, M. *Interpersonal Accomodation* (Princeton, N.J.: D. Van Nostrand Co., 1966).

ARONSON, E. and MILLS, J. "The Effect of Severity of Initiation on Liking for a Group." *Journal of Abnormal and Social Psychology* 67 (1959): 31–36.

ARONSON, E. and WORCHEL, P. "Similarity Versus Liking as Determinants of Interpersonal Attractiveness." *Psychonomic Science* 5 (1966): 157–158.

BAVELUS, A., HASTORF, A. H., GROSS, A. E., and KITE, W. R. "Experiments on the Alteration of Group Structure." *Journal of Experimental Social Psychology* 1 (1965): 55–70.

BEIER, E. G., ROSSI, A. M., and GARFIELD, R. L. "Similarity Plus Dissimilarity of Personality: Basis for Friendship?" *Psychological Reports* 8 (1961): 3–8.

BERGER, E. M. "The Relation Between Expressed Acceptance of Self and Expressed Acceptance of Others." *Journal of Abnormal and Social Psychology* 47 (1952): 778–782.

BERKOWITZ, L., ed. *Advances in Experimental Social Psychology,* vol. 4 (New York: Academic Press, 1969).

BERSCHEID, E., BOYE, D., and DARLEY, J. M. "Effects of Forced Association Upon Voluntary Choice to Associate." *Journal of Personality and Social Psychology* 8 (1968): 13–19.

BERSCHEID, E. and WALSTER, E. *Interpersonal Attraction* (Reading, Mass.: Addison-Wesley, 1969).

BYRNE, D. "Attitudes and Attraction," in *Advances in Experimental Social Psychology,* vol. 4, L. Berkowitz, ed. (New York: Academic Press, 1969): 36–90.

————. "Interpersonal Attraction and Attitude Similarity." *Journal of Abnormal and Social Psychology* 62 (1961): 713–715.

————. *The Attraction Paradigm* (New York: Academic Press, 1971).

BYRNE, D. and CLORE, G. L., JR. "Predicting Interpersonal Attraction Toward Strangers Presented in Three Different Stimulus Modes." *Psychological Science* 4 (1966): 239–240.

BYRNE, D. and GRIFFIT, W. "A Developmental Investigation of the Law of Attraction." *Journal of Personality and Social Psychology* 4 (1966): 699–703.

————. "Interpersonal Attraction." *Annual Review of Psychology* 11 (1973): 317–336.

BYRNE, D. and NELSON, D. "Attraction as a Linear Function of Proportion of Positive Reinforcements." *Journal of Personality and Social Psychology* 1 (1965): 659–663.

CATTELL, R. B. and NESSELROADE, J. R. "Likeness and Completeness Theories Examined by 16 Personality Factor Measures on Stably and Unstably Married Couples." *Journal of Personality and Social Psychology* 4 (1966): 699–703.

Cozby, P. C. "Self-Disclosure: A Literature Review." *Psychological Bulletin* 79 (1973): 73–91.

Deutsch, M. "Some Factors Affecting Membership Motivation and Achievement Motivation." *Human Relations* 12 (1959): 81–95.

Deutsch, M. and Solomon, L. "Reactions to Evaluations by Others as Influenced by Self-Evaluation." *Sociometry* 22 (1959): 93–112.

Dittes, J. E. "Attractiveness of Group as Function of Self-Esteem and Acceptance by Group." *Journal of Abnormal and Social Psychology* 59 (1959): 77–82.

Festinger, L., Schachter, S., and Back, K. *Social Pressures in Informal Groups* (New York: Harper and Brothers, 1950).

Frandsen, K. D. and Rosenfeld, L. B. "Fundamental Interpersonal Relations' Orientations in Dyads: An Empirical Analysis of Schultz's FIRO-B as an Index of Compatibility." *Speech Monographs* 40 (1973): 113–122.

French, J. R. and Rowen, B. "The Basis of Social Powers," in *Group Dynamics,* D. Cartwright and A. Zander, ed. (New York: Harper & Row, 1968): 259–268.

Gerard, H. B. and Rabbie, J. M. "Fear and Social Comparison." *Journal of Abnormal and Social Psychology* 62 (1961): 586–592.

Hastorf, A. H., Schneider, D. J., and Prolefka, J. *Person Perception* (Reading, Mass.: Addison-Wesley, 1970).

Jones, E. E. *Ingratiation: A Social Psychological Analysis* (New York: Appleton-Century-Crofts, 1964).

Jones, E. E. and Gerard, H. B. *Foundations of Social Psychology* (New York: John Wiley, 1967).

Kiesler, C. A. and Kiesler, S. B. *Conformity* (Reading, Mass.: Addison-Wesley, 1969).

Lashbrook, V. and McCroskey, J. C. "Source Valence: An Improved Conceptualization." Paper presented at the annual meeting of the Western Speech Association, Honolulu, November, 1972.

McCroskey, J. C., Jensen, T., and Valencia, C. "Measurement of the Credibility of Peers and Spouses." Paper presented at the International Communication Association Convention, Montreal, Quebec, April, 1973.

McCroskey, J. C. and McCain, T. A. "The Measurement of Interpersonal Attraction." *Speech Monographs* 41 (1974): 261–266.

McCroskey, J. C., Scott, M., and Young, T. "Dimensions of Credibility for Peers and Spouses." Paper presented at the annual meeting of Western Speech Convention, Fresno, California, November, 1971.

Maslow, A. H. Motivation and Personality, 2nd ed. (New York: Harper & Row, 1954; copyright 1970 by Abraham H. Maslow).

———. *Toward a Psychology of Being* (New York: Van Nostrand Reinhold, 1968).

Newcomb, T. M. *The Acquaintance Process* (New York: Holt, Rinehart and Winston, 1961).

Pearce, W. B. and Sharp, S. M. "Self-Disclosing Communication." *Journal of Communication* 23 (1973): 409–425.

Priest, R. F. and Sawyer, J. "Proximity and Peership: Bases of Balance and Interpersonal Attraction." *The American Journal of Sociology* 72 (1967): 633–649.

Richmond, V. P., McCroskey, J. C., and Daly, J. A. "The Generalizability of a Measure of Perceived Homophily in Interpersonal Communication." Paper presented at the International Communication Association Convention, Chicago, April, 1975.

Rogers, E. M. and Bhowmik, D. K. "Homophily-Heterophily: Relational Concepts for Communication Research," in *Speech Communication Behavior,* L. L. Barker and R. J. Kibler, eds. (Englewood Cliffs, N.J.: Prentice-Hall, 1971): 206–225.

Rogers, E. M. and Shoemaker, F. F. *Communication of Innovations: A Cross-Cultural Approach* (New York: The Free Press, 1971).

Sarnoff, I. and Zimbardo, P. G. "Anxiety, Fear and Social Affiliation." *Journal of Abnormal and Social Psychology* 62 (1961): 356–363.

Schachter, S. "Deviation, Rejection and Communication." *Journal of Abnormal and Social Psychology* 46 (1951): 190–207.

————. *The Psychology of Affiliation* (Stanford, Cal.: Stanford University Press, 1959).

Schopler, J. "Social Power," in *Advances in Experimental Social Psychology,* vol. 2, L. Berkowitz, ed. (New York: Academic Press, 1970), 177–215.

Schutz, W. *FIRO: A Three Dimensional Theory of Interpersonal Behavior* (New York: Holt, Rinehart and Winston, 1960).

Secord, P. F. and Backman, C. W. *Social Psychology* (New York: McGraw-Hill, 1964).

Tagiuri, R. "Person Perception," in *The Handbook of Social Psychology,* vol. 3, G. Lindzey and E. Aronson, eds. (Reading, Mass.: Addison-Wesley, 1969).

Tagiuri, R. and Petrullo, L., eds. *Person Perception and Interpersonal Behavior* (Stanford, Cal.: Stanford University Press, 1958).

Warr, P. B. and Knapper, C. *The Perception of People and Events* (New York: John Wiley, 1968).

Wenzlaff, V. "Source Credibility: A Summary of Experimental Research." Paper presented at the Speech Communication Association Convention, San Francisco, December, 1971.

Wheeless, L. R. and Charles, R. "A Review and Reconceptualization of Stereotyping Behavior." Paper presented at the Speech Communication Association Convention, New York, November, 1973.

13

Resolving Interpersonal Conflict: Redeveloping Affinity

Now that you have survived twelve chapters of a book on communication, you are entitled to see how the "experts" communicate. We are fortunate. There is a faculty meeting going on now. Five people from the Communication Department are on a committee asked to decide on the nature of the basic course that the department will offer next fall. Let's listen in.

Margaret: *Well, the first thing we should probably decide is what textbook we are going to use. I'm sure tired of the one we've got.*

John: *Yeah. It is terrible. I don't know what we were*

thinking of when we selected it. I think we should consider Max Black's book.

Wayne: *I'm not very satisfied with the book either, but I think we should decide what it is we want to teach first, and then consider possible books to use. We all have to teach the same course, and I'm not sure we all want to do the same thing.*

Mike: *I agree, Wayne. What we teach is the big question.*

Chuck: *That's right, Wayne. We have to settle that issue first.*

Margaret: *You are probably right, Mike. I'll go along with that.*

Wayne: *I think our main goal should be to help the students to understand the human communication process.*

Chuck: *So far so good. But understanding is not enough. They also have to learn how to do it.*

Mike: *Do what?*

Chuck: *Communicate.*

Mike: *I suppose you mean give speeches, right?*

Chuck: *Naturally, giving speeches is communicating.*

Mike: *That's what I expected to hear.*

Chuck: *What do you mean by that?*

Mike: *Here we go again. All you can ever think of is how many speeches you are going to assign. When are you ever going to realize that speech making died with Daniel Webster?*

Chuck: *That's absurd. I suppose that all you want us to do is talk about interpersonal communication, whatever that is.*

Mike: *Sure, I think that's what we should be teaching. After all, over 90 percent of all of our communication is interpersonal. Since these students will probably only have one communication course in their lives, we should teach what they need most.*

Chuck: *That's a bunch of crap. Just because someone does something a lot, doesn't mean we have to teach them about it. People spend more time watching TV than they do talking to other people. Should we have our whole course on how to watch "All in the Family?"*

Margaret: *Might not be a bad idea at that. Why not?*

Mike: *Most people can already watch "All in the Family." But they can't relate well to other people interpersonally.*

Chuck: *Good Lord! Now I suppose you want us to spend all of our time on
"warm, human relationships." I'm not going to run any infernal encounter
groups in my class!*

John: *Maybe some "warm, human relationships" are just what we need around
here.*

Yes, even the experts have their problems in communicating.
Sometimes there is conflict. While our faculty group was formed as a
decision-making committee, the interaction we have just observed centered
on interpersonal conflict rather than the problem the group was supposed to
solve. Until they can get over that barrier, their real purpose for meeting will
continue to be frustrated. Mike and Chuck will get in the way of resolving
the goal, and will use up the time of everyone involved in the process.

The Nature of Conflict

In order to get a handle on some ways of dealing with interpersonal conflict
in communication, we must understand what conflict is. Conflict between
people can be viewed as the opposite or antihesis of affinity. In this sense,
interpersonal conflict is the breaking down of attraction and the development of repulsion, the dissolution of perceived homophily and the increased
perception of incompatible differences, the loss of perceptions of credibility
and the development of disrespect.

As we define them, conflict and disagreement are not the same
thing. Conflict is characterized by competition, hostility, suspicion, distrust,
and self-perpetuation. Differences of opinion on issues—disagreement—
can prompt conflict, but so can differences in orientations toward life, life-
styles, and personality. The resulting competition and hostility perpetuate
and enlarge the conflict. Not all conflict is bad or undesirable, but to some
extent, all conflict situations tend to be self-perpetuating. Competition and
hostility often lead to stopping attempts at communication. Mike and
Chuck, for example, were not attempting to communicate to resolve their
conflict, they were merely taking potshots at one another. This lack of
communication, in turn, is likely to increase distrust and suspicion, which
continue to feed the conflict. The racial animosities prominent in the 1960s
and the continuing "generation gap" are typical of this self-perpetuating
process on a large scale.

A Model of Interpersonal Relationships

So that you will be able to understand the different kinds of conflict situations that can develop in communication between people, we believe that we need to develop a clear conceptualization of the kinds of relationships people can have in interpersonal encounters. A model developed by Theodore Newcomb is particularly useful for this purpose. Please bear with us while we explain this model; then we will be able to return to our direct focus on conflict.

Newcomb's model is called the "A-B-X" model after the symbols he uses for the elements in the model. Figure 13–1 presents the basic elements of the model. In the figure, "A" represents one person, "B" represents a second person, and "X" represents something that they are communicating about, or are likely to communicate about. The arrows between the parts represent the four possible orientations that the people can have, their beliefs and attitudes toward each other and toward the "X." Any of these orientations can be positive, negative, or somewhere in between (recall our discussion of attitudes and beliefs in chapter 7).

The basic assumption underlying this model, one that has been demonstrated to be accurate in many research studies, is that people strive for balance and consistency in their interpersonal orientations. Our in-

Conflict is characterized by competition, hostility, distrust and self-perpetuation.

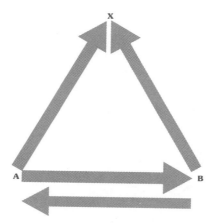

FIGURE 13–1. *Basic elements of interpersonal relationships.*

teraction behaviors, then, either disrupt, maintain, or restore this balance. The need to interact usually arises out of some perception of imbalance, and typically is an attempt to bring things back into balance. Any change in one orientation is likely to be accompanied by a change in another or others. In short, our orientations toward each other and toward the things we talk about are interdependent. Let us look at conflict within the context of this model.

Types of Conflict

To begin let us examine an interpersonal relationship in which there is *no conflict*. The relationship between Margaret and John in our faculty meeting appears to represent such a case. As we see in Figure 13–2, all of their orientations are positive. Both Margaret and John dislike their current textbook, but they show no signs of ill-feeling toward each other. When people hold the same orientations toward each other and the topic, even if their orientations toward the topic are negative, there is no imbalance and no conflict.

The behavior of Margaret and Wayne suggests at the outset there was *topic conflict* between them. Their relationship is represented in Figure 13–3. They disagreed on what the first problem to be resolved should be, the book or the course content. This represents an unbalanced interpersonal relationship, the kind that could lead to trouble. Both Margaret and

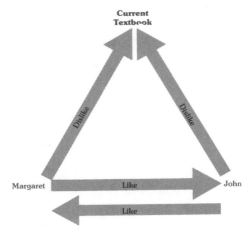

FIGURE 13-2. No-conflict relationship.

Wayne will feel a need to restore balance. This could be done either by changing orientations toward one another, in this case by taking on a negative attitude toward each other, or by one of them changing his or her orientation toward the topic. In this interaction, Margaret resolved the potentially serious conflict by simply going along with Wayne's idea. She changed her orientation toward the topic.

A third type of conflict is *interpersonal conflict.* This conflict is not clearly exemplified in our faculty discussion, so let us read some into it. You

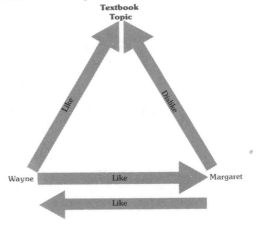

FIGURE 13-3. Topic conflict relationship.

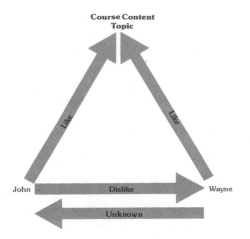

FIGURE 13-4. *Interpersonal conflict relationship.*

may have noticed that Wayne assumed a partial role as leader of the group by channeling the discussion in the direction he wanted it to go. John said almost nothing once Wayne started talking. While everyone else reacted to Wayne's leadership attempt, John remained silent until the end. His silence suggests a willingness to let the discussion go in the direction Wayne wanted, however. But we are going to read into that silence some animosity toward Wayne. This relationship is depicted in Figure 13-4. People can agree on a topic and have a negative attitude toward each other. But this interpersonal conflict creates an unbalanced state. As a result, unless this conflict is resolved, an individual is very likely to change her or his orientation toward the topic. This is, obviously, highly destructive behavior which may cause communication to fall apart.

Finally, we have the most severe type of conflict, *combined interpersonal and topic conflict.* The case of Mike and Chuck, illustrated in Figure 13-5, is a classic example of this type of conflict. They disagree on the topic and they don't like one another. While the two types of conflict above represent unbalanced relationships, and will likely lead to attempts to resolve the conflict (which would make things either better or worse), the conflict between Mike and Chuck represents a balanced relationship. Thus, this type of conflict is less likely to be resolved. Neither person is really motivated to try to resolve it. They both think something like, "I don't agree with him, but that's alright, he's a creep anyhow. I'd worry if I didn't disagree with a creep like him." In fact, any attempts to resolve the conflict tend to

251

push the relationship into an unbalanced state. While such attempts may result in overcoming both the topic and the interpersonal conflict, they may only intensify the problems. Shortly, we are going to look at ways that conflict can be resolved, but first let's go backward in the history of the relationship and see what could be done to avoid conflict in the first place. Early prevention is far better than late solution.

**BLACK BOX
40**

Can you recognize the characteristics of conflict?

Describe conflict using the model of interpersonal interaction.

Can you explain the types of conflict?

Prevention of Conflict

In a sense everything we said in the previous chapter could be restated here. Building affinity in the first place is the best step toward preventing conflict. Affinity and conflict are the antithesis of one another and cannot long endure side by side. There is, however, another step we can take. We can seek to develop a supportive climate for communication with other people.

Supportive climates have several characteristics that work to prevent conflict from arising, or if it arises, to make it easier to resolve. First, supportive climates focus on describing the situation, feelings, and behaviors being discussed, rather than evaluating them. In our faculty meeting, the climate was not supportive in this sense. The discussion jumped right off with evaluation. This was followed by even more intense evaluation. Description of the situation was completely overshadowed.

A second characteristic of a supportive climate is that it is oriented toward solving problems rather than controlling them. Mike and Chuck both seemed more interested in controlling what the other person would teach than in focusing on the real problem the group faced.

Supportive climates are also spontaneous in nature and do not involve formulation of manipulative strategies. What is said is what is meant,

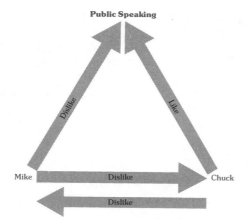

*FIGURE 13–5. Combined interpersonal and topic conflict
relationship.*

rather than used as a device for "conning" someone else. Such manipulation, of course, can often be successful. But over the extended life of a group, such attempts at manipulation, while initially successful, eventually breed an atmosphere of distrust that is fertile ground in which conflict can sprout.

Empathy between communicators is an important characteristic of a supportive climate. Empathy is a concern and feeling for the other person. There appeared to be little of this in our faculty meeting. A supportive climate is also characterized by an assumed equality among participants, not superiority in terms of status, power, or other characteristics. This is the only characteristic of a supportive climate that appeared to be present in our faculty meeting, but by itself it was not enough.

Finally, a supportive climate is characterized by suspended judgment rather than dogmatic certainty. People are willing to hold off making decisions until they have had a chance to consider all the available facts. Our faculty meeting was a classic case of the opposite; everyone seemed to want to make a decision first and look at the facts later.

Generally, we can say that a supportive climate is an open climate. People and ideas are presumed to be worthy, at least until proven otherwise. Such a climate avoids defensiveness, the prime instigator of conflict. To the extent that we can foster supportive climates, we can avoid conflict. To the extent that we can't, we must be concerned with the material in the following section.

> **BLACK BOX**
> **41**
>
> Can you recall relationship(s) from your own experience which have *all* the characteristics of a supportive climate?

The Resolution of Conflict

Before we address specific methods of conflict resolution, we need to make clear the kind of conflict with which we are concerned here. Our focus is on *interpersonal* conflict. Conflict related to the topic under discussion is best resolved by the processes discussed in chapters 18 and 19 that are concerned with decision making. However, rational decision making is often disrupted by interpersonal conflict, like in our faculty meeting, and must be resolved before rational decision making is possible.

The resolution of interpersonal conflict involves breaking down the vicious cycle of self-perpetuation that conflict generates. *We do not argue that all conflict should be resolved, or that conflict is never warranted. There are situations where conflict is appropriate.* However, when conflict is destructive and we want to resolve it, there are several means by which we may attempt to accomplish this. Let us consider these four alternatives.

Leaving the Field

One way to resolve conflict, at least superficially, is to "leave the field" to physically depart. We can "pack up and go home to Mother." We can quit our job. Mike and Chuck could walk out of the faculty meeting. In some cases, such behavior may be appropriate. Although this will not really resolve any conflict, at least it makes it no longer as relevant.

Another way to leave the field is to leave psychologically. This technique is sometimes called "the silent treatment." The dialogue might go something like this: Mike: "What's wrong with you, Chuck? Chuck: "Nuthin'." All the while Chuck is thinking, "I'm right and I know it. I don't want to talk about it." Chuck remains physically present while being psychologically absent. This approach does little to resolve the conflict, but it may help to avoid making it worse.

A third method of leaving the field is more constructive. This method involves changing the topic. Mike: "Well, I don't think we are going to resolve the types of student activities we will have right away, so let's focus on the topics we want to have them learn. I think source credibility is one." Chuck: "I agree. That, to me, is one of the important topics." Not only have Mike and Chuck avoided aggravating their conflict, but they have also begun to lay the groundwork for later resolution. They are likely to find that they aren't as far apart as they originally thought. Talking about areas of agreement goes a long way toward establishing the type of interpersonal relationship needed for people to talk about areas of disagreement without developing interpersonal conflict. When you find yourself in disagreement on a topic, and tension is building between you and another person, change the topic before the conflict becomes interpersonal, if at all possible. After a better interpersonal relationship has been built, you can return to the original topic and make another attempt at rational decision making.

Restoring Trust

When serious interpersonal conflict has developed, one way of breaking out of the self-perpetuating cycle is to deal with suspicion and distrust. The problem is to restore a sufficient amount of trust so that real communication can occur. Trust exists when someone feels free to make a risky decision, to self-disclose, to stick his or her neck out. When trust is present, we are willing to give a little, to take a chance that potentially could result in harm to us.

Trust is more likely to be present when people have had previous experiences of positive orientations toward each other's welfare. If husbands and wives, father and son, or student and teacher previously have acted positively toward each other, then the restoration of trust is more likely. Trust can be developed even when the people in conflict have not previously had a positive relationship; it is just more difficult to achieve.

If we can set up certain conditions, the restoration or establishment of trust can be facilitated. Trust may develop when each person has some guarantee or knows with some certainty what the other person will do before each makes an irreversible decision to trust the other. For example, in marriage problems, the promise or "solemn oath" to not repeat some behavior is often sought. Labor unions seek legal contracts before they return to work after a labor dispute. Trust may also develop when there is opportunity to communicate about mutual responsibilities and the means to be used to deal with violations of trust. Marriage counselors often focus upon these elements. Two people having conflict over a class project they are working on together may discuss such issues. The "father and son talk" (when the father does the talking about the son's behavior) frequently deals with mutual responsibilities and actions that will be taken if trust is violated.

In addition, we can facilitate trust if we have the power to influence the other peoples' choice to trust by rewarding their trustworthy decisions and punishing their untrustworthy ones. This technique is often used in child rearing. At times, mothers tell daughters their responsibility to return home from a date by a particular hour especially if their trust has been violated in the past. Actions that will be taken are also frequently noted. We have a similar ability, if we hold the right position, in complex business organizations or in the military.

Finally, we can facilitate trust through the use of a third party. A third person or agency can point out how losses to either party as a result of violations of trust are mutually detrimental to both people in the conflict. International disputes as well as personal marriage problems are often solved by the instigation of trust through a third party.

Reinstating Communication

A major problem in conflict resolution is reinstating communication between the two parties involved. This problem represents a seeming paradox, or at least a "two-edged sword." Some communication probably started the conflict in the first place—some verbal statement or nonverbal behavior was interpreted in a way as to increase hostility, competition, or distrust. On the other hand, lack of communication tends to perpetuate the conflict. The restoration of communication, therefore, is no guarantee that the conflict will be resolved. It may even be increased. There is some evidence to suggest that too much communication may often be detrimental to interpersonal relationships. For example, as we noted in chapter 11, disclosure patterns in marriage may focus on undesirable elements and high disclosure is often associated with disturbed (in conflict) marriages. Further, in negotiation, completely free communication may be used to convey information such as threats and insults which intensify hostilities rather than reduce them. Consequently, reinstatement of communication must be carefully planned and, to some extent, controlled.

To be useful in resolving conflict, communication must be limited and directed toward actions that are vital to reduction of the conflict.

*Labor union members
restore trust by
seeking a legal
contract after a labor
dispute.*

1. Communication should be directed toward restoring trust. Note the ways we have proposed that this might be accomplished. There is some evidence to suggest that reinstated communication in the absence of trust is not very useful.
2. Communication should focus on common goals. From our previous discussion of factors related to affinity and attraction we would expect common goals to have an effect.
3. Communication should focus on other areas of similarity and homophily such as common attitudes, beliefs, and values.
4. Communication should be as positive and reinforcing as possible. This is particularly true of self-disclosures in conflict situations. Care should be given to positive and reinforcing disclosures.
5. Expressions of cooperation and compliance in areas indirectly related to the dispute should be sought.
6. Past behaviors indicating positive orientations should be discussed.

Free ventilation and disclosure of feelings should not be the essential nature of the communication exchange. These can lead to greater conflict. Recitation of platitudes and principles is seldom helpful. In conflict situations we are seldom influenced by injunctions to "turn the other cheek," or that "it is better to give than receive." The conflict itself indicates that we

257

have abandoned these as working axioms in this particular situation. Likewise, communication which focuses upon the common enemy has only a temporary effect in resolving the conflict and merely transfers the conflict to others.

A now-classic study conducted under the direction of Muzafer Sherif experimented with some of these conflict variables in a secluded boy's camp. The experimenters created two groups in the camp that were in conflict with each other. They tested most of the above methods of resolving conflict and found the common goal approach to work most successfully. When the boys were brought together in the accomplishment of a superordinate goal (survival) the process of conflict resolution was begun. Their cooperation was necessary for achieving the goal which in turn built bonds not unlike the notion of "common fate" which we discussed previously. Through a number of these experiences, the experimenters were able to resolve the conflict between the two groups.

Compromise and Negotiation

Once some measure of trust has been restored and once communication has been reinstated and directed, then it's likely that conflict will still not be resolved except in minor problem situations. But the ground is prepared for compromise and negotiation. Compromise and negotiation assume sufficiently strong mutual interests are at stake. Some common goals must be established at the outset. Marriage partners in conflict frequently compromise by both "giving in a little" or both changing their behaviors because of underlying strong bonds between them and common goals such as child rearing.

In the negotiation setting communication should be directed toward discovering the ranges or latitudes of acceptable and unacceptable solutions to both parties involved. If there is an overlap of acceptable solutions (although not the most desired by either) then compromise in this area of overlap can produce resolution. This frequently occurs in labor-management disputes which are settled fairly quickly. When there is no overlap between each party's range of acceptable solutions further communication must ensue. The two parties must be influenced to expand their range of acceptable solutions so that there is an area of overlap in which compromise can be reached.

Communication in this setting functions in three ways: (1) Communication is used to discover what settlements one's self and the other person will likely accept. (2) Communication is used to influence or persuade one's self or the other person to modify his or her range of acceptable solutions. (3) Communication is used to provide one's self and the other person with rationalizations for acceptance of previously unacceptable positions or solutions.

In the compromise and negotiation setting there is usually mutual pressure for reaching agreement early in the exchange. Communication is usually less threatening and more cooperative at that point. As time goes on for extended periods, however, there is less tendency to agree. Communication may become more competitive and lose sight of common goals. Again, too much communication, especially free ventilation between conflicting parties, may be detrimental to compromise and the restoration of affinity. In the last analysis, some level of tolerance may always be needed.

**BLACK BOX
42**

Can you identify four ways of resolving conflict?

Can you explain how communication should be restored in order to help resolve conflict?

How does communication function in negotiation and compromise?

Summary

Throughout this chapter we have discussed the problems and methods of redeveloping affinity when conflict has arisen. When people have some interdependence upon each other in school, work, play, or marriage, some conflict is almost inevitable. We do not always agree although we are communicating our beliefs and feelings effectively; recall from chapter 1 the misconception of "communication breakdowns." However, perhaps you will now be better able to change the goals of your communication to the goals of resolving conflict and redeveloping affinity when desired. In the next chapter we will examine how likely another person is to expose him or herself to or listen to what you now have to say.

SUGGESTED FURTHER READINGS

1. Gibb, J. R. "Defensive Communication." *Journal of Communication* 2 (1961): 141–148.

   The related idea of defensive and supportive communication environments is discussed in this reading. Gibb's article is a classic, readable essay on this issue. As such, it is strongly recommended to your attention.

2. Jandt, F. E. *Conflict Resolution Through Communication* (New York: Harper & Row, 1973).

   This book of readings provides some interesting essays on conflict. A number of the articles relate conflict to specific, real world contexts. Some discussion of the role of communication in conflict resolution is included. While the book as a whole is generally compatible with the approach taken in this chapter, a number of other views are discussed.

3. Miller, G. R. and Simons, H. W., eds. *Perspectives on Communication in Social Conflict* (Englewood Cliffs, N.J.: Prentice-Hall, 1974).

   An excellent selection of readings are included in this book. The selections incorporated represent a wide variety of approches to social conflict. The relationship of communication to conflict is also discussed. Reading any of a number of the selections can provide useful supplement and expansion of the view of conflict presented in this chapter.

4. Nemeth, C. A. "A Critical Analysis of Research Utilizing the Prisoner's Dilemma Paradigm for the Study of Bargaining," in *Advances in Experimental Social Psychology,* vol. 6, L. Berkowitz, ed. (New York: Academic Press, 1972).

   Many of the studies which examine conflict use simulation and conflict games. This article provides an in-depth criticism of such studies by analyzing their use of the prisoner's dilemma game. Those interested in games and simulations as a means of study should find this reading beneficial and enlightening.

5. Newcomb, T. M. "An Approach to the Study of Communicative Acts." *Psychological Review* 60 (1953): 393–404.

   This essay provides the underlying concept of social interaction upon which this chapter developed the notion of conflict. However, Newcomb's approach has broader applications to human communication in terms of the development of affinity and general interaction.

SELECTED REFERENCES

Abrahamson, M. *Interpersonal Accommodation* (Princeton, N.J.: D. Van Nostrand Co., 1966).

APFELBAUM, E. "On Conflicts and Bargaining," in *Advances in Experimental Social Psychology,* vol. 7, L. Berkowitz, ed. (New York: Academic Press, 1974).

ARCHIBALD, K., ed. *Strategic Interaction and Conflict* (Los Angeles: University of California Press, 1966).

BARNLUND, D. C. *Interpersonal Communication: Survey and Studies* (Boston: Houghton Mifflin Co., 1968).

BERKOWITZ, L. "The Expression and Reduction of Hostility." *Psychological Bulletin* 55 (1958): 257–283.

BIXENSTINE, V. E., CHAMBER, N., POTASH, H., and WILSON, B. V. "Effects of Asymmetry in Payoff on Behavior in a Two-Person Non-Zero-Sum Game." *Journal of Conflict Resolution* 8 (2) (1964): 151–159.

BONACICH, P. "Norms and Cohesion as Adaptive Responses to Potential Conflict." *Sociometry* 35 (3) (1972): 357–375.

BORAH, L. A., JR. "The Effects of Threat in Bargaining: Critical and Experimental Analysis." *Journal of Abnormal and Social Psychology* 66 (1963): 37–44.

BOULDING, K. *Conflict and Defense* (New York: Harper & Row, 1962).

BOVARD, E. W. "The Effects of Social Stimuli on the Response to Stress." *Psychological Review* 66 (1959): 267–277.

BROWN, J. S. "Principles of Interpersonal Conflict." *Journal of Conflict Resolution* 1 (2) (1957): 135–153.

BROXTON, J. A. "A Test of Interpersonal Attraction Predictions Derived from Balance Theory." *Journal of Abnormal and Social Psychology* 63 (1963): 394–397.

CAPLOW, T. "A Theory of Coalitions in the Triad." *American Sociological Review* 21 (1956): 489–493.

DEUTSCH, M. "A Theory of Cooperation and Competition." *Human Relations* 2 (1949): 129–152.

———. "An Experimental Study of the Effects of Cooperation and Competition Upon Group Processes." *Human Relations* 2 (1949): 199–231.

———. "Conflicts: Productive and Destructive." *The Journal of Social Issues* 25 (1969): 7–41.

———. "Trust and Suspicion." *Journal of Conflict Resolution* 2 (1958): 265–279.

DEUTSCH, M. and KRAUSS, R. M. "Studies of Interpersonal Bargaining." *Journal of Conflict Resolution* 6 (1962): 52–76.

ELLIS, J. G. and SERMAT, V. "Motivational Determinants of Choice in Chicken and Prisoner's Dilemma." *Journal of Conflict Resolution* (1968): 374–380.

FESTINGER, L. *A Theory of Cognitive Dissonance* (Stanford: Stanford University Press, 1957).

FISHER, R. J. "Third Party Consultation: A Method for the Study and Resolution of Conflict." *Journal of Conflict Resolution* 16 (1) (1972): 67–94.

FRENCH, J. R., JR. and RAVEN, D. H. "The Bases of Social Power," in *Studies in Social Power,* D. P. Cartwright, ed. (Ann Arbor: University of Michigan Press, 1959).

GALLO, P. S. and MCCLINTOCK, C. G. "Cooperative and Competitive Behavior in Mixed-Motive Games." *Journal of Conflict Resolution* 9 (1) (1965): 68–78.

GIBB, J. R. "Defensive Communication." *Journal of Communication* 2 (1961): 141–148.

GRESELUK, J. and KELLY, H. H. "Conflict Between Individual and Common Interest in a Personal Relationship." *Journal of Personality and Social Psychology* 21:2 (1972): 190–197.

GRINKER, R. and SPIEGAL, J. *Men Under Stress* (Philadelphia: Blakiston, 1945).

HEIDER, F. "Attitudes and Cognitive Organization." *Journal of Psychology* 21 (1946): 107–112.

————. *The Psychology of Interpersonal Relations* (New York: John Wiley, 1958).

JANDT, F. E. *Conflict Resolution Through Communication* (New York: Harper & Row, 1973).

JANIS, I. L. "Decisional Conflicts: A Theoretical Analysis." *Journal of Conflict Resolution* 3 (1959): 6–27.

JANIS, I. L. and KATZ, D. "The Reduction of Intergroup Hostility: Research Problems and Hypotheses." *Journal of Conflict Resolution* 3 (1) (1959): 85–100.

KAHN, R. L. and BOULDING, E., eds. *Powers and Conflict in Organizations* (New York: Basic Books, 1964).

KEE, H. W. and KNOX, R. F. "Conceptual and Methodological Considerations in the Study of Trust and Suspicion." *Journal of Conflict Resolution* 14 (3) (1970): 357–366.

KRAUSS, R. and DEUTSCH, M. "Communication in Interpersonal Bargaining." *Journal of Personality and Social Psychology* 4 (1966): 572–577.

LEVINGER, G. "Kurt Lewin's Approach to Conflict and its Resolution: A Review with Some Extensions." *Journal of Conflict Resolution* 1 (4) (1957): 329–339.

LEWIN, K. *Resolving Social Conflict* (New York: Harper & Row, 1948).

LOOMIS, J. L. "Communication, the Development of Trust and Cooperative Behavior." *Human Relations* 12 (1959): 305–315.

MAZUR, A. "A Nonrational Approach to Theories of Conflict and Coalitions." *Journal of Conflict Resolution* 12 (2) (1968): 196–205.

MILLER, G. R. and SIMONS, H. W., eds. *Perspectives on Communication in Social Conflict* (Englewood Cliffs, N.J.: Prentice-Hall, 1974).

NEMETH, C. A. "A Critical Analysis of Research Utilizing the Prisoner's Dilemma Paradigm for the Study of Bargaining," in *Advances in Experimental Social Psychology,* vol. 6, L. Berkowitz, ed. (New York: Academic Press, 1972).

NEWCOMB, T. M. "An Approach to the Study of Communicative Acts." *Psychological Review* 60 (1953): 393–404.

PEPITONE, A. and KLEINER, R. "The Effects of Threat and Frustration on Group Cohesiveness." *Journal of Abnormal and Social Psychology* 54 (1957): 192–199.

PHILLIPS, B. R. and DeVAULT, M. V. "Evaluation of Research on Cooperation and Competition." *Psychological Reports* 3 (1957): 289–292.

PHIPPS, T. E., JR. "Resolving Hopeless Conflicts." *Journal of Conflict Resolution* 5 (3) (1961): 274–278.

PRUITT, D. G. "Indirect Communication and the Search for Agreement in Negotiation." *Journal of Applied Social Psychology* (1971): 205–239.

RAPOPORT, A. *Fights, Games, and Debates* (Ann Arbor, Mich.: University of Michigan Press, 1960).

SARNOFF, I. and ZIMBARDO, P. G. "Anxiety, Fear, and Social Affiliation." *Journal of Abnormal and Social Psychology* 62 (1961): 356–363.

SCHELLING, T. C. *The Strategy of Conflict* (Cambridge, Mass.: Harvard University Press, 1960).

SHERIF, M. *In Common Predicament: Social Psychology of Intergroup Conflict and Cooperation* (Boston: Houghton-Mifflin, 1966).

————. "Supraordinate Goals in the Reduction of Intergroup Conflict." *American Journal of Sociology* 58 (1958): 349–356.

SHERIF, M., HARVEY, O.J., WHITE, B.J., HOOD, W. R., and SHERIF, C. W. *Intergroup Conflict and Cooperation: The Robbers Cave Experiment* (Norman: University of Oklahoma Press, 1961).

SOLOMON, L. "The Influence of Some Types of Power Relationships and Game Strategies on the Development of Interpersonal Trust." *Journal of Abnormal and Social Psychology* 61 (1960): 223–230.

SUMMERS, D. A. "Conflict, Compromise, and Belief Change in a Decision-Making Task." *Journal of Conflict Resolution* (1968): 215–221.

STAGNER, R. *The Dimension of Human Conflict* (Detroit: Wayne State University Press, 1967).

TEDESCHI, J. T., POWELL, J. LINDSKOLD, S., and GALRAGAN, J. P. "The Patterning of 'Honored' Promises and Sex Differences in Social Conflicts." *Journal of Social Psychology* 78 (1969): 297–298.

TEDESCHI, J. T., SCHLENKER, B. R., and BONOMA, T. V. *Conflict, Power, and Games* (Chicago: Aldine, 1973).

THIBAUT, J. W. and COULES, J.. "The Role of Communication in the Reduction of Interpersonal Hostility." *Journal of Abnormal and Social Psychology* 47 (1952): 770–777.

14

Information Acquisition

Eric loaded Connie's clothes in his car. Both hurried into their seats. He was going to be late for the exam. It was the last final before they left for his folk's home for the holidays. Eric wished he had remembered to put air in the right rear tire.

"Where's Jerry? What the hell is keeping him this time?" Eric thought. "If he doesn't show up in one minute, he's not going to ride to campus with me."

Jerry rapped on the window from behind. Eric let him in and sped away from the parking lot. He didn't notice the stop sign.

Connie began talking subtly about the argument they had last night. He tried to respond but wanted to catch the score of the ball game. He switched on the radio.

"Maybe it isn't such a good idea to take Connie home with me after last night," he thought.

Jerry started reviewing exam items he had with him. Eric knew he hadn't gotten enough information from the book. He just hadn't had time to read it all.

He noticed his speedometer edging up.

"Ah, the score—State won 17 to 14."

Eric scanned his rearview mirror for police.

Connie was no longer subtle, "Well, the whole thing was your fault, you know."

He knew he would never collect his five bucks on the game from Frank. Where was the sign for the River Road exit? All he could see were billboards. One of them indicated it was five minutes until nine.

"Yeah, I'm sorry—but you had something to do with it too, you know."

"What are five characteristics of the strong-mayor system?" Jerry continued to study.

He could cut off five minutes if the River Road shortcut was not busy.

RIVER ROAD EXIT ¼ MILE "How did I miss the first sign?"

"Let's see. Five characteristics. . . ." He glanced over his right shoulder and swung the car quickly into the exit lane. He let his arm rest on Connie's shoulder.

A grey Mustang slammed into the passenger side as both cars slid into the steel-posted railing, and then into the sign—SILVER ROAD EXIT ↗ —and then into the concrete pillar.

Our ability to select, process, and understand information may not always appear to be as crucial as it was for Eric and his passengers. Life or death may not hang in the balance. But from the multiplicity of messages with which we must deal almost simultaneously, we have learned to attempt to select only those that are most valuable to us. We have also learned to process these selected messages, relate them to other information, store that information, and retrieve it when needed. This we can do with little apparent effort. However, as humans, we do make mistakes—many, many mistakes. Sometimes we select the wrong information or pay attention to the wrong things. Sometimes we distort messages to suit our own needs or biases. At other times we fail to perceive (decode) accurately. This and the following chapter explore the process which we go through to obtain information from the multiplicity of messages in our environment. Technically, we refer to this activity as *information processing*. Before we look at information processing itself, we need to explain three important ideas, since they will come up again and again when we talk about information processing. These terms are *information, understanding,* and *selectivity.*

Basic Concepts of Information Processing

Information

We use the term "information" every day, so perhaps it needs little definition. Information is what we derive from both verbal and nonverbal messages. In a more technical sense, information may be viewed as *the meaning we assign to some stimulus that reduces our uncertainty about something.* Information, like meaning, is not inherent in messages; rather, information is the product of messages and the way that we process those

We often have to deal with a multiplicity of messages simultaneously, sometimes with life or death in the balance.

messages to determine their meaning. To the extent that a message has the potential for reducing our uncertainty, then information is present. In the opening illustration, the messages that Connie sent to Eric probably resulted in little information or uncertainty reduction about the previous evening's argument. However, the absence of police cars in his rearview mirror did provide information, in the sense that Eric was able to be more certain about speeding without getting caught. Likewise, the ball game score, the speedometer reading, the billboard, and the road signs all provided messages which resulted in information gain—the reduction of uncertainty.

Understanding

The concept of "understanding" generally refers to how accurately we comprehend verbal and nonverbal messages from others. In a more technical sense, *understanding is the reduction of uncertainty within individuals (and social systems) brought about through accurate processing of messages.* There are many indicants of understanding. We often think of understanding as an indication of our recognition and recall of information. Certainly, retention of information can be a sign that we understand. However, the *accuracy* of this retained information—its fidelity to the original message and the meaning intended by the source of the message—is what we define as understanding. For example, we can also use the term understanding to refer to how accurately we perceive the attitudes and beliefs of the source of a message. In our illustration, Eric understood that Connie was angry with him and blamed him for their fight.

An important distinction needs to be made here. While acquiring information is necessary for understanding to occur, acquiring information does not guarantee that understanding *will* occur. If Eric could recall the five characteristics of the strong-mayor system for the exam, this would indicate he has acquired information. But this would not necessarily indicate that Eric understands how the strong-mayor system works or why it is better than or worse than other systems of city government, which is probably what the course instructor is trying to teach.

Selectivity

One of the crucial things affecting information processing is selectivity. *Selectivity is the degree to which we receive or reject stimuli.* This selectivity *may be conscious or unconscious.* It is the *degree to which we choose to expose ourselves to, attend to, perceive, store, and retrieve messages from others.* The concept of selectivity also implies rejection or distortion of some messages. These choices may be conscious or unconscious. In our illustration, Eric's decisions to read or not to read the textbook, to wait a specified time for Jerry, and to turn on the radio represent examples of *selective exposure* to sources of information. Also, note how he selected among various stimuli such as the stop sign, radio, Connie, Jerry, billboards, rearview mirrors, and exit signs. These choices illustrate *selective attention.* Sometimes what we pay attention to is a result of internal factors (e.g., attitudes and needs); at other times our selective attention appears to be more a result of external factors (e.g., the size and color of the billboards). *Selective perception* refers to how we screen certain bits of information. Connie's statement that the argument was all Eric's fault was probably a result of screening and distorting information. Eric's mistakes in reading the signs and not seeing an oncoming car were examples of his selective perception. Finally, Eric's ability to remember where the exit for an infrequently used shortcut was and remembering information for the examination were probably the result of *selective retention* of information. At this point, it should be fairly obvious that these selectivity processes have significant impact upon our acquisition of information.

The selectivity processes also have a major impact on our level of understanding. The way in which we process messages determines to some extent the accuracy of our understanding as well as the information value of the message—how much it reduces our uncertainty.

There are some useful examples in the illustration with which we began this chapter. Eric's ability to recall information relevant to the upcoming examination indicated to some extent his mastery of the subject.

**BLACK BOX
43**

Can you identify the following concepts?
    information
    understanding
    selectivity

Can you identify the following types of selectivity?
    selective exposure   selective perception
    selective attention   selective retention

His understanding of what Connie was saying, however, was probably best reflected in the accuracy with which he perceived her attitudes from the potential information in the message. This understanding was probably not present in the information which the message produced about the argument itself; there was probably little information on that level. Also, Eric's understanding of the road signs (messages) was reflected in the accuracy with which he processed the amount of potential information which he had acquired. What he had retained or failed to retain from previous trips along this route drastically affected his understanding on this occasion.

A Basic Model of Information Processing

Information processing is what we do to and with messages in our efforts to acquire information and achieve understanding. This process passes through four stages: (1) acquisition of messages from a source(s); (2) recognition of the message codes acquired; (3) interpretation of those messages to obtain meaning; and (4) storage of that meaning in our memory for later retrieval and use. At every stage selectivity is present and can cause distortion or elimination of messages. The model in Figure 14–1 shows the sequential phases of information processing and where the various types of selectivity can impact the process. The remainder of this chapter is devoted to selective exposure and selective attention, the two types of selectivity that have a major impact in the initial stage of information processing—the acquisition of information. Chapter 15 is devoted to the elements in communication that have a major impact on our perceptions and choices to store or reject information that we acquire—information processing.

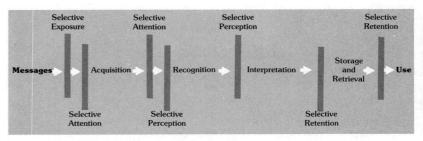

FIGURE 14–1. Stages of information processing and selectivity barriers.

```
┌─────────────────────────────────────────────────────────┐
│                      BLACK BOX                          │
│                          44                             │
│                                                         │
│   Diagram, label, and explain the model of information processing.   │
└─────────────────────────────────────────────────────────┘
```

Acquisition Processes

Selective Exposure

Nature of Selective Exposure.   Selective exposure refers to our conscious or unconscious decision to place ourselves in a position to receive messages containing potential information from various sources. It refers to physical proximity to the message signal. We have at least four options for behavior in this regard. We may (1) select some information, (2) reject some information, (3) not select some information, or (4) not reject some information. These options are illustrated in the following example.

Tom has the choice of turning on a television or not. He may select to expose himself to information or not select to. This does not necessarily mean that he has rejected the information although he *may* have consciously rejected it. Similarly, Tom may also choose between two TV programs, both of which he would like to watch. This represents a choice between selection versus nonselection of information. Clearly he has not rejected the other program and may indeed try to see it during a rerun at a later time. Another possibility is that Tom may choose between a program that he likes and one he would not watch. Here he is clearly selecting one program and rejecting another. Even if he did not choose to select the one he wanted to watch, he would reject or refuse to watch the other one he disliked. Also, Tom may already be watching television and choose among several programs he dislikes. Here his option for selective exposure is best represented by a *not reject* versus a *reject* decision. Although he does not like any of the programs and would not generally select them if he could make that choice, he had made a decision *not to reject* one of them. Finally, Tom has the clear option of *rejecting*—he may turn off the set.

Our selective exposure options, then, include selection, rejection, nonselection, nonrejection, or any combination of choices among those options. Often these choices are made without conscious decision on our

*We often make
predictions about the
nature of a message
through our
knowledge of its
source.*

part. To the extent that we are aware of these possibilities, we will be more likely to exert control over our selective exposure behavior.

Often our choices in this regard are not based upon direct knowledge of what potential information a message may contain. Rather, we make predictions about the nature of the message through our knowledge of the *source* of that message. For example, former President Nixon may come to campus and we may choose to reject or not select exposure to his message. The fact is, we may not know what he is going to say; however, we know the *source* of the message and some of the things he has said in the past. Any of the possible perceptions about others which we discussed in chapter 6 may affect our choice. Based upon this type of knowledge of Nixon, we may reject exposure to him. Most frequently this type of knowledge is instrumental in determining our exposure patterns rather than the actual nature of the message. The source of the communication is a major factor in our selective exposure in such areas as political campaigns, the section of courses to take, attendance of certain campus meetings, editorials we read, and persons to whom we choose to listen in interpersonal settings.

Explanations of Selective Exposure. A number of years ago, Sears and Freedman summarized much of the selective exposure theory and research. They found that one type of research which they classified as studies of *de facto selectivity* produced fairly consistent findings. These studies examined exposure behavior after it had occurred (referred to by researchers as *de facto* selectivity) through the use of surveys and questionnaires. They found that most often people who choose to expose themselves to certain messages or sources of information were in agreement with those messages and sources. For example, people who exposed themselves to Democratic political messages or candidates were also mostly Democrats. These findings tend to support the notion that we generally expose ourselves to sources of information that reinforce or support our view and tend not to expose ourselves to those with whom we are not in agreement. This notion is very consistent with the reasons for interaction among people and our receptivity to feedback which we discussed in chapter 8.

Another explanation of selective exposure behavior is suggested by what has been called *dissonance* theory. Basically, this approach suggests that we often make decisions among fairly attractive options; for example, buying a new car from among several types that we like. Once the choice is made—e.g., we buy the Datsun—we experience dissonance or anxiety about whether we have made the right choice. Afterwards, our selective exposure patterns on this issue are directed toward seeking information that might help us reduce this ambivalent state of dissonance or anxiety; that is, we seek out information that helps us rationalize the decision we made as the right one. We expose ourselves to advertisements and information favorable to Datsuns. This helps us reduce dissonance. On the other hand, we avoid information that would increase our dissonance; for example, advertisements and information on Plymouths, XKE's and Cadillacs that we were attracted to but did not buy. The final chapter on confirmation will expand this explanation as a basis upon which we seek to maintain our previous decisions.

A third plausible explanation of selective exposure behavior is found in *social judgment* theory (sometimes called involvement or ego-involvement theory). This theory notes that on some issues or topics we are highly and personally involved because we see the issue as directly related to our own self-interests. On issues such as these, we use our attitudes as "anchors" by which we accept and assimilate certain information or reject and contrast other information. Chapter 16 will discuss the implications of this process in terms of how we influence and are influenced by others. Here, we are interested only in how it affects exposure to information. On highly involving issues, we have a general range or latitude of acceptable messages. This information cannot be too discrepant from our views. On the other hand, we have another range or latitude for unacceptable message positions. If we anticipate that a message will be too discrepant from our view, then it might fall into this latitude of rejection and we would not expose ourselves to that information. For example, you may be highly involved in course work that helps to prepare you for a specific occupation which is obviously related to your self-interests. If so, you may try to avoid other courses which fall outside this latitude.

If the position taken in the message falls into our range of acceptable positions, then we would expose ourselves to the message. If you are highly involved and favorable to ecology, then you seek out information within some acceptable range of possible positions about ecology. In the same way, we might place sources of information into these latitudes of acceptance or rejection and as a result either expose or not expose ourselves to information from them. This process is also related to how we perceive and process such information once we acquire it. The following chapter will discuss this in detail.

Economic and political theorists have also attempted to explain exposure and information seeking behavior in decisions relating to behavior such as investment and voting. Very simply stated, they feel that getting or exposing ourselves to new information involves certain costs in terms of time and effort expended. Information on one issue is gotten only at the expense of information on another issue. We operate within a context of having more information available than we are able to use effectively. This frequently happens when we attempt to "cram" for final exams. During the semester there was more information than we were willing to spend the effort and time to process; however, new information may reduce uncertainty about some decision we must make. The value of the information to which we might expose ourselves is determined by its ability to reduce our uncertainty. For example, gas mileage and cost of an auto help reduce our uncertainty about which auto to buy. To the extent that the information can reduce our uncertainty, then we perceive the costs of acquiring that information as being low and the potential value of that information as being high. Over a period of time we build up a stock of knowledge or information on the issue. We may study information about all of the autos we are thinking about buying. The more information we have built up, the more costly it becomes to expose ourselves to additional information. Also, the more information we acquire, the less likely it will be that new information will reduce our uncertainty in a significant way. As a result, we expose ourselves only to information which is not too costly and which serves to reduce our uncertainty. At some point, we perceive acquisition of any new information not to be of sufficient value to offset the costs (time and effort) involved. This point is reached when we have enough information so that the addition of further information would not significantly reduce our uncertainty on the issue upon which we must make some decision. We buy a Honda Civic. Perceived costs, value, uncertainty, and our "information stock" determine our exposure and information seeking behavior according to this approach. This *cost-value* theory was well expressed by the fifth-grade boy who was assigned to read a book on penguins and give a report on the book in class. His report was to the point: "The book told me more about penguins than I needed to know." We doubt he will soon pick up another penguin book!

All of these explanations have some value in helping us predict selective exposure behavior; however, no single approach appears to be able to account for all selective exposure. As will be illustrated in the following section, the simple reinforcement explanation appears to be a fairly good predictor of initial exposure behavior when we are confronted with forced choices of selection or rejection of information. However, the last explanation by economists and political scientists may be better in describing how we expose ourselves on an issue over an extended period of time in relationship to other issues that also seek our attention. The social judgment approach may be relevant only when we are highly involved on issues and the dissonance theory approach may be relevant to our exposure patterns following important decisions. Taken together, however, the four approaches do appear to provide a fairly adequate picture for predicting how we will behave in a variety of situations in which exposure to information is a concern.

Predicting Selective Exposure. At this point, what would you say determines your exposure to certain information? Can you predict what information others might seek out? Until just recently the explanations we offered above did not seem to be too helpful in making these kinds of predictions. The large number of studies that tried to predict people's selective exposure produced conflicting results. People just didn't behave the way they were supposed to according to the predictions. Some found that people chose supportive, reinforcing information and others found that people chose nonsupportive, nonreinforcing information. Further studies found that people sought out information that would help them reduce their dissonance following some decision, while others found that people sought information that appeared to increase their dissonance. For example, it has been found that although smokers prefer supportive information, they do not avoid anti-smoking messages. Also, it has been found that when individuals do not prefer supportive information, they still reject or avoid non-supportive information.

Explanations for these inconsistent findings have been advanced. One major theory is that these studies typically provided only two selective exposure options with little freedom of decision. For example, some researchers would only let people select or not select some information. Subjects were not allowed the full range of exposure options that we discussed earlier in this chapter—select, not select, not reject, and reject. A second and equally important problem in most of the research is that the source of the message was also generally ignored by the researchers.

More recent studies indicate that when the full range of exposure options is provided and when the source of the message is considered, the explanations offered consistently predict peoples' selective exposure behavior. You *can* often predict some of your own exposure behavior and the exposure patterns of others. Information that people select often is information toward which they are more favorable; likewise, information that people usually reject is information toward which they are less favorable. But more important, the more involving the issue is, the more likely people are to seek that information. More specifically, people expose themselves to information on topics that they are favorable toward and involved in, *when the source of that information is perceived as competent and similar.* The best predictors of our exposure appear to be our perceptions of the competence of the source, our homophily with the source, and our involvement on the topic. Also, if we have a favorable attitude toward the topic and predict that the information will be useful, we increase the likelihood that we will seek that information. All of these factors must be considered.

What are the implications of these findings for our communication behavior? To the extent that we seek only information that is consistent with our views, then we are likely to avoid much information that would help us change and adapt to our changing world. When we avoid certain sources, for example, those whom we perceive a highly dissimilar to us, we may lose valuable, useful knowledge. Also, we should probably expect that others will respond in similar ways to us and our messages. Is it any wonder that advice given to politicians sometimes includes the following? "Tell then what they want to hear." If the politician doesn't, "they," *meaning we,* may not be listening later. In ancient times in some cultures, when a messenger brought bad news, the messenger was killed. That is certainly an extreme form of selective exposure! But do we not still do the same sort of thing, but in more subtle ways?

BLACK BOX
45

Can you identify and describe the exposure options?

Can you explain the following terms?
    de facto selectivity
    dissonance explanation of selective exposure
    social judgment explanation of selective exposure
    cost-value explanation of selective exposure

Can you explain why selective exposure predictions of research did not work?

Can you identify the best predictors of exposure?

Selective Attention

Nature of Attention.   Attention may be defined as *a selective physiological set to receive a stimulus* (message).   In this sense, then, attention is the tuning of senses (or channels) to selectively sense part of the environment. For example, you are probably not aware of the pressure of your foot against the floor until now as you direct your attention toward that stimulation.   Now, direct your attention to the pressure of your back against the chair.   Although these stimuli were present, you were not aware of them until you "tuned in" your senses or channels on them.   From this example, we can also note that attention involves the selection of certain stimuli in order to facilitate our reception of them and the nonselection and nonreception of other stimuli.

This process involves the accommodation or adjustment of the sensory organs (set) and anticipatory preparation to receive.   This is achieved through lowering thresholds to some stimuli and raising thresholds to others.   As a result, we can attend to a very limited number of stimuli at the same time.   We generally achieve attention to more than one stimulus at a time by one of the following means: (1) shifting our attention rapidly from one stimulus to another (e.g., watching a ping-pong game, watching a number of things that are happening on the TV screen); or (2) widening our focus of attention (e.g., looking at the number 5823 as a whole rather than individual digits, reading words rather than individual letters, or listening to a musical composition as a whole rather than as individual voices or instruments). The duration of attention to a single stimulus without shifting or changing focus falls in the range of two to twenty-four seconds for most people. Most often a five to eight-second duration is representative of our attention to a stimulus. In brief, then, attention serves to focus our perceptual processes. As a result, it is closely related to what information we acquire.

Factors Affecting Selective Attention. Both internal and external factors affect our attention. Internal factors include our physiological abilities, mental set, and anticipatory adjustments. Undoubtedly, these internal factors are related to things such as our general health, sensory capacities, our anxieties, attitudes, physical needs, and social needs. These impinge upon our abilities, set, and anticipations in the selective attention process. For example, if we are hungry we are most likely to attend to (look for?) food, not read a long chapter on information processing.

There are also certain external factors that affect our selective attention. These may be viewed as properties of the stimulus (message, source, channel) which affect the focus, duration, and frequency of our set to respond. As such they are closely linked with involuntary attention—something over which we have little control. For example, if someone slams a door, that gets our attention and we would have difficulty not noticing the event. In a similar manner, skillful sources manipulate our attention. We can also secure more attention to our communication by skillful use of the external properties in our messages. These external properties are designated as the following:

1. The *background* or *setting* in which the object of attention (stimulus) is found affects our selective attention. Any stimulus is attended to in relationship to other stimuli surrounding it. To the extent that surrounding stimuli are more attention demanding, the stimulus or object we are looking for will be more difficult to locate. For example, if you are looking for a particular sheet of paper on a cluttered desk you will have more difficulty finding it than if the sheet were on a neat, clear desk. Similarly, any message or source is attended to in relationship to other surrounding stimuli. Good television directors have developed the skill of directing your attention to particular components on the picture screen by the manipulation of the setting through the use of close-ups, focus, zooms, color, composition of the total picture, lighting, and various other techniques. Similar techniques are used in public rallies, newspapers, dramatic presentations, and the arrangements of chairs at committee meetings. Against the background or setting, various stimuli—often competing messages and sources—vie for our attention and subsequent acquisition of information.

The concreteness and intensity of this billboard would be likely to draw attention.

2. The *intensity* of the stimulus affects our selection for attention. The louder, brighter, or more vivid the stimulus, the more likely we are to attend to it. We notice the louder talker in a social group, the girl in the bright red dress, and the priest when he raises his voice. The intensity of the language we use can have attention value.

3. The *extensity* of the stimulus (message, channel, source, etc.) also directs our attention. Extensity refers to size or amount. All other stimuli being equal, we notice the headlines, larger signs, long words, larger persons, and bigger objects first.

4. The *concreteness* and *complexity* of the stimulus may call attention to it. The more easily recognizable and definite the form of the stimulus the more likely we are to pay attention to it. For example, concrete words are more attention demanding than those that are abstract. On the other hand, the more complex and complicated the stimulus is, the more difficulty we have in maintaining the focus and duration of our attention. We are more likely to shift or change the focus of our attention when the stimulus is complex rather than simple. A

279

billboard with a single word would be more attention demanding than one with a more complex message. A note to someone with the single word, "yes," on it might attract the attention desired.

5. Closely related to the two factors above are *contrast* and *velocity*. These elements refer to the striking quality, variety, novelty, change, movement, activity, and animation that the stimulus (message, source) displays. We attend more readily to a motion picture than a still picture, to a rapidly moving object than a slowly moving one, to a point of change in a speech than other points, to messages with variety than those that are predictable. If a 500-pound mouse walked into the room you would certainly notice it. Sometime, count the number of different pictures or "frames" in a television commercial.

6. The *impressivity* of stimuli also affects our selective attention. Impressivity refers to the repetition and duration of a stimulus. All other things being equal, we will attend to the stimulus that is repeated, is repeated, is repeated, is repeated, is repeated. How many TV commercials have you unintentionally memorized as a result of repetition? In reference to duration, for example, we notice the long stop lights, the long wait for someone, the long siren, and the long pause in speaking.

Importance of Selective Attention. Television advertisers have long known that ads using these principles are going to be noticed or attended; so have interesting teachers and appealing mates. To the extent that the sources, messages, and channels to which we expose ourselves utilize these factors, they generally heighten our attention to them. Obviously, the attention that we give affects the amount of subsequent information that we acquire. Part of effective studying is learning how to control our attention. Selective attention processes affect both the type and amount of information that we acquire. For some time, communication scholars have also suggested that what is best attended is also best understood and remembered. Others have argued that attention also facilitates influence and persuasion. It is

---

BLACK BOX
46

Can you describe selective attention and factors affecting it?

Can you explain how selective attention is important in human communication?

Try to recall instances of selective exposure and selective attention from your own experience that illustrate explanations of both.

---

difficult to be persuaded by a message that you do not pay any attention to. Also, as sources of communication we can facilitate information that others acquire by application of the ideas suggested above to our own encoding of messages (verbal and nonverbal) and our utilization of channels—media for message transmission. Skillful utilization of these factors can also facilitate understanding and retention of that acquired information by others.

Unconscious and Subliminal Communication

We have concentrated to this point on conscious exposure and attention. Another question occurs: Can we unconsciously acquire information? The answer to this question is yes. We do indeed acquire information at varying levels of awareness. There appear to be at least three distinct levels. The first is the conscious, attentive level of information acquisition. This level was discussed above in detail under the topics of selective attention and exposure. The others are unconscious acquisition and subliminal acquisition.

Unconscious Acquisition. The unconscious is an inattentive level of information acquisition. Although conscious attention facilitates acquisition and retrieval of information, we do acquire information that we have not consciously attended. For example, after you have attended a meeting, you may be able to recall the color of the walls, floor, and drapes of the room in which the meeting was held, although you did not consciously pay attention to them. You may also be able to recall the number of persons present, the number of windows in the room, the color and type of clothing worn, and a number of other bits of information that you were unaware that you had acquired. All of these stimuli were above your sensory thresholds for receiving them; therefore, while you did not notice them, they were registering or being perceived by your senses. You acquired information without being aware of it. There is some evidence to suggest that the individual acquires a vast amount of detailed information at this level. The problem appears to be in the retrieval of this information from the memory later. For example, neurosurgeons have used mild electric probes during brain surgery and found that people could picture rooms they had been in many years past and could describe them in detail. Under these conditions, patients recalled vast amounts of information that they were unaware that they had acquired or stored. During normal circumstances, they could not retrieve the same

281

information. Apparently we acquire information without consciously paying attention to it; the difficulty at times is retrieving that information from our memory.

Subliminal Acquisition. A third level is subliminal or subthreshold information acquisition. This level is similar to the unconscious level but explaining it is a bit more complex. As individuals, we have certain sensory thresholds. The stimulus threshold is the level or intensity that a stimulus must achieve in order to be consciously perceived by the individual. For example, a sound must reach a certain level before a person can hear it. This point is called a person's sensory threshold for that stimulus. A number of years ago, before the FCC barred such behavior for TV, some movie theaters rapidly flashed words on the screen below persons' threshold in order to induce them to buy popcorn and soft drinks. There is some dispute as to whether such "tricks" worked or not. Today, however, this practice is illegal in the public media.

Whether or not we can acquire information at this level has been the subject of a large number of research studies. Although there are conflicting results, there is evidence that stimuli presented at this level do register within an individual. For example, two researchers rapidly projected nonsense syllables upon a screen below their subjects' thresholds of perception. Then they gave electrical shocks with some of the syllables. When they showed the syllables to their subjects again, they reacted to the syllables which had been associated with the mild electrical shock. Another researcher found similar results from whispering words to persons who were sleeping. Still another researcher found that by flashing a speaker's credentials on the television screen at subliminal levels increased the watcher's attitude change by increasing the speaker's credibility.

Subliminal communication does register upon the individual. However, the stimulus (message) must be presented at a level *immediately* below the stimulus threshold, which varies from person to person. So it is not surprising that the subliminal technique has not been too effective when applied to mass audiences. If we targeted the subliminal message immediately below the average threshold, then the message would be effective for some, consciously perceived by others, and much too far below the threshold of others to register. If the stimulus level of the message was low enough to be below everyone's thresholds then the message stimulation would be much too low to register on the vast majority of the audience.

The use of unconscious and subliminal levels of information acquisition appears to be quite limited because of these problems. While there is evidence that we can acquire information through this type of stimulation, there is also difficulty in retrieving it from our memory. Apparently, conscious attention is one of the primary facilitators of subsequent retrieval of stored information.

However, if we are interested in effects other than acquisition of information, then these levels may hold some potential. Information may "get by" the usual selectivity processes. For example, the selective attention process might be skipped. Also, while the other selective perception and selective retention processes still function as they do at more conscious levels, their impact on incoming information is reduced or minimized. Our awareness of what is happening allows us to analyze potential information more carefully. When we are not aware that we are receiving information, it tends to "slip by" unnoticed although some selectivity is still occurring at a diminished, unconscious level. If this is indeed the case, then it may be possible to "plant" certain feelings and attitudes in us along with the information. Although the information is hard to recall, the feelings and attitudes may remain. The study using subliminal nonsense syllables along with electrical shocks, as well as the study which influenced attitudes with subliminal credibility cues, indicate that this is quite possible.

**BLACK BOX
47**

Can you explain how unconscious and subliminal acquisition of information occurs?

Discuss why these types of information acquisition are important.

Can you discuss how "extrasensory" information acquisition might occur?

The problems in acquiring information by subliminal means may be similar to those of acquiring information through psi communication. While some people have been found to be very effective in telepathic and/or clairvoyant communication, others appear to have little or no psi communication ability. It is quite possible that we all send and receive messages that could permit us to be telepathic or clairvoyant, but we are unable to process these messages at a conscious level. At some point in the future it may be possible for human communication science to crack the ESP barrier and permit all of us to employ psi communication as a means of information acquisition. While this possibility does not appear to be just around the corner, we should remember that the possibility of talking to someone on the other side of the world, and even being able to see them at the same time, was dismissed only a little over a century ago as the wild speculation of dreamers. Now we accept radio and television as commonplace. Today we know *that* psi communication occurs. Tomorrow we may discover *how* it works.

SUGGESTED FURTHER READINGS

1. Broadbent, D. E. "A Mechanical Model for Human Attention and Immediate Memory." *Psychological Review* 64 (1957): 205–215. Deutsch, J. and Deutsch, D. "Attention: Some Theoretical Considerations." *Psychological Review* 70 (1963): 80–90. Treisman, A. M. "Strategies and Models of Selective Attention." *Psychological Review* 75(3) (1969): 282–299.

   These three articles summarize important concepts and research in the area of selective attention. Also, they present conceptual models of how the attention process works. The Treisman article relates more directly to human communication; however, any of these three would make excellent supplementary reading that provides more depth and concerns not discussed in this chapter.

2. Donohew, L. and Palmgreen, P. "A Reappraisal of Dissonance and the Selective Exposure Hypotheses." *Journalism Quarterly* 48 (1971): 412–420. Sears, D. O. and Freedman, J. L. "Selective Exposure to Information: A Critical Review." *Public Opinion Quarterly* 31 (1967). McGuire, W. J. "Selective Exposure: A Summing Up," in *Theories of Cognitive Consistency: A Sourcebook,* R. P. Abelson, E. Aronson, W. J. McGuire, T. M. Newcomb, M. J. Rosenberg and P. H. Tannenbaum, eds. (Chicago: Rand McNally, 1968), 797–800. Wheeless, L. R. "The Effects of Attitude, Credibility, and Homophily on Selective Exposure to Information." *Speech Monographs* 41 (1974): 329–338.

   These summaries of research and theory in selective exposure offer critical and insightful discussion of the problems in this area of human communication. Also, they provide additional references and sources not listed in our chapter references because of space limitations. People interested in pursuing this area of study in more depth will find these articles to be valuable sources of information and criticism. While the McGuire article is brief, it might constitute an excellent starting point for further reading. Again, any of the remaining three would make excellent supplementary readings.

3. McCleary, R. A. and Lazarus, R.S. "Autonomic Discrimination Without Awareness: An Interim Report." *The Journal of Personality* 18 (1949): 171–179.

This summary and research study is now a classical study in the area of subliminal communication. It would make an interesting and valuable starting point for additional reading. Other related studies and articles are listed below in the chapter references.

4. "Paranormal Communication: A Symposium." *Journal of Communication* 25 (1975): 96–194.

This recent edition of the *Journal of Communication* contains a symposium or series of articles on *Psi,* or "Extrasensory Communication." It represents the most up-to-date summary and critique of the thinking and research in this fascinating area of human communication. Eleven articles are included in the symposium. These articles, in turn, summarize and critique hundreds of studies and approaches to understanding this phenomenon. Reading any of the articles included in the symposium would be an excellent supplement for people interested in this area.

SELECTED REFERENCES

BACH, S. and KLEIN, G. S. "Conscious Effects of Prolonged Subliminal Exposures of Words." *American Psychologist* 12 (1957): 397.

BAKER, L. E. "The Influence of Subliminal Stimuli Upon Verbal Behavior." *The Journal of Experimental Psychology* 20 (1957): 84–99.

BROADBENT, D. E. "A Mechanical Model for Human Attention and Immediate Memory." *Psychological Review* 64 (1957): 205–215.

———. *Perception and Communication* (London: Pergamon Press, 1958).

BROCK, T. C., ALBERT, S. M., and BECKER, L. A. "Familiarity, Utility, and Supportiveness as Determinants of Information Receptivity." *Journal of Personality and Social Psychology* 14(4) (1970): 292–301.

CANON, L. K. "Self-Confidence and Selective Exposure to Information," in *Conflict, Decision, and Dissonance,* L. Festinger, ed. (Stanford: Stanford University Press, 1964), 83–96.

CHAPANIS, N. P. and CHAPANIS, A. "Cognitive Dissonance Five Years Later." *Psychology Bulletin* 61(1) (1964): 22.

CRANE, L. D., DIEKER, R. J., and BROWN, C. T. "The Physiological Response to the Communication Mode: Reading, Listening, Writing, Speaking, and Evaluating." *The Journal of Communication* 20 (1970): 231–240.

DAVIS, W. L. and PHARES, E. J. "Internal-External Control as a Determinant of Information-Seeking in a Social Influence Situation," *Journal of Personality* 35 (1967): 547–561.

DEAUX, K. "Variations in Warning, Information Preference, and Anticipating Attitude Change." *Journal of Personality and Social Psychology* 9 (1968): 157–161.

DEITER, J. "The Nature of Subception." Unpublished Doctoral Dissertation, University of Kansas, 1953.

DEUTSCH, J. and DEUTSCH, D. "Attention: Some Theoretical Considerations." *Psychological Review* 70 (1963): 80–90.

DONOHEW, L. et al. "A Conceptual Model of Seeking, Avoiding, and Processing," in *New Models for Mass Communication Research,* P. Clarke, ed. (Beverly Hills, Cal.: Sage Publications, 1973).

DONOHEW, L. and PALMGREEN, P. "An Investigation of Mechanisms of Information Selection." *Journalism Quarterly* 48 (1971): 412–420.

————. "A Reappraisal of Dissonance and the Selective Exposure Hypothesis." *Journalism Quarterly* 48 (1971): 412–420.

DONOHEW, L., PARKER, J. M., and McDERMOTT, V. "Psychological and Physiological Measurement of Information Selection: Two Studies." *Journal of Communication* 22 (1972): 54–63.

EAGLE, M. "The Effects of Subliminal Stimuli of Aggressive Content Upon Conscious Cognition." *Journal of Personality* 27 (1957): 578–600.

EGETH, H. "Selective Attention." *Psychological Bulletin* (1967): 41–57.

FOX, M. "Differential Effects of Subliminal Stimuli and Supraliminal Stimulation." Unpublished Doctoral dissertation, New York University, 1960.

FREEDMAN, J. L. "Confidence, Utility, and Selective Exposure." *Journal of Personality and Social Psychology* 2 (1965): 778–780.

————. "Preference for Dissonant Information." *Journal of Personality and Social Psychology* 2 (1965): 287–289.

GAITO, J. "Stages of Perception, Unconscious Processes, and Information Extraction." *Journal of General Psychology* 70 (1964): 183–197.

GARNER, W. R. "The Stimulus in Information Processing." *American Psychologist* 25 (1970): 350–358.

GIBB, J. D. "Experimental Study of the Effects of Subthreshold Prestige Symbol in Informative and Persuasive Communication." Unpublished Doctoral dissertation, Wayne State University, 1966.

HENDRICK, C. "Preference for Inconsistant Information in Impression Formation." *Perceptual and Motor Skills* (1969): 459–466.

HILLS, J. W. and CRANO, W. D. "Additive Effects of Utility and Attitudinal Supportiveness in the Selection of Information." *Journal of Social Psychology* 89 (1973): 257–269.

HOVLAND, C. I. and SHERIF, M. *Social Judgment* (New Haven: Yale University Press, 1961).

JECKER, J. D. "Selective Exposure to New Information," in *Conflict, Decision and Dissonance,* L. Festinger, ed. (Stanford, Cal.: Stanford University Press, 1964).

JOHNSON, J. R. "Psychology in Advertising: What Research Says About Subliminal Stimulation." *The Journal of Business Education* 36 (Feb. 1961): 205–207.

KATZ, E. "On Reopening the Question of Selectivity in Exposure to Mass Communication," in *Theories of Cognitive Consistency,* R. P. Abelson et al., eds. (Chicago: Rand McNally, 1968), 788–796.

KENDLER, H. H. and KENDLER, T. S. "Selective Attention Versus Mediation: Some Comments on Machintoch's Analyses of Two Stage Models of Discrimination Learning." *Psychological Bulletin* 66 (October, 1966): 4.

LAVOIE, A. L. and THOMPSON, S. K. "Selective Exposure in a Field Setting." *Psychology Reports* 31 (October, 1972): 2.

LUBROSKY, L., RICE, R., PHOENIX, D., and FISHER, C. "Eye Fixation Behavior as a Function of Awareness." *Journal of Personality* 36 (1968): 1–20.

McCARTHY, M. V. "Commitment, Utility, Relevance, and Supportiveness as Determinants of Information Receptivity." *Dissertation Abstracts* 33A(5) (1972): 2495–2496.

McCLEARY, R. A. and LAZARUS, R. S. "Autonomic Discrimination Without Awareness: An Interim Report." *The Journal of Personality* 18 (1949): 171–179.

McCONNELL, J. V. "Subliminal Stimulation: An Overview." *American Psychologist* 13:5 (1958): 229–239.

McGUIRE, W. J. "Selective Exposure: A Summing Up," in *Theories of Cognitive Consistency: A Sourcebook,* R. P. Abelson, E. Aronson, W. J. McGuire, T. M. Newcomb, M. J. Rosenberg and P. H. Tannenbaum (Chicago: Rand McNally, 1968), 797–800.

MILLER, J. C. "Discrimination without Awareness." *American Journal of Psychology* 52 (1939): 562–578.

MILLS, J. "Effect of Certainty About a Decision Upon Post-Decision Exposure to Consonant and Dissonant Information." *Journal of Personality and Social Psychology* 2 (1965): 749–752.

MILLS, J. and ROSS, A. "Effects of Commitment and Certainty Upon Interest in Supportive Information." *Journal of Abnormal and Social Psychology* 68 (1964): 552–555.

NORMAN, D. A. "Toward a Theory of Memory and Attention." *Psychological Review* 75(6) (1968): 522–536.

PALETZ, D. L., KOON, J., WHITEHEAD, E., and HAGENS, R. B. "Selective Exposure: The Potential Boomerang Effect." *Journal of Communication* 22 (1972): 48–53.

PASCHAL, F. G. "The Trend in Theories of Attention." *Psychological Review* 48 (1948): 383–403.

"Paranormal Communication: A Symposium." *Journal of Communication* 25 (1975): 96–194.

PLAX, T. G. and HAYS, E. R. "A Systems Approach to the Study of Information-Seeking Behavior: A Valuable Area for Communication Research." Paper presented at the International Communication Association Convention, Montreal, April, 1973.

RALEIGH, K. K. "Children's Selective Listening to Stories: Familiarity Effects Involving Vocabulary, Syntax and Intonation." *Psychology Reports* 33 (1973): 255–266.

RHINE, R. J. "Some Problems in Dissonance Theory Research on Information Selectivity." *Psychological Bulletin* 68 (1967): 21–28.

ROBINSON, D. O. "The Limits of Selective Attention in DAF Shadowing." *Physionomic Science* 21(6) (1970): 325–327.

ROSEN, S. "Post-Decision Affinity for Incompatible Information." *Journal of Abnormal and Social Psychology* 63 (1961): 188–190.

SAEGERT, S., SWAP, W., and ZAJONC, R. B. "Exposure, Context, and Interpersonal Attraction." *Journal of Personality and Social Psychology* 25 (1973): 234–242.

SCHRAMM, W. and ROBERTS, D. F., eds. *Process and Effects of Mass Communication,* rev. ed. (Urbana: University of Illinois Press, 1971).

SEARS, D. O. and FREEDMAN, J. L. "Commitment, Information Utility, and Selective Exposure." *USN Technical Reports,* ONR, Nonr-233 (54) NR 171–350 No. 12, (August, 1963).

————. "Selective Exposure to Information: A Critical Review." *Public Opinion Quarterly* 31 (1967): 66–97.

————. "The Effects of Expected Familiarity With Arguments Upon Opinion Change and Selective Exposure." *Journal of Personality and Social Psychology* 2 (1965): 420–426.

SHERIF, M., SHERIF, C., and NEBERGALL, R. *Attitude and Attitude Change* (Philadelphia: Saunders, 1965).

SINGER, J. E. "Motivation for Consistency," in *Motivational Antecedents and Behavioral Consequences,* S. Feldman, ed. (New York: Academic Press, 166), 47–73.

SMITH, G. J., SPENCE, D. P., and KLEIN, G. S. "Subliminal Effects of Verbal Stimuli." *Journal of Abnormal Social Psychology* 59 (1959): 167–176.

STANEK, F. J. "The Effect of Stimulus Complexity on Selective Attention." *Dissertation Abstracts* 31 (11-B) (1971): 6959.

TREISMAN, A. M. "Contextual Cues in Selective Attention." *Quarterly Journal of Experimental Psychology* 12 (1960): 242–248.

————. "Strategies and Models of Selective Attention." *Psychological Review* 75(3) (1969): 282–299.

VERNON, J. A. and BADGER, D. H. "Subliminal Stimulation and Human Learning." *The American Journal of Psychology* 72 (1959): 265–266.

VERNON, M. "Perception, Attention, and Consciousness," in *Foundations of Communication Theory,* K. K. Sereno and C. D. Mortensen, eds. (New York: Harper & Row, 1970).

VIDMAN, N. and ROKEACH, M. "Archie Bunker and Bigotry: A Study in Selective Perception and Exposure." *Journal of Communication* 24 (Winter, 1974): 36–47.

VOHS, J. L. "An Empirical Approach to the Concept of Attention." *Speech Monographs* 31 (1964): 355–360.

VOOR, J. H. "Subliminal Perception and Subception." *Journal of Psychology* 41 (1956): 437–458.

WHEELESS, L. R. "The Effects of Attitude, Credibility, and Homophily on Selective Exposure to Information." *Speech Monographs* 41 (1974): 329–338.

_____. "The Relationship of Attitude and Credibility to Comprehension and Selective Exposure." *Western Speech* 38 (1974): 88–97.

ZAJONC, R. B. "Attitudinal Effects of Mere Exposure." *Journal of Personality and Social Psychology,* Monograph Supplement 9 (1968): 1–24.

15

Information Processing

"When I use a word," Humpty Dumpty said in rather a scornful tone, "It means just what I choose it to mean—neither more nor less."
"The question is," said Alice, "whether you can make words mean so many different things."
"The question is," said Humpty Dumpty, "which is to be the master—that's all."

In our illustration at the beginning of the last chapter, Eric never made it to his exam. He failed to adequately acquire and process the information necessary to get him there. If he had arrived, we would have found out some more things. So let us resurrect the poor fellow and give him another chance.

Eric's car pulled up in front of Woodburn Hall, stopping a lane of traffic behind it. Connie took over the wheel while Eric raced inside. He had taken the wrong turnoff from the expressway and was now twenty minutes late for the exam. The professor frowned at him as he handed out the exam.

"Sorry, I'm late."

"Just so you finish on time," was the reply.

Eric's hands were trembling with anxiety as he opened the exam.

"What does that mean?" he said to himself as he read the first question for the third time.

He had expected the exam to be hard. Sure enough, it was. He hadn't liked the professor or the course from the first day.

The questions were long and rambling. They seemed ambiguous and he had difficulty interpreting them. If he only misread half of them, it would be better than he did on the midterm.

"Why can't this idiot write multiple-choice questions instead of essay questions," Eric thought. He was used to multiple-choice exams in most of his courses.

"Maybe if I would have had time to reorganize and outline" he mumbled as he tried desperately to pull the answers out of his memory.

"Time's up," came a loud voice from the front of the room.

Eric was only a little over halfway through when the professor walked over and took his paper.

He left the room confident that he would be taking this course again next semester. After all, he had even forgotten to put his name on the exam.

"Now where did I tell Connie to meet me?"

Poor Eric has again had difficulty with information processing. If he can remember where Connie is to meet him, we're sure he will make it home for a well-deserved rest. But why all that trouble dealing with information? Was he overloaded with it? Was he stupid? No. He simply had some problems that we all share in processing information. In the following sections we will investigate those problems together.

Recognition, Interpretation, and Storage-Retrieval

We noted in chapter 14 that information processing involves highly interdependent stages. Information acquisition does not merely precede recognition, interpretation, and storage-retrieval; it is integrally involved in these processes. Likewise, the stages of recognition, interpretation, and storage-retrieval are highly interrelated. It is difficult to discuss one of these processes without considering the other. Therefore, in this section we will examine selective perception and selective retention as they relate to recog-

*Sometimes the
subject of our
attention frustrates
information
processing.*

nition, interpretation, and storage-retrieval collectively. The focus of this section is upon how accurately or inaccurately we understand and retain acquired information. We hope you will be searching along with us for factors that will help you improve your information processing ability.

Perceptual Tendencies

Perception is most closely related to our recognition and interpretation of stimuli (messages, sources, etc.). To a large extent, then, how we perceive something determines what we understand or believe. As we have noted previously, what a person perceives or understands to be reality *is* her or his reality. Also, to the extent that any given event is perceived differently by different people, then their understanding of that event is different. As a result, we will subsequently relate, index, synthesize, store and retrieve dif-

293

ferent information although we are exposed to the same event. For example, people in Eric's class perceived the information, the course, and the professor differently. Likewise, people viewing an automobile accident often understand that event differently. Our differences in experience cause perceptual differences as well. That is why human beings can be exposed to the same potential information (messages) and different understanding and opinions can result. Simply stated, perception is interrelated with numerous other elements in human information processing. Some of our more common perceptual limitations and tendencies are noted below.

Sensory Limitations. Perhaps Eric is one of those people who has a hearing, sight, or other perception problem. Their understanding and decoding capacities are likely to be seriously affected. The potential information they can perceive is not the same as that which other, more problem-free people can perceive and share in common as they communicate. However, all humans share a similar limitation. We may not have a specific hearing or sight problem, but we all have only a limited number of senses through which we experience the world. There are more potential stimuli and more potential information than we are capable of perceiving with these limited number of senses. For example, we cannot experience the world the way a bat does; bats have a built-in radar system. As a consequence of our limitations we cannot perceive everything there is to perceive about anything. Through the use of technology such as telescopes, x-ray, radar, laser beams, loud speakers, and TV we have expanded our human sensory capacities somewhat. But our natural sensory limitations distort our perceptions of reality from the outset. Therefore, we should have our sensory capacities (sight, hearing, smell, etc.) checked periodically to assure that we are not attempting to communicate with even more limitations than normal.

Perception Levels. There are also degrees of levels of perception similar to those noted for attention processes. Attention does indeed serve to focus our perceptual processes, and there is also perceptual capacity below our conscious level of awareness. (Note the discussion in chapter 14 of unconscious and subliminal communication.) An important point to make here is that filtering takes place below the conscious level of awareness. Considerable filtering probably took place below Eric's awareness when he was studying for the exam and when he was trying to read the exam questions. Some evidence suggests that different potential information is routed to different areas of the brain. For example, what a person considers to be obscene words do not appear to go through the normal information-processing centers of the brain; rather, these words appear to be "short-circuited" to other, more emotional response areas. Likewise, some subject matter to which we are negatively oriented (as in Eric's case) may be filtered more below the level of our awareness.

Learned Habits. We perceive or misperceive according to learned habits of recognizing and interpreting the *nature of the stimulus* against some *background or setting.* Eric had developed the habit of perceiving multiple-choice questions in his classes. Consequently, he had difficulty adjusting to different forms of questions. Our understanding and interpretation are partly supplied by our habits built up through past experience. As a result of our experience with various stimuli we have built up certain patterning tendencies:

1. *Similarity*—Items of the same size, shape, or quality are more likely to be viewed as a group or pattern than dissimilar elements; for example, we may stereotype people sharing similar racial characteristics.
2. *Proximity*—Items that are close together tend to be grouped in our perceptions. Some people perceive everyone from the south as one group and essentially alike.
3. *Continuity and Closure*—We have a tendency to avoid breaking the continuous flow of a line, design, or pattern. As a result, we fill in the missing information, correctly or incorrectly. We have an organizing tendency to complete an incomplete pattern.

As a result of these tendencies, we have difficulty perceiving groupings of dissimilar and low proximity items. Or we interpret some things as associated or as a group when they are not. For example, we may stereotype individuals as the same because of some similar characteristics. People from "the other side of the tracks" are often grouped because of proximity. We also distort information by filling in and completing discontinuous and incomplete information. We often "read into" a message more than was there because of this tendency. Our learned habits of interpreting stimuli (potential information) affect our recognition and interpretation of them. Figures 15–1 and 15–2 illustrate visually some difficulties caused by these patterned habits of perception.

In Figure 15–1, do you notice anything wrong in the first two illustrations? What is the third illustration? We call it three lines. If you call it a

295

FIGURE 15-1. *Visual illustration of some patterning tendencies.*

triangle that is because you recognize the triangle-pattern and fill in the missing parts of the lines. Do you perceive selectively? What do you perceive in Figure 15-2?

Background or Setting.   The background or setting against which we perceive an event also affect our perceptions of that event. The way we would interpret nonverbal communication through touch by a member of the opposite sex might vary depending upon whether that touching behavior took place in a bar or at church. We have learned habits for interpreting certain cues in relation to the environment in which they normally occur. When the background or environment changes we may interpret the same cue in a different way or we may merely misperceive it. Figure 15-3 illustrates the reliance we place upon the background for our perceptions. The gray circles are the same size. So are the black and white boundaries. Do they look that way to you?

Set or Expectancy.   At this point, it should be fairly obvious that our *attentive* set can facilitate perception; however, if we have strong enough expec-

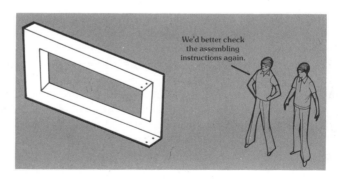

FIGURE 15-2. *Visual example of the effects of perceptual
experience.*

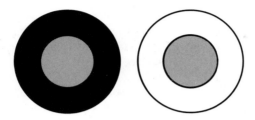

FIGURE 15–3. *Visual example of background or setting effects.*

tancies, these expectancies may distort our perception and understanding. Eric had expected the exam to be hard, and for him it was! Consider the following illustration. A college professor was fond of playing a certain trick on his class. He would uncork a small bottle, smell the liquid inside, and grimace. Then he would tell the class to raise their hands when they were able to smell it and would continue to lecture. After a while some of the confederates he had "planted" in the class would raise their hands and soon other, unsuspecting students would "smell" the liquid and begin raising their hands. Only clear, odorless water was in the bottle, but the students perceived the smells of ammonia, perfume, and other substances. Their expectancy was so high that they perceived odors that did not exist. What they expected to perceive, they *did* perceive. In another case, teachers were told that certain capable, bright students' were actually below average, slow learners. Although the students' work was of the same quality, the teachers rated them lower than other students because they actually misperceived the quality of their work. What they expected to perceive was what they perceived.

Anxiety and Conflict. Under conditions of high stress, anxiety, and conflict we have more difficulty discriminating among certain cues and stimuli. As a result we have more difficulty interpreting communication elements and events (source, message, channel, situation). This produces more error in our decoding. For example, many of us have difficulty reading exam items on a test as Eric did. Because of our anxiety, we often have to read the question several times and occasionally we misinterpret the question altogether. Our anxiety often impairs our perceptual abilities.

Language and Symbols. To some extent, our language structures how we perceive reality and communication events. The language we use partially determines what we will be able to "see" and how we will interpret things. Eric obviously had difficulty perceiving things the way his professor did in reading the test questions. Similarly, one of the basic problems in learning a foreign language is understanding certain words in that language for which there is no English equivalent. People of other cultures may indeed perceive the world differently than we do. As a result, their language reflects that differing perspective.

In the same manner, our language not only reflects our perceptions of reality but to some extent determines how we perceive. Sometimes we find it necessary to invent new words or use metaphors to express new perceptions. The language of mathematics provides a case in point. Conventional mathematics were insufficient to express Einstein's theory of relativity. So he had to develop a new system, a new language in order to be able to perceive and express new relationships.

Social and Physiological Needs. When our physiological or social needs become strong enough, they may affect our recognition and interpretation of communication stimuli. Eric's strong social needs with regard to Connie and his need to get out of town for a while both affected his ability to concentrate. In a now-classic study, researchers directed economically deprived, hungry children to view certain objects through translucent glass. Almost invariably, these children saw food although none was present. Their strong physiological need for food facilitated perceiving what was not there. A number of other studies have found similar results. Our social needs and drives may also affect our recognition and interpretation. Further, if we have a strong need for status, we may interpret innocent remarks by others as a social "slam." If we have a strong need for social affiliation with a group, we have a tendency to perceive things from the perspective of that group. We tend to perceive other sources and messages in line with the perceptions of the group(s) with which we have a strong need to maintain affiliation.

Attitudes, Beliefs, and Values. Probably one of the most heavily researched areas in perception is the relationship of attitudes to recognition and interpretation, as we noted in chapter 7. One very general conclusion we can draw is that the more favorably disposed we are to something the more accurately we recognize and subsequently interpret it. Eric was favorably disposed neither to his professor nor the course. For example, in one study peoples' names were assigned to sets of pictures of blacks and whites. Both blacks and whites of varying degrees of racial prejudice were asked to view the pictures. As we would expect, highly prejudiced individuals (both blacks and whites) had difficulty remembering the names of pictures of persons of another race. Most of us are familiar with this "Archie Bunker perception problem" where "they all look alike." In general, then, we are more receptive to sources and messages toward which we are favorably disposed.

Also, when an issue is highly salient and involving to us we are more likely to distort the potential information from a source. If someone takes a position that is too discrepant from our attitudes and beliefs, we distort the view by contrasting the person and perceiving her or him as even more discrepant than she or he really is. If you have a strong dislike for a professor and the subject matter, it is very likely that you will misperceive that there is anything of value and you will very likely have difficulty understanding and accepting what is said. In the process you will selectively perceive and retain information that may be quite different from the information of someone who is favorably disposed to the course.

On the other hand, when we are highly favorable toward a source and the subject matter and at the same time highly involved on the issue, we may also distort our perceptions. In this case we fail to note differences in views and consequently assimilate that source's position as our own. We misperceive by failing to recognize real differences that do exist in our views.

As noted previously, we are generally more receptive to supportive, agreeing information and less receptive to nonsupportive information. When this tendency becomes strong enough, we distort by contrasting and assimilating other's views. When we are unable to avoid this information, sometimes we will process that information differently by devaluing the importance of the issue. We say, "Well, it isn't very important anyway," thereby dismissing the information. As a result, we do not adequately perceive and retain that information. Later it will be easier to forget it when the issue arises again. And finally, if this technique does not work, then we engage in what is called "differentiation." When we run into discrepant information which we can't avoid, we interpret that information by perceiving some new categories and putting that information into a new category. For example, if you are devoted to the brand of car you drive and run into information about some mechanical or safety defect, you may simply note that the information only applies to the more recent models. The 1967 model that you drive is OK. We engage in this type of differentiation with people when we receive information which violates our stereotypes. In these cases we say something like "Some of my best friends are Jewish."

Improving Perception. A final note on perception tendencies is that they can be changed. Research has demonstrated that many of our perceptual

299

tendencies are learned and, hence, can be relearned. The first step in relearning is conscious awareness of the tendency and attention to it while processing information derived from various stimuli. In the following section we will ask you to become aware of how your perceptions of sources affect your information processing.

**BLACK BOX
48**

Can you describe the elements that affect perception?

Can you explain how these elements affect perception?

Effects of Our Perception of Sources

As we would expect, how we perceive the source of a message affects the resulting accuracy of our understanding and our retention of information. We noted in chapter 6 some important aspects of our perceptions of other communication participants. Some of these variables are: (1) The participant's credibility, including our perceptions of his or her competence, character, composure, sociability, and extroversion; (2) The participant's attraction, including perceptions of his or her social attraction, physical attraction, and task attraction; and (3) The participant's homophily, including perceptions of his or her attitude, morals-values, appearance, and status-class. Most research in perceptual accuracy and retention has not carefully considered all of these components; rather, studies have looked at only broad estimates of credibility, attraction, or homophily. But some interesting results have been found.

Accurate Recognition and Interpretation. When we perceive a source as highly credible, our perceptions of her or his attitudes are more accurate. Also, we perceive the attitude revealed in a message emanating from a person to whom we assign high credibility more accurately. Some research investigated the specific dimensions of credibility that were related to accurate perception of attitudes of others. It was found that higher competence, sociability, and composure were most closely related to more accurate perceptions of the attitudes of public figures. When we perceive a public figure as higher on these dimensions, we are generally more likely to perceive her or his attitudes more accurately. Very little research has looked at the effects of attraction and homophily in this area; however, Rogers and Shoemaker note that homophilous individuals consistently communicate more effectively with each other. Also, to the extent that we are alike, have shared experiences, and communicate more effectively, we are also more likely to accurately perceive each others' attitudes and beliefs.

Retention and Retrieval. More complete research has been conducted in the area of retention and retrieval of information in relation to our perception of the source of the message. For public speakers, competence, character, and extroversion appear to be related to the later retention and recall of message content. When we perceive communicators as higher on these dimensions, we apparently retain and are able to retrieve information from their communication that we have stored in our memory. In a study of classroom learning, perceptions of the communication source (teacher) were also found to relate to our recall of information. Remember poor Eric's perceptions of his teacher. Perceived competence, homophily, social attraction, and task attraction of the teacher are related to immediate recall of information. However, while higher competence and task attraction of the teacher increase students' recall of information, higher social attraction and homophily decrease recall. Apparently, most classrooms are more task-oriented than social-oriented, and higher perceptions of competence and task attraction increase our recall. If we perceive the situation as more social and are socially attracted to a teacher whom we perceive as very much like us, we may not recall as much information. Such perceptions of sources are probably due partly to the source and partly to our own personal characteristics.

Personal Characteristics

Certainly, personality factors (discussed in chapter 7) influence how we recognize, interpret, and store-retrieve information. Characteristics, traits, and types of personality are related to our information processing, but how many personality variables are related is not completely clear at this point. The highly anxious individual, of course, has problems in making discriminations among differing stimuli and has difficulty in perceiving potential information. The exact, specific problem areas are unclear. Treatment of the individual to reduce that anxiety appears to be the most expedient solution to the problem. Communication apprehensives can be treated (as we noted in chapter 5) to improve their encoding. Although some people have high levels of receiver apprehension (decoding anxiety), no particular treatment program has been developed for this specific problem.

We also know that highly dogmatic, closed-minded individuals engage in abnormal information processing. They are more likely to respond to information on the basis of irrelevant inner needs and drives than on the basis of the logic and reasonableness of the message. They are also more likely to perceive the beliefs of those with whom they disagree as much more discrepant than they really are. The highly dogmatic is also more likely to use her or his perceptions of the *source* rather than message content as a basis for processing the information. In general, dogmatics are more receptive to information and sources that fit within their beliefs and are not receptive to those outside of them. This conclusion is fairly consistent with other research on personality that has found that "objective" listeners comprehend more than "egocentric" or self-centered listeners.

People have differing styles that also dictate some information processing tendencies. Some appear to be more analytic in interpreting information while others appear to be more concerned with synthesizing and simplifying. Others appear to filter out more of the rational, logical content and prefer content related to emotional, affective, or "humanistic" information. The latter individuals with *affective life styles* appear to be quite different from others with *cognitive life styles* who prefer the rational, logical type of content and filter out affective or "humanistic" elements.

A closely related area which affects comprehension is *organizational ability*. Individuals who are able to reorganize, grasp main points of a message, and follow general outlines are also able to index, order, and synthesize that material into their memory. These individuals retain and

---

**BLACK BOX
49**

Can you identify the perceptions of sources that increase or decrease your ability to accurately interpret and retrieve information?

What personal characteristics increase or decrease accuracy of interpretation and recall of information?

Do you remember people who had these characteristics and some problems in information processing as a result?

retrieve both oral and visual messages better. Fortunately, people can be trained to increase these organizational skills.

Other personal characteristics such as sensory abilities, intelligence, listening experience, verbal ability (vocabulary, etc.), and motivation are more obviously related to the ways we process rational, cognitive types of information. For example, people who rate higher on intelligence and related characteristics tend to be better able to efficiently recognize, interpret, and retain cognitive information.

Effects of Language-Message Characteristics

Our discussion of information processing indicates that there are certain tendencies that we have as individuals, groups, and social systems that affect the ways we process information. Probably as a result of these tendencies and others we have failed to discern, certain message characteristics also affect our decoding in terms of recognition, interpretation, and storage-retrieval. For example, we have discussed some factors which may affect our attention and perception of potential information. Awareness and control of these factors can facilitate more effective encoding and decoding of messages. The language and specific elements in a message are related to these processes.

The Language/Code of the Message

Much of our language is a rather arbitrary system that has been developed (or has evolved) for communication purposes. As a result, there are some problems with this and other language systems. As we noted in chapter 9, the language or specific word used in a message is often confused with the thing itself. Over a period of time, things and symbols that are used to refer to them become associated in our minds through our life experiences. To the extent that these life experiences vary, the meanings which we hold for the same symbols that others use may also vary. Both the verbal and nonverbal symbol for "the flag" do not evoke the same meanings from different people. Hence, the crux of some of our communication problems.

Lewis Carroll illustrated the problem in *Through the Looking Glass* with an exchange between Alice and Humpty Dumpty:

"I don't know what you mean by 'glory'," Alice said.

Humpty Dumpty smiled contemptuously. "Of course you don't—till I tell you. I meant 'there's a nice knockdown argument for you.'"

"But 'glory' doesn't mean 'a nice knockdown argument'," Alice objected.

"When I use a word," Humpty Dumpty said in rather a scornful tone, "It means just what I choose it to mean—neither more nor less."

"The question is," said Alice, "whether you can make words mean so many different things."

"The question is," said Humpty Dumpty, "which is to be the master—that's all."

Many of the verbal and nonverbal symbols that we use evoke highly discrepant responses from people with differing experiences and beliefs. The use of profanity by some individuals can be a sign of insult, but by others a sign of affection. If we have similar experiences from which we draw the meanings for the words, symbols, signs, and behaviors that we use, then we are more likely to share the same meaning and reach understanding. Language has meaning only in the sense that we have common experiences with that language. In this sense, verbal and nonverbal behavior evoke or elicit meaning from a person's past experiences stored in her or his memory. Language behavior does not "carry" meaning to the other individual. We say that we "understand" each other when our verbal and nonverbal behaviors result in the retrieval of similar or shared experiences from our memories.

Our language systems help us to relate, order, index, and synthesize our communication experiences with other people. Our verbal and nonverbal systems, however, are not completely logical, though often we behave as if they were. For example, if a person says, "I am lying," then he must be lying about lying—or telling the truth, which is that he is lying. If we say that "all statements I make are false" then the phrase itself must be false—but then, it couldn't be or it would be true.

Our language does not allow us to say everything that could be said about anything. We have a limited number of verbal and nonverbal behaviors. We must leave things out. In this sense, we can never really "tell it like it is." Also, although no two things are exactly alike, we must often use the same word or behavior to refer to them as if they were alike. We have a finite number of words but an infinite number of things and ideas about which to communicate.

To compound this problem, we can use language not only to refer to things and ideas but also to refer to itself. We can talk about language with language. The preceding paragraphs have done just that. The further our

The meanings people hold for the same symbols often vary.

language usage gets away from referring to reality, the more abstract it becomes and generally the more difficult understanding becomes. Much of our nonverbal behavior, such as gestures, is used to refer to what we are saying orally. In this sense, these gestures are "talking about or explaining" what we are verbally saying. It should not be surprising that we are often unable to interpret the specific meaning of a gesture used in conjunction with verbal discourse.

Finally, our most frequently used language habits tend to polarize our thinking into either-or categories (dichotomies). We tend to more readily recognize yes-no, good-bad, right-wrong, and black-white kinds of distinctions. Our interpretation of potential information tends to be sorted and synthesized into these types of polarized extremes. Some people would note that there are actually very few mutually exclusive, dichotomous categories in the world. In bad things, some good may exist; in pleasure there may be some pain (e.g., childbirth).

Some have suggested means for remedying some of these problems. They propose that in the processes of both encoding and decoding messages we do the following things:

1. *Index* signs and symbols. Politician No. 1 is not Politician No. 2 and we should note the specific differences when we have to use the same term to refer to both. This helps us overcome the generality of language created by a limited number of terms that must be used for differing things.
2. *Date* signs and symbols. College Student 1976 is not the same as College Student 1970, who was rioting on campus. However, we must still use the same word to refer to both. Noting changes through our specific encoding and decoding helps to clarify.
3. Use *mental quotation marks* for terms that are used in a special manner. We should indicate special meanings for common words that are used in uncommon ways. For example, we use the term "receiver" in a special way in this book, although it is a common term.
4. Use *mental hyphens* to indicate things that are separable verbally but are not separable in reality. For example, we can verbally separate and analyze things such as mind-body, structure-function, and students-university, that are inseparable in reality.

Information Potentials of Language Codes

We have noted previously that messages contain potential information and that when a message reduces our uncertainty it has resulted in information gain for us. To some extent, then, *understanding* is the reduction of uncertainty within individuals and social systems through accurate information processing. You will remember from chapter 10 that when we encode messages designed to create understanding and information gain we have two broad choices to make. First, we can choose the specific content or elements to be included in the message. Second, we have to choose how those elements will be ordered and arranged into sequences, sentences, paragraphs or other structures. The first choice involves the selection of ideas and words (symbols, behaviors) that we will use to express those ideas; we call these *lexical choices*. The second choice involves the order in which we will place these words and ideas; we call these *syntactical choices*. Selections in these two areas which facilitate desirable attention and perception tendencies also aid information acquisition, recognition, interpretation, and storage-retrieval. What are some options in these two general areas? We noted some briefly in chapter 10. Now we will take the time to examine them in more detail so that you will be able to gain more accurate processing of your messages by others.

Important Message Elements

General Characteristics of Messages. In general, verbal and nonverbal messages that utilize factors related to increasing attention (discussed in chapter 14) are more easily acquired, understood, and retained. Channels of communication, particularly the mass media, can be viewed in this context as nonverbal messages or stimuli. They frequently utilize factors related to attention. Some characteristics related to attention that we discussed previously are intensity, extensity, concreteness, complexity (or simplicity), contrast (change, novelty), and impressivity (repetition, redundancy, duration). To the extent that *content* (lexical choices) and *arrangement* (syntactical choices) reflect these characteristics, then the message will be better attended and will focus the receivers' perceptions. However, any one characteristic used too frequently, or any number of characteristics used to extremes, may have detrimental effects on decoding. Exerting control over our own attention tendencies may facilitate our own receptivity to messages which do not contain those attention demanding elements. In like manner, concern for perceptual tendencies (discussed previously in this chapter) may facilitate more accurate encoding and decoding of message stimuli. When messages and channels utilize techniques that facilitate desirable attention and perception tendencies and inhibit undesirable tendencies, then more effective recognition, interpretation, and retention result.

**BLACK BOX
50**

Can you discuss how language affects our ability to process information?

Identify language elements and language potentials that are related to our understanding of messages.

Can you describe the general characteristics of messages?

Organization. We would expect the organization of a message to have considerable impact on our comprehension; however, research has not demonstrated this to be true in typical human communication. If a message is moderately well organized, it usually produces comparable understanding and retention with a very well-organized message. But when a message is extremely disorganized it has a detrimental effect on comprehension. The point at which a message becomes well enough organized to be considered "moderately well organized" is not absolutely known. This is often a matter of judgment. Some scholars have explained that moderately disorganized messages may force listeners or readers to participate more in the communication by requiring them to organize the message by themselves. This may well occur if the message is interesting enough and maintains our attention. Related research has investigated the *order in which important points are placed within a message*. Material you present first and/or last in a message appears to be better retained than material presented in the middle of a message.

Two-Sided Messages. Most of the research on one-sided and two-sided messages has investigated persuasive effects (see chapter 20). A two-sided message mentions opposing ideas or arguments and sometimes refutes them. A two-sided message produces more retention than a one-sided message. This is particularly true when pro and con arguments are juxtaposed: When we present one of our arguments and immediately follow it with an opposing argument, attention and perception are increased through the contrast, change, and novelty created. Hence, there is usually greater understanding and retention.

Syntactical Choices. The order in which we arrange words into sentences and the order in which we arrange particular nonverbal stimuli into meaningful sequences can be labeled *syntax*. There appear to be five syntactical choices available:

a. *Repetition* involves repeating the same or a similar word or stimulus in close proximity or time sequence (e.g., "Of the people, by the people, for the people.");
b. *Antithesis* is using a word or stimulus with opposite meaning in close proximity or time sequence (e.g., "Ask not what your country can do for you, but what you can do for your country. . .");
c. *Inversion* calls for deviation from normal order or sequence so that words or stimuli that normally come first are delayed until later (e.g., "Came spring,");
d. *Omission* involves the condensation of statements or sequences by the elimination of connectives, modifiers, articles, and other elements that do not signifi-

cantly alter meaning (e.g., "Bring home milk," instead of "would you stop by the store on your way home and buy some milk");

e. A *Rhetorical Question* frames an interrogative statement to which we expect no one to actually answer but which seeks to draw the conclusion we imply by the question (e.g., "Wouldn't you really rather have a Buick?").

These stylistic devices are probably most applicable to verbal messages but might possibly be applied to nonverbal stimuli. Potentially, all of these syntactical sequences might increase comprehension and retention. They appear to utilize attention factors related to simplicity, conventionality, contrast, change, novelty, impressivity, repetition, and redundancy.

Research has generally supported this conclusion, particularly in reference to those elements involving redundancy and repetition. Generally, three to four immediate repetitions appear to increase retention and retrieval of information. Immediate repetitions are frequently utilized in television advertising as well as repetitions delayed over time. There is some evidence to suggest that omissions and inversions may potentially reduce redundancy and predictability. This may reduce comprehension, particularly of more complex or difficult material. To the extent that material is simple and concrete, then omissions and inversions may be novel enough to facilitate attention-perception, thereby increasing retention. Antitheses display characteristics of contrast and, to a lesser extent, repetition. Because of this, antitheses appear to increase retention. Journalists and media specialists were quick to remember the phrase "Ask not what your country can do for you, but what you can do for your country." Similar antitheses are used by advertisers quite frequently. Finally, explicit conclusion drawing, rather than rhetorical questions and implied conclusions, appears to facilitate understanding and retention. This effect is probably attributable to the fact that direct, explicit statements are less subject to misinterpretation than implied or interrogative conclusions.

Transitions and Proactive Statements. In verbal messages the use of transitions has been shown to increase comprehension. This is particularly true when the transitions are obvious and explicitly point to the idea or argument. "Proactive statements" in this context may be considered as *very* explicit transitions. Phrases such as "now, get this," "write this down," and "now, don't forget this" have been shown to increase comprehension of the statement immediately following. We also use nonverbal cues for transition, regulation of thought, and proactive emphasis. Nonverbal techniques

such as pausing before a statement, raising the voice, gesturing, and banging on the table may increase comprehension.

Concreteness and Ambiguity. Concreteness and specificity of language appear to increase recall of information. We would of course expect that the more concrete and specific the wording is, the better the intended meaning could be recognized and interpreted. But words which refer to real things (e.g., chair, house, tree) also evoke mental images and produce greater recall than more abstract language (e.g., attitude, love, friendship). Picture words, imagery, and metaphor (e.g., he is a lion) appear to be processed in such a manner as to be more easily retained by individuals. On the other hand, both abstract and ambiguous words-sentences are likely to be distorted by an individual to fit her or his own past experience, attitudes, and needs.

More abstract mental images and metaphors may be more difficult to recall—compare "bird" to Brancusi's "Bird in Space."

*The concreteness of a
word—bird—appears
to increase
information recall.*

Language Intensity. Intense language indicates that a source is not neutral on an issue and that she or he may have varying levels of extreme views. Intensity does not refer to how loud someone speaks. Intense language refers to words which indicate that the source's attitudes deviate from neutral. Qualifiers and modifiers, along with metaphors, opinionated language, and fear appeals may make the language of a message more intense. Although research at this point in time is not conclusive, we can make some tentative conclusions about the effects of intense language on comprehension and retention. Intense language, because of its nature, has the potential of raising the activation level and attention of the receiver. In this sense, it might well increase information and understanding. If too intense, however, our own attitudes might interfere, as noted in the earlier section on perception. Remember the effect that obscenity can have on some people. To some extent the effect of intense language on comprehension is dependent upon the anxiety and activation level which the receiver already has. If she or he enters the communication event with a fairly high anxiety level, then intense language may increase anxiety beyond the limits where she or he can accurately recognize and discriminate among message cues. However, if the receivers are not anxious and at a low level of activation, then the use of intense language may strengthen attention, focus perception, and produce greater retention of information.

Additional Nonverbal Elements.   A person's speaking ability, message delivery and vocal qualities appear to have only a minimal affect on comprehension.   Most research reports only slight differences or no differences resulting from these types of considerations.   Likewise, rate of speech appears to have little impact on understanding and retention until a rate of 275 to 280 words per minute is reached.   We normally speak around 145 to 160 words per minute.   However, visible, meaningful actions and gestures by speakers appear to increase comprehension.   Again, these may draw attention and make receivers more receptive, in addition to being complimentary means of explaining ideas.   Also, eye contact by a source will increase our recall of what she or he has said.   However, if we know someone will test us on what is said, then eye contact does not appear to matter as much.

Effects of Channels, Social Systems, and Feedback

Channels of communication and social systems that facilitate feedback and cross-checking of information increase the probability of accurate perception and understanding.   Dyads, small groups, and small conferences, for example, are often used to facilitate interaction in the careful examination of information and claims.   On the other hand, channels and social systems which inhibit feedback and information cross-checking are more efficient at rapid dissemination of larger amounts of information.   The mass media, for example, are able to disseminate vast amounts of information to millions of people very efficiently.   Television which utilizes more than one channel—sight and sound—allows for cross-checking information between those two channels to facilitate accuracy.   Newspapers, however, may increase understanding with more in-depth explanation provided by the space available.   These mass systems, however, have much less feedback involved.

The time that can be devoted to feedback and interaction in any information system is the crucial variable.   Feedback and cross-checking between participants and channels may increase accuracy, but they also consume time and reduce efficiency in terms of the amount of new information that can be disseminated.   Therefore, there is no magic answer to what kind of communication system is best for information exchange.   Judgments must be made on the desired goals and the sacrifices that the participants are willing to make in information exchange.   A brief review of chapters 3 and 4 on social systems and a quick review of feedback in chapter 8 might be useful to you at this point.

Mass Systems of Information Diffusion

As noted in chapter 4, mass systems of communication are highly efficient in the diffusion of information to large numbers. Some research on mass communication has demonstrated fairly well that the primary effect of mass communication is the diffusion of information about ideas, practices-events, and products. Early researchers argued that we could not determine the effects of mass communication because of individual differences in perception; however, later researchers found that by placing receivers into social categories based on demographic characteristics (status, economic level, etc.) they could predict what information people would select among the options available in the media. Others have noted that the mass media provide information about norms and acceptable-unacceptable behavior in our society and culture. Thus, the media ultimately influence our behavior by establishing norms for that behavior. The diffusion of information from the media involves a multi-cycle, multi-step flow involving interpersonal relationships as well as media. Apparently, the most influence is exerted in interpersonal relationships. But the media also provide an important informative function in the diffusion of new ideas, practices, and products. Mass media systems make people aware of new innovations and provide basic information upon which subsequent interpersonal exchanges can be based. In the subsequent exchanges, cross-checking and reinterpretation of the initial information occur. We would expect similar types of information processing to occur in public speaking, societal, and cross-cultural systems of communication.

In mediated mass communication, the gatekeeper (discussed in chapter 4) is a key element determining what information we are likely to have available. Government agencies (e.g., FCC), government regulations, censorship boards, product sponsors, and news editors all serve to necessarily inhibit some information while facilitating other information. Time and space are not available for all information to receive mass dissemination at one time. These gatekeepers attempt to regulate the flow of information by protecting the good of society as a whole and simultaneously safeguarding the individual's right to know. Mistakes made in the process are often arbitrated by the Supreme Court under amendments guaranteeing freedom of speech and press.

Although mass media are rapid diffusers of information, sometimes they are not fast enough. Highly important news (hot news), for example, is often diffused interpersonally by persons with *immediate* access to the media. When a president is assassinated or some other major tragedy or crisis occurs, large numbers of people learn of the incident in a very short

*Mass systems involve
multi-step flows
through reporters,
gate keepers, media,
and interpersonal
relationships.*

period of time, often only minutes after it occurs. However, only a relatively small number may have heard of the incident initially from the media. We are likely to receive less urgent but still highly newsworthy items from the news mass media first. Depending upon our reading habits, we may first learn that information from interpersonal or mediated communication. Items with very low news value may have very low interpersonal and media exchange. They are more likely to appear in books or in work-related interpersonal exchanges.

Organizational Systems of Information Exchange

Organizations have some of the characteristics of both mass and highly personal systems of information diffusion and exchange (see chapter 3). Mass media in the forms of company news letters, training films, and memos are often used. Interpersonal information exchange, however, is frequently used in day-to-day practical affairs. Committees, conferences, board meetings, and interviews are typical. In addition, channels of communication are highly diverse. The formal structure forms the official channels for information; however, informal channels and "grapevines" assume much of the information diffusion burden. As in mass communication systems, opinion leaders also play an important role in the dissemination of information in organizations.

Generally, there are a number of characteristics of information flow in organizations. Communication from top management down the levels of the organization is not too effective. Likewise, upward communication and feedback to management is generally inhibited by the structure. Each level of an organization serves as a filter or "gatekeeper" by screening out and failing to pass on information that would be harmful to that level. Apparently some combination of both oral and written communication is most effective in the diffusion of information both upward and downward. Written communication alone appears to have even less impact than oral. The grapevine appears to be the least accurate, but a highly rapid channel. It is not surprising that most hear of new information through the grapevine. Most organizational scholars argue that horizontal or lateral channels of information exchange are not used as frequently as needed. The increase in technology has placed a greater demand upon these horizontal information channels.

Dyadic and Small-Group Systems

Dyadic and small-group systems of communication (see chapter 3) are useful in dealing with certain types of information. Information upon which decisions are based can be carefully analyzed in these settings. Opinions, beliefs, and attitude of participants can be cross-checked and tested in a system that allows a high level of interaction; however, information exchange is likely to be more time-consuming than in more linear systems of informa-

---

**BLACK BOX
51**

Can you explain how the following variables affect information processing?
organization
syntactical choices
transitions and proactive statements
concreteness and ambiguity
language intensity
nonverbal elements

Can you discuss the impact social systems have upon people's information processing?

tion dissemination.   In addition, these face-to-face systems are more likely to give rise to personal opinions, psychological states of individuals, and self-disclosive messages (see chapter 11).   These types of information may or may not be desirable depending upon the goals of the participants involved.   But judgments based upon understanding the nature of information exchange in these systems should allow us to utilize them more effectively.

Summary

In this chapter and the previous one, we have explored the ways humans acquire, recognize, interpret, store, and retrieve information.   We have noted various phases of information processing as they apply to individuals, groups, and various other social systems.   The ways in which we are able to effectively and accurately process information are related to our perceptual tendencies, our perceptions of other participants, personal characteristics, characteristics of messages, and social systems of which we are a part. Your own attention to these factors can increase your ability to process information and can make you a more effective source of information for others.   However, effective communication can also be concerned with additional functions.   In the next chapter, we turn our attention to influence.

SUGGESTED FURTHER READINGS

1. Hayakawa, S. I. *Language in Thought and Action* (New York: Harcourt, Brace and Co., 1949).

    Those interested in general semantics and how we use words and meaning will find this book informative and entertaining.   It is a very readable classic in that area of thinking.

2. Kibler, R. J., Barker, L. L., and Cegala, D. J.   "Effect of Sex on Comprehension and Retention." *Speech Monographs* 37 (1970): 287–292.

    These researchers summarize studies which have shown differing comprehension and retention for males and females.   They critique many of the biases in the studies and offer a final study of their own in which no such differences were found.

3. Miller, G. R. "Human Information Processing: Some Research Guidelines," in *Conceptual Frontiers in Speech Communication,* Kibler and Barker, eds. (New York: SCA, 1969), 51–67.

For people interested in more in-depth understanding of information and how we process it, this article will be valuable reading. Although the volume in which it is found is fairly scarce in libraries, someone on the faculty in the speech communication department may have a copy.

4. Thompson, E. "Some Effects of Message Structure on Listener's Comprehension." *Speech Monographs* 34 (1967): 51–57.

This article summarizes much of the research on the effects of message structure. A critique of that literature led Thompson to develop a well-conceived follow-up study that is reported in the article.

5. Vernon, M. "Perception, Attention, and Consciousness," in *Foundations of Communication Theory,* K. K. Sereno and C. D. Mortensen, eds. (New York: Harper & Row, 1970).

A fairly comprehensive summary of studies relating to perception is presented in this discussion. The effects of elements such as attitudes, needs, and expectancies are discussed. This summary presents a number of highly interesting studies and findings.

6. Wheeless, L. R. "The Relationship of Attitude and Credibility to Comprehension and Selective Exposure." *Western Speech* 38 (1974): 88–97.

In this report a number of attitudes and perceptions of sources are considered. Many of them were found to affect how we process information.

7. Zagona, S. and Harter, R. "Credibility of Source and Recipient Attitude: Factors for the Perception and Retention of Information on Smoking Behavior." *Perceptual Motor Skills* 23 (1966): 155–168.

This study is one of the earliest to demonstrate some perception or retention of information to be the result of source credibility. Also, since the study is applied to an important health issue (smoking), the study is worth reading as a supplement.

SELECTED REFERENCES

ADRIAN, E. H. "The Human Receiving System," in *Foundations of Communication Theory,* K. K. Sereno and C. D. Mortensen, eds. (New York: Harper & Row, 1970).

ANDERSEN, P. "An Experimental Study to Assess the Effects of Source Credibility on Comprehension." Paper presented at the Speech Communication Association Convention, New York, November, 1973.

ASHBY, W. R. *Design for a Brain* (New York: John Wiley, 1960).

ATKIN, C. "Instrumental Utilities and Information Seeking," in *New Models for Mass Communication Research,* Peter Clarke, ed. (volume II of Sage Annual Reviews of Communication Research. Beverly Hills: Sage Publications, 1973), 205–242.

AYRES, H. J. "An Overview of Theory and Research in Feedback." Paper presented at the ICA Convention, Phoenix, Arizona, April, 1971.

BEIGHLEY, K. C. "An Experimental Study of Three Speech Variables on Listener Comprehension." *Speech Monographs* 21 (1954): 248–253.

BERSHEID, E. and WALSTER, E. *Interpersonal Attraction* (Reading, Mass.: Addison-Wesley, 1969).

BOWERS, J. W. and OSBORN, M. "Attitudinal Effects of Selected Types of Concluding Metaphors in Persuasive Speeches." *Speech Monographs* 33 (June, 1966): 147–155.

BROADBENT, D. E. *Decision and Stress* (London: Academic Press, 1973).

————. "Information Processing in the Nervous System." *Science* 150 (1965): 457–462.

CARTER, R. R. "Stereotyping as a Process." *Public Opinion Quarterly* 26 (1962): 77–91.

CHALL, J. S. *Readability* (Columbus: The Ohio State University Press, 1958).

CHERRY, C. *On Human Communication* (New York: John Wiley, 1957).

COHEN, A. R. *Attitude Change and Social Influence* (New York: Basic Books, Inc., 1964).

DARNELL, D. K. "The Relation Between Sentence-Order and Comprehension." *Speech Monographs* 30 (1963): 97–100.

DEESE, J. and HULSE, S. H. *The Psychology of Learning* (New York: McGraw-Hill, 1967).

DEFLEUR, M. L. *Theories of Mass Communication* (New York: David McKay Co., Inc., 1970).

DEVITO, J. A. "Comprehension Factors in Oral and Written Discourse of Skilled Communicators." *Speech Monographs* 32 (1965): 124–129.

EHRENSBERGER, R. "An Experimental Study of the Relative Effectiveness of Certain Forms of Emphasis in Public Speaking." *Speech Monographs* 12 (1945): 94–111.

GANGE, R. M. *The Conditions of Learning* (New York: Holt, Rinehart and Winston, 1965).

GARDINER, J. C. "A Synthesis of Experimental Studies of Speech Communicaton Feedback." *Journal of Communication* 21 (1971): 17–35.

GILLIE, P. J. "A Simplified Formula for Measuring Abstraction in Writing." *Journal of Applied Psychology* 41 (1957): 214–217.

GOSS, B. "The Effect of Sentence Context on Associations to Ambiguous, Vague, and Clear Nouns." *Speech Monographs* 39 (1972): 286–289.

GURWITSCH, A. *The Field of Consciousness* (Pittsburgh: Duquesne University Press, 1964).

GUTHRIE, M. L. "Effects of Credibility, Metaphor, and Intensity on Comprehension, Credibility, and Attitude Change." Unpublished Masters' Thesis, Illinois State University, 1972.

HANEY, W. V. "A Comparative Study of Unilateral and Bilateral Communication." *Academy of Management Journal* 7 (1964): 128–136.

HARRELL, M., BOWERS, J. W., and BACAL, J. P. "Another Stab at 'Meaning': Concreteness, Iconicity and Conventionality." *Speech Monographs* 40 (1973): 199–207.

HASTORF, A. H. SCHNEIDER, D. J., and POLEFKA. *Person Perception* (Reading, Mass.: Addison-Wesley, 1970.)

HAYAKAWA, S. I. *Language in Thought and Action* (New York: Harcourt, Brace, 1949).

HENNEMAN, R. H. "Vision and Audition as Sensory Channels for Communication." *Quarterly Journal of Speech* 38 (April, 1952).

HILL, W. F. *Learning* (Scranton: Chandler Publishing Co., 1971).

HOVLAND, C. I. "A Communication Analysis of Concept Learning." *Psychological Review* 59 (1952): 461–472.

HOVLAND, C. I., HARVEY, O. J., and SHERIF, M. "Assimilation and Contrast Effects in Reactions to Communication and Attitude Change." *Journal of Abnormal and Social Psychology* 55 (1957): 244–252.

HOVLAND, C. I. and MANDELL, W. "An Experimental Comparison of Conclusion-Drawing by the Communicator and by the Audience." *Journal of Abnormal and Social Psychology* 47 (1952): 581–588.

HOVLAND, C. I. and SHERIF, M. *Social Judgment* (New Haven: Yale University Press, 1961).

HOVLAND, C. I. and WEISS, W. "Transmission of Information Concerning Concepts Through Positive and Negative Instances." *Journal of Experimental Psychology* 45 (1953): 175–182.

JANIS, I. L. and MILHOLLAND, W. "The Influence of Threat Appeals on Selective Learning of the Content of a Persuasive Communication." *Journal of Psychology* 37 (1954): 75–80.

JERSILD, A. T. "Modes of Emphasis in Public Speaking." *Journal of Applied Psychology* 12 (1928): 611–612.

JONES, R. W. and GRAY, J. S. "Systems Theory and Physiological Processes." *Science* 140 (1963): 461–466.

JORDAN, W. J., FLANAGAN, L. L. and WINEINGER, R. W. "Novelty and Recall Effects of Animate and Inanimate Metaphorical Discourse." *Central States Speech Journal* 26 (1975): 29–33.

KAMIN, L. J. "Predictability, Surprise, Attention, and Conditioning," in *Punishment and Adversive Behavior,* B. A. Campbell and R. M. Church, eds. (New York: Appleton-Century-Crofts, 1969).

KNAPP, M. L. *Nonverbal Communication in Human Interaction* (New York: Holt, Rinehart and Winston, 1972).

KIBLER, R. J., BARKER, L. L., and CEGALA, D. J. "Effect of Sex on Comprehension and Retention." *Speech Monographs* 37 (1970): 287–292.

KORZYBASKI, A. *Science and Sanity: An Introduction to Non-Aristotelian Systems and General Semantics,* 3rd ed., revised (Lakeville, Ct.: The International Non-Aristotelian Library Publishing Co., 1948).

KURTZ, K. H. and HOVLAND, C. I. "The Effect of Verbalization During Observation of Stimulus Objects Upon Accuracy of Recognition and Recall." *Journal of Experimental Psychology* 45 (1953): 157–164.

LASHBROOK, W. B., HAMILTON, P., and TODD, W. "A Theoretical Consideration of the Assessment of Source Credibility as a Function of Information Seeking Behavior." Paper presented at the Western Speech Communication Association Convention, Honolulu, November, 1972.

LIVINGSTON, H. M. "An Experimental Study of Effects of Interest and Authority Upon Understanding of Broadcast Information." Unpublished Doctoral Dissertation, University of Southern California, 1961.

LURIA, A. R. *Higher Cortical Functions in Man* (New York: Basic Books, 1966).

MABRY, E. A. "A Multivariate Investigation of Profane Language." *Central States Speech Journal* 26 (1975): 39–44.

MACKAY, D. J. and BEVER, T. "In Search of Ambiguity." *Perception and Psychophysics* 2 (1967): 193–200.

MACKAY, D. M. "Information Theory in the Study of Man," in *Readings in Psychology,* J. Cohen, ed. (London: Allen and Unwin, 1964).

MCCROSKEY, J. C. "Measures of Communication Bound Anxiety." *Speech Monographs* 37 (1970): 269–277.

MCCROSKEY, J. C. and COMBS, W. H. "The Effects of the Use of Analogy on Attitude Change and Source Credibility." *Journal of Communication* 19 (1969): 333–339.

MCLAUGHLIN, B. "Effects of Similarity and Likableness on Attraction and Recall." *Journal of Personality and Social Psychology* 85 (1971): 51–64.

MILLER, G. A. *Language and Communication* (New York: McGraw-Hill, 1951).

———. "The Magical Number Seven, Plus or Minus Two: Some Limits on Our Capacity for Processing Information." *Psychology Review* 63 (1956): 81–97.

MILLER, G. R. "Human Information Processing: Some Research Guidelines," in *Conceptual Frontiers in Speech Communication,* Kibler and Barker, eds. (New York: SCA, 1969), 51–67.

MILLS, R. G. "A Relative Frequency Principle in Processing Contingent Information." *Psychonomic Science* 18 (1970): 215–217.

MINSKY, M., ed. *Semantic Information Processing* (Cambridge, Mass.: MIT Press, 1968).

NICHOLS, A. C. "Effects of Three Aspects of Sentence Structure on Immediate Recall." *Speech Monographs* 32 (1965): 164–168.

NICHOLS, R. G. "Factors in Listening Comprehension." *Speech Monographs* 15 (1948): 154–163.

OSGOOD, C. E., SUCI, G. J., and TANNENBAUM, P. *The Measurement of Meaning* (Urbana: University of Illinois Press, 1957).

PAGANO, D. F. "Information-Processing Differences in Repressors and Sensitizers." *Journal of Personality and Social Psychology* 26 (1973): 105–109.

PAIVIO, A., YUILLE, J. C., and MADIGAN, S. A. "Concreteness, Imagery, and Meaningfulness Values for 925 Nouns." *Journal of Experimental Psychology, Monograph Supplement* 76 (1968): 1–25.

PASCHAL, F. G. "The Trend in Theories of Attention." *Psychological Review* 48 (1948): 383–403.

PAULSON, S. "The Effects of the Prestige of the Speaker and Acknowledgment of Opposing Arguments on Audience Retention and Shift of Opinion." *Speech Monographs* 21 (1954): 267–271.

PETRIE, C. R., JR. "Informative Speaking: A Summary and Bibliography of Related Research." *Speech Monographs* 30 (1963): 79–91.

PINES, H. A. and JULIAN, J. W. "Effects of Task and Social Demands on Locus of Control Differences in Information Processing." *Journal of Personality* 40 (1970): 405–415.

REDDING, W. C. and SANBORN, G. A. *Business and Industrial Communication: A Source Book* (New York: Harper & Row, 1964).

ROGERS, E. and SHOEMAKER, F. F. *Communication of Innovations,* (New York: The Free Press, 1971).

ROKEACH, M. *The Open and Closed Mind* (New York: Basic Books, 1960).

ROSENKRANTZ, P. S. and CROCKETT, W. H. "Some Factors Influencing the Assimilation of Desperate Information in Impression Formation." *Journal of Personality and Social Psychology* (1965): 397–402.

SCOTT, M. D. YATES, M., and WHEELESS, L. R. "An Exploratory Investigation of Communication Apprehension in Alternative Systems of Instruction." Paper presented at the International Communication Association Convention, Chicago, April, 1975.

SEILER, W. J. "The Effects of Visual Materials on Attitudes, Credibility, and Retention." *Speech Monographs* 38 (1971): 331–334.

SHAMO, W. G. and BITTNER, J. R. "Information Recall as a Function of Language Style." Paper presented at the International Communication Association, Phoenix, Arizona, April, 1971.

SHERIF, M., SHERIF, C., and NEBERGALL, R. *Attitude and Attitude Change* (Philadelphia: W. B. Saunders Co., 1965).

SPIELBERGER, C. D. *Anxiety and Behavior* (New York: Academic Press, 1966).

THISTLETHWAITE, D. L. and KAMENETSKY, J. "The Effect of 'Directive' and 'Non-Directive' Communication Procedures on Attitudes." *Journal of Abnormal and Social Psychology* 51 (1955): 3–12.

THOMAS, G. L. "Effect of Oral Style on Intelligibility of Speech." *Speech Monographs* 23 (March, 1956): 46–54.

THOMPSON, E. "An Experimental Investigation of the Relative Effectiveness of Organization Structure in Oral Communication." Doctoral Dissertation, University of Minnesota, 1960.

———. "An Experimental Investigation of the Relative Effectiveness of Organizational Structure in Oral Communication." *Southern Speech Journal* 26 (1960): 59–69.

———. "Some Effects of Message Structure on Listener's Comprehension." *Speech Monograph* 34 (1967): 51–57.

TOCH, H. and MACLEAN, M. S., JR. "Perception and Communication: A Transactional View." *Audio Visual Communication Review* 10 (1967): 55–77.

TUCKER, C. O. and MCGLONE, E. L. "Toward an Operational Definition and Measurement of Understanding." *Central States Speech Journal* 21 (1970): 41–45.

VERNON, M. D. "Perception, Attention, and Consciousness," in *Foundations of Communication Theory*, K. K. Sereno and C. D. Mortensen, eds. (New York: Harper & Row, 1970).

———. *The Psychology of Perception* (Baltimore: Penguin Books, 1963).

WHEELESS, L. R. "An Investigation of Receiver Apprehension and Social Context Dimensions of Communication Apprehension." *Speech Teacher* 24 (1975): 261–268.

———. "The Relationship of Attitude and Credibility to Comprehension and Selective Exposure." *Western Speech* 38 (1974): 88–97.

———. "The Relationship of Four Elements to Immediate Recall and Student-Instructor Interaction." *Western Speech* 39 (1975): 131–140.

WHEELESS, L. R. and CHARLES, R. "A Review and Reconceptualization of Stereotyping Behavior." Paper presented at the Speech Communication Association Convention, New York, November 1973.

WHEELESS, L. R. and McCROSKEY, J. C. "The Effects of Selected Syntactical Choices on Source Credibility, Attitude, Behavior, and Perception of Message." *Southern Speech Communication Journal* 38 (1973): 213–222.

WHEELESS, L. R. and WILLIS, M. "The Relationship of Attitudes Toward Course and Instructor to Learning and Student-Instructor Interaction in Instructional Assessment." Paper presented at the Speech Communication Association Convention, Chicago, December, 1974.

WHORF, B. *Language, Thought, and Reality* (Cambridge, Mass.: The Technology Press, Massachusetts Institute of Technology, 1956).

YUILLE, J. C. and PAIVIO, A. "Abstractness and Recall of Connected Discourse." *Journal of Experimental Psychology* 82 (1969): 467–471.

ZAGONA, S. and HARTER, R. "Credibility of Source and Recipient Attitude: Factors for the Perception and Retention of Information on Smoking Behavior." *Perceptual Motor Skills* 23 (1966): 155–168.

ZIMBARDO, P. "Verbal Ambiguity and Judgmental Distortion." *Psychological Reports* 6 (1960): 57–58.

16

Influence: Basic Theories

Tom tunes in a football game and is told about a brand of shaving cream he should try.

Ellen asks her mother how she prepares au gratin potatoes.

Carol attends a commercial art exhibit.

Velma goes to church and hears her priest explain the Catholic position on artificial birth control.

Mike calls Randi and suggests that they attend a movie this evening.

Leonard reads an editorial in the local newspaper.

Rocky gives a speech to the local Kiwanis.

Pete goes to an interview for a new position.

There is a staff meeting held to determine what the new policy ought to be.

These are brief descriptions of communication events. All of these incidents have one thing in common: they involve influence or attempts at influ-

ence. We could go on listing more and more such communication examples. In fact, some people contend that all human communication involves influence. We are sympathetic with that view, but our concern with influence in this chapter will narrow that definition of influence somewhat. We will examine influence having to do with ideas or behaviors. The four previous chapters were concerned with communication related to affinity and information acquisition. In a very real sense, the development of affinity and the acquisition of information are also examples of influence. However, at this point we are excluding these two forms of influence communication and are focusing on the type of influence that results in change or retention of beliefs, attitudes, values, or behaviors.

The Definition of Influence

Influence is so much a part of our everyday lives and our total communication experience that it may seem unnecessary to define it. However, as is the case with most things that we consider to be "common sense," not everyone thinks of influence in the same way. Consequently, it is important for us to have a shared meaning for influence so that the remainder of this chapter will make some sense.

In general, influence has been defined in the past from either of two orientations: intent or effect.

Intent

Many writers concerned with the process of persuasion, particularly in a one-to-many context, look at influence from the intent orientation. Essentially this orientation holds that influence exists whenever one individual consciously intends to alter the attitudes, beliefs, values, or behaviors of another individual or individuals. An advertisement on television is clearly an example of an intentional attempt to influence. Approached from this orientation influence can be either successful or unsuccessful. If the influence that was intended occurs, then we have successful influence. If the intended influence does not occur, or some other outcomes occur, the influence attempt is judged as unsuccessful. This is a very source-centered orientation, but it can be expanded to include a receiver orientation. Although we may not think of it as often, people do consciously seek communication with other people in order to be influenced as well as to influence the other people. This is particularly true in a communication system where an opinion leader is present. Very often we turn to our opinion leader to ask her or his advice about what we should think and what we should do. Such influence seeking would also fit this intent-oriented definition of influence.

Effect

The effect orientation to influence holds that whenever change of attitudes, beliefs, values, or behavior occurs or is prevented from occurring, influence exists. Examining influence from this orientation excludes the concept of intent. Whether one or more people involved in the communication system intend to influence another or be influenced by another is irrelevant. The only concern is with whether or not such change or prevention of change occurs. Thus, the concept of successful as opposed to unsuccessful influence is not relevant in this orientation. In its place is the concept of influence or no influence. Those who argue that violence on television increases violence in our society do not usually claim that this is the intent of the networks; rather, they merely argue that this influence occurs, regardless of the intent.

Our Orientation

Our preference is for the effect orientation toward influence. This is not to deny that there is intent in many human communication systems and this intent is sometimes followed by desired influence and in some cases is not followed by that influence. But we despair of determining how to discover the intent of other people, at least with much accuracy. Further, it is clear that much influence occurs through human communication with no real intent involved. Consequently, we prefer to examine the influence process in its totality to determine how people are influenced through human communication rather than to narrow our orientation to intentional influence.

Models of the Influence Process

Before we begin to consider the relationship between communication and influence, we need to examine the influence process itself. We will first look at three general models of the influence process that view this process from different vantage points. In the next section we will consider the three major theories concerning how influence occurs.

There have been three major models employed by most scholars to describe the influence process. These are the adoption model, the intellectual assent model, and the behavioral compliance model. We will consider each of them in turn.

The Adoption Model

The adoption model was developed by communication researchers concerned with the diffusion of innovations, particularly agricultural innovations. It has been very influential on the kind of research that has been done concerning the acceptance of new ideas, techniques, and products. The model involves six steps or stages (see Figure 16–1).

1. Awareness. The first step of the adoption process is awareness. During this stage the individual learns of the existence of some new idea, technique, or product, but may know very little about it. This model suggests that awareness must be the first stage, because until we are conscious of a new idea, technique, or product, we cannot possibly be influenced to accept or reject it. An example of this stage of the adoption process in operation would be observing a new brand of toothpaste in a friend's home. Or we might see a television advertisement describing this new toothpaste. Prior to this time we were not aware of its existence; consequently, we had neither adopted nor rejected the new toothpaste.

2. Interest. The second step of the adoption process is the development of interest in the new idea, technique, or product. People are aware of many things in which they are not at all interested. Presume, for example, that I had a complete set of dentures. The existence of a new brand of toothpaste would not be likely to draw my interest. The possibility of me adopting the new product would be remote indeed. However, presume that I do have a normal set of teeth, and become aware of the new toothpaste; during the interest stage I would be very likely to seek more information about the new toothpaste. I might read advertisements in magazines about the toothpaste, or watch television advertisements about the toothpaste, or even more likely I might turn to a friend of mine and ask if he or she has tried it, and if so how good it was. In short, during the interest stage people frequently expose themselves voluntarily to influence attempts concerning the new idea, technique, or product.

3. Evaluation. During the evaluation stage of the adoption process the individual makes a mental application of the new idea, technique, or product to see how well it might serve his or her needs. During this period normal influence attempts by outside interests may affect the evaluation that is made of the innovation. Further, our interaction with our friends or opinion leaders who are acquainted with the innovation may have considerable influence over how we ultimately evaluate the innovation. For example, I may attend to an advertisement that compares the new toothpaste with other brands and projects the consequences that would result from adopting the new toothpaste. This may influence what I think about the new toothpaste. Similarly, I may talk with my friends or an opinion leader about their experience with the new toothpaste and project from their experience to what my experience would likely be.

4. Trial. During this stage of the adoption process the individual makes a tentative adoption of the new idea, technique, or product. The results of this temporary adoption are carefully evaluated to determine the desirability of the outcome. I might buy a tube of the new toothpaste and try it out. Then I evaluate whether my teeth are brighter, or my breath is fresher, or maybe just whether the toothpaste tastes better than what I have been using.

5. Adoption. If the new idea, technique, or product survives the trial stage, the individual will adopt it as a relatively permanent choice. In our toothpaste example, I would become a regular user of the new brand.

6. Continuance-Discontinuance. New adoption does not necessarily mean permanent adoption. Once an individual has adopted an innovation, the testing of that innovation will still continue. Over a period of time the new idea, technique, or product may prove unworthy and thus be discontin-

FIGURE 16–1. The adoption model.

ued.   Similarly, over a period of the time the innovation may prove to be
very worthy indeed, and thus be continued indefinitely.   Very often, however,
another innovation comes along that would require discontinuance of the
previous innovation for adoption.   In such circumstances, the adoption
process starts all over again.   In our toothpaste example, I might become
aware of a still newer toothpaste, become interested in it, evaluate it as
possibly beneficial, give it a trial, and decide to adopt it in place of the earlier
toothpaste.

BLACK BOX
52

**Can you distinguish between the "intent" and the "effects" orientation
to influence?**

Can you identify the six stages in the adoption model of influence?

**Try to generate an example of each stage based on your own adoption of
new ideas, techniques, or products.**

Throughout the entire process, there is potential for influence either
to change from current attitudes and behaviors to adopt new ones or to
remain with current attitudes and behaviors.   Although the individual ultimately makes the decision on whether or not to adopt and whether or not
to continue the adoption, external influences are very important in all of the
other stages of the adoption process.   All of these external influences relate
to communication between human beings.   We will discuss how this process
operates later in this chapter.

The Intellectual Assent Model

While the adoption model attempts to describe the steps a person goes
through when deciding whether or not to accept an innovation, the intellectual assent model tries to describe simply the intellectual processes that the
individual goes through in determining his or her behavior.   Four terms
need to be clarified in this model (see Figure 16–2).

1. Behavior.   Behavior is any overt act that an individual chooses in which
to engage or not to engage.   Behavior is the only element in the intellectual

FIGURE 16–2.   Intellectual assent model.

assent model that is directly observable by someone else. We can tell what a person's behavior is by observing it, but we cannot tell what a person's beliefs, attitudes, or values are by observing them, since they are elements inside the mind and are not directly observable by anyone else. If I donate money to a worthy cause, that is my behavior. If I don't donate money to a worthy cause, that is my behavior.

2. Attitudes.   Attitudes are learned predispositions to respond to an object or a class of objects in a favorable or unfavorable way. More simply, our attitudes are our evaluations of potential behaviors in which we might engage. The intellectual assent model suggests that, other things being equal, if we have a positive attitude toward a given behavior, we are likely to engage in it, but if we have a negative attitude toward that same behavior, we are unlikely to engage in it.

3. Beliefs.   Belief is the term we use to describe the way people view reality. If I think donating money to the American Cancer Society will lead to a cure for cancer, that is my belief. If I believe that donating money to the American Cancer Society is unlikely to lead to a cure for cancer, that is my belief. The assumption underlying the intellectual assent model is that, other things being equal, the stronger my belief that a given behavior will lead to desirable consequences, the more likely I am to have a positive attitude toward that behavior; or, on the other hand, the more I believe that a given behavior will lead to undesirable consequences, the more likely I am to have a negative attitude toward that behavior.

4. Values.   Our values are our conceptions of the nature of good and bad. While an individual may have an almost infinite number of attitudes and beliefs, people hold very few values. On the basis of this limited number of values we evaluate all potential beliefs, attitudes, and behaviors. People with vastly different values are very unlikely to engage in the same behaviors, or to hold the same beliefs or attitudes. People structure their values into an hierarchical arrangement. By that we mean that while we may hold ten to twenty values, they are not all equally important. We can rank order them, particularly when it is time for us to make a decision about our behavior. Consider the following values: comfortable life, achievement, peace, equality, freedom, national security, salvation, friendship, and wisdom. These are some of the most commonly held values in the American culture. But not everyone adheres to all of these values, and they are not in this particular order for everyone. To understand this point, you might take this list of values and present it to several different friends of yours or several acquaintances who are not friends. Ask them to rank order these values and then compare the rankings that you get. Unless something very unusual occurs, you will find major differences in the way your friends and acquaintances will rank these values. The intellectual assent model of the influence process specifically takes into account this kind of difference in value structure that people hold. Further, the intellectual assent model stresses that values mediate or influence everything else in the intellectual assent process.

An examination of the intellectual assent model (Figure 16–2) indicates that as information is acquired it has an impact on a person's beliefs. As a person's beliefs are affected this alteration has an influence on the

A decision about how to deal with Arab oil countries will rest on information, beliefs, and attitude in the intellectual assent model.

person's attitudes which in turn influence the person's behavior. The model also indicates that a person's value system interacts with the information that is acquired in order to affect beliefs. Similarly, a person's values interact with his or her beliefs to determine that person's attitudes, and the values interact with the attitudes to determine the person's behavior. Let us take an example to see how this model functions. Presume that I have acquired the information that: (1) it is vital for our country to have oil for us to maintain our current standard of living; (2) most of the oil that we need must be imported from Arab countries; (3) the Arabs are not going to sell us as much oil as we need. Now presume that I hold three relatively important values: (1) a comfortable life, (2) peace, and (3) salvation. The interaction of this information and my value system could result in the following beliefs: (1) our country will be short of oil; (2) the Arabs are unfriendly toward us; (3) my way of life is threatened. Now to continue our hypothetical case, presume that two behaviors have been recommended for our nation: (1) ration oil so that we can survive on what we have; or (2) invade the Arab countries and take over their oil supplies. The question: What will my attitude be toward those two behavioral choices? Since I have ordered my values with a comfortable life being first and peace being second, this value system is likely to interact with my beliefs about the threat to my comfort and the unfriendliness of the Arabs to result in a positive attitude toward invading the Arab countries and a negative attitude toward rationing. Now let us presume that there are two political candidates running for President of the United States. One of them advocates the invasion of the Arab countries, and the other advocates rationing instead. For whom am I likely to vote? My attitude toward invasion is positive, and my attitude toward rationing is negative, so we might conclude that I will vote for the former candidate. However, my values for salvation and peace may interact with my attitudes at this point and cause me to select the rationing candidate. My choice will depend upon what other information I obtain and additional beliefs and attitudes that I have formed.

This extended example is designed to make one simple point: the intellectual assent model suggests that my behavior is based upon how I respond intellectually to my environment. In short, the way I think determines the way I act. Communication is involved because communication is the means by which the way I think is influenced to change or remain the same. In fact, the intellectual assent model will suggest that the *only* way that behavior can be altered is through influence via human communication. We will discuss this process later in the chapter.

333

The Behavioral Compliance Model

In the intellectual assent model information is presumed to be the primary element enabling beliefs and attitudes, and subsequently behavior, to be influenced. In that model, information has to do with the external world. The behavioral compliance model does not include a reference to information, but the element is still there. In this model (see Figure 16-3) the assumption is that a behavior at one point in time will influence the beliefs and attitudes that lead to subsequent behavior. We can word that differently so we can see that the concept of information is still present. We could say: information about our prior behavior influences our beliefs and attitudes, which impact our subsequent behavior. Examined in this way the intellectual assent model and the behavioral compliance model may seem to be highly similar. In a sense they are, but there is one major distinction. In the intellectual assent model the assumption is that the individual always chooses his or her behavior on an intellectual basis related to information about the external world. But the behavioral compliance model assumes that the basis for our decision concerning behavior is primarily centered on information about our own previous behavior. In essence, this model suggests that the primary element influencing our beliefs and attitudes—and consequently our behavior—is our previous behavior. Thus, if we wish to influence a man, we can do that most easily by getting him to engage in a behavior similar to the one that we want him to continue in the future. This might be done either through force or voluntary cooperation on the part of the other individual. Let us consider an example. Presume that we are members of a business corporation and it is in the corporation's interests for us to speak well of the corporation's product wherever we might be. One of the managers of the corporation takes it upon herself to influence us to engage in that desired behavior. If the manager were to operate under the intellectual assent model, she would be very likely to provide us with infor-

---

**BLACK BOX
53**

Can you explain and distinguish between the *intellectual assent* and
behavioral compliance models of influence?

Can you distinguish among beliefs, attitudes, and values? Can you
provide examples of each from your own orientations?

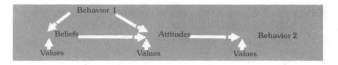

FIGURE 16–3. *Behavioral compliance model.*

mation about the company's product that would show it in a favorable light and would indicate that it could satisfy one or more of our strongly held values. We can predict that we would develop a positive attitude toward that product and engage in desired behavior, such as talking in a favorable way about the product to friends. Presume, however, that the manager decided to employ the behavioral compliance model to influence us. Then she might encourage us to write a positive message about the product, either under real or presumed-real conditions for presenting that message externally. We might be asked to write a publicity release, a variety of trial advertisements, or a response to a testing agency explaining the good qualities of the product. The behavioral compliance model would suggest that because we have engaged in this behavior that we would indeed develop positive beliefs about the product and positive attitudes about the product which should subsequently result in speaking favorably about the product to our friends.

While we have attempted to compare and contrast the intellectual assent model and the behavioral compliance model, we wish to make clear that we don't want to indicate that one model is correct and the other model is incorrect. Both are models of how influence occurs, but influence can occur in more than one way and thus both models are appropriate for different types of influence. To explain how people are influenced under any of these models, we will direct our attention to major theories of influence.

Major Theories of Influence

For many years learning theorists and social psychologists have been very concerned with the process of influence. Specifically, their concern has been with how people's behavior is altered as a result of interaction with their environment. As a result of almost a half-century of research, three major theoretical explanations of the influence process have been developed. We

will consider each of these theories in turn, and then turn our attention to
how you can use communication to produce influence according to each
approach.

Reinforcement Theory

One of the first theoretical explanations of how human behavior is altered
was reinforcement theory, and it is still a very predominant basis for many of
the explanations of influence in human communication systems. The underlying assumption of reinforcement theory is that organisms seek to attain
rewards and to avoid punishments. More simply, we will engage in behaviors for which we are rewarded and tend to discontinue behaviors for which
we are not rewarded or receive punishment. As noted in a previous chapter,
our communication behavior is significantly affected by our need for
rewards. We will seek communicative relationships that are supportive of
our beliefs, attitudes, values, and behaviors, while we will tend not to expose
ourselves as often to communication which has a low probability of reinforcing us. When we apply reinforcement theory to the process of influence,
we can observe that people who are rewarded for their behavior tend to
continue that behavior while people who are rewarded for new behaviors
tend to adopt those new behaviors. If we apply the adoption model that we
discussed above, we can see that reinforcement applies very strongly during
the trial and adoption stages of the process. If we try out a new idea,
technique, or product (our new toothpaste) and are rewarded for that (our
mouth feels fresher, friends comment on our bright teeth), we are much
more likely to continue to utilize that innovation. On the other hand, if we
engage in a trial of an innovation but are not rewarded for that attempt, we
are likely not to adopt the innovation or discontinue it subsequently.

Consistency Theory

The essence of consistency theory is that human beings strive for consistency among their cognitions. People want their attitudes to be consistent
with their behaviors; their beliefs to be consistent with their attitudes; and
their behaviors to be consistent with each other. So long as we are not
aware of any inconsistency, we are likely to continue to behave in a constant
manner. However, when we recognize that our behavior is inconsistent with
our attitudes and/or our beliefs and/or our values, we are likely to seek

some way to resolve that inconsistency. The interrelationship of the need for consistency and influence is strong. This theory suggests that to get people to maintain their behavior, they must be shown continually that the behavior in which they are engaging is consistent with their attitudes, beliefs, and values (we must keep being complimented on our bright teeth). Similarly, in order to get people to change their behavior, it will be necessary to get them to realize that their behavior is inconsistent with their beliefs, attitudes, or values ("How come your teeth are turning brown, Tom?").

Involvement Theory

Involvement theory, sometimes referred to as ego-involvement theory, posits that the degree to which a person can be influenced is heavily dependent upon the importance of the influence target to them. If something is extremely important to an individual, his or her behavior is probably very strongly habituated toward that element and will be very difficult to change. Unimportant behaviors may, however, be changed quite easily. Thus, this theory will suggest that in order to influence someone, the individual's level of involvement with the target must be increased or decreased, or at least rechanneled.

With these relatively simple explanations of the major theories in mind, let us turn our attention to the relationships among these theories and communication in the influence process.

Inducing Influence: Communication and Reinforcement

Whenever we talk to another human being we have the potential to provide reinforcement for that other person. Similarly, that person has the potential for reinforcing us. In fact, communication itself is a very strong reinforcer. The mere act of being willing to talk with another person itself provides some reinforcement to both people involved. Some people even take the position that reinforcement of human beings is impossible *without* communication. Be that as it may, our concern here will be with the content of the communication between people rather than the fact that communication occurs. More specifically, we will direct attention to the messages and the sources involved in the communication.

Messages

What we say and the way we say it will determine a major portion of the degree of reinforcement that we provide for another person when we are communicating with that other person. When another person says something with which we agree, we will be very likely to engage in two forms of reinforcing communication. First, we will probably indicate our approval through our nonverbal behavior, such as smiling, nodding, and making sounds like "uh huh." Second, we are very likely to provide a positive verbal message, such as "Yes, I agree. That's right." If the other person receives similar responses from other people with whom she or he communicates, this pattern of reinforcement will tend to influence the individual to maintain that idea and to act on it when the time is appropriate. On the other hand, we may withhold reinforcement from another person with whom we are communicating when he or she expresses an idea with which we are not in agreement. We may simply remain silent, or we may express verbal disagreement. Similarly, our nonverbal behavior may be nonreinforcing. The absence of a smile, much less the presence of a frown, may be a strong indication of nonreinforcement to another. These very elementary verbal and nonverbal responses occur constantly throughout the interaction of human beings. In some cases the individual responding may be intentionally trying to reinforce or not reinforce the other person. In many other instances she or he is just responding. However, even though the communicator may not intend to either reinforce or not reinforce the person, her or his behavior will almost certainly have one of those effects anyway.

In addition to the normal interaction discussed above, reinforcement is provided or withheld in communication in a number of other ways. The first is by use of tangible rewards. Consider for a moment a business setting. There is a supervisor and a subordinate. The subordinate engages in a certain kind of work activity. The superior may reinforce that activity by providing an increase in pay, a positive written evaluation for the files, or possibly a promotion. Along with these fairly tangible reinforcements, of course, are likely to come more intangible reinforcements in the form of positive words and nonverbal behavior directed toward the subordinate. On the reverse side, the subordinate may engage in that same behavior but receive no recognition of it from the superior. This produces a lack of reinforcement, and the subordinate may be influenced through this absence to try other behaviors which would produce reinforcement. The key point here is that communication is involved whether there is tangible or intangible reward provided, and even no reward provides strong communication.

These two examples relate to comparatively subtle influence through reinforcing communication. In other circumstances there may be overt attempts to influence people. For example, one person may present a systematic argument to a person suggesting that she or he ought to maintain or alter present beliefs, attitudes, or behavior. If these arguments are perceived as supporting ideas which the other person values, influence is very likely to be the result. The major point to remember, however, is that whenever we communicate with another person we provide reinforcement or lack of reinforcement. It is simply impossible to avoid influencing the other person if we communicate with her or him at all. Of course, the influence that we exert may not be great, nor may the other's be great on us, but to communicate at all will insure that either reinforcement or lack of reinforcement is perceived by the people involved. In either event, beliefs, attitudes, and behaviors are most likely to be either strengthened or changed as a result.

Reinforcement can be provided through group indentification.

Sources

The source of a reinforcing or nonreinforcing message in communication has a major impact on the degree of reinforcement or nonreinforcement supplied. Positively viewed souces have much more potential for a reinforcement, and much more devastating impact for nonreinforcement, than do negatively viewed sources. Most people like to associate themselves in their own mind with people whom they perceive to be credible, attractive, and powerful. If such a person indicates that what the person believes or what the person does is right, this in itself is very reinforcing. On the other hand, if the sources with whom the individual identifies hold views or engage in behaviors different from the individual, there is no reinforcement for engaging in normal behavior. It is likely that the individual will seek other behavioral options that might produce greater reinforcement. To understand the import of the source in providing reinforcement to an individual through communication, we should turn our attention to the opinion leader. You will recall that an opinion leader is a person to whom an individual turns for advice or information. When the opinion leader indicates she or he is in agreement with an individual's beliefs, attitudes, or behaviors, this is strongly reinforcing to the individual. On the other hand, an indication of lack of agreement is a major withholding of reinforcement that will stimulate the individual to seek other attitudes, beliefs, or behaviors that would be more in line with those of the opinion leader. Often communication between an individual and her or his opinion leader is not direct. Rather, it may occur as a result of modeling. By that we mean that the individual observes what the opinion leader does and then imitates that behavior and is reinforced internally because that behavior is identified with the positively evaluated individual. A similar type of modeling occurs for an individual within a positively evaluated group. Sometimes these groups are referred to as "reference groups." A reference group is one with which an individual identifies, even if the individual is not a member of that group. For example, the football fan may like to emulate the attitudes, beliefs, and behaviors of members of the football team, even though the individual is not a member of the team. Or an individual might find that the members of her sorority or his fraternity engage in certain behaviors and she or he will model that behavior and receive reinforcement for identification from the group membership.

To summarize, reinforcement is provided through communiction in two primary ways: through verbal and nonverbal messages; and through identification with positively evaluated sources, either individuals or groups. In a sense, therefore, to communicate is to insure some degree of influence. We will influence other people and other people will influence us through the process of reinforcement that is inherent within human communication.

Inducing Influence: Communication and Consistency

When we receive messages that indicate agreement with us, particularly from positively evaluated sources, we are reinforced. We can also say that these messages are consistent. Indeed, we seek messages in our environment which are consistent and rewarding. When we do this, however, we are often confronted with messages, sometimes from positively evaluated sources, that are not consistent with our beliefs, attitudes, or behaviors. In either event, we are confronted with situations where communication and our need for consistency interact to produce influence. As was the case with reinforcement, communication and consistency interact to produce influence through messages and sources.

**BLACK BOX
54**

Can you explain the major assumptions underlying these schools of thought?
reinforcement theory
consistency theory
involvement theory

Do you know how messages and sources function to produce influence according to each of these theories?

Messages

Probably the simplest message which activates the principle of consistency and produces influence is an indication that a person's beliefs and attitudes, or attitudes and behavior, or two or more behaviors, are in direct conflict. For example, if it is pointed out to a man (as it was once pointed out to the senior author as a result of a previous book) that while he often verbally

expresses support for the liberation of women, he always uses the masculine
pronoun form when talking about either men or women, there is a strong
likelihood that this will create enough inconsistency in the individual's mind
that he will alter one of his two behaviors. Either he will reduce the frequency with which he verbally supports women's liberation, or he will attempt
to modify his pronoun usage. As this example may indicate, the main way
that consistency and communication interact to produce influence is by
creating an inconsistency, or on the other hand, by preventing it from occurring. Of course, the simple communicative statement that the two behaviors
are in conflict may not create enough inconsistency to produce influence.
Remember that the individual always strives to be consistent and this includes misperceiving the world around her or himself in order to do so.
Thus, the tendency is to reject such simple, straightforward descriptions of
our own inconsistencies. It will often take a fairly extended argument to
convince us that we are indeed inconsistent. Consequently, we may not
need only fairly convincing arguments but also substantial evidence that the
argument is correct. Simple nonverbal elements in our environment are
much less likely to have an impact. While the message is crucial in creating
inconsistency, we must also consider the source of that message because it
is also crucial.

Sources

The perceived credibility, attractiveness, and powerfulness of a source of a
message that is designed to create inconsistency is the most crucial predictor of how much inconsistency will be generated. If we do not highly value
the source of a message which points out our inconsistencies, we will have a
very strong tendency to reject that message and continue to perceive our
attitudes, beliefs, and behaviors as consistent with each other. This linkage
of a positively evaluated source with a message that argues for inconsistency
is central to producing influence through communication under the consistency theory. Whether the source is a distant individual, our opinion leader,
or a reference group, unless that source is very positively evaluated, little
inconsistency will be generated, and thus, little influence to change will occur.

If we may compare what we have said concerning *communication
and reinforcement* and *communication and consistency,* we may be able to
see how these two theoretical positions operate in different ways. We
believe that the reinforcement theory probably best explains why people
maintain their attitudes, beliefs, and behaviors with relatively little change

under most circumstances. Most people seek communication environments where they will be reinforced; find those environments; are reinforced; and thus maintain their attitudes, beliefs, and behaviors. On the other hand, we believe that consistency theory explains why in some cases people are influenced to change their attitudes, beliefs, and behaviors. When a very positively evaluated source points out our inconsistencies, we have really only two alternatives, since it is difficult for us to simply ignore the situation. We can either think less of the source, which we will probably try to do, or we can accept the fact that we are inconsistent and try to resolve that inconsistency by modifying our attitudes, beliefs, or behaviors. To the extent that we perceive the source as very high in credibility, power, and/or attraction, it is increasingly difficult for us to simply reject the source's message and derrogate her or him. Consequently, we are forced to reevaluate our situation and modify our attitudes, beliefs, and/or behaviors. When trying to influence someone else, we must keep in mind that if we want to maintain his or her current attitudes, beliefs, and/or behaviors we must provide some reinforcement through our communication. If we wish the other person to change his or her attitudes, beliefs, and/or behaviors, we must be perceived in a very positive way and call attention strongly to the fact that his or her attitudes, beliefs, and/or behaviors are not consistent with one another. Even then, little change may occur, because of the problem of involvement.

Inducing Influence: Communication and Involvement

A large number of research studies have indicated that people who are highly involved with a topic are very unlikely to change their attitudes, beliefs, or behaviors concerning that topic. A simple example: the chairman of the Student Republican Party is not likely to be convinced to vote for the Democrats in the next election, no matter what we say or do in the interim. Involvement, therefore, is a very crucial variable in the process of influence through communication. To put it as simply as we know how, if we wish to prevent people from changing their beliefs, attitudes, or behaviors, we will seek to increase their involvement with their present orientations. However, if we wish to change people's beliefs, attitudes, or behaviors, we must alter their involvement level, or at least redirect it. In either event, the main focus of our communicative efforts must be on the consequences of the particular belief, attitude, or behavior.

Messages

Messages seeking to alter levels of involvement or to redirect them must focus on the consequences of a particular belief, attitude, or behavior. By this we mean that the belief, attitude, or behavior must be linked with what will happen to the person holding that particular orientation. Messages seeking to lower involvement will normally attempt to show the lack of consequences stemming from the already held belief, attitude, or behavior, or to direct attention to the negative consequences that may occur. If nothing ever happens as a result of an attitude, we are very likely to lower our involvement with that orientation and be much more susceptible to influence designed to get us to change our orientation. When we wish to get people to increase their involvement, our message will normally focus on the extent of the consequences which occur as a result of a belief, attitude, or behavior, with particular focus on the choice between positive and negative consequences given a particular orientation. As we have noted before, the message and the source of the message are very highly related.

Sources

For one person to influence the level of involvement of another person on any topic requires a particularly high positive evaluation of the source of influence. For a person to be merely credible is generally not enough. The variables of homophily and power are much more important. If a person whom we perceive to be very similar to us in many respects suggests that we should alter our involvement level, this provides a potent argument for us to change. Similarly, if someone has a great deal of power over us, the mere fact that she or he suggests that something is more or less relevant to us than we had believed may actually make it so, particularly if we perceive her or him to have the direct power to make it so.

One of the reasons that it is very difficult to alter a person's involvement level in many instances is that our involvement with any particular attitude, belief, or behavior is generally rooted in our value system, which we have noted before is very resistant to change. Since it is so difficult to alter people's values, the strategy for influence that is most likely to work is rechanneling involvement to other values. At any rate, the likelihood of lowering a person's involvement level substantially in a short period of time is very slim, no matter what strategy is employed. On the other hand, a person who has a very low involvement level with a topic can be influenced to raise that involvement level very sharply if it can be demonstrated that desirable consequences can result and that demonstration is provided by an attractive, credible source.

Throughout this chapter we have focused on the variety of theoretical orientations about how influence occurs. We have noted the central position of communication in the production of influence, no matter what theory is being applied. Influence is the product of the interplay of sources, messages, and receivers. The next chapter will focus on these three elements.

SUGGESTED FURTHER READINGS

1. Hovland, C. I., Janis, I., and Kelley, H. H. *Communication and Persuasion* (New Haven: Yale University Press, 1953).

   A classic book on influence research. The first major work of its kind.

2. Kiesler, C. A., Collins, B. E., and Miller, N. *Attitude Change* (New York: John Wiley, 1969).

   An excellent summary and critique of the major theories of attitude change. Includes extensive summaries of research in each theoretical area.

3. Miller, G. R. and Burgoon, M. *New Techniques of Persuasion* (New York: Harper & Row, 1973).

   This brief book synthesizes a substantial body of recent theory and research in a clear, practically oriented manner.

4. Zimbardo, P. and Ebbesen, E. B. *Influencing Attitudes and Changing Behavior* (Reading, Mass.: Addison-Wesley, 1970).

   A brief, clear summary of influence theory and research.

SELECTED REFERENCES

ABELSON, R. P. "Psychological Implication," in *Theories of Cognitive Consistency: A Sourcebook,* R. P. Abelson, E. Aronson, W. J. McGuire, T. M. Newcomb, M. J. Rosenberg, and P. H. Tannenbaum, eds. (Skokie, Ill.: Rand-McNally, 1968).

ARONSON, E. "Dissonance Theory: Progress and Problems," in *Theories of Cognitive Consistency: A Sourcebook,* R. P. Abelson, E. Aronson, W. J. McGuire, T. M. Newcomb, M. J. Rosenberg and P. H. Tannenbaum, eds. (Skokie, Ill.: Rand-McNally, 1968).

BEM, D. J. "An Experimental Analysis of Self-Persuasion." *Journal of Experimental Social Psychology* 1 (1965): 199–218.

————. "Self-Perception: An Alternative Interpretation of Cognitive Dissonance Phenomena." *Psychological Review* 74 (1967): 183–200.

CARTWRIGHT, D. and HARARY, F. "Structural Balance: A Generalization of Heider's Theory." *Psychological Review* 63 (1956): 277–293.

CHAPANIS, N. P. and CHAPANIS, A. "Cognitive Dissonance: Five Years Later." *Psychological Bulletin* 61 (1964): 1–22.

FEATHER, N. T. "A Structural Balance Model of Communication Effects." *Psychological Review* 71 (1964): 291–313.

FESTINGER, L. *A Theory of Cognitive Dissonance* (New York: Row, Peterson, 1957).

FISHBEIN, M. "A Consideration of Beliefs, Attitudes, and Their Relationship," in *Current Studies in Social Psychology,* I. D. Steiner and M. Fishbein, eds. (New York: Holt, Rinehart and Winston, 1965), 107–120.

HEIDER, F. "Attitudes and Cognitive Organization." *Journal of Psychology* 21 (1964): 107–112.

HOVLAND, C. I., HARVEY, O. J., and SHERIF, M. "Assimilation and Contrast Effects in Reactions to Communication and Attitude Change." *Journal of Abnormal and Social Psychology* 55 (1957): 244–252.

HOVLAND, C. I., JANIS, I., and KELLEY, H. H. *Communication and Persuasion* (New Haven: Yale University Press, 1953).

HOVLAND, C. I., LUMSDAINE, A. A., and SHEFFIELD, F. D. *Experiments on Mass Communication* (Princeton, N.J.: Princeton University Press, 1949).

HOVLAND, C. I. and SHERIF, M. *Social Judgment* (New Haven, Conn.: Yale University Press, 1961).

KATZ, D. "The Functional Approach to the Study of Attitudes." *Public Opinion Quarterly* 24 (1960): 163–204.

KELMAN, H. C. "Compliance, Identification, and Internalization: Three Processes of Attitude Change." *Journal of Conflict Resolution* 2 (1958): 51–60.

KIESLER, C. A., COLLINS, B. E., and MILLER, N. *Attitude Change* (New York: John Wiley, 1969).

MILLER, G. R. and BURGOON, M. *New Techniques of Persuasion* (New York: Harper & Row, 1973).

MILLS, J., ARONSON, E., and ROBINSON, H. "Selectivity in Exposure to Information." *Journal of Abnormal and Social Psychology* 59 (1959): 250–253.

OSGOOD, C. E. and TANNENBAUM, P. H. "The Principle of Congruity in the Prediction of Attitude Change." *Psychological Review* 62 (1955): 42–55.

SHERIF, M., SHERIF, C., and NEBERGALL, R. *Attitude and Attitude Change* (Philadelphia: W. B. Saunders Co., 1965).

SKINNER, B. F. *Verbal Behavior* (New York: Appleton-Century-Crofts, 1957).

TANNENBAUM, P. H. "The Congruity Principle Revisited: Studies in the Reduction, Induction, and Generalization of Persuasion," in *Advances in Experimental Social Psychology,* L. Berkowitz, ed. (New York: Academic Press, 1967), vol. 3, 270–320.

WHITTAKER, J. O. "Resolution of the Communication Discrepancy Issue in Attitude Change," in *Attitude, Ego-Involvement and Change,* C. W. Sherif and M. Sherif, eds. (New York: John Wiley, 1967), 159–177.

ZAJONC, R. B. "The Concepts of Balance, Congruity, and Dissonance." *Public Opinion Quarterly* 24 (1960): 280–296.

ZIMBARDO, P. and EBBESON, E. B. *Influencing Attitudes and Changing Behavior* (Reading, Mass.: Addison-Wesley, 1970).

17

Influence: Sources, Messages, and Receivers

In earlier chapters we took considerable effort to explain the people and message variables that can affect communication. In this chapter our attention will be directed toward how many of these variables are related to the outcome of influence. We will not set forth the "five easy steps to influence," because no such formula exists. But we will highlight variables with which you must be concerned, whether you desire to influence someone else or you simply want to know what is going on so you can control whether or not you will allow someone else to influence you.

Common Elements of Influence

In the preceding chapter we attempted to explain how influence occurs through communication among human beings according to several different theories. In the course of that discussion we mentioned several important source and message variables.   At this point we wish to look directly at some of these source and message variables in terms of how they function regardless of what theoretical explanation is applied to them.   We will then turn our attention to the receiver, the target of influence.

Credibility

Probably the clearest conclusion from the hundreds and hundreds of research studies investigating the process of influence in communication is that the credibility of a source of a message has a major impact on the degree to which that message influences the receiver.   As we indicated in chapter 6, credibility is a perception of one person on the part of another.   If I perceive you to be credible, you are; if I do not perceive you to be credible, you aren't.   When we judge another person to be credible, that person has considerable potential for influencing our beliefs, attitudes, and behaviors; however, when we do not perceive another person to be credible, the potential influence of that individual is greatly reduced, if not completely eliminated.   When we wish to influence other people, therefore, it is important that we are perceived as credible in their eyes.   If we are not, our communicative efforts may prove completely fruitless.   In fact, research indicates that if we are not credible we are very apt to influence in a direction opposite from what we intended.   Prime examples at opposite ends of the political continuum were the campaigns of Senator Goldwater in 1964 and Senator McGovern in 1972.   For the large majority of Americans, neither of these men was credible enough.   Consequently, as the campaign wore on and they continued to express their ideas, fewer people identified themselves as supporters, rather than more and more as was intended.   Credibility, therefore, should be looked upon as a central element that determines the impact of communication on influence.

Attraction

Attraction to another person operates in a manner very similar to credibility.   We are quite willing to expose ourselves to communication from credible and/or attractive people, but those whom we perceive to be less credible or attractive we tend to avoid communicating with.   Research has indicated that we are much more susceptible to influence attempts on the part of attractive people than we are from attempts that emanate from unattractive people. You will recall from our earlier discussion of attraction in the chapter concerning participant variables that we are not talking here only about physical attractiveness; we are concerned with social attractiveness and task attractiveness as well. People with whom we want to socialize or with whom we want to work have greater potential for influencing us than do those whom we see as less socially or task attractive. Because of this relationship between attractiveness and influence we must keep in mind that if we wish to influence another person we must first establish in that other person's mind that we are attractive (recall methods for doing this discussed in chapter 12). Otherwise, our attempts at influence will probably be useless.

Homophily

Perceived similarity, or homophily, particularly in interpersonal communication systems, is equally as important as perceived credibility and attraction. We tend to communicate most with those people whom we perceive to be similar to us. Consequently, these people have the greatest opportunity to

For a large majority of Americans the 1972 campaign of George McGovern was simply not credible enough.

351

influence us. On the other side of the coin, since we communicate mostly with people similar to us, these are the people whom we have the greatest opportunity to influence. Simple frequency of communication is not the only reason that people who are highly similar tend to have the most influence on one another. Communication is more likely to be successful between similar people because they have shared backgrounds and orientations which lead to much more commonality in language and meaning. Our opinion leaders are generally quite homophilous with us, although probably being a little bit more credible on the given topic with which we are concerned. And a very clear finding from the research on diffusion and adoption of new ideas, techniques, and products is that the opinion leader is the crucial source of influence in the adoption process. Simply put, people tend to believe and do what their opinion leaders say they should believe and do, not *always* but *usually*.

Power

The degree to which we perceive that another person has power over us is a very good indication of the extent of influence that person is probably capable of having over our behavior, and to a lesser extent over our beliefs and attitudes. If we perceive a person to have power over us, this will tend to magnify the way we perceive her or his credibility and attractiveness. If we approve of that power—consider it to be legitimate—this will tend to enhance her or his credibility and make the individual more attractive to us as well. On the other hand, if we do not approve of the power the other person has over us—we consider it illegitimate—this will seriously detract from the other person's credibility and will also make association with him or her even less attractive.

Power functions as a source of influence in the intellectual assent model and the behavioral compliance model in very different ways. In the intellectual assent model, we react to the power source on the basis of the legitimacy of the source's power. If we perceive the source of power to be legitimate we are very likely to look upon that source as a model to emulate. Consequently, the very fact that the power source believes that something is true and suggests that it is an appropriate way to behave is often reason enough for us to conclude that it is a behavior in which we should engage. On the other hand, negatively perceived power sources are also likely to be negative models. If the boss we don't like suggests it should be done, that is frequently reason enough for us to conclude that the opposite is true.   Under the behavioral compliance model, we engage in the behavior upon which the power source insists.   At the outset we do not necessarily agree or disagree with the behavior, we just do it because we are told to. This behavior on our part may have little effect on our beliefs or attitudes in the short run.   However, if a power source can continually influence our behavior over a sustained period of time, we are also very likely to modify our beliefs and attitudes so that they come in line with the behavior in which we are forced to engage.   Thus, over a period of time, we no longer perceive that we are being forced to engage in a behavior; instead, we engage in it since we actually believe we should be engaging in it.   At this point the power source becomes less relevant with relation to our behavior, but the effect of that power source is continuing.

Membership and Reference Groups

As we have noted previously, our identification with groups in our environment can have a strong impact on our attitudes, beliefs, and behaviors. We tend to look to the typical behavior of group members of which we are also a member, and to groups with which we identify but are not a member, as models of appropriate behavior.   Consequently, we are often influenced by the attitudes, beliefs, and behaviors of these groups without anyone attempting consciously to influence us.

The orientations of this group may also be used by a communicator to influence someone who identifies with the group in a very conscious way. The "everyone else is doing it" argument that is so often employed among adolescents is a good example of the conscious use of this source of influence by a person desiring to modify someone else's behavior.   Adoption of such behaviors as smoking or drinking, as well as our choice of clothing style, are examples of behavioral choices that are very often made primarily as a result of identification with membership or reference groups, and such behavior is certainly not limited to adolescents.

Data or Evidence

To this point we have looked primarily to people as sources of influence on other people.   This has been appropriate since very little influence occurs without the involvement of another person.   But there are other sources of influence as well.   One of the most obvious, and most important, sources of

influence is facts or what we perceive to be facts. When two people communicate, there are many allegations of what one person believes to be true
that are passed on to the other person. Items of alleged fact are frequently
referred to as "data." Data serve as a basis for all rational argument.

There are at least three different types of data. The first are data
that we already accept or believe. We are influenced by this type of data
only if it is applied in a manner different from our previous applications.
The communicator who is going to influence us with this kind of data will
show us a new relationship between facts that we have already accepted and
beliefs, attitudes, or behaviors to which we have not related that data previously. The second type of data is the type which we accept as true
because a communicator suggests that it is true. This type of data is
dependent upon our perception of the other person, particularly in terms of
that other person's credibility. If a person whom we perceive to be highly
credible says that automobile prices are likely to increase from 7 to 10
percent in the next year, we are very likely to accept that as true. Then that
other person may use that data to influence us to purchase a new car. The
third type of data is often referred to as "evidence." We may define evidence as matters of fact or opinion that are attested to by a source outside
of the immediate communication transaction. Person A is talking to Person
B and quotes Person C. The quotation from Person C is the evidence.
Evidence is particularly important in the influence process when the communicator attempting to exert influence on the other person is not perceived
to be particularly highly credible. In interpersonal communication between
highly homophilous individuals, therefore, evidence can be an extremely
important source of influence.

A number of other message variables, particularly language intensity and message structure, can have a major impact on the degree of influence in a given communication transaction. The impact of these message variables is not directly on the influence process itself, but on information acquisition which in turn impacts influence. Since these variables were discussed extensively in the chapter concerning information acquisition (see chapter 14), we will not repeat that discussion here.

Communication and Influence: Individual Variables

In the preceding section our attention was focused on common elements that operate to impact influence in communication, regardless of who the people are that are involved in the process. Knowing how these variables operate will help us to understand the influence process better and to control it when we need to do so. But influence is still a highly individual matter. Placing two people in the same communication context will not necessarily result in the same amount of influence occurring. The reason is probably obvious: people differ greatly on individual variables. Our concern in this section will be to examine some of these individual variations in people, mostly thought of as personality characteristics, to see how they relate to the influence process.

Self-esteem

A person's level of self-esteem may be the most important individual variable in determining the amount of influence that takes place in a given communication encounter. As we noted in an earlier chapter, self-esteem is essentially a person's attitude toward her or himself. People with high self-esteem perceive themselves as being competent, composed, and pretty much in control of their own lives. People with low self-esteem see themselves in essentially the opposite manner. All things being equal, therefore, people with high self-esteem are much less susceptible to outside influence than are people with low self-esteem. The reason for this is fairly simple. People with high self-esteem see themselves as equal to or superior to most of the people with whom they come in contact and who attempt to influence them. People with low self-esteem, however, perceive other people in their environment as more credible and better informed than they are, and as a result they tend to be very susceptible to influence from these credible outside people.

Although it is not universally true, people with high self-esteem are generally perceived more positively by people in their environment than people with low self-esteem. In short, our images of ourselves are projected to other people and consequently, are likely to be accepted by them. You will recall our earlier discussion of communication apprehension. We noted that highly apprehensive people tend also to have low self-esteem and to be perceived in a negative light by other people in their environment. People with low communication apprehension tend to have high self-esteem and to be perceived more positively by other people in their environment. Although there has been little research directly involving this question, we may strongly speculate that because of the interrelationship of communication

The high esteem represented by this billboard's caption changed radically after political events influenced the electorate's view of the president.

apprehension and self-esteem that highly apprehensive individuals are probably much more highly prone to be influenced than are people who are less apprehensive.

Machiavellianism

The Machiavellian personality characteristic is strongly related to the influence process. Highly Machiavellian individuals want to influence people and generally are quite good at doing so. People who are low Machiavellians operate in the opposite way: they do not care much for trying to influence other people, and even when they try to they generally fail. On the other side of the coin, the highly Machiavellian individual is much less prone to be influenced by others than is the low Machiavellian.

While all of these patterns are consistent, knowing them may not help us to improve our functioning in the influence process very much. It is difficult for us to perceive another person's Machiavellian level unless it is unusually extreme. Machiavellians tend to control their environment, but do not dominate it in such a way that other people recognize that they are in control. If we analyze our own orientations, however, we can generally perceive quite accurately our own level of Machiavellianism. If we enjoy influencing others and are moderately successful at it, we can guess that our Machiavellian level is reasonably high. This would also indicate, as we have noted above, that we are probably less susceptible to influence by other people than the typical person would be. If our self-analysis indicates a fairly low level of Machiavellianism, however, we should take this as a warning that we may be easily influenced by other people, and since it is probable that some influence is not in our best interests, we should guard against it.

Dogmatism

A person's level of dogmatism will have a major impact on the degree to which that person can be influenced and the means by which that person can be influenced. In general, high dogmatics adhere to their beliefs, attitudes, and behaviors very rigidly, while low dogmatics are much less rigid and more open. On the face it would appear, as a result, that low dogmatics would be much easier to influence than would high dogmatics. This is only partially true, and in some instances completely false. Low dogmatics are best influenced by rational argument supported by evidence. High dogmatics tend to reject rational argument; however, high dogmatics are much more susceptible to influence than are low dogmatics if the influence attempt comes from a person with high power and authority. High dogmatics tend to accept the ideas and behaviors of people in authority; low dogmatics tend to view such people with considerable suspicion and are not strongly influenced by them unless there is a good rational reason for accepting them and their behavior. While Machiavellianism is probably easier to perceive in ourselves than it is in other people, the exact reverse is true with dogmatism. Few people would be willing to acknowledge that they are dogmatic, but most of us can readily perceive this characteristic in other people. When we recognize that another person is highly dogmatic, a sort of Archie Bunker type, we should recognize the futility of attempting to influence that person through normal rational means. We will need the influence of a person in authority or strong group conformity pressure to sway this dogmatic figure. For the highly dogmatic individual not only conforms to the desires of people in authority, but also has a strong need to conform to the behavioral patterns of her or his reference groups. If the dogmatic can be made to perceive that the reference group is in disagreement with her or him, considerable influence is usually attainable.

Individual Needs

People differ greatly in what they need in order to be happy. The element that provides individual reinforcement will differ from person to person. Two of the more significant desires that have a major impact on the influence process are the need for approval and achievement.

People with a strong need for approval react to other people in communication quite differently from people with less need for approval. Simply put, people with a high need for approval are people-oriented; people with a low need for approval are self-oriented. People with a high need for approval, consequently, are particularly prone to be influenced by others. They tend to conform more quickly and more often when compliance would gain the reward of other people's approval. People with less need in this area, however, are more independent in their behavior choices. The fact that the rest of the group is not doing something is not looked upon as any good reason why this person should not do it. People with a low need for approval are scarcely influenced by appeals to the behavior of their reference groups, because their reference groups are of considerably less importance to them than those of people with a higher need for approval.

Similarly, people with a low need for approval are less influenced by power figures in their environment than are people with a high need for approval.

**BLACK BOX
56**

What is the relationship of each of the following individual variables to the outcome of influence?

self-esteem   dogmatism
Machiavellianism   individual needs

Can you identify people in your own environment who are particularly high or low in any of these areas? Explain how you would need to adapt your communication to them to increase the probability that you could influence them.

The need for achievement is also a strong factor in the influence process. People with a high need for achievement are very prone to being influenced if they perceive that adopting a new belief, attitude, or behavior will get them a leg up on their environment. They are constantly seeking practical means to success, and are strongly influenced by anything that appears to fulfill this need. People with a low need for achievement, however, are almost immune to influence attempts of this kind. Very often they will look upon advancement in the hierarchy of their field as a disadvantage rather than an advantage and make comments such as "who needs it."

Adopter Categories

In recent years it has become increasingly apparent that the degree to which a person is likely to be influenced and the amount of time it would take to influence a person are determined by a wide range of personality variables. While we have enumerated some of the more important personality variables above, it is probably more useful to look at people in terms of their total personality rather than to look at any individual characteristic. A very thorough review of several hundred research studies that investigated the process of influence leading to the adoption of innovations has resulted in a particularly useful categorization system. This system is based upon the

359

point in time at which one person is likely to adopt a new idea in comparison with other people. Researchers have examined the personality characteristics of people in relation to the general point in time at which they adopt new ideas. This has led to a fairly descriptive profile of the kinds of people who adopt behavior early and those who adopt during later periods. The pattern seems to hold whether it takes six weeks or sixty years for an innovation to be adopted widely throughout a population. The five categories of adopters are labeled *innovators, early adopters, early majority, late majority, and laggards.* We will examine some of the relevant characteristics of people in each of these categories.

1. *Innovators* can best be described as "venturesome." The innovator is willing to try things, in fact, is anxious to try them. He or she tends to be rash and daring and to take high risks even though they may be very hazardous. The innovator is willing to fail, and then try again with some other new idea. These are the people who adopt new ideas, techniques, and products first. For them it is a positive value to change, to try something new, even to try something new and fail. Innovators constitute a very small percentage of the population. They are generally recognized very easily because of their adoption behaviors. Innovators tend to communicate a lot with one another, even though they may be hundreds of miles apart. They are not looked upon with great positive regard by the rest of the people in their society. They often become very rich as a result of their willingness to try new things but they are also likely to become very poor as a result of trying new things that don't work. They tend to have a very high self-esteem, to be somewhat Machiavellian, have a very strong drive for achievement, a low need for approval, and are quite open-minded. About all you have to do to influence an innovator to adopt something new is to let them know that it is new.

2. *Early adopters* are usually "respectable." Whereas innovators tend to have a very national or world orientation, early adopters tend to hold significant roles in their local community. Most opinion leaders in a society are early adopters. These are the people to whom others look for advice and information about new ideas. Early adopters tend to be models for other people; respectable, successful models. Early adopters always keep an eye on the innovators to see what they are doing, and when they see them doing something that seems to be working, they try the new idea, technique, or product. Like innovators, early adopters tend to have high self-esteem, to be somewhat Machiavellian, to be quite open-minded, and to have a strong need for achievement. Early adopters differ from innovators in that

they have a very strong need for approval and status in their environment. Early adopters do not like to take risks; they leave those to innovators.

3. The *early majority* may be described as "deliberate." The early majority are very seldom leaders, but they are very conscious followers. They tend to keep an eye on the early adopters to see what the respectable people are doing and then check to see if it works. If they perceive that it does, they then will try the new idea, technique, or product. Generally, they try something for quite a while before they make a decision to adopt it on a relatively permanent basis. They are somewhat reluctant to discontinue an old idea in favor of a new one, particularly until they are quite certain that the new idea is better. The early majority tend to have a moderate level of self-esteem, to be relatively low in Machiavellianism, and to be quite low in dogmatism. They have only a moderate need for achievement but a very high need for approval, particularly among other people like themselves.

4. The *late majority* can be labelled "skeptical." These people view any new idea with suspicion. Before they will even try a new idea they have to be reasonably certain that the majority of the people in their environment have already tried it and it has worked for them. This is a cautious group of people who are particularly prone to influence by members of their peer group. When the majority of their peer group has adopted a new idea, they will be willing to give it a try. Their adoption will be speeded considerably if the peer group puts pressure on them to adopt. The late majority have very low levels of self-esteem, are generally low in Machiavellianism, and moderate in dogmatism. They have a very high need for approval, but a very low level of need for achievement. They recognize that it is necessary for people to stick their necks out for progress, but they will assure you that they won't do it.

5. The *laggards* are "traditional." These are the last people to adopt any new idea, technique or product. There are no opinion leaders among this group. They are totally provincial in their outlook, and may be social isolates. Their behavior is conditioned by whatever has been done in the past. They will continue standing custom indefinitely if they can. Laggards tend to interact primarily with other laggards and have little contact with people in other adopter categories. By the time they adopt a new idea, technique, or product the innovation is no longer new; in fact, it may have already been replaced by another innovation. Laggards tend to distrust and avoid anybody who is in favor of anything new. Laggards are very often alienated from the society in which they live, and create a vision of a society that did exist in the past but is not typical of the real environment in which

they must operate. For the most part laggards are quite low in self-esteem, low in Machiavellianism, extremely high in dogmatism, have little need for achievement, and only a moderate need for approval. While it is almost impossible to influence laggards to change their beliefs, attitudes, or values, trying to convince laggards to maintain their present orientations can cause you to perceive yourself as a much better agent of influence than you deserve!

BLACK BOX
57

Can you identify and distinguish among the adopter categories?

How should messages differ for people in the various catgories so that influence would be more likely?

For the most part, the greatest economic and social rewards with the least likelihood of punishment come to the early adopters. They don't have to take the risks of the innovators, but they are in on things while they are still relatively new. For our part we would like to be thought of as fitting into this category, but self-analysis suggests that we may be somewhat further down the line. You should ask yourself where you fit in this categorization system. More importantly, whenever you engage in communication designed to influence someone else, the most important question you can ask is where that other communicator fits among these categories. This knowledge will help you to adapt your communication behavior to what would be appropriate for that person.

SUGGESTED FURTHER READINGS

1. Andersen, K. and Clevenger, T, Jr. "A Summary of Experimental Research in Ethos." *Speech Monographs* 30 (1963): 59–78.

An excellent synthesis of the early research on source credibility.

2. McCroskey, J. C. *An Introduction to Rhetorical Communication,* 2nd ed. (Englewood Cliffs, N.J.: Prentice-Hall, 1972), chapters 7–10.

   These chapters are devoted to methods of developing messages for influence. They provide extended practical advice for employing the theories discussed in this and the previous chapter.

3. Rogers, E. M. and Shoemaker, F. F. *Communication of Innovations: A Cross-Cultural Approach* (New York: The Free Press, 1971).

   This book includes an extensive discussion of adopter categories and how they relate to the influence process.

SELECTED REFERENCES

(The references for chapter 16 also apply as references for this chapter.)

ANDERSEN, K. and CLEVENGER, T., JR. "A Summary of Experimental Research in Ethos." *Speech Monographs* 30 (1963): 59–78.

BERSCHEID, E. and WALSTER, E. *Interpersonal Attraction* (Reading, Mass.: Addison-Wesley, 1969).

LEVENTHAL, H. and PERLOE, S. I. "A Relationship Between Self-Esteem and Persuasibility." *Journal of Abnormal and Social Psychology* 64:5 (1962): 385–388.

MCCROSKEY, J. C. *An Introduction to Rhetorical Communication,* 2nd ed. (Englewood Cliffs, N.J.: Prentice-Hall, 1972), chapters 7–10.

————. "A Summary of Experimental Research on the Effects of Evidence in Persuasive Communication." *Quarterly Journal of Speech* 55 (1969):169–176.

————. *Studies of the Effects of Evidence in Persuasive Communication,* Report SCRL 4–67, Speech Communication Research Laboratory, Michigan State University, 1967.

NEWCOMB, T. M. "Attitude Development as a Function of Reference Groups; The Bennington Study," in *Readings in Social Psychology,* E. E. Maccoby, T. M. Newcomb, and E. L. Hartley, eds. (New York: Holt, Rinehart and Winston, 1958), 265–275.

ROGERS, E. M. and SHOEMAKER, F. F. *Communication of Innovations: A Cross-Cultural Approach* (New York: The Free Press, 1971).

18

Receptive
Decision Making

Every day we receive thousands of messages calling for decisions. The media editorialize, attempt to sell us products, and subtly influence our social values in dramatic presentations. Professors sell us ideas and practices in the classroom. We seek out our respected friends for their opinions and help in making decisions. They, in turn, seek our advice.

We spend a great deal of our time consuming messages related to new ideas, practices, courses of action, products, and solutions to problems. The ability to analyze these messages critically is essential. If we can understand the problems, weakness, and fallacies of these messages, then we ought to be more critical receivers and decision makers. And comprehending rational elements in messages helps us in the analysis of problems and solutions. Chapters 9 and 10 have discussed some of the essential elements of messages and chapter 17 has discussed the persuasive impact of those elements. There are additional components and relationships

365

which we ought to examine if we are concerned specifically about the communication outcome of rational decision making. We ask you to look at them carefully with us because they can help you become a more intelligent and analytical decision maker when you receive messages.

Arguments in Messages

We often use informal arguments in our daily message exchanges with others. Arguments are *not* simply our highly verbal disagreements with others. *Argument is the process of leading someone—a receiver—to infer or draw a conclusion from certain data or evidence.* We can distinguish argument from reasoning on the basis that argument is interpersonal (between at least two people) and reasoning is intrapersonal (within one individual). Therefore, argument is a type of communication based upon rational or cognitive processes for its effect. Because of this characteristic, arguments in messages are most related to our beliefs and information about reality and about each other.

Understanding the nature, types, and tests of arguments is useful in the consumption of messages from editorials, politicians, business associates, and friends. This understanding is also helpful in the analysis of problems, issues, and information upon which we base our important decisions.

The Structure and Function of Argument

Stephen Toulmin, a British philosopher, developed a model of argument used in everyday human communication. This description has gained wide acceptance because of its general clarity and usefulness in analyzing arguments in messages. Although there are other methods for analyzing arguments and messages in general, this is one pragmatic way to apply some of the possibilities for messages that we discussed earlier. With some modifications, the model and explanation are presented in Figure 18–1.

These four basic message elements—data, warrant, claim, and qualifiers—are the essential components of an argument. A source of communication makes certain *claims* (or draws certain conclusions) with the receiver

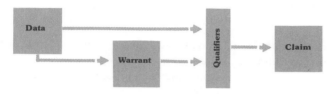

FIGURE 18-1. *Model of argument.*

by presenting or utilizing *data* (beliefs, evidence) from which she or he draws
or infers the claim. The underlying assumption (or type of inference) that
allows her or him to make claims based on that data is called the *warrant.*
The *qualifiers* refer to the degree of certainty or the reservations with which
the claim is made. Any one of these components may be actually stated or
merely implied by the source. But all of them, whether stated or implied,
are essential components in every argument.

Consider the following example of an argument: "I saw Jane out with
a strange man last night (data). She and Bill might have broken up
(claim)." The phrase, "might have" indicates the degree of certainty or
reservation with which the claim is made; it is the qualifier. The underlying
assumption that allows the claim to be made from the data is that "going out
with another person of the opposite sex is a sign that a couple has broken
up"; the warrant. Although implied, rather than stated in this argument, the
warrant is an essential part of the argument. These elements are present in
messages ranging from formal government policy statements to television
commercials, casual conversations, classroom lectures, and business
memos. The essential nature and possible weaknesses of each of these
components are examined in the following discussion.

BLACK BOX
58

Can you briefly identify the following elements?
    argument   warrant
    claim   qualifier
    data

Do you recognize these components in messages that you hear or read?

Data and Evidence

The bases of argument are data and evidence. On the basis of certain data or evidence we attempt to draw some conclusions or make some claim. What we observe about the world and each other (data) serves as the basis of our beliefs. Phenomena which exist or existed in the world (including ourselves) we call *facts*. Data and evidence consist of beliefs about these facts. A bottle of "El Stingo" mouthwash may exist as a fact. Beliefs about that mouthwash—its effectiveness and pleasant taste—are beliefs offered as data and evidence.

There are generally three types of data which can serve as the basis of claims that we attempt to make. One type of data consists of the *beliefs of the receiver*. As receivers of communication about "El Stingo" we may believe that it irritates our tongue and tastes bad. This type of observation is generally labeled *first-order data*. These beliefs are probably the most important in decision making. Ultimately all decisions that we make as receivers are based upon *what we believe to be true* about the world and events in it, whether these beliefs are accurate or not. If we believe that a certain politician is dishonest, that will affect our decisions regarding voting for her or him.

Another type of data is the *beliefs of the source* of communication. This is labeled *second-order data*. These are beliefs that the communicator states in a message that receivers have not believed previously. For example, the TV announcer, dressed in a white medical coat, says that the taste of the mouthwash is really dirty germs and particles being washed away and the slight irritation really makes it effective. He notes further that "El Stingo" smells pleasant. To the extent that the communicator is credible to us, we may accept some of those beliefs, converting them into our own. At that point they become beliefs of the receiver—first-order data. If we suspend judgment upon those beliefs or if we reject them, they remain second-order data. For example, if a communicator states a belief that smoking marijuana is harmful, our decision regarding that practice may be affected depending upon whether we hold that belief or if we accept that belief as our own as a result of the communicator's credibility.

Third-order data is called *evidence*. These are beliefs and opinions originating from sources outside of the message source and receiver. Our announcer reads a short recommendation from the Dental Association stating that "El Stingo" is "an effective decay preventer that can be of substantial value...." Communicators generally incorporate the beliefs or opinions of others into their messages when insufficient common beliefs are held between them and their receivers. Essentially, these other beliefs consist of various types of observations about the world made by different sources. The types of evidence which communicators utilize most frequently are *peer or majority opinion, authoritative opinion, definitions, statistical materials,* and *examples.*

Peer or *majority opinion* consists of evidence of others' beliefs. These beliefs may originate from the groups and individuals we associate with or they may form some estimate of what the majority of people believe (polls, news items, etc.). Research generally indicates that we have some susceptibility to group pressure and majority opinion. As we noted in the last chapter, other people with whom we identify also influence our beliefs.

Authoritative opinions are the considered beliefs or observations of people we consider to be experts on the issue at hand. Authorities are credible sources whom we tend to believe because of their special training and experience. A number of years ago, Crest Toothpaste cited evidence from a recognized dental association certifying the effectiveness of its formula containing fluoride. This evidence was credible enough to convert large numbers of people to use of that brand. But authoritative opinion not only consists of endorsements of certain products, practices, and ideas, but also the reasoning underlying those endorsements. We should also examine the reasons behind an authoritative source's beliefs.

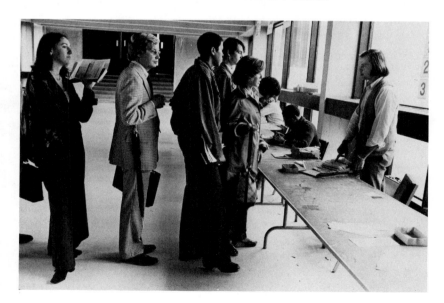

The registrar makes a claim to a student (receiver) by showing her the class rosters.

Definitions of key concepts and issues, as well as examples or specific instances of the point at issue, are also used as evidence. To the extent that those definitions and examples are reasonably clear, authoritative, and representative, they serve as a basis for claims made by a communicator. Statistical descriptions of things and events are also used to make claims and predictions which the receiver is often asked to accept. How these data and evidence serve as the bases of various claims is discussed in some detail in the subsequent section on warrants. However, if we are to evaluate critically the data and evidence in messages, there are some questions or tests that we can apply.

Tests of Data and Evidence

Suppose for a moment that you are reading an article in the local newspaper. The article presents the Secretary of Defense's case for a 15 percent increase in military spending in the next federal budget. He notes that inflation has consumed much of the dollar's buying power and costs have increased. He states that recent technological advances by other world powers have made many of our weapons obsolete. In addition, he emphasizes worsening crises in the world, the need for balance of power, and cites numerous statistics and sources that agree with his view. Finally, he mentions the "cold war" with other countries.

Tests of data from which conclusions (claims) are drawn can help us to determine the worth of that material. To the extent that the data used meet these tests, these data become more adequate bases for the claims made by the communicator.

1. Are my beliefs reasonably consistent with reality? Are they logical? First you must check the reasonableness and validity of your own beliefs on military spending.
2. Are there sufficient data to prove the point or support the claim? This is especially important in the use of examples and other evidence. One example of an obsolete weapon may not be enough.
3. Are the examples, quotations, and other evidence typical? Is there contrary or inconsistent evidence? The recent TV news special on the development of weapons may offer another set of examples and quotations that demonstrate inconsistency or atypicality.
4. Are there contradictions and inconsistencies within the expressed data and evidence? Did the Secretary also say that the U.S. is the strongest nation in the world?

5. Is it the most recent evidence available? Maybe the world situation has really changed or new advances have offset the problems mentioned.

6. Are the data and evidence really relevant to the claim made or conclusion drawn? Even if all the evidence is accepted you must determine if it justifies a 15 percent increase in military spending.

7. Are the statistics used a clear index of what you want to know in order to accept or reject the claim? The total number of certain weapons or the percentages of them in relation to another country may be offset by differences in the quality of the weapons.

8. Are the data and evidence clear and understandable? If they can't be understood there are reasons to suspend your judgment until you can understand what is going on.

9. Is the evidence documented and referenced so that you can validate it if needed? Did you find out how you could "check out" all of the information for yourself?

10. Are the data and evidence cumulative? Often a single belief or opinion is insufficient for supporting a claim. However, sometimes a number of pieces of data taken together can establish a conclusion that no one or two pieces can by themselves. Maybe the Secretary built up the number of obsolete weapons and a substantial number of problems.

11. Is the source of the data and evidence credible? We would ask this question about the communicator and about the sources of evidence which she or he uses in the message. Maybe he relied only upon military men who want to advance their own cause. More specifically, we would ask the following:

   A. Is this person competent or expert in the area being considered by the message? For example, what are the Secretary's qualifications in this area?

   B. Was or is this person in a position to observe or know what is being talked about? Does the Secretary really observe the problem at first hand?

   C. Was or is that person capable of observing accurately? Is he physically and psychologically sound?

   D. Is this person respected by other experts in the area? What do former defense secretaries, financial experts, and congressional defense committees say?

   E. Does this person have reason to be biased? The Defense Secretary might see the federal budget in terms of his own interests.

   F. Has this person been reliable in observations and predictions in the past? Perhaps the Secretary issued unwarranted fear appeals in the past or has spent money for the development of weaponry that was immediately obsolete.

12. Is the source of the reporting of the data and evidence credible? Here we refer to source—magazine, newspaper, grapevine—from which the information is obtained. Now, how reliable and accurate is your local newspaper in reporting information in general? All of the tests in item 11 apply here also.

While this discussion of data and its tests is not exhaustive, it does provide some basis for us to analyze the information that comes to us in messages more critically. To the extent that we can apply some of these tests, we can refine the critical decision making upon which our beliefs rest.

**BLACK BOX
59**

Can you list and describe the various types of data and evidence?

Can you use the tests of data-evidence by applying them to messages that you receive?

Warrants

A *warrant* is the underlying assumption or type of inference that allows conclusions or claims to be drawn from data. You may question whether our earlier example that Jane's "going out with another person of the opposite sex" warrants drawing the conclusion that Jane and Bill have broken up. Perhaps too often we accept conclusions without questioning the validity of unstated warrants; however, the warrant, which expresses the relationship between two of these elements—data and claim—in a message, is seldom examined carefully. Unstated warrants are often insinuated quite persuasively into the receiver's mind. The source's intent is irrelevant.

Three specific types of warrants are frequently employed in messages: *motivational, authoritative, and substantive.*

Motivational warrants are generally based upon emotions, needs, drives, and values of the individual. The argument, "The new grading system for the university should replace the present one (claim) because we will have better grades under the new system (data);" rests on the assumption that (motivational warrant) "We want better grades."

Authoritative warrants are based upon the credibility of the source of the data. Our example illustrates: "The President says that our energy resources are completely adequate for the winter (data); the President is traditionally considered a credible source (warrant); therefore, government rationing of energy resources will be unnecessary (claim)." Claims made through authoritative warrants appear to be circular because of the similarity of the data and the claim. Understanding the nature of the warrant, however, allows us to make a rational judgment about the acceptability of that claim.

Substantive warrants are probably the most complex because they indicate more clearly how we perceive the relationship of things and events in reality. These warrants directly express the interdependent, systemic relationships among things which allow us to draw conclusions from data. You will remember from chapters 2, 3, and 4 that the relationships that exist among components of any system allow us to make inferences about that system. In a message, the *relationship* is the warrant for a claim. These warrants take the form of *definition, generalization, signs, sequence, causation,* and *analogy.*

In the process of making claims or drawing conclusions, we sometimes assume that (1) something should be categorized or labeled in a particular way—*definitional warrant.* For example, "Abortion after a certain number of months of pregnancy is certainly (qualifier) murder (claim). After a certain number of months of pregnancy the fetus is capable of surviving outside of the mother's body (data). A fetus that is capable of surviving outside of the mother's body should be classified or defined as a separate human being (definitional warrant)." Definitional warrants also allow us to classify a specific thing or event as belonging to a more general class (called classification warrants by some). These kinds of warrants are most often implied; however, examination of the warrant is essential to an adequate decision on the issue.

Very frequently we draw a conclusion based upon the warrant that (2) some generalization is true because of the examples existing that are typical of the thing or event referred to in the claim—*generalization warrant.* "Detective series will possibly (qualifier) be taken off television next fall (claim). The detective shows 'Head Honcho' and 'Black Gun' are being cancelled for the fall (data examples)." The implied *generalization warrant* is that " 'Head Honcho' and 'Black Gun' are representative of detective series in general." Although similar to definitional warrants which categorize or label a single event or thing as belonging to a general class, *generalization warrants* attempt the opposite. Generalization warrants predict what will happen to a general class (e.g., detective series) based upon representative examples (e.g., "Head Honcho" and "Black Gun") or subsets of that general class.

At other times we draw a conclusion by assuming (warranting) that (3) two or more things or events are related in such a way that the presence or absence of one may be taken as proof of the presence or absence of the

*An analogical
warrant asserts that
two strip mining
companies have the
same problems with
costs and
conservation.*

other—*sign warrant.* Consider the following illustration: "A large number of students' cars are being ticketed and towed away on campus (data). There are probably (qualifier) inadequate parking facilities for students on campus (claim). This large amount of ticketing and towing of students' cars signifies the absence of adequate parking facilities for students on campus (sign warrant)." Through examination of this warrant we might decide that the claim is acceptable or we might reject it in favor of other warrants: "The towing and ticketing of a large number of cars is a sign of lack of adequate traffic regulations;" or "The towing and ticketing of a large number of cars is a sign of too many student cars." One event need *not cause* the other to occur to be a sign relationship, although causation is not precluded. High unemployment may be a sign of a recessed economy but would not necessarily be the cause of that recession.

Certain arguments are based upon sequential relationships. In that case the argument is warranted by assuming that (4) certain events precede other events in a time order—*sequential warrant.* In the following statement, note how this assumption warrants the claim: "Final registration for fall classes is occurring this week (data). Fall classes will begin next Monday (claim)." The argument is based upon the *sequential warrant* that "fall registration precedes the weekend which in turn precedes the first fall classes." The implied *certainty* of the conclusion illustrates the degree of qualification used. Understanding the assumed sequential relationship helps us to evaluate the acceptability of the claim. This is similar to the sign warrant but stipulates a time-ordered sequence in the sign relationship. Again, causal relationships are not necessary between the two events.

Causal warrants assume that (5) one or more things are the cause of other things or events. "Jane and Bill will probably (qualifier) get a divorce (claim). They are having irreconcilable problems in their marriage (data). Irreconcilable problems in marriage frequently lead to divorce (causal warrant)." Seldom are causal relationships simple. There are usually a number of possible causes or effects. Often sign and sequential relationships are misinterpreted as causal. Careful perusal for causal warrants in these types of statements allows us to examine them for more complex or misinterpreted relationships.

Substantive warrants based upon *analogy* assume that (6) some event will occur or something is true because it occurred or was true in a comparable event or thing—*analogical warrant*. At the heart of this method of inference is a comparison to two highly similar things or events. They must be equal members of the same general class. To the extent that the two things are similar in all crucial aspects, the warrant supports the claim made by analogy. For example: "Increasing costs and decreasing personnel productivity are producing a drop in net profit in the 'Strip Coal Company' (data). Increasing costs and decreasing personnel productivity will produce a drop in net profit in the 'Scalp Coal Company' (claim)." The

---

**BLACK BOX
60**

Can you name and explain the differences between the three general types of warrants?

Can you describe the types of substantive warrants and how each works?

Can you recognize the different warrants in the messages you receive and send?

implied *analogical warrant* is that Strip and Scalp Coal companies are similar in all crucial aspects. If, however, Scalp Coal Company has mechanisms for absorbing increased costs or relies more on technology than personnel, the claim may not be properly warranted. Again, the implied certainty of the conclusion is indicative of the degree of qualification attached to the claim.

Qualifiers

The qualifier in an argument is the degree of certainty with which we hold that claim. These *degrees of* certainty (traditionally labeled "probative force") are: *possible, plausible, probable, and certain* (or their synonyms). Any claim is qualified, implicitly or explicitly, with one of these levels of certainty. In analyzing statements, we should examine the stated or implied qualifier of the claim and supply the appropriate level when needed.

There are two basic sources of qualification made on a claim. One source is actual argument supplied by a communicator. In this case, the qualification is determined by examining how good the data and warrant are in supporting the conclusion drawn and by examining the appropriateness of the qualifier as stated or implied by the communicator. Remember our example of Bill and Jane and the other man she was seen with last night? The qualifier was that she and Bill "might have" broken up. This qualifier probably represents the *most* that we could claim from the data actually given in the brief message. On this basis, perhaps even a weaker qualifier is needed, such as "might possibly have."

Another source of qualification to a claim is external to the data, warrant, and claim used in the argument. The qualification to the claim cannot be found by looking only at the argument that the communicator is presenting or using. In this case, we would add or change a qualifier to the claim if there are other data or warrants available that might produce differing claims. Other data, for example, could offer the information that Jane's older brother happened to be passing through town. Or we might also discover that she and Bill have had a "fight" and that she had been secretly dating this other fellow for several months. In this case, we might change the claim to the following: "Jane and Bill will probably never get together again." These findings would, of course, modify the degree of certainty of a claim offered by the source. Specifically, the source of these reservations about the claim results from discovering the following information: (1) other motives, (2) other credible sources, (3) other definitions, (4) other generalizations, (5) other sign relationships, (6) other causes, (7) other comparisons, and (8) other incompatible data. As the level of certainty of these reservations *increases,* the level of certainty of the original claim *decreases.*

Claims

The claim of a statement refers to a stated or implied conclusion that a source and receiver draw from data by means of a warrant. One type of claim attempts to establish the existence of a fact or event. It answers the question, did something occur or does something exist? For example, are grades at this university above national norms? This type of claim is called *designative.* Another type of claim attempts to define and classify. It tries to answer the question, what do we name it? Or what category do we place it in? Return to our previous example: Do we call abortion "murder" or "a woman's control of her own body?" This type of claim is labeled *definitive.* A third type of claim, *evaluative,* attempts to assess the value of some thing or event; it answers the question of how good or bad something is. For example, evaluative claims might be concerned with the desirability of open marriage or the value of compact automobiles. *Advocative* claims concern policy and future courses of action in terms of our beliefs, practices, or product adoption. These types of conclusions might be concerned with whether we should vote for a certain candidate, buy a particular car, become engaged, or chose any number of courses of action.

> **BLACK BOX
> 61**
>
> **What are qualifiers and claims?**
>
> **Can you recognize them in messages?**
>
> **Try to use the tests of arguments by applying them to messages you receive. (See below.)**

Tests of Arguments in Messages

Any system of meaningful statements (messages) involving the elements discussed above can be analyzed critically by assessing the relationships among those components. Some basis for doing that analysis has been provided. Also, assessing the quality of each component and its importance to a particular argument and to the message as a whole is useful. We have explored the crucial components of a message; however, we can refine this critical ability by utilizing certain tests. Recall our illustration of the Secretary of Defense's request for a budget increase and try the following questions:

Data. Is the data complete? Is it accurate? Is it clear? Was the data actually given? How credible is the source of the data? (See previous tests of data and evidence.) Do you remember all of this! If not, flip back a few pages.

Motivational Warrant. Is the warrant actually given? Is it relevant to the claim? Does the need or value really exist? Has the need or value been interpreted and labeled correctly? Does the need or value necessitate a means to resolve the problem that is suggested by the claim? (Fifteen percent increase needed in defense spending?) Does the need or value apply in this case? Are there overriding or more important values or needs that supersede this one (domestic needs for food or energy)? Is there another value that will continue to satisfy the needs and is consistent with accepted norms? Do urgent demands or needs necessitate the acceptance of other values? For example, you might consider whether there are other foreign aid programs and negotiations that could better accomplish defense goals.

Authoritative Warrants. Is the warrant actually given? Is it relevant to the claim? Is the authority credible? (See previous tests of sources of evidence.) How believable is the Secretary, the sources he cites, and your local newspaper?

Substantive Warrant: Definition. Is the definition fair and unprejudiced? What did he really mean when he said national defense or Mideast crisis? Does the definition exclude words that need definition? Does the thing or event identified belong to the established general class? Does the definition differentiate the thing defined from all other things? Does the definition simply and briefly classify? Does it fit the context of the claim? Is it relevant to the claim? Is it actually stated? For example, do you and the Defense Secretary agree on the names of things and has he really put events in the right perspective?

*Ford and Brezhnev
sign an agreement
at Vladivostok, a
series of warrants
allowing claims to be
made by the U.S. and
the U.S.S.R.*

Substantive Warrant: Generalization.   Is the warrant actually stated?   Is it relevant to the claim?   Are the examples typical and representative?   Are enough examples cited?   Are opposite examples accounted for?   Is the Defense Secretary aware of the TV special and the columnists in the paper?   Is the relationship between example(s) and claim apparent?   Do the examples cited meet the tests of good evidence (see previous section on evidence)?   For example, was the Secretary deliberately selective in his examples or were they really representative of the current state of our military preparedness?

Substantive Warrant: Sign.   Is the warrant actually stated?   Is it relevant to the claim?   Is the sign relationship accidental or is it consistently present?   Is the sign relationship reciprocal with the presence or absence of either component indicating the presence or absence of the other?   Does this obsolete weapon indicate that we are in danger?   Have other conditions intervened to alter normal sign relationships so that the sign is not completely reliable?   Are other collaborating signs unnecessary to the acceptance of the claim?   Are there other signs that confirm the conclusion?   In our illustration, do the problems noted indicate weakness or willingness to seek peace and compromise?

Substantive Warrant: Sequence. Is the warrant actually stated? Is it relevant to the claim? Is the time-ordered sequence consistent and reliable? Are there other sequences of events that would explain the relationship? Is it really a sign relationship? Are there intervening events that are absent in the sequence? Again in our illustration, might the Defense Secretary's expenditures only produce more obsolete weapons because of the poor planning or time required to develop them?

Substantive Warrant: Causation. Is the warrant actually stated? Is it relevant to the claim? Is there a direct relationship between the alleged cause and effect? Are there other, more important causes? Have other conditions intervened to prevent the functioning of the cause or that break the relationship between cause and effect? Are there other more important effects? To what extent is the cause capable of producing the effect? Are there multiple causes and multiple effects involved that obscure the relationship? Maybe there are other causes of the problems which the Secretary mentioned besides military preparedness.

Substantive Warrant: Analogy. Have things changed since the "cold war" of the 1950s? Is the warrant actually stated? Is it relevant to the claim? Are the compared cases significantly similar in essential or crucial aspects? Are the similarities important? Do differences not accounted for negate the comparison? Are we still engaged in a cold war? Are enough points of comparison drawn to support the claim? Are the things or events that are compared members of the same general class of events?

Qualifiers. Is the actual qualifier the one that is stated? Is it stated? Does the quality of the data used justify this qualifier? Does the quality of the warrent justify this qualifier? Are there other warrants that might produce differing claims, thereby necessitating a different qualifier for the claim stated? Are there other data that would necessitate a different qualifier? Note the columnists, senators, and TV specials! Have other reservations to the claim been ignored? You may have to examine how much the case for increased defense spending has been overstated.

Claims. Is the claim stated? Is the claim stated the actual one that should be drawn? Is the claim justified by the data and warrant? Is the claim fair and unprejudiced? Is the claim clear and unambiguous? Does the claim relate to the rest of the message? Is the claim overstated or understated?

Has the absence of a stated qualfier resulted in an overstated claim? What kind of claim is being made? In short, is a 15 percent increase in defense spending really warranted?

Additional Defects: Fallacies. Another way of examining arguments for defects is to look for fallacies. Fallacies are defects in argument and/or evidence which render a claim improbable or invalid. They are similar to weakness discussed above. These fallacies or defects can also be viewed as stratagems that divert rational decision. They are used in messages consciously and unconsciously as substitutes for rational argument. *They are fallacies only when they are used as such substitutes.* They rely upon our uncritical acceptance for their persuasive impact.

One such fallacy is personal abuse or ridicule of others *(ad hominem).* For example, a politician might state the following: "My opponent has not responded adequately to my argument. Obviously, he does not understand it. Perhaps, he may some day be able to take an elementary course in political science which will help him to understand such things." This type of fallacy is often more subtly expressed. A classic example appeared in the 1960 election debate between Kennedy and Nixon. Democrats circulated a picture of Nixon with a heavy "five o'clock shadow" of a beard and put the following caption under the picture: "Would You Buy a Used Car from This Man?"

Another very similar type of fallacy involves "playing the gallery" through the uses of popular argument and appeals to special interests, prejudices, and irrationality. This may involve arguing that something is beside the point, stopping arguing altogether, and displaying indignant anger. This category of fallacies is labeled *ad populum* or *ad misericordiam.* For example, men have been heard to comment in answer to women's statements, "I'll never understand female logic." On other hand some women have stated that "men carry their brains between their legs."

Uncritical appeals to authority, force, prestige, or status in the absence of the reasoning of the authority is another category of fallacies, *ad verecundiam.* Although similar to authoritative warrants, fallacies represent a substitute for rationality. Generally, the forms of the defect are the following: "The President says so, so it must be right." "This must be the right way because this is the only way the boss allows." Or this defect may take the opposite stance and allege that some claim is not right because of the source of that claim. If we do not like the source, then what he or she says cannot be right *(genetic fallacy).* For example: "Russia has proposed this new nuclear treaty. Therefore, it must be bad."

The fallacy of assertion involves the statement of normally accepted or unaccepted conclusions without subargument or data. Advertising, of course, is often guilty of this fallacy: "Bayer Aspirin is better."

Overgeneralization involves making sweeping claims, hasty generalization, or what we might label weak hypothesizing. This is closely related to generalization warrants based on too few or atypical examples. For example: "The Premier of India and the Prime Minister of Burma have made strong statements criticizing the United States' foreign aid programs. So we can see that our foreign policies are generally unpopular among world leaders."

Another defect involves drawing a conclusion from data and warrant that is irrelevant to the data and warrant in the assertion. We say, in this case, that the claim does not follow from the data and warrant; it is a *non sequitur*. Note the following examples: "Inflation is soaring; therefore we need a tax increase." "Women are generally weaker than men; therefore, women's place is in the home."

A related defect involves arguing in a circle by drawing a conclusion (claim) from a different wording of the same statement (data). This has also been labeled *begging the question* or *tautology*. For example: "Belief in God is universal, for everyone believes in Him." Or consider this popular example: "American politicians have always been crooked through history. They entered politics because it is crooked too. Today our politicians are still crooked. They still enter politics because it is crooked." The conclusion is that "politics and politicians are and always have been crooked." This example, of course, has bits of *ad hominem* and *ad populum* defects mixed in.

The common fallacy of inconsistency (noted above) involves making statements and drawing conclusions that are inconsistent with each other. This fallacy is quite popular in the media if one takes the time to examine messages carefully. For example, "Blight Guard is an anti-perspirant that stops wetness and will not stain when you sweat." Often news and editorial statements contain information such as the following: "Over ¾ths of the prices on commodities rose 15 percent last month. This is one reason for inflated prices. A maximum of 35 percent of the prices on commodities remained stable."

Another fallacy involves forcing ideas into arbitrary, either/or classes, using opposites in wording for concepts that are not opposites, or using false alternatives. For example, "Music is either intellectual or emotional. On the basis of the reactions we must conclude that this music is emotional." Or consider the following statement: "During the summer of 1975, food prices advanced rapidly. This was due either to food scarcity or to inflation which made increased prices inevitable."

Defects involving causation have been discussed in some detail above; however, we can note some forms this type of logical fallacy takes. Wrong cause, confusion of cause and sign, confusion of cause and sequence, and failure to recognize multiple causes are the most common mistakes made. Let us restate a previous example to fit this problem area: "During the summer of 1975, food prices advanced. This was due to food scarcity which alone produced the upward trend."

The fallacies of false division and false composition occur when during analysis of an issue, the arguments are organized or divided in such a way as to invalidate the conclusions drawn. For example, "It would be advisable for the people of our whole country to favor a new international organization of noncommunist countries; therefore, it would be wise for the people of Chicago to approve it." What is wise for the whole class is not necessarily wise for all the components of that class. This fallacy also proceeds in the opposite direction. For example, "Local agencies cannot solve the problem alone. State agencies cannot solve the problem alone. Regional agencies have not been able to solve the problem. Therefore, the federal government must assume the responsibility for solving the problem." Note that the possibility of local, state, or regional agencies solving the problem together was never considered.

The defect of using imperfect analogy has been discussed above. This involves drawing a conclusion or making a claim by comparing two things that are not essentially alike. We have supplied tests to examine claims for false analogies. However, we should note the difference between literal analogies and figurative analogies. Literal analogies involve the comparison of two things of the same class such as states, felony laws, universities, or people. Figurative analogies involve metapohoric comparisons of things of different classes such as linking people with animals, government with machinery, and business cycles with weather conditions. For example: "John is a tiger." "American government is like a steam engine and it should operate like a computer." "The business cycle has hit its winter and profits are down. Everything will be OK if we wait until spring." While these figurative analogies are useful in clarification and persuasion, they do not constitute rationally acceptable argument. They do not provide reasonable warrants for claims.

A number of other defects we should be aware of are related to our use of language. One of these involves taking material (evidence in particular) out of the context in which the intended meaning is clear and, as a

result, distorting what the source intended.   Another involves using the
same word in two different ways within the same argument, *equivocation.*
For example, "*Some* people are homosexuals.   His roommate is *some*
person."   Ambiguity is another form of parlance using highly abstract language or double talk.   For example, "Churches in this University city have
some form of respectable fellowship *every* evening except Sunday."   "I
favor the American way of doing things."   Loaded language and "tricky"
questions are further types of language fallacies in argument.   Loaded
language is often used in *ad hominem, ad populum* and arguing in a circle.
Note our previous examples of name calling and ridiculing terminology.
Trick questions, on the other hand, ask yes or no questions for which there is
no adequate alternative given.   In this sense, they are similar to fallacies
involving false alternatives.   For example, consider the following questions:
"Have you stopped cheating on exams?"   "Has the Democratic Party rid
itself of communists yet?"

A final defect which we should consider involves attempting to prove
a negative statement or asking someone to attempt it *(ad ignorantiam).*   For
example: "God must exist because no one can prove that He doesn't."

**BLACK BOX
62**

Can you identify the concept of *fallacy?*

Can you recognize fallacies in messages you receive and send?

"People must live on other planets because no one can prove that they
don't."   The logical impossibility of proving such negative statements pre-
cludes valid claims based upon them.

Understanding the nature of argument in messages, the components
of argument and their relationships, and the utilization of the tests supplied
should provide a fairly adequate basis for the rational analysis of messages
that emanate from the large variety of sources in our society.   Decisions
based upon such analysis should be more effective and functional for the
individual or social system involved in decision making.   Our ability to engage in coherent analysis is not only dependent upon our understanding of
these elements and relationships, but also upon conscientious practice and
application of principles.   Some research relevant on this issue follows.

Some Relevant Research

Research has fairly well established that the common notion that emotional arguments are irrational is simply not true. Arguments may be logical or illogical, rational or irrational, and emotional or unemotional. Arguments in messages may also consist of different combinations of these features. For example, we can make rational decisions with emotional arguments that are also logical. Also, there is some research that suggests that through training we can increase our ability to judge the validity of arguments and our ability to think critically and analyze messages. These findings about us as humans are particularly important in light of most of the conclusions of most of the research in persuasion and attitude change discussed in previous chapters.

Most of the research in regard to evidence has been conducted in the context of persuasion and attitude change; however, some of the findings are relevant to our discussion here. While good evidence presented by a highly credible source does not appear to increase attitude change, it does appear to affect our perceptions of the credibility of that source. Apparently, although we believe this source already, we can modify our judgments about her or his credibility based upon whether or not she or he uses good evidence. It follows that we can rationally assess the credibility of a source of communication based upon her or his use of good or bad evidence. The fact that a less credible communicator can improve perceived credibility and increase attitude change through the use of good evidence seems to indicate that we make judgments about sources and decisions regarding our beliefs based upon the quality of data and evidence that the communicator uses. Some research has indicated that we also assess the sources of the evidence a communicator uses.

Research in the area of qualifiers and reservations has produced some mixed interpretations. Studies on the level of certainty expressed by qualifiers has shown that the qualifier used directly affects the certainty with which we *believe* the claim. This appears to indicate that we do evaluate or limit claims and that the qualifier is indeed an essential component of argument. However, research further indicates that the stronger or more certain the qualifier used by the communicator, the more we believe what she or he claims. This would indicate that we are not generally very critical of qualifiers that are used. Research results are similar in the area of *reservations* we have about the claim. To the extent that a communicator deals with the reservations we have or potential reservations that might come up in the future, she or he is generally more effective in changing our

385

beliefs and attitudes in a more permanent, enduring way. Again, this suggests the importance of reservations in messages, but does *not* indicate that we critically evaluate those qualifications and reservations in reaching decisions. Hopefully, careful attention to this component can improve your critical consumption of messages and subsequent decisions.

There is also research dealing with our abilities to draw rational and valid conclusions. This research is directly related to the process by which we make inferences, draw conclusions, and warrant claims. Studies in this area indicate that the order of the components in the arguments and their familiarity or abstractness affect our abilities to draw conclusions. The less expected or conventional the arrangement and the less familiar the terms are, the more difficulty we have in recognizing valid claims. Also, the acceptability of the claim appears to be influenced by the arguments that precede it. If we have a "feeling" that the arguments are logical and if the statements are presented in a way to "appear" logical, then we generally accept the conclusions. This tendency is called the *atmosphere effect*.

Further research in this area has demonstrated fairly substantially that attitudes, prior knowledge, and personality affect our critical ability to examine arguments and their claims. If we have strong favorable attitudes toward an issue, we are much more likely to accept claims uncritically and draw conclusions that are consistent with those attitudes. The same is true regarding strongly unfavorable attitudes toward the claim. Also, how directly relevant the issue is to our self-interests—how involving the issue is—determines to some extent the range of claims that we might accept. If we are highly involved, we are likely to have a smaller range of acceptable claims and a larger range of unacceptable ones which we would, despite the argument, accept or reject. In a similar way, we tend to distort arguments and claims to fit within the context of our previous knowledge and beliefs.

**BLACK BOX
63**

Can you explain what research says about these aspects of arguments?
    critical thinking
    evidence
    qualifiers
    reservations
    the atmosphere effect
    the effect of attitudes, prior knowledge, and personality

This tendency, while common to all of us, is most pronounced in the dog-matic, closed-minded individual we have seen in earlier chapters. For the dogmatic, the nature of the data, warrant, and qualifiers is of less importance than the authority of the source (as in authoritative warrants) and whether the claim fits into that person's existing beliefs. This research is not ob-viously optimistic about our critical abilities and decision-making capacities. But knowledge and application of the components and their relationships in messages can improve those capacities.

Finally, we should refer you back to chapters 14 through 17. There we noted numerous message variables that intentionally or unintentionally affect our beliefs, attitudes, and behavior. Research was discussed which demonstrated the persuasive impact of message elements such as evidence and message-sidedness as well as message structure, conclusion drawing, statements of intent, fear appeals, message discrepancy, opinionated lan-guage, and language intensity. To the extent that we are aware of these persuasive components and their usual effects, we can more completely bring our responses into the realm of intentional, conscious decision. Therefore, we recommend the examination of messages for such persuasive strategies in addition to analysis of data, warrants, qualifiers, and claims. You can only become a more intelligent, critical consumer of the informa-tion that is important to you and the society in which you live.

SUGGESTED FURTHER READINGS

1. Brockriede, W. and Ehninger, D. "Toulmin on Argument: An Interpretation and Application." *Quarterly Journal of Speech* 54 (1968): 252–259.

   This brief article discusses, in some detail, the Toulmin model used in this chapter. The article provides a more in-depth analysis and a consideration of relevant issues neglected above.

2. Gore, W. and Dyson, J. W. *The Making of Decisions* (New York: The Free Press, 1964).

   This text offers several chapters of interest. Approaches to decision making and processing information are discussed. Since the approaches in this text are considerably different from those we presented, this reading constitutes an excellent supplement.

3. McCroskey, J. C. *An Introduction to Rhetorical Communication* (Englewood Cliffs, N.J.: Prentice-Hall, 1968).

Chapter 5 in this text presents another treatment of the Toulmin approach. In here, persuasive argument in a variety of contexts, with differing examples, is discussed.

4. McCroskey, J. C. "A Summary of Experimental Research on the Effects of Evidence in Persuasive Communication." *Quarterly Journal of Speech* 55 (1969): 169–176.

This article summarizes much of the research on evidence. The typical persuasive effects of evidence along with division of sources of evidence is developed.

5. Miller, G. R. "Some Factors Influencing Judgments of the Logical Validity of Arguments: A Research Review." *The Quarterly Journal of Speech* 55 (1969): 276–286.

This article offers an excellent summary and critique of research on argument and logical validity. Since this material was not discussed in detail in this chapter, this article constitutes an excellent supplementary reading. The ability of individuals to draw logical conclusions from arguments–messages is the focus of the discussion.

6. Toulmin, S. *The Uses of Argument* (Cambridge: Cambridge University Press, 1958).

This short volume is the source of the central notion underlying this chapter. Complete development of the model with underlying philosophical assumptions is presented. As the primary source, this reference is highly recommended for your reading.

SELECTED REFERENCES

ANDERSON, L. J. and ANDERSON, K. E. "Research on the Relationship of Reasoning and Evidence to Message Acceptance." Paper presented at the Speech Association of America Convention, New York, December, 1969.

BREMBECK, W. L. "The Effects of a Course in Argumentation on Critical Thinking Ability." *Speech Monographs* 16 (1949): 177–189.

BROCKRIEDE, W. and EHNINGER, D. "Toulmin on Argument: An Interpretation and Application." *Quarterly Journal of Speech* 54 (1968): 252–259.

CRANE, E. "Immunization; With and Without the Use of Counter-arguments." *Journalism Quarterly* 39 (1962): 445–450.

CRONKHITE, G. L. "Logic, Emotion, and the Paradigm of Persuasion." *Quarterly Journal of Speech* 50 (1964): 13–18.

EDWARDS, W. and TVERSKY, A., eds. *Decision-Making* (Middlesex, England: Penguin, 1967.)

EHNINGER, D. and BROCKRIEDE, W. *Decision by Debate* (New York: Dodd, Mead, 1963).

FEEZEL, J. D. "Verbal Qualifiers in Argument as a Factor in Receiver Acceptance of the Claim." Paper presented at the International Communication Association Convention, Minneapolis, May, 1970.

GORE, W. and DYSON, J. W. *The Making of Decisions* (New York: The Free Press, 1964).

HOVLAND, C. I. and MANDELL, W. "An Experimental Comparison of Conclusion-Drawing by the Communicator and by the Audience." *Journal of Abnormal and Social Psychology* 47 (1952): 581–588.

JACKSON, T. R. "The Effects of Intercollegiate Debating on Critical Thinking." (Ph.D. Dissertation, University of Wisconsin, 1961).

KEPNER, C. H. and TREGOE, B. B. *The Rational Manager* (New York: McGraw-Hill, 1965).

KOEHLER, J. W. "Effects on Audience Opinion of One-Sided and Two-Sided Speeches Supporting and Opposing a Proposition, Examining Opinions on Speaker's Ethos, the Topic, and the 'Open-Mindedness' of Listeners." Doctoral Dissertation, Pennsylvania State University, 1968.

LUMSDAINE, A. A. and JANIS, I. L. "Resistance to 'Counter-Propaganda' Produced by One-Sided and Two-Sided 'Propaganda' Presentations." *Public Opinion Quarterly* 17 (1953): 311–18.

MANIS, M. and BLAKE, J. B. "Interpretation of Persuasive Messages as a Function of Prior Immunization." *Journal of Abnormal and Social Psychology* 66 (1963): 225–230.

McCROSKEY, J. C. *An Introduction to Rhetorical Communication* (Englewood Cliffs, N.J.: Prentice-Hall, 1968).

————. "A Summary of Experimental Research on the Effects of Evidence in Persuasive Communication." *Quarterly Journal of Speech* 55 (1969): 169–176.

McGUIRE, W. J. "The Effectiveness of Supportive and Refutational Defenses in Immunizing and Restoring Beliefs Against Persuasion." *Sociometry* 24 (1961): 184–197.

————. "Resistance to Persuasion Conferred by Active and Passive Prior Refutation of the Same and Alternative Counterarguments." *Journal of Abnormal and Social Psychology* 63 (1961): 326–332.

MILLER, G. R. "Some Factors Influencing Judgments of the Logical Validity of Arguments: A Research Review." *The Quarterly Journal of Speech* 55 (1969): 276–286.

PAPAGEORGIS, D. and McGUIRE, W. J. "The Generality of Immunity to Persuasion Produced by Pre-Exposure to Weakened Counter-Arguments." *Journal of Abnormal and Social Psychology* 62 (1961): 475–481.

SMITH, C. R. and HUNSAKER, D. M. *The Bases of Argument: Ideas in Conflict* (Indianapolis: Bobbs-Merrill, 1972).

PHILLIPS, G. M. "Effects of Debate on the Student." *AFA Register* 10 (Spring, 1962): 15–20.

TRENT, J. D. "Toulmin Model of and Argument: An Examination and Extension." *The Quarterly Journal of Speech* 54 (1968): 252–259.

TOULMIN, S. *The Uses of Argument* (Cambridge: Cambridge University Press, 1958).

WARREN, I. D. "The Effect of Credibility in Sources of Testimony on Audience Attitudes Toward Speaker and Messages." *Speech Monographs* 36 (1969): 156–458.

WEAVER, R. M. *The Ethics of Rhetoric* (Chicago: Henry Regnery Co., 1965).

19

Active Decision Making

A couple of years ago a faculty senate debated and discussed a new proposal for grading in the university. As you would expect, the issue was hotly contested on both sides. Finally, unable to reach an agreeable solution, the senate turned the problem over to a special committee. This committee was to study the issue, sample campus and business-world opinion, and recommend a solution when the senate met again in three weeks. The committee attempted to be open-minded as it agonized and weighed options. But a division of opinion arose, some hostility and conflict surfaced, and the committee became bogged down in the process. Finally, unable to reach consensus, they decided to take a vote. The proposal calling for the elimination of "F's" passed by a narrow margin of 5 to 4.

At the next meeting of the senate, the committee made its report and presented its proposal. The senate discussed the proposal and promptly voted it down. Debate again emerged in the senate

393

and a counter-proposal was presented. Discussion continued sporadically for the next three meetings and the issue was finally tabled. The old grading system remained.

Unfortunately, this example is typical of most decision making that affects us. Those actively involved in decision making usually know little about it. They possess neither the elementary skills of decision making nor the ability to communicate effectively in order to achieve that goal. Consensus is even more rarely arrived at, and, consequently, group decisions are undercut. In our example, this was the case. As a result, we will never know if the best action was taken.

In this chapter we will deal directly with decision-making systems and skills you need to make decisions effectively. We will discuss problems and recommend communication principles for you to use.

The Nature of Rational Human Decisions

Bases of Rational Decision

We are both consumers of information and participants in the process of decision making. At times we listen to advocates—politicians, advertisers, friends—as they attempt to convince us of the value of their ideas, practices, or products. At other times we become the advocates. Frequently we sit down with another person or group of others and reflect in an orderly way upon courses of action or solutions to problems.

This chapter deals with the roles we play every day in decision making: consumer, participant, advocate, bargainer, reflective thinker, and analyzer. We will look at some of the important variables that affect decision making and pay particular attention to how we can work with others to reach decisions. Hopefully, our decisions will become better as a result.

The main assumption underlying this whole discussion is that *rational decisions are better than irrational ones*. This does not mean "unemotional" decisions. Rational decisions may also involve the emotions. We may make rational decisions about emotional issues such as Vietnam, impeachment of a President, marriage, or termination of a marriage. Rational decisions are merely those which are beneficial to individuals or groups of individuals. Decision making may have varying degrees of rationality and emotionality involved.

Premature Judgment. In order to make our decisions more rational, it is helpful to understand several factors initially. The first of these is personal *suspension of premature judgment.* Too often we say (although seldom out loud) "my mind is already made up; don't confuse me with facts." Suspending judgment means avoiding this tendency. At *some* time we must make a judgment and decide; however, we want to remain open to new information and views until that time. Suspending judgment so that we do not *prematurely* decide can be useful in arriving at rational decisions. This openness should not be confused with indecisiveness. Necessity sometimes dictates that we must make decisions before we are ready—before we feel we have enough information and have assessed the situation adequately.

Scientific attitude. Another useful factor is adopting a *scientific attitude.* This attitude is characterized by objectivity in dealing with information that we seek out and receive. It demands hard evidence and good reasoning. Careful, orderly, systematic thinking is helpful in making decisions. Often it is hard for us to "stand back" from what is going on and assess it objectively, as a scientist would. Some people appear to have a natural knack for rationality; others' life styles and ways of thinking seem to preclude this approach. But everyone's ability in this area can be improved with certain information and training.

Knowledge of Variables. A third factor useful to decision making involves some knowledge of communication variables, processes, and systems. For example, up to this point much of this book has discussed how messages are exchanged. You have noted that certain message elements seem to influence our decisions without our awareness. Remember the influence of source credibility, attraction, homophily, and power on our conscious and unconscious decisions? (chapters 6 and 7). Can you recall how attitudes (chapter 16), feedback (chapter 8), personality elements (chapter 17), and opinion leadership (chapter 4) influence you? To the extent that you are aware of the variables and processes that normally affect you unconsciously, you can make your decisions more conscious and rational. The remainder of this chapter will extend your understanding of some of the more crucial elements involved in making decisions.

Potential Barriers to Rational Decisions

A number of psychological, social, and cultural tendencies can become barriers to *rational* decision making. The three factors discussed above can be detrimental when they are absent. The tendency toward premature judgment based upon preconceived attitudes can short-circuit rational processes. Lack of objectivity and systematic thinking can lead to less desirable decisions (chapter 18). While ignorance of communication variables, processes, and systems may not completely preclude effective decision making, knowledge in this area is certainly useful and helpful. Other potential barriers, however, warrant consideration.

Lack of Tolerance. Most manipulative attempts at persuasion appeal to certain physical and social needs or attempt to create some kind of inconsistency among our attitudes, beliefs, values, and behaviors (chapter 16). By doing so, these persuasive attempts create some kind of imbalance or apparent inconsistency for which we have varying degrees of tolerance. We generally need to resolve this imbalance, and the effective persuader provides the way for us to deal with that imbalance. In so doing, she or he gets us to believe or do what she or he wants. The persuader gains acceptance of an idea, practice, or product by showing how it resolves the imbalance or inconsistency that we are experiencing. All of us have greater or lesser tolerance levels for imbalance in our needs, attitudes, beliefs, values, and behaviors, as we noted in chapter 7. To the extent that our tolerance level is high, we are able to maintain imbalance long enough to examine the matter more closely and come to a more rational decision. To the extent that our tolerance level is low, we are more likely to seek premature means of resolving the imbalance in some unsatisfactory manner.

Anxiety and Conflict. When our anxiety or fears are at a high level, our tolerance for imbalance is decreased. We are more likely to rush to a solution when we are highly anxious or fearful. Also, as we noted in chapter 15, anxiety and conflict impede our ability to make careful distinctions. We do not see things as well or as clearly under these conditions. In a *social climate* of anxiety, fear, conflict, and hostility (chapter 13), we have a strong tendency to seek resolution of a problem quickly or to avoid an issue altogether. This tendency, while "natural" and understandable, can be detrimental to careful decision making. The decision-making process also varies within groups depending upon the socio-emotional climate. If there is a supportive atmosphere present and the group is cohesive and interested in reaching agreeable decisions, then there will be more participation and satisfaction involved in the process.

Attitude Response Tendencies. Our attitudes toward others and their ideas produce tendencies to respond in certain ways that may preclude effective decision making. If these attitudes are strongly unfavorable, we may avoid or misperceive information from that source even though that information may be useful. On the other hand, we may seek out only sources and information that support our preconceived attitudes. As you will recall from chapters 14 and 15, these tendencies to distort or avoid information are related to several things: (1) how intense our attitudes are; (2) how involved and self-interested we are; (3) how competent we think the source is; and (4) how similar to ourselves we perceive the source as being. We know, for example, that if we perceive the source negatively, then we are likely to contrast or distort her or his views on issues that involve us personally.

Personality Characteristics. Undoubtedly, a number of the personality characteristics which we discussed in chapter 7 affect the way we make decisions. As a result people have different "life styles" and different ways of deciding issues important to them. Some people are cognitively oriented; they are thinkers who enjoy mental tasks and problem solving. Others may be considered to be more affectively oriented; they are more concerned and motivated by emotions, feelings, and personal concerns. Some people may be classified as *levelers;* they like to synthesize and simplify ideas and problems. Still others might be labeled *sharpeners;* they prefer to analyze and tear apart ideas, issues, and concepts. A brief review of chapter 7 would suggest a number of personality characteristics that could be related to the ways human beings are likely to process information in order to reach decisions. Perhaps, however, the dogmatic characteristic represents the greatest potential threat to rational decision making. Recall that the dogmatic individual is very likely to be closed-minded and rigid in her or his approach to other people. The dogmatic's ideas are generally less open to change except by those whom she or he perceives as an authority figure. The substance of evidence and logic may have little impact upon the dogmatic's decisions.

Language and Semantics. Language can pose barriers in decision making. Certainly, people who do not "speak the same language" are going to have difficulty arriving at a mutually agreeable decision. Not only does this

*Socio-cultural
background can have
a strong effect on
decision-making
processes: these
people support the
calls of the American
Indian Movement.*

pose problems in cross-cultural communication, but also in communication among subcultures in our own society. Subcultures and ethnic groups often build their own language to which others have little access. Witness the terminology of the black ghetto versus Wall Street. Because different individuals have varying meanings for the same word, our ability to understand each other and arrive at solutions is hampered. Also, as we noted in chapters 9 and 15, the nature of the language itself tends to obscure important issues. Careful definition of concepts is often absent in group decision making. In addition, our language is rather static and changes less rapidly than the pace of the events the words describe. This hinders how we process information about those events. The categories and labels of our language are often inadequate (or inadequately used) to describe the problems, ideas, or practices about which we need to make decisions. Labeling the deliberate abortion of a fetus "murder" is quite different from naming it "woman's control of her own body." This type of language use is bound to affect decision-making processes.

Socio-cultural Factors. Differing cultural practices are likely to have some impact upon the decision-making processes that are allowed. In some cultures, for example, independent decisions by members of the same family are not allowed. In Asian cultures, what we would regard as authoritarian decisions by a parent are the quite acceptable norm. Even within our own culture, differing social systems discussed in chapters 3 and 4 have impact on the decision-making processes. A large organization or business obviously does not go about making decisions the same way that families do.

People in certain subcultures allow differing degrees of freedom in making decisions. For some time in our culture, for example, women were not allowed to make certain decisions, and decisions involving women were arrived at through a process much different than they are, hopefully, today. Ethnic and racial groups still protest their exclusion from the decision-making process in our political and economic systems. If full understanding of problems and representative participation are desirable to decision making, then these cultural factors may be viewed as potential barriers.

**BLACK BOX
64**

Can you discuss the bases of rational decision?

Can you explain how each of the following elements may be a barrier to
    rational decision making?

lack of tolerance	personality characteristics
anxiety and conflict	language and semantics
attitude response tendencies	socio-cultural factors

All of these numerous factors, and others, can affect the decision-making process significantly. To the extent that we are aware of these elements and take time to assess their impact upon our decisions, we are more apt to arrive at decisions that will be functional and realistic. The recognition and assessment of these variables alone, however, is not sufficient for complete understanding of how we arrive at decision outcomes.

Decision-Making Processes and Systems

In our discussion of the communication outcome of decision making, we need to examine and understand the social communication processes through which we actually arrive at decisions. Some of these decision processes are rather "natural" kinds of occurrences; others are prescribed by convention or law. Still others are recommended by specialists and scholars in our society. All of these processes can be viewed as systems that we use in social communication aimed at decision outcomes. They are the means we use to analyze ideas and issues, practices and courses of action, as well as products and solutions to problems. They are systematic, communication processes of analysis and decision making.

The Advocacy System

In certain segments of our society the advocacy system is utilized as a basis for analysis and decision making. This approach assumes that the best way to reach a decision is to have worthy and competent advocates argue against each other. By the creation of the best cases representing the sides involved and by the critical exchange of these views, the best answer or solution will win out. Necessary to this system are (1) a disputed claim, (2) capable advocates and opponents, (3) some rules for interaction, and (4) some mechanism for finalizing and implementing the decision. In the advocacy system, the advocates support some change in ideas, beliefs, values, or policy. The opponents argue against change in favor of things as they are. The assumption is that we will believe and act as we have before until the advocate demonstrates sufficient need and means for change. We engage each other informally in this type of transaction in a variety of social settings. Our legal system of plaintiff, defendent, and jury-judge is, of course, one of our society's most formalized representatives of the advocacy system of decision making. Legislatures, elections, institutions and businesses, and differing social groups rely upon this process at times.

The essential function of the advocacy system is to provide a basis for analysis and decision regarding the acceptability of new or disputed claims. As we noted in chapter 18, these claims may be about (1) *fact* (e.g., designative claim—Did the new manufacturing processes produce more profit?); (2) *definition* (e.g., definitive claim—Is it "murder" or "manslaughter?"); (3) *value* (e.g., evaluative claim—Is the Christian ethic valuable in our society?); or (4) *policy* (e.g., advocative claim—"should the new grading system be adopted?"). Claims regarding definition are involved in questions of fact. Claims regarding definition and fact are involved in questions of value. Claims regarding definition, fact, and value are involved in questions of policy. These claims, then, are related to each other in an ordered hierarchy or pyramid with facts (or designative claims) at the base and policy (or advocacy claims) at the peak. Making a decision about one type of claim requires that relevant types of claims under it must be considered. An *advocate* of a particular claim has the burden of proof to consider all relevant subclaims or questions relevant to the claim he or she is advancing. The *opponent* in the advocacy system must attempt to maintain "things as they are," without significant change. This is done by defending the existing claims or present system (things as they are) and refuting the advocate's definitions, facts, and/or values. Thereby, the advocacy system is designed to answer crucial questions and establish or demolish subordinate claims upon which the main question or main claim rests. When this process has been completed, according to some means of critical exchanges between the advocates and their opponents, decision upon the acceptability of the main question or claim is made, often by vote or some similar action.

Seldom are we participants in such formalized disputes. We are usually receivers of messages and exchanges between advocate and opponent. However, understanding the analysis of possible claims in this system allows us to make more functional and useful decisions. Also, understanding of the method of analysis in the advocacy system gives us tools for analyzing our own problems involving definition, fact, value, and especially policy involving future courses of action.

The advocacy system of analysis and decision making is probably best illustrated by examining the questions used in deciding policy claims. Since policy claims represent the broadest types of demands, the following list of questions will be used to illustrate the basic questions upon which the critical transactions in this decision-making process are based:

1. What is the extent and nature of the present system (things as they are)? How does it work? (e.g. a grading system)
   A. What facts and definitions best describe the present system?
   B. What are the values of the present system? What good is there about it?
2. Are there inherent problems or evils in the present system?
   A. Do these problems really exist? How do you define them or name them?
   B. Are they really harmful problems? Can they be viewed as advantages under some circumstances?
   C. Are the problems or evils inherent to the principle or structure of the present system? That is, must we change the principle or structure of the present system in order to correct the problems?
   D. Can the problems be corrected?
   E. How significant are the problems?
   F. What are the causes of the problems?
3. Will the proposed changes correct the problems or evils? (e.g., a proposed, new grading system)

    A. Do the proposed changes remove the causes of the problems?

    B. What are all the values involved in the proposed changes? What values in the present system would be eliminated by adoption of the proposed changes?

    C. Which of the values involved are most important?

    D. Are there better proposals for change available?

4. Will the proposed changes produce the alleged advantages or benefits?

    A. Is the plan for change capable of producing the advantages?

    B. Are these really advantages? Can they be viewed as harms or disadvantages under some circumstances? Do they exist? Will they exist? What will you name them?

    C. Are more important advantages of the present system (values) eliminated by the adoption of the proposed changes?

    D. Do the alleged advantages result from the proposed changes? Or do the advantages result from some minor repair of the present system?

5. Will the proposed changes produce new problems or harms?

    A. What are the disadvantages or harms of adopting the proposed changes?

    B. What values of the present system would be eliminated?

    C. Are they really disadvantages? Could they be viewed as advantages or benefits under some circumstances?

    D. What are all of the values involved? Which are the most important?

    E. Will the harms exist? What will you call those harms?

This set of questions underlies claims advanced and criticized in the advocacy system of decision making. To the extent that we have capable advocates and opponents, much of the analysis may be done for us; however, we must often apply or use these questions to test the claims made by advocates and opponents. At other times we must analyze problems by ourselves. To the extent that we are capable of doing this, we can make more critical rational decisions.

The competitive environment in which this decision making occurs heightens the initiative of both advocate and opponent to develop the best case available. Once a person becomes an advocate "suspension of judgment" is dropped. This competition often becomes so strong that alternate information and solutions are not sought after freely. In addition, consensus on the resulting decision may be hard to establish because of the competition among the sides in the controversy.

Closely related to the advocacy system is that of bargaining. The bargaining process, however, is more closely akin to persuasion and even coercion. It involves primarily the discovery of the range of acceptable and unacceptable solutions on both sides, and modification through persuasion and coercion of those ranges of acceptable solutions. To the extent that

> **BLACK BOX**
> **65**
>
> Can you identify the components necessary for an advocacy system?
>
> Can you give examples of the advocacy system in our society?
>
> Can you explain how claims are related to decision making and advocates as compared to opponents in the advocacy system?
>
> Can you analyze a contemporary issue or claim using the set of questions provided for decision-making systems?
>
> Can you describe the effect of this competitive environment on final decision making?

issues above are considered, however, the value and long-term acceptance of the decision will be more likely to prevail.

Reflective-Agenda Systems

Small-group communication scholars have suggested systems for decision making that are traditionally labeled "reflective processes" or "agenda systems." These structures consist primarily of a systematic set of procedures and processes to be followed in the analysis of problems and the decision on specific solutions. These systems are generally useful for decision making in small groups, committees, conferences, and similar social settings. However, utilization of these reflective agendas can be helpful for the individual if they are carefully applied to problems he or she wishes to solve. Reflective-agenda systems can be applied to decisions ranging from purchasing a car to government foreign policy. Their primary utility appears to be in groups that have some decision-making goal. For example, problems involving such things as business decisions, family financial problems, and programs of study for students lend themselves readily to decision making via the reflective-agenda systems.

At the heart of this approach is the concept of "reflective thinking" advanced by John Dewey a number of years ago. Reflective thinking "is the active, persistent and careful consideration of beliefs..." in terms of the grounds that support those beliefs. Many small group scholars have argued that effective small-group decision making requires an attitude of suspended judgment, effective methods of searching for information, systematic protracted inquiry, and maintenance of a state of doubt. Seldom are we as individuals capable of living up to these kinds of expectations. Fortunately, utilization of the reflective-agenda itself helps to direct our communication and analysis in these directions. Even where a cooperative, objective attitude is absent, such as those situations discussed in chapter 13, these agendas provide focus on critical components of decision making, supply a structure for communication, and tend to facilitate rational, analytical processes.

Dewey's description of this process is reflected in his five stages of reflective thinking: (1) occurrence and recognition of a felt difficulty; (2) definition and specification of the difficulty; (3) suggested explanations of the difficulty and cultivation of a variety of solutions through rational exploration of suggestions; (4) selection of optimum solutions through rational elaboration of the ideas and suggestions; and (5) acceptance and implementation of the solution or ideas by testing their effects through experimental corroboration. This sequentially related system for problem solving has served as the basis of most agendas proposed by small-group scholars. However, no single agenda for decision making is appropriate in all situations. An agenda must be selected which is appropriate to the group and the type of problem or question involved.

Composite Agenda for Group Decision Making. The following agenda represents a composite or synthesis of a number of systems recommended by contemporary scholars. Not every item will be useful in every process of group decision making. Care should be taken to select the stages and processes which are most appropriate to the problem under consideration, the nature of the group members, and the social-emotional climate present.

1. *Recognition of a felt difficulty.* This involves recognition by group members that there is some problem. In some situations some participants do not recognize that a problem exists.

2. *Ventilation of feelings and hidden agendas.* Often problems are so personally involving that participants cannot easily analyze the situation. Some time may be needed to allow group members to "get things off their chests." Also, some participants may be harboring certain feelings, attitudes or personal goals—hidden agendas—that prevent decision making and the progress of the meeting or conference. Their behavior may block the progress toward analysis and solutions. Ventilation of these problems may be essential. However, a new problem-solving task may arise in the process of this type of ventilation which will require another agenda and problem

solving. We call this a "hidden agenda." Ventilation of hidden agendas may first occur at this point in any discussion. However, this stage may reoccur at any point in the remainder of the decision-making process at the will of group members.

3. *Definition of the Problem.* This process involves the wording of the question or problem and specification of the main question or claim involved. The main problem may center around any of the types of questions or claims with which you are now familiar: fact, definition, value, or policy (chapter 18). By examining the context and wording and selecting the central type of problem involved, participants can identify subclaims or questions and eliminate others that are not relevant. (At this point you may wish to review the advocacy system or chapter 18 for more detailed discussion of types of questions or claims.) In defining the problem it may also be necessary for participants to identify past, present, and future goals of the system in which the problem has occurred. This may involve identifying the past, present, and future goals of the decision-making group itself.

4. *Limitation of the problem.* Often, after defining a problem or problems, a group may find it necessary to limit its decision making to some subproblem or question. This may occur when the group finds that its authority over the problem is limited, that the question is too large to handle, that time-limitations prevent effective discussion of the broader problem, or that separating the problem into a series of smaller problem-solving attempts is a better decision-making process. This phase is normally recommended for inclusion early in an agenda but may also be included at later times in the process if needed.

5. *Searching for information.* After a problem has been defined and limited, seeking information on the problem can be more efficient. Differing methods may be needed depending upon the nature of the problem. If the problem involves some question highly relevant to participants, the method may demand reconsideration of information which group members share. However, some questions may involve library research, opinion polling, interviews, or bringing an expert into the group. Attention to what critical types of information are needed and some division of responsibility among participants can make this stage more efficient and productive. The successful discovery of crucial information, as opposed to quantity of information, is essential to effective problem analysis. (A review of chapter 14, on selective exposure behavior, might be helpful at this point.)

6. *Analysis of the problem.* This stage involves consideration of information selected by careful isolation of facts, definitions, values, and subproblems involved in the main question or problem at hand. (Review of

questions suggested for analysis of problems in the preceding advocacy system would be useful at this point to sharpen your analytical tools.) Depending upon the level of the main problem (fact, definition, value, or policy), different analytical questions must be answered. As we noted previously, analysis of questions of fact requires isolating possible things that exist or events that occur in the past, present, and future of the problem. Questions of definition call for categorization and labeling of these things or events. Analysis of value questions involves investigation of facts and definitions plus isolation of crucial values and arranging them in order of importance. Once this is done, selection of appropriate values is more efficient. Questions of policy involving desirable courses of action or practices require analysis of the ills or problems of the present system and isolation of the multiple causes and antecedents of those ills. Again the past, present, and possible future conditions of these problems should be considered through analysis of subordinate values, definitions, and facts involved in each ill analyzed. Careful consideration of *probable* relationships such as causes and effects is essential. Seldom are we *certain* of all the complex relationships that exist within problems. Some careful estimates of probabilities and our levels of certainty are useful. At the same time, remember that some problems may be beyond our competence and training; then expert or specialized help and information may be needed.

7. *Reformulation of the problem.* After analysis it is often useful to summarize and synthesize what has transpired. This can be thought of as reformulating the problem. Sometimes we discover in this process that the problem is quite different from what we thought it was when we began. After this reformulation, changes in our thinking may require that we define and limit the problem again.

8. *Proposal of solutions.* The generation and proposal of solutions is an important stage in decision making and may be approached in numerous ways. In some cases, "brainstorming" by quick suggestion and recording of all possibilities that "pop" into participants' minds is best. *None*valuation of the solutions at this point is essential. "Brainstorming" often produces a large number of possibilities which can be accepted, rejected, or modified in future stages of the decision making process. At other times, careful consideration of the preceding analysis and suggestion of solutions relevant to all phases of the problem is most important. Again, however, actual evaluation of the proposed solutions is usually reserved for later consideration.

9. *Establishment of solution criteria.* Before actual evaluation of proposed solutions, it is frequently useful to establish the criteria or stan-

*This small group at a
summer camp is
exploring solutions
for an entertainment
proposal.*

dards which the solutions must meet or fulfill in order to be accepted. This
process involves defining and limiting the standards and arranging them in
order of importance. Seldom can a single solution meet a large number of
criteria. More often a solution may fulfill some standards and not others.
The arrangement of criteria in order of importance allows later evaluations
of criteria against solutions for the selection of the best. Some "stock"
criteria include the following:

1. The solution(s) must best solve the problem or "cure the ills."
2. The solution(s) must not "cost" us too much.
3. The solution(s) must not produce significant new problems or disadvantages.
4. The solution(s) must be workable and feasible.

Additional criteria which are directly relevant to the specific question at hand
should also be generated. The criteria or standards should be formulated

keeping in mind not only the appropriate standards for the present but the appropriate criteria for the future too.

10. *Evaluation of proposed solutions.* We evaluate solutions by comparing them to (1) the stock criteria, (2) the generated criteria, and (3) the problem as analyzed. By testing the solutions in this way we can select or reject appropriate resolutions that are relevant to the problem. The previous arrangement of criteria in order of importance is helpful at this stage. Seldom will a single solution fulfill all the standards established; however, solutions which meet the most important criteria may be acceptable. Also, a number of solutions is often needed to fulfill the requirements of all the criteria. The selected solutions take the form of claims regarding facts, definitions, values, or policy. Some care should be given to the wording of these claims.

11. *Decision and selection of solutions.* Sometimes a separate phase is required for actual decision upon solutions. This process may take several forms. Sometimes voting or majority decision is sufficient. At other times, the process involves seeking and reaching consensus by all participants. The actual decision on solutions may require trial testing of the solutions. This may take the form of some small-scale trial or testing of tentative solutions for a short period of time. Sometimes it is possible to simulate the trial testing through role playing or other devices. Computers are being used more frequently for simulated testing of solutions to major problems.

12. *Implementation and further testing of solutions.* The final stage in many decision-making tasks is implementing the solutions or putting them into action. In the process the solutions may be checked for their effectiveness. This stage may require a completely new problem-solving process. If implementation requires strategies, problem solving, and decision making, it may constitute a whole new problem which requires the same care as the original problem.

Some Suggestions from Research

Although no single agenda system is universally "best," failure to follow some agenda or "getting off the track" appear to be the most common reasons for breakdowns in group decision making. However, when some agenda is followed, more good ideas appear to evolve from patterns that allow for suggesting solutions *before* the establishment of criteria for the acceptance of solutions. Apparently criteria can inhibit suggestions by some participants. Although the amount of time allowed for decision making has not been explored in depth, limited research suggests that more time produces better decisions. This conclusion should, of course, be tempered with consideration of the complexity of the problem. But this added time is particularly valuable in decision making which requires consensus of the participants.

Social pressure and cohesion also affect decisions. Majority opinion and social pressure within groups generally reduce divergent opinions and decisions. Individuals express fewer divergent judgements about facts and values in group conditions; however, the social reinforcement provided by groups to their participants normally produces higher-risk decisions by groups than by the individuals alone who make up the group. The more attracted participants are to the group, the more cohesion the group has among its members. The more cohesion or attraction (chapters 6 and 12) there is, the more likely it is that group pressure and high-risk group decisions will occur. These phenomena also appear to be somewhat responsible for the generally superior decisions of groups over individuals (there are exceptions). Estimates by groups often tend to be more accurate than those of individuals. Also, groups appear to produce a larger number of "correct" decisions and solutions than the individual and do not tend to err in presenting incorrect solutions as soon as the average individual does. Some research tenuously suggests that the general quality of the group decision is superior to individual decision making, although this may have resulted from biases and wishful thinking in the research itself.

**BLACK BOX
66**

Can you explain the usefulness of the reflective-agenda system?

Can you describe Dewey's description of reflective thinking?

Can you name and explain each stage in the composite agenda for group decision making?

Can you formulate and use an appropriate agenda for a process of group decision making?

Can you think of any other factors that can inhibit or facilitate group decision making and satisfaction with those decisions?

Supplementary to quality of a decision is its durability. Individuals are likely to abide by group decisions if they are attracted to the group and it reinforces them in some way. To the extent that an individual maintains contact with the group, then, the decision for the individual will be most lasting. Ultimately, those decisions that an individual makes and accepts him or herself are most lasting.

Consideration of these factors might well improve our decisions. Awareness of general barriers and some adaptive uses of reflective agendas should be helpful in our decision-making tasks. Thoughtful, critical utilization of these suggestions is recommended for your use in individual and group decision-making attempts.

Functional Approach

Functional Leadership. Another "approach" to decision making has been suggested by scholars and practitioners in the area of *leadership*. Recommendations on this approach have emerged from research in the small group setting. *Basically, this approach states that doing and saying certain things is instrumental to problem solving and decision making.* Specifically, *if a person performs certain functions for a group, then effective decision making is facilitated.* These "things" that an individual does or performs are called *leadership functions.* This approach to leadership defines a leader as one who performs guiding functions to which others respond. A leader, then, is one who carries out definite goals which lead the group closer to its goal—in this case decision making. Although status, prestige, or appointment may be sources of leadership designation, they may not produce *functional* leadership within a group. From a functional viewpoint *negative leadership* moves the group further away from decision; *nonleadership* consists of comments that do not significantly help or hinder the group. Functional leadership must be responded to—there must be followers. However, any member may become a functional leader by performing leadership functions, if only for a brief period of time.

There are two broad categories of leadership functions. The first types are called *task functions.* These are related to information, content, agendas, analysis, problem solving, ideas, and other factors leading to decision making. The second category consists of *social functions.* These roles are related to group cohesion, morale, feelings, attitudes and the general human climate of the group. Both are important at times in the decision-making process. In private closed groups, task functions *can* generally receive more attention, but not necessarily *will* receive that attention. Public meetings generally force additional attention toward social functions.

Leadership Functions. Generally, *task functions consist of intellectual and procedural statements* that facilitate decision-making processes in the group. *Intellectual functions* are roles that involve information and critical analysis. Examples of intellectual functions are:

1. contributing ideas and information;
2. asking for ideas and information;
3. analyzing the ideas and information of others;
4. asking for analysis of ideas and information;
5. evaluating the beliefs and values of others;
6. asking for evaluation of beliefs and values;
7. clarifying concepts and ideas with definition, examples, principles, or other means which reduce abstraction.

Procedural functions are statements that facilitate discussion, utilization of an agenda, and progress through an agenda. Examples of procedural functions are:

1. initiating discussion;
2. formulating the goals and purposes of the meeting;
3. making or suggesting agendas;
4. summarizing the progress of the discussion;
5. directing attention back to the agenda when discussion has strayed;
6. verbalizing areas of consensual aggreement when disagreement has stopped the progress through the agenda.

Social functions can be considered as a single category. *Social functions* as noted above are related to human dimensions such as feelings, attitudes, and morale of group members. Often these factors interfere (see previous section on "barriers") with analysis, procedure, and decision-making processes. When a person makes statements which help the group deal with these factors, social functions are being performed. Some examples of social functions are:

1. regulating participation in the decision-making process;
2. providing emotional support for group members;
3. discussing attitudes and needs of participants;

4. managing conflict among participants;
5. providing relief or reduction of anxiety and stress;
6. initiating group self-analysis.

To the extent that these functions facilitate decision-making processes, they are worthy of our consideration. Although they do not constitute a decision-making system they do appear to be helpful to the process.

BLACK BOX
67

Can you explain the ideas behind these types of leadership?
  functional leadership   negative leadership
  leadership   nonleadership

Can you identify leadership functions?
  intellectual functions
  procedural functions
  social functions

Try to recall examples of these leadership functions from your own experience.

Perform these functions in a small-group communication aimed at decision making.

Summary

In this chapter we have attempted to expose you to some helpful systems for decision making. We have also tried to make you more aware of some of the factors that can inhibit or facilitate rational decisions. You should have gained some practical skills to help your communication with others in achieving this outcome. In the next chapter we turn to a consideration of how we confirm or discontinue our decisions once they are made.

SUGGESTED FURTHER READINGS

1. Barnlund, D. C. "Experiments in Leadership Training for Decision-Making Discussion Groups." *Speech Monographs* 22 (1955): 1–14.

    In this article, some of the early studies on functional leadership are summarized. Also, a leadership training program is described and its effectiveness in small-group decision making is assessed.

2. Brock, B. L., Chesebro, J. W., Cragan, J. F., and Klumpp, J. F. *Public Policy Decision-Making* (New York: Harper & Row, 1973).

    Several chapters of this brief text will be of interest. The advocacy system of decision making is discussed in more detail as it relates not only to collegiate debate but also other public communicaton systems. The text adopts a "systems" approach in the analysis of public issues.

3. Edwards, W. and Tversky, A., eds. *Decision-Making* (Middlesex, England: Penguin, 1967).

    The book takes a considerably different approach to decision making; therefore, it expands on a number of approaches not discussed in this chapter.

4. Phillips, G. M. *Communication in the Small Group* (Indianapolis: Bobbs-Merril, 1973).

    This short text has a couple of chapters devoted to a system for planning and implementing decisions. This innovative program (PERT) is worth attention by those who are likely to be involved in decision making and implementation of programs, actions, etc.

5. McGrath, J. E. and Altman, I. *Small Group Research: A Synthesis and Critique of the Field* (New York: Holt, Rinehart and Winston, 1966).

    An early chapter in this volume summarizes much of the research in small-group communication. Some attention is devoted to decision making in the small-group system and to elements affecting group decisions.

SELECTED REFERENCES

ANDERSON, L. R. and FIEDLER, F. E. "The Effect of Participatory and Supervisory Leadership on Group Creativity." *Journal of Applied Psychology* 48 (1964): 277–281.

BALES, R. F. *Interaction Process Analysis: A Method for the Study of Small Groups* (Cambridge, Mass.: Addison-Wesley, 1950).

_____. "Task Roles and Social Roles in Problem-Solving Groups," in *Working Papers in the Theory of Action*, R. F. Bales, T. Parsons, and E. A. Shils, eds. (New York: The Free Press, 1953.)

_____. "Task Roles and Social Roles in Problem-Solving Groups," in *Readings in Social Psychology*, E. MacCoby, ed. (New York: Holt, Rinehart and Winston, 1958).

_____. "How People Interact in Conferences," *Communication and Culture*, Alfred G. Smith, ed. (New York: Holt, Rinehart and Winston, 1966).

BALES, R. F. and STODTBECK, F. "Phases in Group Problem-Solving." *Journal of Abnormal and Social Psychology* 46 (1951): 485–495.

BARNLUND, D. C. "Experiments in Leadership Training for Decision-Making Discussion Groups." *Speech Monographs* 22 (1955): 1–14.

_____. "Consistency of Emergent Leadership in Groups with Changing Tasks and Members." *Speech Monographs* 29 (1962): 45–52.

BARNLUND, D. C. and HAIMAN, F. S. *Dynamics of Discussion* (Boston: Houghton Mifflin, 1960).

BAVELAS, A. and LEWIN, KURT. "Training in Democratic Leadership." *Journal of Abnormal and Social Psychology* 37 (1942): 115–119.

BAYLESS, O. L. "An Alternate Pattern for Problem-Solving Discussion." *Journal of Communication* 3 (1967).

BERG, D. M. "A Descriptive Analysis of the Distribution and Duration of Themes Discussed by Task-Oriented Small Groups." *Speech Monographs* 34 (1967): 172–175.

Bibliography: PERT and Other Management Systems and Techniques (Washington: Bolling Air Force Base, 1963).

BLACK, E. B. "A Consideration of Rhetorical Causes of Breakdown in Discussion." *Speech Monographs* 22 (1955): 15–19.

BRAYBOOKE, D. and LINDBLOM, C. *A Strategy of Decision* (London: The Free Press, 1963).

BRILHART, J. K. and JOCHEM, L. M. "Effects of Different Patterns On Outcomes of Problem-Solving Discussion." *Journal of Applied Psychology* 48 (1964): 174–179.

BROCK, B. L., CHESEBRO, J. W., CRAGAN, J. F., and KLUMPP, J. F. *Public Policy Decision-Making* (New York: Harper & Row, 1973).

CARTWRIGHT, D. and ZANDER, A. *Group Dynamics: Research and Theory* (Evanston: Row, Peterson, 1960).

COHEN, A. R. *Attitude Change and Social Influence* (New York: Basic Books, 1964).

COLLINS, B. E. and GUETZKOW, H. *A Social Psychology of Group Processes for Decision Making* (New York: John Wiley, 1964).

DEWEY, J. *How We Think* (Boston: D. C. Heath, 1910).

EDWARDS, W. and TVERSKY, A., eds. *Decision-Making* (Middlesex, England: Penguin, 1967).

FISHER, B. A. "Decision Emergence: Phases in Group Decision Making." *Speech Monographs* 37 (1970).

———. "Communication Research and the Task Oriented Group." *Journal of Communication* 21 (1971): 136–149.

GOLOMB, S. W. and BAUMERT, L. "Backtrack Programming." *Journal of Associated Computer Machines* 12 (1965).

GORDON, T. *Group-Centered Leadership* (New York: Houghton Mifflin, 1955).

GORE, W. and DYSON, J. W. *The Making of Decisions* (New York: The Free Press, 1964).

GOURAN, D. S. "Conceptual and Methodological Approaches to the Study of Leadership." *Central States Speech Journal* 21 (1970): 217–223.

———. "Group Communication: Perspectives and Priorities for Future Research." *Quarterly Journal of Speech* 59 (1973).

GULLEY, H. E. *Discussion, Conference, and Group Process* (New York: Holt, Rinehart and Winston, 1963).

HAIMAN, F. S. *Group Leadership and Democratic Action* (Boston: Houghton Mifflin, 1957).

HARE, A. P. *Handbook of Small Group Research* (New York: The Free Press, 1962).

HARNACK, R. V. and FEST, T. B. *Group Discussion: Theory and Technique* (New York: Appleton-Century-Crofts, 1964).

JENNESS, A. "The Role of Discussion in Changing Opinion Regarding a Matter of Fact." *Journal of Abnormal and Social Psychology* 27 (1932): 279–296.

KATZ, E. et al. "Leadership Stability and Social Change: An Experiment with Small Groups." *Sociometry* 20 (1957): 36–50.

KATZ, D. and KAHN, R. L. *The Social Psychology of Organizations* (New York: John Wiley, 1966).

KELLEY, H. and THIBAUT, J. "Experimental Studies of Group Problem Solving and Process," in *Handbook of Social Psychology,* G. Lindzy, ed. (Reading: Addison-Wesley, 1954).

KEPNER, C. H. and TREGOE, B. B. *The Rational Manager* (New York: McGraw-Hill, 1965).

KIESLER, C. A., COLLINS, B. E., and MILLER, N. *Attitude Change: A Critical Analysis of Theoretical Approaches* (New York: John Wiley, 1969).

KRECH, D. and CRUTCHFIELD, R. *Theory and Problems of Social Psychology* (New York: McGraw-Hill, 1948).

McGRATH, J. E. and ALTMAN, I. *Small Group Research: A Synthesis and Critique of the Field* (New York: Holt, Rinehart and Winston, 1966).

MILLS, G. E. *Reason in Controversy,* 2nd ed. (Boston: Allyn and Bacon, 1968).

PARNES, S. J. "The Creative Problem Solving Course and Institute at the University of Buffalo," in *A Source Book for Creative Thinking,* S. J. Parnes and H. F. Harding, eds. (New York: Scribner's Sons, 1962).

PHILLIPS, G. M. *Communication in the Small Group* (Indianapolis: Bobbs-Merrill, 1973).

Planning and Scheduling with PERT and CPM (Newburyport, Mass.: Entelek, Inc., 1964).

PRYER, M. W., FLINT, A. W., and BASS, B. M. "Group Effectiveness and Consistency of Leadership." *Sociometry* 25 (1962): 391–397.

ROKEACH, M. "The Nature and Meaning of Dogmatism." *Psychological Review* 61 (1954): 194–204.

———. *The Open and Closed Mind* (New York: Basic Books, 1960).

ROGERS, C. R. "Some Observations on the Organization of Personality." *American Psychologist* 2 (1947): 358–368.

ROSS, R. S. *Speech Communication,* 3rd ed. (Englewood Cliffs, N.J.: Prentice-Hall, 1974).

SEILER, J. A. *Systems Analysis in Organizational Behavior* (Homewood, Ill.: Irwin, 1967).

SERENO, K. K. and MORTENSEN, C. D. "The Effects of Ego-Involved Attitudes on Conflict Negotiations in Dyads." *Speech Monographs* 36 (1969): 8–12.

SCOTT, M. D. and BODAKEN, E. M. "Backtrack Programming: A Computer-Based Approach to Group Problem Solving." Paper presented at the International Communication Association Convention, Montreal, April, 1973.

SHARP, H., JR. and MILLIKEN, J. "Reflective Thinking Ability and the Product of Problem-Solving Discussion." *Speech Monographs* 31 (1962): 124–127.

SHAW, M. E. "A Comparison of Individual and Small Groups in the Rational Solution of Complex Problems." *American Journal of Psychology* 44 (1932): 491–504.

SPIELBERGER, C. D. *Anxiety and Behavior* (New York: Academic Press, 1966).

THOMPSON, W. E. *Modern Argumentation and Debate* (New York: Harper & Row, 1971).

UTTERBACK, W. E. and FOTHERINGHAM, W. C. "Experimental Studies of Motivated Group Discussion." *Speech Monographs* 25 (1958): 268–277.

VON BERTALANFFY, L. *General Systems Theory, Foundations, Development, Applications* (New York: Braziller, 1968).

WATSON, G. B. "Do Groups Think More Efficiently than Individuals." *Journal of Abnormal and Social Psychology* 23 (1928): 328–336.

WHEELESS, L. R. *Tournament Debating: Fundamentals for Novices* (Normal, Ill.: Illinois State University Press, 1970).

Young, O. R. "A Survey of General Systems Theory." *General Systems Yearbook* 9 (1964): 61–80.

Zagona, S. V. and Zurcher, L. A. "Participation, Interaction, and Role Behavior in Groups Selected from the Extremes of Open-Closed Cognitive Continuum." *Journal of Psychology* 58 (1964): 255–264.

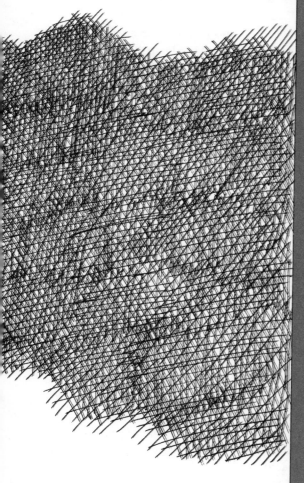

20

Confirmation

The meeting began at 1:15 and broke up at 4:30. Everyone was about talked out. The decision was made to open a new store in Greenville. Martha and Bill are walking down the hall to their offices.

Martha: *I didn't think we would ever get a decision. Some of those people just love to hear themselves talk!*

Bill: *And how! I don't ever care to hear about Greenville again! Do you think we made the right decision?*

Martha: *Well, only time will tell; but Greenville seems to be as good a prospect as Morgantown, and our store there is doing all right.*

Bill: *Yeah. Well, I hope so. It's too late to change our minds now.*

At some point a decision is made. Information has been acquired. Influence has occurred. A new idea, technique, or product has been adopted or

419

rejected (or a new store scheduled to be built). Communication has occurred and change has occurred or the status quo has been preserved. We may think, "that is that." We may never care to hear about Greenville again. But that is not the end, and it may be just the beginning. Poor Bill will probably hear a lot more about Greenville. Did you notice that right after he indicated he didn't want to hear anymore, he asked Martha a question that would insure that he would hear more?

Bill's behavior is not unusual. When a decision is reached, and for some time thereafter, the individual or the group who has made the decision will have an increased need for communication. This communication will be sought in order to confirm that the decision made was the correct one. Influence that has occurred may be either temporary or permanent, depending upon the amount of confirmation that the individual receives subsequent to decision.

Increasing Confirmation

Dissonance

One of the best explanations for why people seek communication about the decision they have made is provided by dissonance theory. Dissonance theory suggests that the act of making any decision to accept a new idea, technique, or product necessitates rejecting alternate decisions, some of which may have been perceived in a very positive light. Presume, for example, that you have just purchased a new Plymouth. Prior to purchasing that Plymouth, you looked at Fords, Chevrolets, Volkswagens, and Cadillacs. You found all of these automobiles to have certain advantages. Probably most of them have at least one advantage over the Plymouth that you purchased. Maybe you even owned one of these other types of cars before buying your Plymouth. You recognize that the automobile that you purchased is not a perfect automobile. Dissonance theory suggests that this recignition will cause you to be in a stage of discord or imbalance. It is necessary for you to try to get all of your beliefs and attitudes into consistency with the behavior in which you have engaged. One of the ways to do this is to increase your communication about automobiles. You may seek to talk with other Plymouth owners to find out reasons why they like their Plymouths. You may read advertisements for Plymouths to find out good things about Plymouths. Similarly, you may seek to communicate with other people who own other kinds of cars and are unhappy with them, or you may read advertisements about other kinds of cars and look to see what's wrong with those cars.

The unique characteristic of communication of this type is the active search for confirmation for an idea or behavior to which you are already committed. All of the selectivity processes that were discussed in the chapters concerning information processing will be in operation. In short, you will do almost everything possible to get information that will confirm your behavior. Similarly, you will try to filter out information that does not confirm the wiseness of your decision.

In most instances this type of communication behavior leads to confirmation and the continuance of the behavior which you have chosen. However, in other instances you cannot escape information which suggests that your decision is incorrect; for example, you have your Plymouth back in the shop nine times in the first six weeks that you own it. When communication after decision does not lead to confirmation of that decision, the likelihood of discontinuance is very high. In the case of your Plymouth, you will be looking forward to the opportunity of trading it in on another car. And the likelihood of that other car being a Plymouth is remote indeed.

Seeking confirmation is a very important element for us to consider when we are attempting to influence another person. Once we have gotten him or her to agree with us or to engage in the behavior that we are recommending, the tendency may be for us to cease communicating since we perceive that we have accomplished our purpose. But our purpose may be only temporarily accomplished if the person does not receive adequate confirmation that what we have encouraged him or her to do is right. Thus, it is usually important for us to continue our influence attempts in order to guarantee against discontinuance later. One of the authors recalls having purchased a new Ford at one point in his life. He had not intended to purchase a new Ford, but the Ford salesman had convinced him that it was the best buy. After driving the new Ford home he experienced considerable dissonance because the car that he really wanted was an Oldsmobile. But the Ford salesman knew what he was doing. Over the next year the author received a call every month from the Ford dealer asking about how satisfied the author was with the Ford and suggesting if there were any problems to be sure and bring the car into the shop so they could be taken care of. By the end of that year the author was firmly convinced that he had made a wise decision and when it came time to trade in that car on another new one, you can probably guess what dealer had the first chance to sell him another new car.

Behavioral Commitment

Confirmation of a decision can also come as a result of something that has very little to do with communication. We observe our behaviors and know that other people observe them as well. Consequently, once we have adopted a new behavior, it is public. To the extent that we express new beliefs or attitudes that we have acquired, we make a public commitment to those beliefs and attitudes. Research suggests that the more publicly we are committed to something, the less likely we are to change it and the more strongly we will become committed to it. The skilled influence agent, consequently, will attempt to get people whom she or he has influenced to engage in public behavior indicating the adoption of the idea, technique, or product that the influence agent has been pushing. To the extent that the public behavior is communication behavior, that communication behavior also commits the individual to our orientation. The skilled Ford salesman mentioned above recognized this and induced other potential customers to call the author and ask his opinion of his Ford and of the Ford dealership. Every time the author expressed his pleasure with the Ford and the dealer, he became more and more committed to the decision that he had made and more likely to repeat it.

Preventing Disconfirmation

After a person has been influenced and made a decision, the need to seek further communication to confirm that decision is strong. While the decision maker will employ selective exposure, attention, and perception in the attempt to acquire information supportive of the decision, it is almost inevitable that some information will be acquired that will challenge the correctness of the decision. When this happens, we have disconfirmation, and the possibility of reversing the original decision or making a new decision contrary to the previous one is increased. Let us put our influence agent's hat on for a moment and see what we can do about this problem.

We have already noted two follow-up behaviors that we could use—continue to provide positive information and encourage a public commitment. But we could also use a strategy in our original influence attempt that would help to prevent later disconfirmation. This has been called the strategy of *inoculation.*

Communication and Inoculation

In previous chapters on influence we have focused our attention on two types of influence: inducing people to change their attitudes, beliefs, or behaviors and influencing people not to change their attitudes, beliefs, or behaviors. There is a third form of influence to which we should direct some attention so that we do not lose sight of a very important part of the relationship between communication and influence. This is influence that is designed to *prevent* influence at a later time.

The theory of inoculation was developed on the basis of a medical analogy. In medicine there are certain diseases for which the body can build a natural immunity. The body may need some help in order to accomplish this feat, so a small amount of the disease-causing virus is inserted into the body. Not enough of the virus is inserted to cause the disease, but just enough to stimulate the natural body function of developing defenses against that virus in the system.

The same principle of induced immunology can apply in the process of influence. There are many topics about which there is very little communication. So people have attitudes and beliefs and engage in behaviors related to those topics without ever thinking much about them from one day to the next. People are highly susceptible to influence on these topics because they are living in an essentially "germ-free environment." They accept statements such as: we should brush our teeth after every meal; we should wear seat belts when riding in or driving a car; there is a God; honesty is better than dishonesty; a college education is an extremely valuable step toward success in life; smoking is hazardous to our health. Most people can probably not remember the last time they heard a serious argument on the other side of any of these questions. They have become "cultural truisms" to most people in our society. Research has indicated that because of the absence of contrary opinions against these propositions, when we are exposed to such argument most of us are very susceptible to influence. Very often, people wish to prevent other people from being influenced on such important questions. This is where the process of inoculation comes in.

Inoculation against future counterargument operates very much like inoculation against future disease; some of the other side of the case is introduced so that the individual can build up immunity against that side. When the immunity is built up, a strong attack from a person on the other side will tend to be rejected rather than accepted. The process of inducing inoculation through communication normally proceeds in one of two ways.

The first is by directly presenting arguments on the opposite side of the truism and then refuting those arguments, or encouraging the other person to refute them. This is probably the strongest way of inducing inoculation. The second method is to present strong arguments in favor of the truism. While this has been found to produce some inoculation against later argument, it is generally inferior to considering the opposing arguments and refuting them.

We have referred to the type of issues that are important for inoculation as "cultural truisms." By that we mean that within any given culture, most of the people believe the proposition to be true but may not have much of an argument that they can present in favor of it. At first it may seem like there are not too many of these topics. But if we examine various subsets of the American population, we can see a very large number of these topics that are specific to one or more of the subsets. In some cases, the beliefs held by an individual group can be reasonably easily demonstrated to be true in the light of cold hard facts; in other cases such proof is next to impossible. When comparing two different subsets of the population, we may even find cultural truisms that are exactly contrary to one another, but are held as cultural truisms by the opposing groups. For example, a very large portion of the adult population of the United States believes that marijuana is a harmful drug. A similarly large group of young people believe that marijuana is a harmless drug. Most people in both groups have little information to support the truism to which they adhere, and thus, they are potentially highly subject to influence by a skilled persuader.

Or consider, on a less political level, the view held by many people with a liberal arts orientation to education that the study of a foreign language is a very liberalizing experience. This is countered by more technically oriented people who believe that the study of a foreign language is quite useless. Branding such views as cultural truisms does not suggest that everybody who holds any one of these views holds it as a cultural truism. Remember, a cultural truism is something that is believed by a group but which the individuals in the group have little to support their belief. Those people who hold any of the beliefs that we have discussed above and have strong, reasoned arguments to support that belief are not holding to a cultural truism, and there are many in each case. However, we all hold certain cultural truisms, and in many cases are not even aware that we are doing so. Similarly, our social group may hold cultural truisms that if attacked will fall like ten-pins. Influence through communication designed to produce inoculation, therefore, it is a very important element in the total communication and influence process.

> ## BLACK BOX
> ## 68
>
> Can you explain how a communicator can increase the probability of confirmation of a decision on the part of another person?
>
> Can you explain how an influence agent can prevent disconfirmation by employing inoculation?
>
> Can you provide examples of dissonance, behavioral commitment, and inoculation from your own experience?

Recently researchers have investigated the possibility that the inoculation approach could be used to prevent later disconfirmation on topics other than cultural truisms. Important political topics as well as highly involving campus topics have been examined. The results have been most encouraging. Inoculation strategies have been found to work even on these highly controversial topics on which people have been exposed to many arguments.

The use of the inoculation strategy is fairly straightforward, and involves a direct choice of messages to present to receivers. When we are designing our attempt to influence another person we can choose to present only those messages that are supportive of the position that we want them to accept (one-sided messages). Or we can include some messages that support the position we are advocating and some others that are not supportive (two-sided messages). Inoculation involves the latter approach, and usually goes further to present other messages that show what is wrong with the arguments that are in opposition to our position.

Once people have been inoculated, they tend to reject subsequent communication from other sources that includes the arguments to which they have been exposed and which have been shown to them to be faulty. But equally important, they also tend to reject new arguments to which they have not been previously exposed. Apparently, when we have been made suspicious of some of a source's arguments, we tend to become suspicious of her or his other arguments as well.

As with most communication strategies which we have discussed in this book, the existence of the inoculation strategy is a double-edged sword. As sources we can delight in having this tool in our arsenal, for it will help us to influence others and get them to stay influenced long after we are done. But as receivers we must recognize that when we are inoculated by some other influence agent, our critical abilities in decision making are put to a severe tese.

Is inoculation a good thing? Well, it is like communication itself, isn't it? It all depends on what it is used for.

SUGGESTED FURTHER READINGS

1. Festinger, L. *A Theory of Cognitive Dissonance* (New York: Row, Peterson, 1957).

   This is the original work on dissonance theory.

2. Miller, G. R. and Burgoon, M. *New Techniques of Persuasion* (New York: Harper & Row, 1973).

   This brief book provides an excellent discussion of recent research and theory concerning both inoculation and dissonance.

SELECTED REFERENCES

CRANE, E. "Immunization; With and Without the Use of Counter-Arguments." *Journalism Quarterly* XXXIX (1962): 445–450.

FESTINGER, L. *A Theory of Cognitive Dissonance* (New York: Row, Peterson, 1957).

FESTINGER, L. and CARLSMITH, J. M. "Cognitive Consequences of Forced Compliance." *Journal of Abnormal and Social Psychology* 58 (1959): 203–210.

FESTINGER, L. and MACCOBY, N. "On Resistance to Persuasive Communications." *Journal of Abnormal and Social Psychology* 68 (1964): 359–366.

KIESLER, C. A., COLLINS, B. E., and MILLER, N. *Attitude Change* (New York: John Wiley, 1969).

KOEHLER, J. "Effects on Audience Opinion of One-Sided and Two-Sided Speeches Supporting and Opposing a Proposition, Examining Opinions on Speakers Ethos, the Topic, and the Open-Mindedness of Listeners." Unpublished Ph.D. Dissertation, Pennsylvania State University, 1968.

McCROSKEY, J. C. "The Effects of Evidence as an Inhibitor of Counter-Persuasion." *Speech Monographs* 37 (1970): 188–194.

McCROSKEY, J. C., YOUNG, T. J., and SCOTT, M. D. "The Effects of Message Sidedness and Evidence on Innoculation Against Counterpersuasion in Small Group Communication." *Speech Monographs* 39 (1972): 205–212.

McGuire, W. J. "Inducing Resistance to Persuasion: Some Contemporary Approaches," in *Advances in Experimental Social Psychology,* L. Berkowitz, ed. (New York: Academic Press, 1964): 191–229.

————. "Nature of Attitudes and Attitude Change," in *Handbook of Social Psychology,* G. Lindzey and E. Aronson, eds. (Reading, Mass.: Addison-Wesley, 1968).

————. "Persistence of the Resistance to Persuasion Induced by Various Types of Prior Belief Defenses." *Journal of Abnormal and Social Psychology* 64 (1962): 241–248.

————. "Resistance to Persuasion Conferred by Active and Passive Prior Refutation of the Same and Alternative Counterarguments." *Journal of Abnormal and Social Psychology* 63 (1961): 326–332.

————. "The Current Status of Cognitive Consistency Theories," in *Cognitive Consistency,* S. Feldman, ed. (New York: Academic Press, 1966).

————. "The Effectiveness of Supportive and Refutational Defenses in Immunizing and Restoring Beliefs Against Persuasion." *Sociometry* 24 (1961): 184–197.

McGuire, W. J. and Papageorgis, D. "The Relative Efficacy of Various Types of Prior Belief-Defense in Producing Immunity Against Persuasion." *Journal of Abnormal and Social Psychology* 62 (1961): 327–337.

Manis, M. and Blake, J. B. "Interpretation of Persuasive Messages as a Function of Prior Immunization." *Journal of Abnormal and Social Psychology* 46 (1963): 225–230.

Miller, G. R. and Burgoon, M. *New Techniques of Persuasion* (New York: Harper & Row, 1973).

Papageorgis, D. and McGuire, W. J. "The Generality of Immunity to Persuasion Produces by Pre-Exposure to Weakened Counter-Arguments." *Journal of Abnormal and Social Psychology* 62 (1961): 475–481.

Thistlethwaite, L. and Kamenetsky, J. "Attitude Change Through Refutation and Elaboration of Audience Counter-Arguments." *Journal of Abnormal and Social Psychology* 51 (1955): 3–12.

Author Index

428

Subject Index

434